Date Due

BRODART   Cat. No. 23 233   Printed in U.S.A.

CAGED:
Eight Prisoners
and Their Keepers

CAGED

Eight Prisoners and
Their Keepers

BEN H. BAGDIKIAN

HARPER & ROW, PUBLISHERS

New York, Hagerstown, San Francisco, London

For my wife, Betty Medsger

FIRST EDITION

Designed by Dorothy Schmiderer

Library of Congress Cataloging in Publication Data

Bagdikian, Ben H
  Caged: eight prisoners and their keepers.
  1. United States. Northeastern Penitentiary,
Lewisburg, Pa. 2. Prisoners—Pennsylvania—Lewis-
burg—Case studies. 3. Corrections—Pennsylvania—
Lewisburg. I. Title.
HV9474.N6B33 1976   365'.9748'48   74–20398
ISBN 0–06–010174–1

76 77 78 79 10 9 8 7 6 5 4 3 2 1

CONTENTS

PART THREE

PART FOUR

"They had me in prisons for 25 years and all they taught me was how to live in prisons."

WILLIAM RYAN IRWIN

"Who does society put in cages? Animals and prisoners."

RONALD TRACY PHILLIPS

"Every effort is made to discover those human values which lie within every individual and to make them available as guides to a more successful life."

Public Relations Pamphlet
of United States Penitentiary,
Lewisburg, Pennsylvania

FOREWORD

All of this book is, to the best of my ability, factually accurate. Names of all major persons involved are real. In the case of a few secondary persons, a different name has been substituted, indicated by using quotation marks on first use. But these, too, are real people depicted doing things that actually happened. Descriptions of all events are as I or the subjects actually saw them. All conversations are as reported by those speaking or by a party to the conversation whose accuracy of recollection I had reason to believe.

None of the people and none of the events have been invented or fictionalized. Information came from prisoners and prison officials, from hundreds of interviews, from diaries and journals kept by some of the prisoners, from hundreds of letters held by their relatives, from court records and trial transcripts all over the country, and from innumerable letters between me and imprisoned men. I viewed the scenes of some of their crimes and interviewed some of their victims.

With few exceptions, the Federal Bureau of Prisons did not cooperate in the research for this book. Whatever information the book contains about the Bureau comes from public records and from a few confidential interviews with some individuals connected with Lewisburg penitentiary. The rest was obtained by me over a protracted six-month inquiry of the Bureau under the Freedom of Information Act, which the Bureau answered only in part.

The Bureau of Prisons refused information unless I paid for it. It denied access to some records and said that other records had been destroyed.

Correspondence with the men in prison was facilitated by their use of a new regulation permitting uncensored letters to members of the "press" while I was still an assistant managing editor of the *Washington Post*. I think that most of these letters went out according to regulation, unread by the prison censor. This was important because the men were telling me about events in prison and in their past lives that would put them at a disadvantage if some of the events were known to their keepers and to other prisoners. A few of the "privileged" letters to me clearly had been opened by someone between the time the prisoner had sealed the letter and its delivery to me. All my letters were censored.

Some of their letters failed to reach me and some of mine failed to reach them. When it was clear that correspondence had been interrupted, I would have to send the prisoner a certified return-receipt letter in which a United States Postal Money Order was enclosed, a standard technique to discourage arbitrary interference with mail by federal staffs.

I left the *Post* when I began this book. Under the rules of the Federal Bureau of Prisons I then visited the prisoners involved as a friend under the usual visiting-room rules. This meant that I could not take notes, could not show anything to the prisoner and he could not show anything to me. I would visit for the maximum time permitted, usually five hours, and immediately afterward record events of the visit on a tape recorder in my car.

Even visits as a friend were interrupted. I had only one visit with Lumumba Jones in Marion penitentiary. When I appeared at the institution, an officer at the door had a list of every letter I had ever written Jones and every letter he had written me, and knew every address from which my letters had been mailed. Immediately after my visit—which had been unexceptional and strictly following the rules—Jones was called to the office of the associate warden and threatened with punishment because of my visit. I was denied further visiting privileges with Jones.

Fortunately for the disclosure of public information, some of the prisoners involved sued their keepers on the constitutionality of the punishment the prison staffs imposed on them. The result was an extraordinary four-day trial. Personal attendance at the trial and the 1251 pages of the trial transcript were invaluable sources of information on official actions that might otherwise have remained secret.

BEN H. BAGDIKIAN

Berkeley, California

PROLOGUE:
OF RATS AND MEN

Whatever people may feel about the common Norway rat, the animal does better than most of the human race at achieving civilized life. The rats have stable families, are considerate toward their mates and offspring; when able to get sufficient space and food, they are friendly with their neighbors, diligent in the gathering of meals, mutually happy in their mating, productive of healthy births, kindly in their training of the young and peaceful in their cooperation with the rest of the community.

Some years ago John B. Calhoun at the National Institute of Mental Health changed only one element in his healthy experimental rat colonies. He let them become overcrowded. Six times he repeated the test, observing results through glass walls, and six times the community disintegrated into savagery. There was enough food for all, but individuals became bizarre. Males for the first time committed acts of homosexuality and rape. Pregnant females miscarried. Colonies divided into two groups: gangs who terrorized everyone else and the intimidated who clustered like beaten sleepwalkers.

If the crowded rats were later removed to a normal colony, the impact of their early life experience was so profound that males retained their distortions and females continued to miscarry.

Dr. Calhoun observed, "It is obvious that . . . the Norway rat . . . break[s] down under the social pressures generated by population density. . . . Refinement . . . of these studies may advance our understanding to the point where they may contribute to the making of value judgments about analogous problems confronting the human species."

There is no observation window in the compacted slums of America nor in the American prisons where so many slumdwellers are further compressed.

The twenty-six acres behind the wall of the United States Penitentiary in Lewisburg, Pennsylvania, comprise the total life space of about
1500 prisoners. This is the equivalent of 37,000 people per square mile,
twenty-four times more densely packed than the average small community, two and a half times more crowded than the most crowded city
in the country.

To the casual eye viewing the central corridors and dining halls of
Lewisburg the human scene is disarming. There is no stereotype of old
prison movies: prisoners shackled, dressed in stripes, marching in lock-
step to the rockpile or to filthy dining halls where they swallow nauseat-
ing beans and warm water, guarded by potbellied sadists in uniform
snarling at their captives.

There are prisons in the United States where some of those conditions
exist. But not Lewisburg. Prisoners do not march in formation. The
officers have an easygoing manner; they wear blazers instead of uni-
forms. Most of the prison employees are not even guards, but administrators, chaplains, secretaries and shop foremen.

During the day prisoners work inside the factories, or work in the
stainless-steel kitchens, or clean and paint their institution. Those with
white-collar skills perform clerical work and a few others learn and
assist at specialized jobs like dental technician. Between jobs they stroll
the corridors in quiet conversation, play ball or lift weights in the
exercise yards, where there are tennis and handball courts and even a
miniature golf course.

In the evening a prisoner may be in his "house"—the universal
prison term for personal quarters—where he may listen to earphones
plugged into the institution radio circuit that offers two local radio
stations. Others watch television in group units, or take part in noisy
card games or quiet chess matches. A few attend Alcoholics Anonymous, a Toastmasters speech club or one of the fundamentalist Protestant religious sessions, or group therapy, or the Junior Chamber of
Commerce chapter, whose prison Jaycees plan institutional entertainment. On weekends there are movies, where prisoners, like any college
audience, cheer and applaud when the main feature is preceded by Bugs
Bunny or Roadrunner. Some of the scenes could be in a community
college; some prisoners have even been allowed to attend classes at
nearby Bucknell University.

Lewisburg is a showplace, a monument to the builders of the new
federal prison system nearly forty years before the events in this narra-
tive. The institution was designed with loving care by men who wished
prisons to look better. Just north of the small town of Lewisburg (6376

population), off Route 15, a hardly noticeable country road leads two miles to the federal prison reservation, where there is, suddenly, a highway lined with elegant hemlocks leading to a parking area framed by giant sycamores. Here you see the penitentiary's central tower, done in the style of the Torre del Mangia in the fourteenth-century Palazzo Pubblico in Siena, concealing the prison smokestack.

The main buildings have Romanesque windows framed in elaborate red brick recesses and curvatures with no ugly bars to spoil their exterior. Inside the prison's main concourse there are further architectural surprises—cast-concrete gothic arches and oak paneling with wrought-iron studs, giving the appearance of a penal Yale. When it opened on November 15, 1932, Lewisburg Federal Penitentiary was a triumph in the art of prison decoration.

The complex was considered a classic in prison planning, one of the first major American prisons built neither in a large hollow square nor with radial wings, but in the French "telephone pole" design. Its central corridor is an incredible 750 feet long, the "telephone pole," intersected by living quarters and other buildings that form the crosspieces of the "pole." It was one of the first modern prisons to be totally self-contained within its high wall—housing units, factories, steam plant, hospital, administration headquarters, classrooms, visiting rooms, chapel. It was built with six open dormitories, with the idea that the openness "promotes rehabilitation by teaching men how to get along with each other."

The institution is close and decorative enough to exhibit to Washington politicians, at least those not so unfortunate as to enter as inmates. Visitors are shown the gothic corridors and oak-paneled dining rooms and then retire to the softly lighted office of the warden, where they can drink good coffee served in delicate china.

Behind the scene of strolling prisoners in khaki and the chess games there is a different reality.

Even the splendiferous design was less than a functional triumph. Retaining the architectural purity of the Northern Italian Renaissance required windows too small and too high to provide natural light for the prisoners. To keep the windows in style required bars placed inside, which gave the interior of the prison a more grim look, intensified by the gothic arches and dark paneling. The deep basements where prisoners are punished were a serious fire risk, and in them it was, as a later official report observed, "hard to get equable temperature and good ventilation."

Even without these aesthetic complications, Lewisburg is no exception to the nature of penitentiaries.

Prison, as operated in the United States, is a machine to control every minute of every day in the life of every prisoner.

The machine has powerful physical mechanisms of control: thirty-foot walls, gun towers occupied by guards equipped with binoculars, spotlights, .38-caliber revolvers, shotguns, high-powered 30.06 rifles. Miles of barbed wire, steel plates, unnumbered rods and grilles segment every visible space, the steel made to specifications to resist penetration by six successive bits in a power drill. Concrete by the thousands of tons. There is a control center where the administration building meets the main prison, like an airport control tower placed on the floor, its panels filled with lights and switches to open and close doors in sequences that do not let anyone move ahead until the door behind has been locked, operated by officers in semidarkness behind tinted bullet-proof glass.

Inside the machine are sluggish parts called prisoners.

It is not a stable machine. The human personality is not readily reduced to such meticulous control. Even the massive hardware does not explain the working of the prisoner-machine, given the fact that the captives overwhelmingly outnumber their captors. Because a seized gun could reverse the balance of power, it is against regulations for an officer to bring a weapon inside the walls.

It is not weapons that keep the many prisoners from their few guards, nor the physical enclosures of concrete and steel—both keepers and kept are trapped in them. A state of mind keeps the machine working, mechanisms of bureaucracy, rewards and punishments, the power to take away those small amenities that in their ridiculous way help sustain sanity in constricted life—or the crucial power to deny early release. These are the official mechanisms that create the desired state of mind.

There are other mechanisms that are not official and are not openly discussed—private psychological and physical torture in dark places, "accidental" injury and death, arranged or tolerated by guards in the secret warfare of prisons. In the basement there are loneliness, sensory deprivation and other deliberate pressures that produce psychosis, augmented by occasional beatings by cadres of brutal guards, "the goon squads."

Some guards in Lewisburg are decent men who like many prisoners and abhor their savage associates. Most work at their jobs with no more feeling than most Americans with boring occupations. And there are some who, in the solitude of segregation, usually at night, send away the prisoner-orderlies who do the cleanup work, and beat prisoners they dislike. "Falling down the stairs" on the way to segregation is the euphemism for a beating by guards, or by another prisoner instructed by guards. But all—the decent, the bored and the sadistic—work obediently in the machine.

There are more subtle dangers from above. Despite public proclamations about prisoner study, the number permitted to study at colleges is minuscule, often as a reward for informing. Lewisburg's most famous college student was Boyd Douglas, a prisoner in "study-release" whose real mission was laid down by the FBI—to infiltrate the Bucknell University peace movement and to inform on his fellow prisoner "friend," the Reverend Philip Berrigan. "Rehabilitation" is a hated word among prisoners, cynicism toward it universal.

Most prisoners come from impoverished worlds where physical and verbal treachery are survival techniques that help shape the personality that becomes criminal. Prison intensifies these same pressures, from their keepers above, and from their fellow prisoners reacting to cynicism and corruption.

There is danger to a prisoner from others who are powerful, who control money, who are sexual aggressors or leaders of internal rackets. In Lewisburg, as in every other prison, there is smuggling by guards or with guard acquiescence. Narcotics flow inside, distributed in the early 1970s by a prisoner with a privileged job, a white man about thirty who liked to boast that he had addicted or readdicted a large portion of blacks in "the jungle," the prison name for the violent open dormitories in E and F blocks. Some men became addicted for the first time inside prison. The prison operator's heroin and amphetamines were carried inside the wall by prisoners in minimum custody who worked on the nearby prison farm. Addicts arranged with outside friends or family to pay the dealer's agent on the outside. The dealer's own prisoner goon squad beat drug customers who failed to pay or talked too much.

Money and liquor, both contraband if possessed by a prisoner, flow easily through the visiting room by way of privileged prisoners, such as chieftains of organized crime, who are treated with respect.

If smuggled liquor is too expensive, prison-made alcohol is available —"pruno," fermented in plastic bags filled with fruit, potato peelings, raisins and sugar, tied inside ventilators and drained off for celebrations.

Prisoner fights are usually over informing, money, drugs or homosexuality.

In prolonged all-male life homosexuality is almost inevitable. Most prisoners masturbate to relieve sexual deprivation. Others run miles every day or lift weights endlessly trying to sublimate sex.

The most violent form of sexual "adjustment" is gang rape, usually in "the jungle," the prime target young white prisoners inexperienced in violence. Special venom is directed at white draft resisters, a long line of whom have been duly assigned to "the jungle" and duly raped.

The prison has over 400 employees, but at night only one guard watches six separate dormitory wings on three different floors. As the guard leaves his desk for another floor there is a quiet scuffling in the newly unwatched wing as the rape gang moves to the victim, stuffs a sock in his mouth and beats him until he is terrified and semiconscious. They take the sock from his mouth and hold him down while they take turns at penetrating his anus and mouth with their penises. When they are through, they beat him again, with the threat of death if he talks. It is an event seen or heard by hundreds, maybe thousands, of Lewisburg prisoners who have lived in the dormitories designed to promote "rehabilitation by teaching men how to get along with each other."

Homosexual couples in voluntary association are known throughout prison as "husband and wife." When there is a fight over possession of an attractive "female," the administration may, if it wishes to do the "husband" a favor, lock him up with his "wife," but if it wishes to punish him, it may lock "her" up with the rival.

It is not difficult to understand the growth of homosexuality in an atmosphere of artificial sexual deprivation. A prisoner in Lewisburg told me, "There are some prisoners who adopt the female role and every day, every week they look more and more like a woman to you and pretty soon there is no doubt in your mind that they are a woman. It's that simple. They believe it. You believe it."

It is less easy to understand the unrelenting tradition of puritanism and vengeance applied to sex in American prisons. I asked an official in Lewisburg why conjugal visits are not permitted.

"That would be all right for the married men, but what would you do about single men?"

I suggested that it be left to the single men to decide.

"But that would mean the possibility of prostitutes, and the American people aren't ready for that."

Are the American people ready for forced homosexuality?

"Quicker than prostitution."

A Lewisburg prisoner found attempting sexual intercourse with his wife in the ladies' room of the visiting hall was arrested and sent for psychiatric examination.

Hostility and tension among prisoners are not altogether distasteful to their keepers. Unity among captives is always feared by the controlling minority. Whites are traditionally set against blacks, blacks against Latins. Aggression comes easily to rural-bred white guards who exert power over city-bred criminals.

Spontaneous unity among prisoners is rare. Racial and religious bigotry is at least as common among prisoners as among their guards, producing self-segregation. Most prisoners have spent their lives in cultures where distrust is a strategy of survival. Among the ethnic groups blacks alone have some sense of cohesion, exceeded only by the mafiosi.

If officials want a prisoner to cause trouble, they have powers of persuasion. An uncooperative prisoner can be put in quarters with an enemy, or in a dormitory known for gang rapes, or found guilty of an infraction that is false or perhaps genuine but tolerated until the staff needs to use it as a weapon. The manipulation of its own solemn regulations by prison systems contributes to the massive prisoner cynicism that greets official declarations.

The pamphlet Lewisburg gives to inquiring citizens states, "There are many parallels between the free community and an institution such as Lewisburg Penitentiary. Men come to prison from all walks of life. . . ."

Men come to prison overwhelmingly from one walk of life—the poor.

The booklet says, "They represent a fair cross-section of the contemporary American scene."

A fair cross-section of the American scene, according to the *Statistical Abstract of the United States*, is 51 per cent female. Lewisburg's population is 0 per cent female. The American nonwhite population is 13 per cent, Lewisburg's about 50 per cent. The country and Lewisburg prisoners have about the same average IQ, Lewisburg's 104, but the free adult population has an average of 12.7 years of schooling, the Lewisburg prisoner only 7.3 years.

The official book says, "At Lewisburg a chapel is maintained for all faiths in which an atmosphere of religion can be continuously maintained, with a revolving altar for Protestant, Catholic, Jewish and other traditions."

One of the most popular places for homosexual acts is between the pews of the chapel, blessed by the trinity of revolving altars.

"Every effort is made," the official Lewisburg booklet tells the inquiring public, "to discover those human values which lie within every individual and to make them available as guides to a more successful life."

THE PRISONERS
AND THEIR KEEPERS

John T. Alger, Prisoner No. 37102–133, white, age 27; offense, interstate transportation of forged securities; sentence, five years.

William Ryan Irwin, Prisoner No. 36234–133, white, age 42; offense, armed robbery of a bank; sentence, twelve years.

Lucky Johnson, Prisoner No. 36791–133, black, age 25; offense, armed robbery of a bank; sentence, four to six years.

Clarence Jones, Prisoner No. 36218–133, black, age 26; offense, armed robbery of a bank; sentence, twenty years.

Edward Mason, Prisoner No. 36035–133, black, age 30; offense, possession of stolen bank funds; sentence, seven years.

Joel S. Meyers, Prisoner No. 23429–145, white, age 28; offense, failure to report for induction into the military service; sentence, three and a half years.

Ronald T. Phillips, Prisoner No. 33074–136, white, age 34; offense, bank robbery; sentence, fifteen years.

Ronald L. Tucker, Prisoner No. 33582–118, black, age 23; offense, armed robbery of a bank; sentence, four to six years.

OTHER PRISONERS

Michel Guy Buyse, Prisoner No. 35712–133, white, age 32; offense, armed robbery of a bank; sentence, fifteen years.

Anthony DiLorenzo, Prisoner No. 72735–158, white, age 44; offense, interstate transportation of stolen property and conspiracy; sentence, ten years.

Miguel Estrada, Prisoner No. 69694–158, Latin, age 27; offense, receiving, concealing and transporting heroin; sentence, five years.

William Genco, Prisoner No. 37290–133, white, age 30; offense, conspiracy to possess counterfeit money, and escape; sentence, eight years.

Luis Pedro Hernandez, Prisoner No. 33541–134, Latin, age 40; offense, receiving, concealing and selling heroin; sentence, five years.

James C. Hilty Jr., Prisoner No. 37070–133, white, age 29; offense, bank robbery; sentence, ten years.

John Moore, Prisoner No. 37483–133, black, age 37; offense, possession and sale of marijuana; sentence, ten years.

Richard Moore, Prisoner No. 70209–158, black, age 41; offense, mail theft; sentence, three years.

Walter J. Scully, Prisoner No. 35648–133, white, age 54; offense, armed robbery of a bank; sentence, twenty years and $5000 fine.

Marcello Vivero, Prisoner No. 34357–133, Latin, age 36; offense, buying, selling and transporting narcotics; sentence, fifteen years.

John Wagner, Prisoner No. 83938–132, white, age 33; offense, bank robbery; sentence, fifteen years.

Robert Wolcott, Prisoner No. 23247–145, white, age 25; offense, interstate transportation of stolen motor vehicle; sentence, two years, eleven months and twelve days.

Dr. Z, Prisoner No. 18461–175, white, age 43; offense, mail fraud; sentence, four years.

THE KEEPERS

Noah L. Alldredge, white, former guard, age 55, warden of the United States Penitentiary, Lewisburg, Pennsylvania.

George W. Cansler, white, former guard, associate warden, Lewisburg penitentiary.

Paul Dodd, white, former guard, captain, Lewisburg penitentiary.

Norman A. Carlson, white, former guard, Director of the Federal Bureau of Prisons, Washington, D.C.

PART ONE

Cage (kāj) *n.* [OF., fr. L. *cavea* cavity, cage, fr. *cavus* hollow. . . .]

1. A box or enclosure, wholly or partly of openwork, in wood or metal, used for confining birds or other animals.

2. A place of confinement for malefactors. *Archaic.*

Webster's New International Dictionary,
Second Edition, Unabridged

1

POPULATION, FEBRUARY 15: 1491

Eddie Mason opened his eyes. The long window was a ghost of gray winter light. He reached for his cigarettes. Through the first puff of smoke he stared at the cold dawn and tried to remember why today was supposed to be so special. He said out loud, "Damn!"

Then to himself, It's my birthday!

It was February 15, 1972.

A voice nearby said, "All right, Motor Mouth, time to get your ass out that rack."

Mason couldn't see the speaker, whose bed was hidden by the chest-high partition in the privileged dormitory. He propped his head on the pillow. His hair was short, unlike the high Afros of militant blacks, consistent with his short, slender frame and round, amiable face that made him a pleasant but not memorable presence, an unaggressive peacemaker who could take part in the constant banter of insults and still be friendly. He looked at his watch.

"Shit, man, I got a whole hour before I get to the iron house."

"Iron house" was a factory in Lewisburg Federal Penitentiary, where Edward Mason, citizen of Jersey City's black ghetto, was Prisoner No. 36035–133.

It would be another five hours before Eddie Mason would discover that his thirtieth birthday would dissolve in events that would alter his life and the lives of seven other men he hardly knew.

Prisoner No. 36234–133 also opened his eyes that morning with a special expectation, a daily expectation of support and renewal. In a reflex as automatic as Eddie Mason reaching for a cigarette, William Ryan Irwin reached for his Bible. He read aloud and prayed silently. Then he picked up *Twenty-Four Hours a Day,* the slender black book

3

used by members of Alcoholics Anonymous to manage one day at a time.

Irwin was managing better than ever. Irish, curly-haired, huskily handsome, passionate, he was an oddity in prison. He was trusted by everyone who knew him.

Irwin often spoke with the eloquence of his Bible. This morning he laid it back on his table and opened his AA book to the page marked "February 15."

"I pray that I may be an instrument of the Divine Power. I pray that I may do my share in remaking the world."

At that moment his remade world seemed to him to be one that would cleanse his thoughts of indulgences like meat and cigarettes, women and robbing banks. And alcohol. He put the AA book on the table and walked to the window. He was in J wing, an honor block, the most privileged quarters. He had a private cage with a solid door and a small window. Most prisoners spend years with their vision limited to a few dozen feet, to the dull colors and hard lines of impervious surfaces like concrete, brick and steel. Irwin had an outside cage on the third floor and his window was higher than the thirty-foot wall that enclosed the prison. His eyes could escape daily. He could see the elaborate gabled mansion that was the warden's house, rolling Pennsylvania farmland, the undulating valley of Buffalo Creek and in the distance along the Susquehanna River the Bald Eagle range of the Allegheny Mountains. He loved the wild colors of the autumn trees, the first flowers in spring, the sensuous foliage and fat pheasants in summer.

But this morning the air was sullen, the trees crooked skeletons against an aluminum sky. There was no softness. The most dramatic shapes that fixed the limits of the world were the upslanted lines of the tinted glass of the gun towers along the wall.

Irwin sat down on his plastic chair and picked up a book, *Think on These Things,* by his favorite philosopher, Jiddu Krishnamurti:

"Life is very beautiful. . . . And you can appreciate its richness, its depth, its extraordinary loveliness only when you revolt against everything, against organized religion, against tradition, against the present rotten society so that you as a human being can find out for yourself what is true."

He heard the rattle of the morning guards unlocking the steel grille that barred the end of the wing. He hurried out, anxious to reach the dining hall before the crowd. He liked solitude in the morning. He took only cereal and fruit. An hour after reading Krishnamurti on the need for revolt, when the work whistle blew, Irwin marched without conscious objection to his job as a captive laborer working at thirty-seven cents an hour to produce goods sold for a net profit to the free citizens of the United States.

Long before Eddie Mason and Bill Irwin awoke, a guard walking through D block on the other side of the prison rapped his key against the steel door of a cage. It was five in the morning, still black in the February gloom before dawn. The door, like all the others on that tier, had a narrow opening just big enough for a man to stick out his hand.

The guard released one lock on the door and looked through the opening to make sure the occupant was awake. The prisoner was already out of his cot, naked, stretching sleepily.

This prisoner did not reach for a cigarette, certainly not for a Bible. Joel Simon Meyers, indefatigable communist missionary, was ready to start another day in the kitchen of the capitalist prison where he had been sent for disrupting conscription into the armed services of the United States.

He put on his T-shirt and jockey shorts and went to his sink. There were two spring-loaded buttons, one for hot water and one for cold. And no stopper. You could have cold alone or hot alone and catch what came out with the other hand. Meyers pushed the cold water button and splashed his face. There was no point in washing more thoroughly. After a day in the kitchen he would have a shower.

He put on his white uniform. As he pushed his foot into the high brown boots he hit a carton under his cot. There were three cartons, two more than officially permitted. But the guards were not strict. They knew what was in the boxes, of course. It all came through the mail and was duly inspected, and the cage was shaken down regularly for a thorough inventory. Meyers made no secret of the contents of his cartons or of his brain. Both were full of the works of Marx, Engels, Lenin, Castro, Guevara, Fanon, and his mentor, Leon Trotsky. There were copies of the newspaper of his splinter of the Trotskyist movement, *Workers World.* And a set of books on mathematics and physics.

Meyers put his hand through the small opening of the door and waved. In response he heard an unseen guard at the end of the block shake out a key and insert it into the master switch. An answering "click" electrically unlocked all the second locks of cage doors on the tier. Meyers pushed his door open and closed it behind him. The guard turned his key the other way and a "click" told him all the doors were double-locked again.

Meyers turned left into the polished main corridor and walked the hundred feet to "Red Top," the red-tiled concourse at the center of the prison. He was one of the few prisoners who always walked fast. Short, bushy-haired, with a perpetual expression of childlike glee, he always moved as though he were late for a victory celebration. One of the guards had said, "Joel would go to the gallows with that goddamn grin on his face." This morning he moved toward a rendezvous with a tray-washing machine in the prison kitchen.

As a kitchen worker he enjoyed the usual advantage of unofficial access to extra food, but his vegetarian demands were simple and he filled a stainless-steel bowl with raw Quaker Oats, a fistful of raisins, and ate them dry.

Dirty trays, emptied of solid remains by each prisoner, began to pile up at Meyers' machine. He set each dirty tray on pegs in a moving belt that went through the washing tunnel.

After his two hours of breakfast duty, Meyers returned to his cage to change clothes. He wanted to do his daily weight-lifting in the inside recreation room, but it was forbidden to wear kitchen whites anywhere except the kitchen. While he waited at the guard's station he watched a hand appear through a door opening. The guard unlocked the master lever. The prisoner opened his door. A second prisoner came out of a cage two doors away and the guard ordered him back to his cage.

"Why?"

"You got to signal."

"I got to come out to go to work and I'm out already."

"You know you got to signal first. One at a time. You know that."

"For Christ sake, I got to get out and I'm out!"

"I said get back."

The prisoner cursed and stomped into his cage and pulled the door shut behind him. The guard turned the key locking all the cage doors. The prisoner's hand appeared through the opening. The guard turned the key. The prisoner came out.

Meyers grinned at the guard. "He doesn't know how to play 'Giant Step.' He forgot to say, 'May I?'" Meyers spoke with the adenoidal inflection of central Brooklyn.

The guard said nothing. Meyers was always saying things you couldn't be sure of.

Meyers spent almost two hours on his back on the recreation room floor, slowly lifting a 170-pound barbell up and down to develop bulky muscles. Then it was time to get back into his kitchen whites for ten o'clock lunch duty.

William Irwin, at ten o'clock, was working to the slow rhythm of the factory. On Irwin's floor a line of huge presses dominated the scene. He and another prisoner lifted and positioned a slab of steel under the jaws of their machine. Irwin used both hands to depress the safety trigger, the press slammed down, punching holes and bending one side of the slab, the two men lifted it out and slung it toward two other prisoners, who turned the slab around and duplicated the shaping on the other side.

It was a standard scene in any factory except that all the workers were dressed in the products of their own world, their khaki shirts and trousers from Lewisburg, their gloves from Danbury prison, their shoes from Leavenworth penitentiary.

At ten o'clock William Irwin received the first clue that this day would be unlike all others. Out of the corner of his eye he noticed two white prisoners going to certain machines and whispering to their operators. He did not know them well but he knew enough to dislike them. They worked in another building of the factory. They avoided his machine.

There are almost no good surprises in prison, so Irwin went to the operator of another machine. "What the hell was that all about?"

"They said the guys in the shops ain't goin' back to work after chow."

"Why not?"

"The motherfuckin' shit yesterday, docking us two motherfuckin' hours' pay while they had a motherfuckin' staff meeting."

Irwin snorted. There was always strike talk. The gripers never acted. He didn't trust the two men. Acting like bigshots. Or playing some complicated staff game to smoke out rebellious leaders who could be watched, punished or transferred. His instincts told him Lewisburg was not in a rebellious mood. He finished a stack of steel slabs before he left for lunch.

A full hour earlier, shortly after nine o'clock, George Cansler, associate warden for programs, which included security, walked into the office of Warden Alldredge.

Cansler had small dark eyes and pursed lips. He closed the door behind him. "Billy Joe says two separate informers tell him the men in the shops are planning a strike after chow."

Prison keepers dread the word "strike" as ship captains dread the word "mutiny." It was particularly unwelcome now. Six months earlier the New York State Prison in Attica, only 150 miles away, had exploded in rebellion. Prisoners had seized staff members as hostages. When state police stormed the prison in a military attack, forty-three men had been killed, nine of them officers. Thereafter when wardens heard the words "strike" or "protest," the words "riot" and "hostages" and "Attica" came quickly to mind.

The warden did not react at once. He was wary from thirty years in the trade of guarding criminals, a stiff and uneasy man. Stiff from his early years in the military, where most older prison officials came from, his chin still upthrust, his hair still close-cropped. He was uneasy from periodic doubts about his trade and the institution of prison. He vacillated between military formality and studied friendliness.

But he had no doubts about his reputation. He was the successful product of the federal bureaucracy that incarcerates enemies of society in a system that held itself the best in the world, and he could approach retirement in a couple of years as the best warden in that system, holder of the prize appointment as warden of Lewisburg Federal Penitentiary, "the country club" of tough penitentiaries.

Prisons must move with undeviating rhythm, so prisoners must remain passive. Prisoners obey for interim rewards and hope of early release, or fear that their scream of "No!" fantasized every day by every prisoner will bring retribution. The word "Attica" comes as often to the minds of prisoners as to their keepers'. Each time a whistle is blown, a bell rung, an order shouted, there races through the mind of each prisoner, consciously or subconsciously, a calculation of obedience versus disobedience, a calculation that results in mass obedience almost every day in almost every prison.

February 15, 1972, began with the morning shift of prison employees arriving as they would in any factory. Some came from the stucco and frame houses on the private streets of the prison reservation, out of sight of the prison, shielded by fields and trees, like officers' quarters on a well-tended military base. Others drove from their homes in town, onto the obscure-looking road, past the JPM Company, manufacturers of wire and cable assemblies, the fourth largest employer in the city of Lewisburg, toward the penitentiary, the city's third largest employer. The employees, depending on their occupational status, carried brown paper bags or lunch buckets or attaché cases, and like most workers in factories they made their daily morning jokes and complained about the miserable weather, hardly conscious anymore that they passed through checkpoints, sally ports, double gates and locked compartments.

Key to the rhythm of the machine was the big day shift of guards, fifty-six of them, each officially designated in the euphemism of prison as a "correctional officer," but called by everyone "guard," "hack," "cop" or "screw." They take the vital census of every prison, "the count," a meticulous locating of every prisoner in the institution, to be seen by eye and recorded against the list of prisoners assigned to each enumerating guard, the count to be taken precisely at six A.M., four P.M., eleven P.M. and three A.M. It is an inventory more repetitious and tense than the counting of gold in Fort Knox, all the guards at the appointed minute walking each tier, eying each cage, each work area, in the dark segregation chambers, in the hospital. The results are transmitted to the control center, which checks it against the records, sends the results to the associate warden, who tells the warden's secretary, who posts it on the special board on the rear wall of her boss's office where he can see at any time the count in the main institution, Lewisburg, the separate one in the Lewisburg farm outside the wall, and in Allenwood, the satellite minimum-security camp fourteen miles away. The final number is "the population." The population never includes secretaries, guards, executives, but only the citizens of the prison who spend their years behind the wall, the prisoners.

In Lewisburg that morning Betty Smith, Warden Alldredge's secretary, posted the morning count on her boss's wall: "Population, Main Institution, February 15, 1972 . . . 1491."

At morning's start nothing disturbed the habitual rhythm. No one reported the classic symptoms of trouble. Inmates were not huddled together and scattering when guards approached. Normally talkative prisoners had not stopped talking to guards. There was no sudden increase in prisoners asking for protective segregation, hinting that they knew of impending trouble, no increase in commissary sales indicating hoarding of cigarettes and food in anticipation of institutional disruption.

The week before there had been the usual radical hand-lettered sheets calling for prisoner unity behind strikes in other prisons but that was normal. Prisons are perpetually paranoid. Just to be safe the warden had reported it to the weekly staff meeting and reminded everyone to be on the lookout for problems, to follow the rules when there was danger or tension—to be cool, relaxed, avoid arguments with prisoners. Nothing seemed to come of it all. Sales in the commissary had actually declined.

But now Associate Warden Cansler stood waiting, his face cold and expressionless. Behind the passive faces of prisoners there might be a sudden change. The delicate equilibrium of control might be about to disintegrate. The warden knew that in any crisis someone had to test the invisible shield that kept 1491 prisoners from conquering their fifty-six guards.

In a prison crisis the grapevine can make the difference between life or death. The morning of February 15 was no exception.

"Grapevine telegraph" was the American Civil War label for rumor circuits that beat official channels with urgent information. Appropriately in the endemic civil war between keepers and the kept, the "grapevine" has become part of prison vocabularies. Inside the wall both sides have their grapevines, and it is a romantic assumption that the prisoner grapevine is superior to the warden's.

The prisoner grapevine reaches into official files through docile-looking inmates who work in the front office. It works among alumni of reformatories, jails and prisons of the past whose residents go in and out of institutions passing word from distant people and places. Prisoners learn how to read faces, note changes in the atmosphere, detect weaknesses and subtle alterations of procedures. They are capable of the most earnest-looking deceit; a look of simple innocence or confused ignorance helps to conceal information from their keepers. They can be brutal with other prisoners who fail to cooperate.

Prisoners pass information through walls, dispatch innocent couriers with magazines carrying notes inside, drop messages to a floor below on string manufactured from lint, manipulate plumbing to pull property and communications through piped channels designed for human wastes. And they bribe.

The prisoner grapevine is capable of miracles of communication with no visible means of transmission. But it is seldom better than the warden's system.

Keepers of prisons are obsessed with the need to learn the thoughts of prisoners, and they penetrate the life of a prisoner to a degree unknown in other human habitations. They read his incoming and outgoing mail, whether from wife, lover, parent, child, lawyer, judge or priest. They know every book, newspaper and magazine received. They watch him eating, working, crying, laughing, having bowel movements and masturbating. They periodically shake down his cage and look at all his photographs, read his diaries, check his books. They monitor embraces with his wife in the visiting room and afterward strip him naked and examine his mouth and anus for contraband.

They know fragments of the prisoner subconscious through the countless variants of "counseling" and "group therapy" that probe the lives of convicts like psychiatric aphids.

Even strong-willed and shrewd prisoners are not able to conceal everything. Guards walk their rounds and sit at desks through the long boring hours of the night shift. The doors to most cages and dormitories are open, the walls concrete and steel, sounds echoed and amplified. In their sleep, prisoners talk, cry out, scream old fears and obsessions, relive horrors and joys, all heard by those awake and listening to the ricocheting sounds of the cellblock.

Wardens have another grapevine, a secret one of informers, or snitches. It is a complex and subtle system. Some prisoners try to learn everything from the population and tell everything to their keepers. Some prisoners inform only under duress, like the threat of endless segregation, of transfer thousands of miles away, or prosecution for earlier untried crimes, placement in a cage with a mortal enemy or in a dormitory notorious for gang rapes. Some inform only to the FBI, which maintains an office near every penitentiary for the purpose. If the prisoner does not inform, he is threatened from the official side by intensified punishment and extended imprisonment. If he does inform, he may be threatened from the prisoner side by the code of death to informers.

The conventional wisdom that prisoner grapevines are superior to wardens' was not true at Lewisburg the morning of February 15.

The warden needed to know as quickly as possible any evidence of a strike or riot. But so did a special small group of prisoners.

The first week of February was one of intense activity for the Political Education Committee. Strikes were breaking out all over the country after Attica's exposure of prison conditions gave prisoners self-consciousness. In the previous six months eight federal institutions had strikes or prisoner protests, some of whole populations for days. The committee put out hand-lettered sheets: "The Whole Federal System —On Strike!" But the propaganda seemed to disappear without a trace of reaction.

"Political Education Committee" was the ironical name given to themselves by a small band of five or six radical prisoners. In the evening when other prisoners watched penitentiary favorites on television like *The FBI Story* or played cards or read in their cells, the half dozen radicals met in the indoor recreation area to discuss current events, interpret them with Marxist analysis, suggest reading for each other or for newer members of the group, and talk about actions that would politicize other prisoners. It was a group known to the warden if for no other reason than that some of its members came into the institution as open political radicals, a class of convict hated by official-dom and by most prisoners.

Mario Moorhead, now head of a radical party in the Virgin Islands, in Lewisburg for robbery, was one of these, and a member of the discussion group.

Lucky Johnson, former addict and bank robber, from the Philadel-phia ghetto, was another member, emotional, intense, his gigantic Afro affronting officialdom, his speech peppered with "You know?," not a Marxist but a bitter black nationalist. He spoke in Muslim slogans, but after he embraced African nationalism he wrote his name, "Olaudah Ano Nkrumah."

Clarence Jones, also a former addict and bank robber, from Long Island, was tall and proud, his hair in a debonair butterfly Afro, his granny glasses giving him the air of a seventeenth-century scholar-aristocrat. He and Johnson had been profoundly moved by reading the Soledad letters of George Jackson. Jones had been a nominal Muslim when he first came to Lewisburg and had adopted the name Abdullah but later pursued African socialism and changed his given name to Lumumba.

Ronald Phillips, former addict and bank robber, was tall and swarthy, a Californian self-educated in literature, philosophy and, now, Marxism. He was quick of mind, ironic and witty, proud of his Russian-Georgian background and his East Los Angeles upbringing.

Joel Meyers loved the discussion group. He was effusively communis-tic, his name on the mailroom hot list of prisoners whose incoming and outgoing letters were held to be read and recorded by the FBI. He was recognized as "hot" from the start. When he first entered Lewisburg he was assigned to the jungle, where he was a perfect target for rape —a draft resister, Jew, communist, physically short. But his first night, after work in the kitchen, he carried a copy of the New York *Times* under his arm, inside the *Times* a large pointed French kitchen knife. At his bunk he let the most talkative prisoner in the dormitory peek at the knife, whispering to the gossip that he always slept with the knife under his pillow. The next morning the guard asked with a smile if Meyers had felt any "sexual pressure." Meyers pretended he didn't understand.

Meyers' brainchild was a secret publication, *The First Step*. It was designed to counter the official prison paper, *The Friday Flyer,* which like most prison papers was a careful blend of innocuous gossip, praise of athletic heroes and inspirational messages from the warden. *The First*

Step was the Lewisburg samizdat, like the underground communications against the regime in the Soviet Union. It had a logotype of three simple lines at right angles forming the outline of a step, drawn by Meyers with a Magic Marker. He used carbon paper given prisoners for their legal documents to make four copies of the twelve- to twenty-four-page editions. Contents included articles about world events from a radical viewpoint, copies of articles from Meyers' party at the time, Workers World, a column called "Law of the Lawless" with items about corruption in government, and periodic campaigns to mobilize prisoners for outside programs like shunning citrus fruits in support of striking agricultural workers.

Under the logotype he put in handwritten block letters, "No rights reserved. All material in this publication may be reproduced without the permission of the author."

The author, of course, was not identified.

Each of the four copies of the paper would be given to a trusted inmate who would make four more copies and in turn give one copy to four more inmates. The paper would disappear into the grapevine, usually through most of three cycles, so that eighty-four copies could have been circulating. Later the distributors would have the satisfaction of hearing arguments among prisoners about articles in *The First Step*. Black prisoners tended to be sympathetic, whites hostile, Latins neutral. Prisoners, except for younger blacks, were usually nationalistic, pro-war and politically conservative.

The first issue was circulated in the summer of 1971. It had not gone far before someone had changed Meyers' design of the step into a swastika, the symbol used by prison "nazis," the small group of white prisoners who organized against nonwhites. On the next issue Meyers redesigned the logotype by enclosing the step, making alteration to a swastika less satisfactory.

After the massacre in Attica there was a special issue. It noted the guards killed in Attica and added, "To any officer who might confiscate this magazine—remember what happened to hacks at Attica. Don't allow yourself to be used."

The Christmas issue had a large cartoon of policemen nailing a prisoner to a cross. The legend was "Merry Xmas."

Shortly before the strike Meyers produced his most inspired creation. *The Friday Flyer* frequently ran photographs of the warden in various poses. Meyers collected copies of an issue of the *Flyer* that carried a photograph of Warden Alldredge seated at his desk. Meyers altered the picture to show the warden with one fist outstretched with a crumpled copy of *The First Step* and the other hand holding the hypodermic needle and spoon used by drug addicts.

Warden Alldredge knew about the Political Education Committee. He received a copy of each *First Step* almost as quickly as he got his copy of *The Friday Flyer*. The sheets of paper with "The Whole Federal System—On Strike!" were delivered to him within an hour of their appearance. He knew where it came from and he tested the reaction. He got the same reading as the Political Education Committee. The population was ignoring it. Nevertheless, he thought it prudent to tell his weekly staff meeting on Monday that the sheet was circulating and remind them to use the usual procedures when there was a possibility of trouble. Be watchful, report inmate incidents but don't get involved, be cool, relaxed, use humor with prisoners, avoid confrontations that might trigger violence. Humor, humor, humor. A joke will prevent more trouble and give you more information than an order.

Both the Political Education Committee and Warden Alldredge had an intense interest in any rumor about a strike. But the warden heard first. His first word came on Tuesday morning, minutes after nine o'clock, a full hour before any member of the Political Education Committee heard.

At his lunch break Bill Irwin decided he would try the commissary line in hopes that the usual long wait would be minimal at this hour. He wanted greeting cards for the two women he corresponded with and he wanted some citrus fruit. He was uninterested in the citrus boycott by the radicals. He didn't like radicals. There was a short line at the commissary counter. The man in front turned to him. "Hear about the strike?"

"Yeah. I heard some bullshit about it in the shop."

"No bullshit, Irwin. You're in industry. What you gonna do?"

"Shit, I don't know."

Irwin walked away without waiting to buy his commissary goods. He hadn't really believed there would be a strike. He didn't want trouble. The idea irritated him. He was "doing his own time," staying out of trouble, following the rules, avoiding inmate fights and inmate rackets, speaking politely to guards when they spoke politely to him. He had never had a misconduct report.

All of this gave him maximum prison privileges; as chairman of the prison chapter of Alcoholics Anonymous, he was one of the few prisoners permitted to make talks on the outside to nearby community AA groups. The staff liked and trusted him. His work supervisor had invited him to his home for Thanksgiving dinner and afterward let Irwin take the supervisor's children to a nearby park.

Irwin had a perfect work record, so this month, for the first time in his forty-two years, he was eligible for a week's vacation with pay—a week in his room or the library or the exercise yard, free to run or read or meditate all day and still get his industry wages.

All of this had let him compile an impressive collection of that precious commodity in prison, "good time," the days of good behavior that permit early release. As of that morning Irwin had 586 days of good time that could be subtracted from his twelve-year sentence. The law gave him "statutory good time," ten days a month for every month without a misconduct report. The prison regulations gave him an additional "extra good time" for efficient work in the factories. It was a vital statistic. If he continued at this rate he would be released six and a half years early, when he was forty-four years old instead of when he was fifty. And maybe sooner. The only commodity of greater value than good time was parole—early release to the free world under occasional supervision. It could come theoretically if the parole board was impressed with continual good behavior and preservation of his good time, though in fact no one knew how the parole board made its decisions. If the prison staff took back even one day of accumulated good time, the United States Board of Parole would not consider an application for release. The prison staff, by its own power to bring misconduct reports and revoke days of accumulated good time, controlled parole, or freedom, though nothing in the Constitution said they could.

All of this would explain why Irwin was liked by the prison staff. Ordinarily it would make him hated by his fellow prisoners. The strict followers of rules, the polite talkers to guards, the religious observers, were assumed, at best, to be playing a game of false subservience to make an impression, possibly a little crazy, and at worst informers. Cynics were tolerated, clever ones admired. Snitches were not.

But Irwin was respected by his fellow prisoners because he had passionate feelings that periodically broke out in powerful protests of absolute sincerity that even the most belligerent prisoner might fear to voice.

A few weeks earlier, Irwin was denied parole for the third time in a row, with the usual unstated reasons despite his perfect record. The result had been an impassioned declaration before his group therapy class that became known to others in the institution.

It was shortly after he had received the form letter from the parole board merely saying he was set off for another year, with no reason given. At about the same time a friend in his cellblock, a man with no homosexual desires, had confided to Irwin that he would do anything for a parole including commit a homosexual act with a guard. Irwin was horrified, but for him it symbolized the humiliating groping for parole.

He told his class, "This mad drive for parole is cruel destruction from the very beginning. From the first day you enter prison, you are subject to abject slavery, you start on your knees, and gradually your bonds get heavier. With each new degradation you tell yourself you must accept it, and you're weighed down until finally you're on your belly like a snake. But unlike a snake, you're not free. . . .

"Granted, there are a few who rebel, they go to the hole in preference to humiliation. I used to feel sorry for these guys. All the time in trouble. Real jerks. But now I see they're the ones who are honest. They can't live with this lie."

Irwin had written out his declaration to be sure he said exactly what he wished, and to eliminate the natural profane idiom of prison talk, in deference to Olymp Dainoff, the staff member conducting the class, whom he considered his friend. The polite words made clear to everyone that he was abandoning conformity to the expected image of "rehabilitation," that he was tossing away the bonds of insincerity. It was a personal freedom of sincere expression longed for but feared by hundreds of other prisoners doing their own time.

Irwin let years of frustration burst out: "I can remember the many times during my incarceration that I was forced or felt I was forced to do things or say things I didn't want to say. It's the humiliating treatment by brutal, sadistic guards who insist on being right regardless of the circumstances."

He told the stunned audience he finally felt free.

"I'm no longer willing to pay the price that I've paid in the past. My self-respect is more valuable to me than parole. What good is a parole to me if my heart and soul are still in chains? If I can't allow myself freedom, how in hell can anyone else give it to me?"

Now that he had given himself to God, he said, he had stopped running. He had found peace.

But if there was a strike he could continue his peaceful inner withdrawal, or express his honest feelings. He had to choose one or the other.

As much to delay a decision as anything he went to see his best friend on the staff. Mr. Dainoff, a refugee Jew in the 1930s who came to Lewisburg and whose work in the prison was chief of classification and parole. He had been looked down upon by the regular staff, especially in the beginning, and the tougher guards and officers still were contemptuous of his unmilitary ways. But over the years he had become tougher and over the years there had been more staff members like him. He liked Irwin. For Irwin, Dainoff was the man in prison he most trusted.

Irwin wanted to be transferred back to Southern California. It was a better climate. And Terminal Island, the federal prison at Long Beach, was more relaxed than Lewisburg penitentiary. He had had thirty-two members of the staff endorse his transfer application and now he planned to ask Dainoff for his signature. Dainoff read the application. He had talked to Irwin many times about it. He signed.

As Irwin left Dainoff's office a prisoner walked alongside: "The guys in the shops are going to stop off in the slot after chow. They ain't gonna go back until they get taken care of. You gonna be there?"

Irwin grunted noncommittally and kept walking.

After his talk at group therapy, how could he be a scab? The last two years of his life had been different because he had learned to be honest with himself. He had stopped faking elaborate worlds constructed for others and had found it exhilarating and liberating.

He remembered what he told the therapy class: "If I can't allow myself freedom, how in hell can anyone else give it to me?" And this very morning's reading in Krishnamurti on the need to discover truth by rebelling against rottenness. His AA paragraph for the day, "I pray that I may do my share in remaking the world."

God knows the industries were rotten. They made goods inefficiently. They took advantage of men who were imprisoned and penniless in order to make a profit. They dangled time off their sentences and the maddening possibility of parole if they would work for thirty-seven cents an hour while the industry turned back a $5 million profit it didn't even spend on job training the prisoners needed. They did it all telling the world that they were training the prisoners for gainful employment after release. But grown men spent eight hours a day sewing the left inseam of a chino trouser on a machine no outside industry used anymore, or stamping metal parts that cost half as much as those made by better machines in private industry on the outside. They worked overtime and Saturdays for a few extra days off their sentences so that the industry could complete a contract and make extra money.

But Irwin had determined to stay out of trouble. And who the hell was talking up this strike anyway? A lot of prisoners were boasting loudmouths; they strutted around, jived at the top of their lungs, every other word tough-guy violence, trying to sound like fearless rebels. Usually it was the weakest ones who talked the most. Some of them were plain crazy, not nice crazy like Dr. Z, but dangerous crazy, hungry for violence of any kind. He hated loudmouths. He had been that kind of a person once and like most converts he hated people who were like his old self.

He was deep in his own thoughts when he entered the dining hall. He carried his tray toward the tables. He saw Ron Phillips sitting alone, his head bent over a plate of spaghetti.

"Mind if I sit here, Phillips?"

"Uh, hi, Bill. Sit down."

Phillips had seen Irwin out of the corner of his eye and had hoped he would find another table. He found Irwin's constant Bible talk irritating. Their closest association had been a chess match during which they had a fierce argument. Phillips loved arguments that were tests of knowledge or wit. But not the way Irwin argued, quoting the Bible as his proof for everything.

Besides, Phillips wanted to save the table for himself and Meyers. Phillips worked up in the central dental lab as a trainee and he used lunch to catch up on events and to carry on their endless political jousting. Meyers was so serious about Marxist analysis of everything that occurred in the world that he was an easy target for Phillips' practical jokes. Phillips would concoct a false radio report that refuted a prediction Meyers had made about capitalist collapse. Only after Meyers had gone deep into complicated explanations for the non-event and Phillips had started to laugh would Meyers look hurt and start laughing too.

Phillips had another, less political motive. Meyers could bring extra food from the kitchen.

A white-uniformed prisoner came out with a hot sandwich that he put wordlessly in front of Phillips and walked away, a sign that Meyers couldn't get away from the tray machine. Phillips concentrated on his meal, hoping that Irwin was not in a soul-saving mood. He didn't encourage conversation.

Irwin said, "Heard about the strike?"

Irwin seldom made small talk. Phillips put down his knife and fork and gave his full attention. "No. What strike?"

"In the shops. For not getting paid for the time lost in yesterday's fucking lockup when the staff had its meeting."

What did it mean? Why a strike now? Nobody had been in the mood last week. And the word had gone around only yesterday that the warden had come back from Washington with a lot of liberal policies to announce. He had told the staff about them at yesterday's meeting. Maybe that was it. The strike talk could be a plot by the old-line hacks, "Cansler's boys," to sabotage the new rules. A riot would do it. Send a couple of creeps around getting an incident started and then blame it all on being too easy on the prisoners. Or was this just his own paranoia? Does it make any difference? If there's a strike, what response should he make? Phillips asked Irwin, "When's it coming down?"

"They say right now. After lunch. Everyone's supposed to get together around the dock area instead of going back to work. What about the rest of the population, the guys who don't work in industry? Do they know about it? What are they gonna do?"

Phillips said they hadn't heard in the dental lab, and obviously Joel hadn't heard.

Irwin said, "I thought you might—I mean, knowing how you feel about politics and things like that, I thought you might want to help spread the word around and see how the guys feel."

That sounded like a challenge to Phillips' constant rhetoric for militancy. "Yeah, of course. Let's see what's happening."

They emptied their trays and went outside to the dock area. Between the big dining-hall building and an adjacent dormitory wing, each three stories high, there was an open space leading to a loading platform, the dock serving the kitchen storage room. The dock turned the corner of the building into "the slot," the angled space between the main building and the industrial shops.

The sky was threatening and cold but about a hundred men were gathered around the dock, most huddling deep into their jackets. Irwin went inside to his room for his pea jacket. When he came out, a friend handed him a cup of ice cream.

Phillips walked into the crowd and talked to the men he knew. "What's up?"

"We're not goin' the fuck back till they give us the two motherfuckin' hours' pay they docked us yesterday. They closed the fuckin' shops, not us. They got paid for those two fuckin' hours. Why the hell shouldn't we?"

He asked another man what was wrong.

"Everything! Every fuckin' thing! The fuckin' pay is slave pay. The fuckin' parole board sits on its ass and tells you what to do and you do it and they say wait another fuckin' year. And that fuckin' Cansler . . ."

Almost everyone mentioned Cansler.

One man said he was for the strike, but he was afraid "Cansler's boys" would use it to move in on the warden.

"Alldredge's a fuckin' hypocrite like all the rest but he's got enough sense not to push us too far. The goons are badmouthin' him all the time. Maybe if we go down the goons will take over and we'll all be shit."

An acquaintance said, "This is it, Phil. This is it, man. We are not going to work."

Phillips felt exhilarated. One hundred unified prisoners was amazing. He was uncertain for a moment what to do. The radicals had hoped for a strike and now the conservative workers in Federal Prison Industries had started it.

He went back into the dining room. He went to a few tables and spread the word to men he knew. Only kitchen workers could go inside but Phillips' white dental lab uniform was the same as the kitchen workers' and no one stopped him there. Meyers was stacking dirty trays on the moving belt.

"Joel! They're getting ready to strike at industries!"

Meyers smiled. "Really?"

Phillips regretted all the times he had tricked Meyers. "Jesus, Joel! This is no shit! They're really out. Go look at the dock. At least a hundred guys. I'm going to let the guys in dental lab know."

Meyers was wiping his hands on his trousers and already eying the exit as Phillips left to alert the central dental lab. Inside the lab Phillips walked past his civilian boss, found Jones and told him to get down to the dock right away.

As he headed back out his boss yelled, "Hey, Phillips! Where the hell you think you're going?"

Phillips kept going without answering. At the dock the crowd was bigger. He looked around for Meyers. He could see him nowhere. But he did see Captain Dodd.

Paul Dodd, big, composed, easy in manner, almost but not quite fatherly, tough, was respected more than most captains in prisons. Captains maintain order for the associate warden. Paul Dodd was not hated by the prisoners, something unusual for a captain. He strolled calmly toward the men scattered near the kitchen dock.

Phillips was increasingly excited as he saw the looks on men's faces. Suddenly Attica came to mind. Instinctively he looked toward the gun towers. He was relieved to see that most of the area was shielded by surrounding buildings. But from the center of the kitchen dock there was a clear line of fire from the edge of the gun tower at the center of the west wall. Toward the rear on the north you could see parts of the gun tower at the center of the north wall but it was hard to guess about line of fire, because freight cars and truck trailers on the metal industry siding made an irregular barrier.

As he looked around he noticed staff members in upper windows of buildings taking photographs. That meant the institution was on alert and they were going to identify people for future punishment. He saw a man in white uniform pushing through the crowd. It was unmistakably Jones, walking with a smile, looking, Phillips thought, like a black prince.

"Lumumba!"

"*All right,* Ron! *All right!* Looks like we're really going to get down!"

"Right. But everyone's holding back. Nothing's happening. You got any copies of the Bill of Rights we can hand around?"

Jones nodded. "Be right back."

Phillips looked through the crowd again. Where was Meyers?

Irwin came over again. Incongruously he was eating ice cream with a wooden spoon. There wasn't going to be much help from him.

"Danny," a socialist, came over. "Goddamn, Phil. If something isn't done soon, this crowd is going to break up."

People who didn't know Phillips well called him Phil, but Phillips thought he was going to know Danny better.

Irwin didn't know Danny at all. "You got to be crazy to take the lead," he said to Danny. "That's all they want, see who's leading this thing and bust him and end the strike."

Danny disagreed. "No, you guys are wrong. You guys are experienced. The guys respect you. Once you speak up, they'll follow and the administration won't dare touch you."

Irwin laughed. "You're out of your fuckin' head. Ron's done a lot of time and so have I. When something like this comes down, there's one main thing the screws want—Who are the ringleaders? And once they see who takes the bait to come up front, bang! The ringleader goes into the hole, gets busted, loses good time, gets transferred, and no one else is going to go up front for a long time. How the hell do you know?

Maybe this is just a bunch of fucking snitches smoking out leaders for the screws."

Danny looked at Phillips. Phillips nodded agreement. Yes, the administration's watching to see who takes the first step. He'll be the ringleader and he'll be all through. The protest will be all over. Better go easy until you see who's really leading this thing. Could be some crazies or snitches.

Irwin said to Danny, "If you're so goddamn sure, then go up there yourself."

For the first time Danny looked doubtful. It was true. No one was taking the lead.

The sky was darkening. Spits of rain made spots on the concrete.

Meyers, walking in quick, short steps, came with his arms loaded with a conglomeration of literature. He passed out papers as he approached.

"What the hell kept you, Joel?"

"Those fucking scabs in the kitchen! I was trying to get them out here. But they've got cold feet. And I had to go to my room for this stuff. Hey, a good crowd!"

Jones appeared, his hands also full of papers. Danny grabbed some of the papers and started handing them out, calling, "Strike! Everybody strikes!"

The papers were copies of the United Prisoners Union "Bill of Rights," a document originating in Folsom State Prison in California and instantly popular in prisons all over the country. The Bill of Rights had appeared in Danny's Socialist Workers Party paper, *The Militant,* three months before. An agreeable prisoner with access to the prison mimeograph had run off copies.

Phillips turned to Meyers. "Give me a copy of the Bill of Rights."

Joel handed him a sheet of paper. Phillips took it and headed toward the cluster of men closest the dock. Suddenly he turned back to Meyers. "Joel! For Christ sake! This is a fucking article on the economy of Bangladesh."

2

THE KEEPERS

When his deputy told him there were rumors of a strike, Warden Alldredge had to be cautious. If the rumors were not true and the staff showed anxiety, that by itself might trigger a riot. Hundreds of men held in close custody survive by suppressing their instincts, but those emotions—frustration, anger, hatred, claustrophobia—are held behind a fragile barrier. A wrong move could break the dam. He had to test, but with subtlety.

He knew that some staff members would be so bitter at the thought of a strike, or so fearful, that they could create an incident with violent consequences. On the other hand, he had to warn the staff they might find themselves isolated, possibly taken hostage. How could they make sure that reliable informers in the population were in the right place at the right time?

If hostages were taken, what about the women who worked in the office? More than one warden had cursed the architect of Lewisburg. The beautiful idea of putting everything inside the wall meant that despite the locked grilles between the administration offices and the prisoners, an attack upon the control center might give them access to everyone inside the wall, including the women. In prison strikes women hostages were almost never hurt, but it made for a bad press.

Everyone who went to work in the prison was told that an escaping prisoner holding hostages would be fired at with guns shooting to kill even if it meant killing the hostages. "No prisoner walks out of this institution illegally." But it was not a rule that most wardens liked to think about.

Every emergency had a contingency plan: a fire, a massed open attack, armed rebellion with smuggled weapons, coordinated seizing of hostages at a given moment, riots between whites and blacks, diversions while a few prisoners tried to escape. The defenses were all on file, with key people instructed. But they were for situations that had already erupted.

Should he notify Washington? The Director of Prisons in Washington was the leader of the prison empire. But in fact his wardens were powerful barons who ran their own fortresses. They were expected to handle their institutions by themselves. The Director gave them latitude, the courts gave them latitude, Congress gave them latitude, the press gave them latitude—everyone gave them latitude. If they had trouble, it was up to them to handle it. Only if their institution was out of control would outside help be sent in, and for a warden outside help means defeat. His standing never recovers.

If he notified Washington too soon, it would be a sign of panic. If it got into the newspapers, it would put him in an even worse light, tempting the Director to take over. Or stimulating the prisoners to take dramatic action. Warden Alldredge wanted nothing in his record to show that he lost control of his institution.

But just as wardens' power is seldom challenged by the distant Director, the barons themselves are forever being tested by their knights, the staff. The warden's deputies were divided. The older men, hard-nosed, remembered the days of locksteps, total silence, condoned beating of prisoners, open racial slurs, prisoners standing at attention when spoken to, no cards, no games. For them, all the new liberal looseness was stupid, an intrusion on their duty to punish the prisoner. Washington was regarded as soft-headed and so was Warden Alldredge. The hard-noses were mostly from the South. Guard service had paid poorly, but it was better than the greater poverty of the South.

The knights were not unified. Some despised the hard-noses, knew of their slurs, the beatings and Macings in the basement, were repelled by their private talk and private behavior. They tended to be younger, with some college and from less rural areas. Most liked the warden, compared with his predecessors.

The warden could not lose control of his institution, but the key to that was to maintain control over his staff. The staff could frustrate any order of his, just as he could frustrate an order of the Director. Most of them had been in ˙he military and they all knew how to make a superior fail.

Warden Alldredge considered his greatest strength his standing with the prisoners. He was disliked by prisoners on grounds that all prisoners dislike their keepers. But he was liked on grounds that he was better than almost any warden the prisoners had known before.

In 1944, when Warden Alldredge started as a guard at the Terre Haute penitentiary, he had no doubts about the rightness of its prison life. Prisoners were mostly rural illiterates who accepted everything. Prisoners marched single file every place they went. They lived in silence. If they left a bread crumb or a pinch of pork fat on their trays, they were thrown into the hole. They had no newspapers or radios. No games, including cards, were permitted. Prisoners could not gather in groups.

He knew that some of his officers longed for "the good old days." Riots and violence were constant. At least twice a year, usually spring and fall, there was a riot with killings, knifings, gang fights. The public seldom heard about them, unless the population set the place on fire. Guards were seldom touched by rioting prisoners. It was inmate against inmate, and almost always, especially at Terre Haute, white prisoners beating and killing black prisoners.

In those days no one kept statistics on the added crime committed by American prisoners after they were released to society.

Months before the strike I had a long, discursive interview with the warden, talking about prisons in general. It was in his comfortable office. We sipped coffee. The Quaker book, *Struggle for Justice,* showing the futility of most prisons as a deterrent of crime, was on his desk. He said it expressed the doubts he had developed about prisons over his career.

"Prisoners are better educated today. They react to events in the outside world. They're more militant and bitter. I can understand some of their bitterness. They know they're convicted more often than middle-class offenders, they get longer sentences, and all the rest. They know these things and they're bitter about them."

He believed in the new relaxation and he was certain that no one yet had the answer to ending criminality, certainly not prisons.

"I don't believe that we're ever going to change most prisoners under the present system. There's no real interaction among people. Prisons like this are too large, too tight. Ninety per cent of my regulations are written for 10 per cent of the population who are real problems."

Warden Alldredge believed prison sentences are too long in the United States and too indefinite, letting the prison staffs decide when to free the prisoner.

"It gives too much control to the prison administration. It's self-defeating and frustrating to the inmate. It creates problems for the administrator that he doesn't even realize, because his staff has too much control over the lives of prisoners and this produces extreme tension among inmates."

The warden had doubts about "treatment," the group therapies and other programs that were supposed to "rehabilitate" prisoners.

"I don't know whether we have the right to treat people, whether it is an appropriate concept. If we decide the prisoner is 'sick,' we are deciding he is sick by our standards. I question whether it is effective or moral."

But, Warden, I protested, you pursue treatment in your own penitentiary.

He nodded thoughtfully. "I pursue it, but I question it. The longer I'm in prison, the less I know about prisoners. What's the right thing to do with prisoners? I don't know. Things I used to believe, I no longer believe."

He was sure that as far as the safety of society was concerned, 75 per cent of his prisoners did not need to be there. What we need, he said, are small places where prisoners and staff can interact.

"Everything depends on personal interaction." He paused and said unexpectedly, "I don't believe in the use of informers."

Long after the events of February 15 I called Warden Alldredge, in his retirement in Missouri. I wanted to talk to him about the events. He refused.

Warden Alldredge had a habit that gave him support among prisoners. He strolled among the men. He listened to their complaints. He granted privileges and accelerated petitions, like a good politician building credit for favors done, but on an individual basis so that the obligation was to him alone. He spent a lot of time walking around Red Top, the tiled concourse in front of the dining hall, midway between the two halves of the prison. He asked prisoners about sick families, listened to their entreaties for changes of housing, jobs and support for parole. He had learned how to exude an air of relaxed amiability that was unusual for the warden of a major penitentiary.

The shrewd use of minor changes had gone far in developing loyalty among the prisoners. The day he had arrived as warden in 1970 there had been a strike of industry workers. He had sent his captain among the milling men to find out why they were unhappy. They disliked the wages, the rigid rules, and limitations on smoking. The warden knew that additional pay for some industry workers had already been decided in Washington but not yet announced. So he promised change. He instructed his captain to tell the men to give the new warden a chance, that this warden had a reputation of being a "prisoners' warden," a man on their side. If they continued the strike, it would undercut the liberalizing changes the warden planned. The strike was over in forty-five minutes.

There was a slight increase in industrial pay, for which the warden got credit. The warden permitted buying of soft drinks at the commissary, a privilege previously limited to machines in the visiting room. He let men smoke in areas formerly off limits. He enlarged recreation areas. He ordered especially good food for the week afterward. Over the years he had made small relaxations of rigid rules.

Now he had to test the tension in the population, to find out if the strike plans were real and organized. He couldn't send Cansler, because he knew his deputy was disliked. Paul Dodd was perfect.

Paul Dodd had worked the big penitentiaries—Terre Haute, Leavenworth, Marion. He followed the manner of Warden Alldredge, moving with controlled casualness, exuding assurance and amiability. So now he strolled down the corridor on the west side, down past the jungle, by the semi-honor blocks and the honor blocks. Then he strolled back across Red Top to the east end, "across the tracks," to the closer-custody cages. He knew where "his boys" were, the ones who could talk to him casually in the corridor without stopping long enough to make it look bad.

Captain Dodd, his innocent stroll down the main corridors completed, returned to the warden's office. Alldredge and Cansler were waiting for his conclusion. He reported that something was in the air but nothing very big or clear. Warden Alldredge said he had to have more than that. Dodd had to squeeze his sources harder.

At eleven o'clock Captain Dodd returned. He had taken the risk of seeing some prisoners privately. The talk had evolved in the last hour. There was no question, some men planned a strike to begin at the slot after the noon meal. The supervisors in the industry were hearing pressure being put on passive prisoners.

The warden placed his call to Washington.

The Director sat in Washington on the sixth floor of an undistinguished building near the United States Courthouse and headquarters of the Teamsters Union. The building, home of the Federal Home Loan

Bank Board, at 101 Indiana Avenue, N.W., was one of the innumerable antheaps of human affairs that control federal establishments.

His office was modest by standards of other bureaucratic chieftains, an expansive wooden desk, flags on either side, a large picture of the President of the United States directly flanked by at least one picture of his immediate superior, the Attorney General of the United States, photographs hung on standard hooks for quick changes, of which there would be many in the Director's reign.

He sits at the center of a new organism in the Republic, a national prison system, the American archipelago of more than fifty concrete-and-steel islands sprinkled across the land, enclosing at any one time 24,000 men, women and youths convicted of violating federal laws, the largest prison system in the Western World.

This archipelago is no massive Stalinist madness. It does not corral uncounted millions, or exterminate its captives like Hitler's concentration camps, or match the systematic barbarities of a hundred prisons around the globe.

The American prison system is the measure of a different social order, a social order that says its soul is a civilized standard of human behavior. The prisons of a civilized society can never punish by murder, though murder happens. Or torture, though torture happens. Or deliberate destruction of individual spirit, though that, too, happens. All in the name of a civilized society.

Norman Carlson, the Director, may have thought about such things. But he had built an empire that did not encourage introspection. Through his gates and sally ports during his reign there had passed over 100,000 men, women and young people found guilty of violating some federal law. Up to the time the court passed sentence on them there was at least a public procedure that governed their fate. There had to be "reasonable cause" for arrest, a judgment that the evidence warranted trial, a right to a lawyer, a trial by trained attorneys before a judge held to decorum and confirmation by the Senate of the United States.

But 120 days after the judge has passed sentence, the fate of the prisoner passes out of the courts and into the hands of the prison keepers, who decide where the prisoner will go, into what kind of institution, under how severe custody, in what job he will be forced to work, what kind of associates he will sleep with, the size of the cage he will live in, how and when he will be punished for displeasing his keepers, and how long he will remain imprisoned.

The keepers, unlike the courts, operate in secrecy, with the cooperation of a citizenry grateful to be shielded from unpleasantness. It is a bureaucracy with powers rare even in a totalitarian world. It has total control over an individual. It exercises this power behind an outer vocabulary of social work and therapeutic benevolence, but inside it insists on secrecy and complete control and is as resistant to basic change as the steel it buys in large quantities from the manufacturers of prison supplies. The secrecy is enhanced by placing most of its institutions in remote rural areas. If there are barbarities and injustices, Americans could say, "We never knew it."

Prison is a Christian invention. Until recently jails kept the citizen until the king or duke or bishop decided on guilt and innocence. Punishment was a single act—flogging, cutting off hands, tearing out tongues, branding foreheads, or castrations, or killings. Aristocrats and priests were exiled.

Quakers and others in the late eighteenth century, appalled by the conditions of jails and the brutality of punishment, invented the prison in the spirit of Christian sin and redemption. A criminal was a person with a sick soul. Souls were cleansed by solitude, meditation and penitence. So criminals were sent to isolated institutions to work and live in austere surroundings where they could cleanse their souls and become penitent. The place would be called a penitentiary. Charles Dickens visited this new American invention and noted that whatever it might do for the soul it frequently unhinged the mind. Insanity and suicide were common.

With the best of intentions the trade of prison keeper was established. Tradesmen like to ply their trade. If their trade relieves the average citizen of the need to view an unpleasantness, then the trade becomes secret by default. So it is not surprising that modern prison keepers do not believe in public accountability.

New York State, shaken first by rebellion in Attica and then by the discovery of brutality and corruption throughout its prison system, created a commission charged by law to break the secrecy of prisons by visiting them without notice. Three years later it was disclosed that one of the first acts of the head of the new commission was to agree privately with prison keepers to notify them in advance of inspection visits, contrary to law.

When I was writing this book, I wished to view scenes in the federal prison where the major events occurred. One place was in segregation cages. I was not permitted to view even an empty one. The prison official in charge said, "You are here as a private citizen, so it is not appropriate that you should be permitted to see that part of the prison."

The archipelago is a law unto itself.

The United States went 114 years without a federal prison system. States, territories and counties had their own prisons, and if someone broke a federal law, the federal court sent him to his local institution and paid for his incarceration in his own community. Many of the local prisons are horrors. But they are local, near the prisoner's home and family and visible to his own community. A federal prison is by definition non-local, its residents unrelated to any human concern for hundreds of miles around. A federal prison combines the worst of the ancient practice of exile and of the contemporary practice of bureaucratic imprisonment.

The first penitentiary in the American federal archipelago is literally an island, McNeil Island, Steilacoom, Washington. It was named after William Henry McNeill, a Boston ship captain who sailed into Puget Sound with trinkets to trade for furs with the Indians. He retired a rich man after helping accomplish what is known in the history books as "subduing" the Indians. An expedition named a seven-square-mile island after him, misspelling the name by dropping the last "l." Indians were pushed out of the territory by cheating on treaties or killing them. They rebelled and a prison was needed. The first appropriation by Congress was used by the territorial governor to speculate in land and timber. The prison was further delayed when it was used in real estate and political deals. It was delayed even longer because sheriffs made more money without a prison by hiring out convicts as slave labor. The place was finally opened in 1875, a product of corruption, politics and racism. Its first prisoner was Abraham Gervais, an Indian.

Thus began federal prisons. The tradition has lasted. The most modern federal penitentiary is a replacement for Alcatraz. It was opened in 1963, and violates all contemporary rules for effective prisons. It is too big—it has over 500 prisoners in tight and brutal security. It is in the remote countryside eight miles from Marion, Illinois, population 12,899. It has no public transportation. Its prisoners are almost all poor and from distant cities, effectively cut off from family ties. It is difficult to recruit the kind of prison staff that is talked about on appropriation requests—psychiatrist, teachers, counselors, vocational training specialists.

The official reason for building the prison in that location was the security of a rural site. The real reason was that the minority leader of the United States Senate, Everett Dirksen, was also ranking Republican on the Judiciary Committee with jurisdiction over federal penitentiaries. Senator Dirksen's strength was in southern Illinois, and in the late 1950s and early 1960s his area was suffering a recession. Senator Dirksen needed a money-spending federal facility to guarantee his re-election. Prisons are a recession-proof, depression-proof growth industry.

For half a century after McNeil Island the federal system consisted of seven prisons, each run by an independent warden who made his own money request to Congress. Immigration from Europe was putting poor and despised people into cities, and these—Irish, Germans, Italians, French—filled the prisons. The first penitentiary designed by the federal government was Leavenworth, fronted with a ridiculous Cecil B. DeMille marble facade with forty-three marble steps. In back are the usual grim walls and one of the worst human warehouses. Its crown is a large dome, at the time of its building second in size only to the one over the United States Congress. Atlanta penitentiary, another warehouse, was built in 1902.

In the 1920s the push into centralized prisons mushroomed. The Eighteenth Amendment made it a federal offense to manufacture or drink liquor, and among other pathologies it began filling the courts and prisons with bootleggers and gangsters spawned by prohibition. Narcotics laws against private use of drugs did the same. J. Edgar Hoover was chief of the new Federal Bureau of Investigation and an irrepressible empire builder who not only expanded the federal detective force but pushed to have more offenses labeled federal rather than local. In the next decade the federal government started imprisoning people who used to be kept by the states—kidnappers, prostitution operators, automobile thieves and bank robbers.

In 1930 Herbert Hoover, Republican prophet of minimal government, created the new Federal Bureau of Prisons, "responsible for the safe keeping, care, protection, instruction and discipline of all persons charged with or convicted of offenses against the United States."

The federal system began to grow. One more prison in 1930, two more in 1932, two in 1933, one in 1934, one in 1938, six in 1940, one in 1955, one in 1958, two in 1959, one in 1962, two in 1963, one in 1968 . . .

Richard Nixon, Republican prophet of decentralized government and reduced bureaucracy, in five years tripled the budget of the Federal Bureau of Prisons and projected $750 million in new prisons, the details of which no outsider could learn. The federal prison budget in 1930 was

$6 million, in 1975 more than $200 million.

The Director was fourth in a line of directors. His three predecessors, all of whom are seen as leaders in humane penology, were Sanford Bates, James V. Bennett, and Myrl E. Alexander, reformers and academics. They inherited massive prisons that had been run by incompetent, unmanaged staffs, imposing medieval and pointless discipline with bad food and bad housing. They changed that. They were pioneers in their inheritance, going beyond the practices of their own day and promoting the idea of more humane institutions. But they did not acknowledge the proven failure of prisons or try to build alternative systems. They inherited ugly warehouses for human beings and replaced them with ordinary warehouses for human beings. They are still warehouses.

By the 1960s it became clear that whatever else prisons might do they do not stop crime, either in its spread through society or in the behavior of the individual prisoner. As prison sentences have grown longer in the United States, the longest in the Western World, crime has become worse. The longer an individual stays in prison, the more crime and the more serious crime he commits afterward.

Imprisonment of the poor and outcast who commit known violent crimes does not deter them. It makes them more violent. It puts the criminal out of circulation only for the period of his incarceration. Society buys a few years' security at the cost of something worse later on.

Punished crime comes mainly from the abandoned segments of society, from the ghettos, urban and rural, from the places with wretched schools, violent neighborhoods, unemployed families. As long as these exist, there will not be enough prisons to contain the individuals distorted by them. Increasing the harshness of punishment only raises the level of violence in the society. During the reign of Queen Elizabeth armies of the unemployed poor wandered over the countryside stealing and trespassing. It became illegal to be a vagrant. The Queen hanged vagrants in groups of hundreds at a time. It did not stop vagrancy. Henry VIII hanged 72,000 persons in the name of domestic tranquillity.

It costs society about $10,000 a year to keep a person in prison. If a youth goes to a juvenile prison at age fifteen, it is not unusual for him to spend ten years thereafter in a series of imprisonments for increasingly serious crimes. That is $100,000 for the punishment of one criminal. There are better and less expensive ways. They have been tried in South Carolina, Minnesota, Wisconsin, California and other states, where teams work intensively in the free world to repair the damage done to the individual by violent and impoverished backgrounds and with less future crime by the individual and more productive work and family life.

For the 15 or 20 per cent of presently imprisoned convicts who are physically dangerous to society nobody has a convincing answer, and for them prisons will be in existence for a long time. These are, in the opinion of every warden I have talked to, the only ones who need to be imprisoned for the safety of society or their own good.

But large bureaucracies justify their own existence, and the prison bureaucracy is no exception—more than fifty autocratic institutions with more than 8000 employees with something approaching life-and-death powers over 24,000 individuals. Their operators are often sincere, as sincere as the blacksmiths who wished to make horseshoes after everyone had automobiles.

Their work is frosted with euphemisms that make their trade more pretentious. They run not prisons but "correctional institutions." They are not guards but "correctional officers." Their charges are not prisoners but "residents." They punish their "residents" not by solitary confinement in harsh darkness but in "control units." Men spend years not in cages but in "cells" or "housing units."

Bureau of Prisons Director Norman Carlson presided over an empire with famous names like Leavenworth and obscure ones like the prison for women in Alderson, West Virginia, over a system with 212 numbered institutions, some not yet built, others closed like the famous No. 139 for Alcatraz, and a few not yet opened like No. 177, the prison for "experiments" being built in Butner, North Carolina. The most impressive numbers in status for experienced toughness are in the 130s, the maximum-security penitentiaries, 131 for Atlanta, 132 for Leavenworth, 133 for Lewisburg, 135 for Marion, 136 for McNeil Island, and 138 for Terre Haute.

Each prisoner entered the empire with a last name, the number of his institution, and from that steel family was given a first name, his personal number, his new identity.

Eddie Mason's number was No. 36035–133, his identity within the system. The last three digits meant Lewisburg, where he had been committed in June 1969. His "first name" in the hidden empire was No. 36035, which meant that he was the 36,035th individual to have been officially committed to Lewisburg.

Joel Meyers' name in the empire was No. 23429–145. His "last name"—145—meant Danbury Federal Correctional Institution in Connecticut, where he was first committed, and his "first name"—No. 23429—meant he was the 23,429th prisoner to be entered into that institution's rolls.

In 1971 and 1972 the Director's Teletypes and mail brought in alarming messages from many of his numbered islands, messages of failure—riots, protests, strikes. Every prison keeper knew the epidemic threat of rebellion. And the ruination of reputation if the rebellion became public news. Governors wanted prison keepers to prevent political problems, whether it meant iron repression or liberal policies. Rational attitudes toward convicts did not make for votes, and directors of prisons knew that. Bad publicity was the first blemish when a riot occurred or word of mass protest leaked to the outside world or if the National Guard or state police were called in.

There is a red thread of desperation that runs through American prisons, a thread of failure and cynicism of the system, of conditions intolerable to the human personality, of compacted explosiveness, of the bomblike nature inherent in any large penitentiary. Each is like an individual tree in a forest fire, bursting into flame not because anyone has gone with torch from tree to tree but because each is always near the ignition point of human endurance, and perceived heat even from a distance causes spontaneous combustion.

It is not difficult to follow the trail from the killing of George Jackson in San Quentin, and thence, nineteen days later to Attica, on September 9, a massacre to end in forty-three deaths. And from Attica a week later a riot in Indiana reformatory; three days later one in Florida; a day later in San Jose jail, California; a week after that in the state penitentiary at Lansing, Michigan; the same day the Norfolk State Prison in Massachusetts; two days later in the state prison at Walpole, Massachusetts; the same day in the state prison in Vermont; three days later the state prison in Pontiac, Illinois; two days after that Dallas County Jail, Texas; the same day the state reformatory in Green Bay, Wisconsin; a day afterward Lehigh County Jail in Pennsylvania; and the next day a state prison in Santa Fe, New Mexico; two days later a riot in Suffolk County Jail in California; the following day Cumberland County, Pennsylvania; three days after that Joliet State Penitentiary in Illinois; and two days later the state penitentiary in Nebraska; the same day Solano County Jail in California; the next day Contra Costa jail in California; five days afterward Rahway State Penitentiary in New Jersey; and three weeks later Yardville, New Jersey.

Director Carlson had seen the epidemic in his own system—four strikes and stoppages at McNeil Island, the last just two months earlier, with 116 inmates striking for a week. His prisons at Petersburg, Virginia; women at Alderson, West Virginia; men at Springfield, Missouri; in La Tuna, Texas; in the youth prison in Ashland, Kentucky; in Tallahassee, Florida; two strikes at Leavenworth, one of the entire population; three in the months before January at Marion, Illinois; a four-day racial disturbance at Lompoc, California; a total strike at Allenwood, Pennsylvania.

There were and are many theories on the causes of crime and prison riots. If there is such a massive growth of crime, it is not unreasonable to ask if there may not be something fundamentally wrong in the structure of a rich society that produces such pathologies while other rich societies, like Sweden, do not. And with such astonishing epidemics of prison protests, ask if there may be something fundamentally wrong with the institution of prison.

After each major prison riot in the United States there has been an investigation. As far back as prisons were invented, the investigations have revealed the same reasons: overcrowding, brutality by guards, arbitrary rules unfairly imposed, lack of outside contact, bad food, humiliating practices, indefinite sentences and capricious parole, unaccountability of prison keepers, lack of reason and no due process in punishing prisoners inside their institutions.

A century ago at the founding of the American Correctional Association, the official prison keepers' organization, the charter noted the need for less crowding, for more freedom for prisoners to learn to cope with the normal world, and better training of a realistic kind. A century later the same organization found the same needs.

After Attica the New York governor who succeeded Nelson Rockefeller said of his own prison system, "There's so many things wrong, I could write a book." In Rahway, New Jersey, two months earlier, 500 prisoners, unable to get action on their grievances presented peacefully, seized six guards as hostages. After the hostages were freed, Governor Hughes looked at the prisoners' grievances—ignored as long as the prisoners remained peaceful—and said, "I can't fault any of them."

There is a terrible and stupid ritual in American prison keeping. After every major riot there is a study commission. Their results over the decades can be summarized: Months and years of legitimate grievances peacefully presented by prisoners are ignored. Prisoners reach a breaking point and rebel. The rebellion is put down, often with loss of life on both sides. A study commission investigates and finds that most of the grievances are reasonable and were violations of the prison's own rules or the laws of the state. Nothing substantial is done. Prisoners begin making appeals again. There is no response. There is another riot. There is another study. The grievances are found to be legitimate. Nothing is done. There is another riot.

Even John Mitchell, once Attorney General of the United States and more recently a convicted felon, while still speaking as the Nixonian voice of vindictive law-and-order, told an audience a few weeks before February 15, 1972, "In characterizing most American prisons I need only use the same language that the Wickersham Commission used forty years ago: 'We conclude that the present prison system is antiquated and inefficient. It does not reform the criminal. It fails to protect society. There is reason to believe that it contributes to the increase of crime by hardening the prisoner.' "

Thus spoke the man who at that moment headed the department in charge of the federal prison system and who, in the long tradition of verbal acknowledgment of the futility of his system, insisted on making it worse.

Occasionally prisoners or investigators suggest a mechanism by which elected prisoner representatives can peacefully work out problems with the keepers of their institutions over a council table. But this violates the spirit of total control. It shakes a prison keeper more profoundly than the threat of violent rebellion. He can always win a battle of guns. He cannot always win an argument.

The Director who received the call from Warden Alldredge the morning of February 15 was less well known than any of his predecessors but more powerful. He had more money, a larger empire, and more sophisticated politics. Unlike his predecessors, who were academic in personal style, Norman Carlson was in the style of modern prison keepers—tall, military in bearing, brush-cut hair, rigid in resisting change, but with a full social-work vocabulary acquired with a master's degree in criminology from the University of Iowa. And he knew how to enlarge a bureaucracy.

But neither power nor money nor multiplied institutions brought peace to Director Carlson's empire. When Warden Alldredge called Washington that morning to warn that he had reason to expect "an incident" in a few hours, he could not get through to the Director. Director Carlson was on the phone to his most tightly disciplined prison, Marion, Illinois, where every prisoner had been on strike for a full week.

3

"THE JOINT'S COMING DOWN"

An hour after his first patrol, Captain Dodd walked the corridor again. A prisoner walked by slowly and said, "Better get out to the dock, Captain. I think the joint's coming down."

Captain Dodd walked back to the warden's office. The warden had already heard from a dozen different points. More than a hundred men were gathered at the kitchen dock, and industry supervisors were reporting absentees from their machines. A break in prison routines can produce unpredictable effects on men suddenly released from iron regimentation.

More than anything else, Warden Alldredge needed to know who was behind the strike and what the men wanted. If he knew the grievances, he might dissolve the whole problem in an hour, as he had two years ago. Some concessions, some promises, a reasonable attitude, expression of sympathy with problems originating in Washington, using his personal credit with individual prisoners—and by nightfall, with an especially good meal, the strike talk would be gone. If ringleaders were trying to make serious trouble, they would disappear into segregation or get transferred across the country. He ordered Captain Dodd to the dock: Find out what's eating the men. And find out who's leading the strike.

Captain Dodd walked out again. He could have been a humble gardener strolling pleasurably among his flowers. Though the temperature was just above freezing and the drizzle was chilling, he ambled out to the dock with his suitcoat unbuttoned, his hands in his pockets, relaxed and friendly.

He walked toward a prisoner he liked. Before the captain reached him the prisoner discovered someone twenty feet away that he had to talk to. A bad sign. The captain's expression did not change and he pretended that he was going toward the industrial dock fifty feet away but suddenly turned to a prisoner who hadn't expected the captain to stop. He asked the prisoner, "Why aren't you at work?"

The prisoner turned his head and stared at an upper window of the metals factory.

The men were serious. Turning away when approached and refusal to answer an officer's question were traditional gestures of passive protest. He approached a group of men he knew were not militant and probably against the strike, there only out of curiosity.

"Why's everybody standing around? What's the problem?"

Other prisoners watched. The men, embarrassed, would not speak to the captain. Staff members were watching—about twenty industry supervisors on the metals factory dock and other officers spotted in the upper windows of the surrounding buildings. The guard in the gun tower in the center of the north wall could make out some action at the dock, using his binoculars, his view badly interrupted by freight cars on the metals factory siding. Not very good shotgun clearance. The guard in the tower in the center of the west wall, if he stood at the far corner of his glassed-in station, could get a partial view of the dock, but only partial. Within seconds the warden had calls from half a dozen locations with one essential message: The prisoners in the slot won't talk to Captain Dodd.

By the time Dodd got back to the warden's office both Alldredge and Cansler were already grim. The men were serious, but there didn't seem to be much leadership, which could be good or bad. The failure of leaders to take over might make the thing dissipate if handled right. But the failure of leaders meant that things could turn violent and irrational. Cansler called the shop supervisor: Get the men the hell out of the shops and watch the dock.

Cansler told Dodd to find out the gripes. He didn't care what Dodd had to do to get them. Dodd sauntered out to the slot again. It was even colder and darker now, but he still walked with his jacket unbuttoned and his hands nonchalantly in his pockets.

Lucky Johnson, who six days earlier had insisted to the Political Education Committee that they must find a way to unify the prisoners, was standing passively in a line at the clothing exchange unaware that nonpolitical prisoners had already started a strike. He had just received his clean clothes for the week when a prisoner came by with word that prisoners were gathering at the kitchen dock. Johnson handed his pile of clothes to a friend and walked rapidly toward the kitchen.

Edward Mason, on the first day of his thirty-first year, was doing what he did every weekday; he finished his lunch and began walking across the open roadway to the metal industries shop. He saw a group of men gathered and stopped to see what was going on.

John Alger, son of a prominent family in eastern Massachusetts, serving time on a check charge, blue-eyed, dark-haired, earnest-looking, big talker and sporty dresser, was standing in the chow line with his friend John Wagner discussing rumors about new liberal policies. Alger, a guitar player, followed the magazines closely and liked to be in the latest style. He asked Wagner if it was true that the new policy statement was going to permit mustaches and long hair. He thought that would be cool. Wagner had recently been named prison correspondent for a new publication, *Penal Digest International,* published in Iowa by ex-convicts and, after a long lawsuit, given recognition by the Bureau of Prisons. Alger thought his friend might know. Wagner didn't know, and other men in the line around him argued the truth of the hair-style rumor. During the argument someone mentioned that there was talk of a strike, but this was not a militant group and the remark passed casually. After his lunch Alger walked toward the clothing factory where he worked. There were men gathered at the kitchen dock, but Alger walked through them to his industry station. The sewing room and office were almost empty.

Officer Walter Guzek told him, "John, you better leave work. We can't watch you guys inside and watch the people outside."

Alger went back out in the cold drizzle and stood with the men waiting to see what would happen.

Phillips and Irwin were watching Danny handing out literature, wondering who the real ringleaders were. They heard someone shouting from the dock.

The kitchen dock formed a right angle, a concrete platform four feet high with large rubber blocks to soften contact with tailgates of trucks delivering food. A black prisoner they didn't know was up on the dock holding out his hands.

Eddie Mason had stopped on the way to his shop. He found his brother Sam and together they were watching the men mill around the dock. They knew the black inmate slightly. His name was Bob Saunders, assigned to the hospital.

Saunders shouted, "All right, all right! Hold it down! Hey, man, let's hold it down."

Men in the crowd started shouting for silence. It became quiet except for the gusts of wind blowing around the dock.

Saunders yelled, "Y'all remember what kind of motherfucking cigarettes I smoke when the fucking screws come to lock me up. Now dig this. We been standing out here in this shit since noon and nobody'd come up front to let them know what this is all about."

A few feet from Eddie Mason a man said, "Man, that fucking dude must be crazy. Ain't nobody puts themself on front street just like that."

"Okay," Saunders shouted. "So this fucking joint needs a strike. We got to be treated like fucking men. But we got to go to The Man and tell him things gotta change. What do we tell the warden?"

Now the crowd, grown to between 150 and 200, had turned toward the center of the dock where Saunders spoke.

"Come on! We got to speak up! I'm sticking my fucking neck out! How about some help? Am I goin' to the hole alone? Who's gonna stand up? Who's gonna be up front?"

Irwin and Phillips looked at each other. Someone really was running this show. Someone really was taking the risks while they were just talking. Phillips looked at the paper in his hands, the United Prisoners Union Bill of Rights. He shouted, "I got some grievances."

Phillips pushed through the crowd.

When he reached the dock, he climbed to the platform. "The man's got a point. We've been out here since noon and it's one-thirty now. So far we haven't done anything but tell each other what we all know." He unfolded the four sheets of paper. Someone yelled a joke to a friend across the crowd.

A large black man turned and shouted, "Somebody shut that motherfucker up so the man can talk."

Phillips continued. "For the benefit of guys who don't know me, my name is Ron Phillips. I work in the dental lab. I'm tired of the bullshit treatment I'm getting and I'm tired of the bullshit treatment I see my fellow convicts getting. These people don't give a damn about anybody."

Someone shouted, "Rap on, baby!"

"The paper in my hand is the Prisoners Bill of Rights—and we do have rights whether the pigs know it or not. The prisoners in California drew up this document."

Phillips began to read: " 'We, the people of the convicted class, locked in a cycle of poverty, failure, discrimination and servitude, do hereby declare before the world our situation to be unjust and inhuman.' "

Behind him someone roared, "Right on!" He looked around, startled. It was Irwin, his fist high in the air. Peace-loving, Bible-quoting Irwin!

" 'Basic human rights are systematically withheld from our class. We have been historically stereotyped as less than human, while in reality we possess the same needs, frailties, ambitions and dignity indigenous to all humans.' "

Irwin raised his fist and shouted again, "Right on!"

Men on the ground began to lose interest and talk among themselves. Phillips read faster.

" 'All persons unwillingly conscripted into military service are members of the Convicted Class and this Bill of Rights shall apply to them as well. We demand an end to the draft and to the Vietnam War, which is a subtle and discriminatory form of capital punishment.' "

Someone in the audience shouted, "Fuck that shit about the war and let's talk about the fucking industries."

Phillips hastened to other parts of the Bill of Rights.

" 'Due process of law, right of prisoners to legal representation in all matters pertaining to their destiny . . . An end to all forms of human degradation, leg irons, handcuffs, gags, segregation and isolation . . .' "

Men were beginning to cheer again. The loudest was Irwin, standing beside him.

" 'The right of all members of the Convicted Class to exercise all forms of peaceful dissent and protest without threat and coercion . . . No restriction on the right of convicts and ex-convicts to vote. The right to hold membership in professional groups, unions and related organizations.' "

He looked up. The men were coming closer. Phillips did not speak loudly.

" 'Conditions of prison labor shall include all the rights of union members in the outside world, that is, minimum wage standards, disability compensation, vacation periods, pension plans, retirement benefits, life insurance . . .' "

The crowd cheered again.

" 'The right to conjugal visits.' "

Men roared approval.

Alger, a man drawn to strong personalities, had pushed his way to the edge of the dock.

Phillips finished with demands for a minimum wage, for some way of representing grievances, for changes in parole practices.

Irwin was flushed, his eyes shining. He went to the edge of the dock.

"My name is Irwin. I work in industry. I'm doing twelve years for robbery. I stole some money and I'm in the joint doing time for it. But I've been going into that shop over there"—he pointed to the metals factory—"and working eight hours a day and Saturdays at thirty-seven cents an hour. That's thirty-seven cents an hour, making heavy shelves. And do you know what profit they make on the industries? Five million dollars! Five fuckin' million dollars last year alone! We work for thirty-seven cents an hour and they make five million dollars. We get shit and they get five million bucks! That's stealing!"

The crowd was wild. "Right on!" "Go on, baby, go on."

"I got twelve years for stealing $1745. They stole five million dollars from us. If I was guilty for stealing $1700 on the street, then they're guilty for stealing five million from prisoners.

"If I robbed a bank on the street, they robbed me in this penitentiary.

"If I'm guilty of a crime, they're guilty of a crime!"

The crowd was alternating between silence of electric attention and roars of a new unity. Irwin waited for the silence to return. He spoke with Old Testament power. "If I belong in prison, they belong in prison!"

The roar erupted again.

Until now Captain Dodd had been standing laconically, even nodding as though in agreement, as Phillips spoke. The industry supervisors on the metals shop platform had been grinning in open contempt. But now the staff were grim. Captain Dodd was not smiling. In the windows of buildings staff members could be seen with Polaroid cameras.

Irwin drove on. "And the parole board . . ."

A sound almost like a sob rose out of the crowd, as though a nerve too deep to hurt had finally been reached. It sounded like a cumulative "Oh!"

"The parole board sits in Washington and lets us rot in prison without telling us why!"

"Oh, right on, man!"

"The parole board tells us what kind of people we should be. We should not fight. We don't fight. We should work hard. We work hard. We should improve our education. We go to class. We should go to group therapy. We go to group therapy. We should join AA. We join AA. We should go to church. We go to church. Then we apply for parole again. What happens?"

A prisoner on the ground yelled as though in an irrepressible religious transport, "Fucked! Fucked! Fucked!"

"What happens?" Irwin yelled. "Not a fucking thing. The parole board says, 'No.' It doesn't say why. It doesn't say what we did wrong. We crawl, we beg, we rub our faces in the mud pleading with them to tell us what they have in mind. We do our shit and they pick it up and throw it at us."

The crowd joined in obscenities and shouts of anger.

Irwin shouted, "Rehabilitation!"

The crowd yelled and words emerged like stones thrown in the air: "Shit!" "Fuck!" "Crap!" "Jiveshit!"

"Rehabilitation. Big fucking word. The staff here tells us we got to learn a trade and we work our asses off six days a week in industry. The staff says we're doing fine. They recommend parole. They see us every day. Every fucking night. They know us inside and outside. And they say, Yeah, we're rehabilitated. The parole board is in Washington, D.C. They never saw us. They never even heard of us. They look at our record, they look at our crime, they look at the institution that says we're rehabilitated, and what do they say? Set off for another year."

The crowd was shouting like a single organism.

"When I robbed a bank a judge gave me a sentence. When I apply for a parole the board sits in Washington and looks at the same papers the judge made out and says, 'Stay in prison.' I got imprisoned by the judge for robbing a bank and I'm kept in prison for robbing the bank. That's double jeopardy! That's getting fucked twice!"

The crowd urged him on.

"I've stopped begging. I've decided I'm a man. I'm not a child. I'm not taking any more shit that says I'm not ready but won't tell me why. We are through crawling on our knees. We're standing up like men!"

Irwin stood back, exhausted. He wasn't sure what had happened to him. It hadn't been a conscious decision. He was barely aware of some men helping Captain Dodd onto the platform.

Captain Dodd came over and said quietly, "You got a little carried away, didn't you, Irwin?"

"Yes, I did, Captain."

Phillips came over and grinned at Irwin. There was no question any more that the prisoners were unified.

Phillips felt a tug on his trouser leg. It was a small Puerto Rican prisoner on the ground. "Please, I wish to speak."

"Come on up, amigo. It's a free country." Phillips helped pull the man to the platform and led him to the edge to speak.

The Puerto Rican was suddenly galvanized. "I ask you, please. You want to strike? We strike!"

The men cheered.

"You want to riot? We riot!"

More cheers.

"You want to kill? We kill!"

Some cheers.

"But I ask you, please. Do not take the Lord's name in vain!"

Wild cheering and applause. Upthrust arms helped the man down from the platform as laughter pulsed through the crowd. It was an interlude that a dramatist might have designed to relieve the tension that grew out of Irwin's impassioned talk. The religious appeal, while relief from bitterness, had another effect. For the first time, perhaps loosed by the Puerto Rican's priorities of riot before blasphemy, yells of violence began to be heard.

"Burn the fucking place down!"

"Off the pigs!"

Each shout would be followed by fists in the air and "Right on!"

A tall, slender black man in white uniform pushed his way to the dock. Phillips recognized the unbending grace of Clarence Jones. There were now many men on the platform, including John Alger and Lucky Johnson. Hands helped Jones upward. His piercing look and poised stance created an immediate calm.

"Wait a fucking minute. Cut out all this shit about kill and burn and off the pigs. We didn't come out here for that kind of bullshit. We got a beef, right?"

A murmur of agreement came up from the crowd.

"We want something done about it, right?"

Someone yelled, "Right, man, right!"

"Okay. We can't get a motherfucking thing done with any bullshit about riotin' and all that shit."

Jones paused and looked at the crowd from the edge near the maintenance shop to the left to the other side near the industrial dock. Then he held his finger pointed at the center of the crowd.

"That's exactly what the pigs want! That's what they're waiting for us to try! They *want* us to do something violent. They're gonna *try* to make us do something violent. They *know* how to deal with violence. They *know* what to do when we scream about burning and killing and hostages. They *want* us to talk that way. *Then* they can come in here with their guns and nightsticks and gas. *Then* they can tell the world what a bunch of wild animals we are. *Then—then—they will wipe us out! Then* we lose everything."

It was now so quiet that a paper skidding in the frigid wind was the only sound as Jones paused and everyone else—the men on the ground, Captain Dodd and the prisoners on the kitchen dock, the grim-looking officers standing on the industrial dock—was frozen in attention.

Jones's voice rose in pitch. "What these motherfuckers *don't* know how to deal with is what they think we aren't. They believe we're a bunch of stupid animals, a bunch of idiot children, a bunch of dumb sheep. These motherfuckers don't believe that we are men, that we have brains, that we can think for ourselves, that we can understand a situation and be intelligent about it. *That,* brothers, *that* they don't know how to deal with!"

Men were nodding involuntarily, still silent.

"So all those dudes got nothing on their minds except burning and hostages and killing, get the fuck out of here! Now!"

A prisoner standing at the foot of the dock laughed loudly and said, "Right on, brother!"

Jones looked down at him contemptuously. "Right on, my motherfucking ass! I'm cold serious. Now anyone wants to get violent, get the hell out! Right now! Go back to your house and jerk off, because that's all you're doing with that talk."

Jones stepped back from the edge of the platform. It was a different spirit than before, fewer spontaneous yells, a new look on faces. Two other men spoke briefly from the dock. Eddie Mason repeated the need for nonviolence because the warden was a reasonable man. Joel Meyers stepped forward. Despite his long experience at harangues, talks at rallies and public debates, he started in a fumbling way.

"Like Phillips said, for the benefit of you who don't know me, I'm Joel Meyers. I was shipped here from Danbury because of a strike we had there last year. I was called a ringleader and they shipped me here and put me in the hole for a few months and told me to change my ways. They also denied me parole. So I got a beef, too."

Phillips came forward again. He said men from each housing unit should come to the platform to list their grievances. It was what Captain Dodd had been waiting for. The crowd was more solemn than an hour ago. Men started speaking to Phillips, who crouched his long frame downward to hear them. He turned over the Prisoners Bill of Rights to write on the blank back of the sheets and asked for a pen or pencil. Alger handed him a ballpoint pen.

Men were stating what block or dormitory they represented, others were shouting grievances to them. The calls to unknown representatives were wildly incongruous.

"Parole. For Christ sake"—a quick look at the Puerto Rican— "sorry, buddy—put in about motherfuckin' parole."

"Why can't we have color television? Black and white's nowhere on the outside any longer."

"The food. Hey, brother, tell him about food."

"Shit, man, first get down about the fuckin' minimum wage."

Phillips held up his hands in frustration. "This is too confusing. We got to get it organized better."

Now that the speeches were over, the men on the ground and on the dock noticed that it was very cold. The drizzle was now mixed with snow. The wind blowing around the corner from the east had suddenly shifted and was coming in punishing gusts from the west wall. Suddenly men were shivering, rubbing their arms and holding their palms over their faces.

Someone yelled, "Do we have to stand outside in this shit? Let's go inside!"

Someone else yelled, "Hey, the auditorium."

Phillips turned to Captain Dodd. "Captain, how about going inside? It's cold here and we need to get this thing in shape so we can collect the grievances."

"I'll have to get permission from the warden."

One of the men on the platform announced that permission was being asked for use of the auditorium.

Minutes later Dodd came out, walking along the kitchen wall and up onto the platform. Now he had his suit jacket buttoned. He told the men to quiet down. "It's obvious you aren't going back to work. I'll let you go to the auditorium and you can get your complaints or gripes or whatever together, and give them to me and I'll take them to my superior. If you do this and there is no violence I will take no reprisals against you."

This is what, at a later and more crucial date, Captain Dodd would say he said. Others who heard him remember different words. The exact wording, in all its innocuous semantics, would control a few years of eight men's lives.

The men poured onto Red Top, out of the cold.

"Going to the auditorium?"

"You crazy? That's just a shit-eating trick to get us all in one room where the fucking screws are waiting to bust heads. All of us there and only two motherfucking exits and cops all along those stairways? It's a set-up."

Everywhere clusters of men argued over the threat.

Unknown to the prisoners, officers had the opposite worry. A gathering of a few hundred men in the yard was one thing. They could be locked out in the exposed outdoors. The staff had windows in the surrounding three-story buildings. Gun towers controlled the wall. The logical implements for attack—tools and materials inside the industrial buildings—had been considered by the warden an hour ago when he had ordered all prisoners out of the shops, including those who said they wanted no part of the strike. All the shops were locked and secured.

But prisoners in a rebellious mood inside the prison were something else. And the auditorium. Despite all the careful policies worked out over the years for prisoner control, the auditorium was always a threat. The basic strategy of prisoner control was to move small numbers at any one time, to segment them by grilles along the corridor, by barriers at ends of dormitories and blocks and, ultimately, to seal them off individually in their cages.

The risky areas were places where prisoners could gather in large numbers—in the dining hall, in the recreation room, in the exercise yard, in the shops and especially in the auditorium, which had the largest capacity of any single chamber in the prison. There was no way to compartmentalize the population into separate groups. The evaluation report of Lewisburg seventeen years after it opened had noted that the auditorium location on the third floor with several hundred prisoners moving up and down the stairways constituted "acute security problems."

A few hundred men mounted the three floors. The auditorium was a prime display of the Lewisburg desire for distinctive decoration. Horizontally across the high roof were three mammoth crossbeams carved and painted in fourteenth-century Italianate curves. The benches, long rows reaching down the sloping floor to the stage, were of carved wood. The windows, of course, were gothic.

Men came and went restlessly, warily. At any one time there might have been 150. They speculated on how long it would be before "the cops will come busting heads."

Eddie Mason and his brother Sam had control of the microphone, explaining that the administration was acting reasonably and so should the prisoners.

Most of the men who had spoken from the dock were now on the auditorium stage. In the end about seventy-five prisoners remained. One of them yelled that they ought to start things by staying away from the four o'clock count.

Eddie Mason took the microphone. "Say, bro, you there, talking about not going in for count. I thought you had something on the cap. Don't you realize that's what The Man wants? For you to show some act of defiance to a count? One of the most important things in a joint is the count. You miss that and it gives The Man the excuse he wants to walk in and do some pick-handle therapy."

"Shit, man. I'm not talking about us rioting. Just show 'em we mean business and fuck their four o'clock count. They won't use guns just to count."

Eddie Mason shouted back, "What's the matter with that dude? First he talks that shit about not going in for count. Then he says he ain't riotin'. If you ain't in your crib for count, you're an escapee. They'll come in with night sticks and Mace and tear gas. They got shotguns, riot guns, and we got a dude talking a lot of shit about defiance. They been reasonable and we gotta be reasonable. The warden and his guys can be talked to. They know we got to have changes and I think they're gonna make them."

A prisoner named Richard Moore, serving three years for mail theft, took the microphone, backed by the Masons, and urged less strong talk, reminding them that the staff would react badly to militancy.

Meyers and Phillips watched the exchange and Meyers became increasingly nervous. He was an old hand at microphone control and crowd mood and he didn't like it. He turned to Phillips. "These guys are terrible. We've got to get that microphone away from them before they turn this into a Jaycee meeting."

Phillips walked to the Mason brothers and asked if he could speak. The brothers stepped back, reluctantly.

"Look, we got to make the four o'clock count. We don't gain anything by missing it and it's just the excuse they'll want to bust heads. But that's not the point. We got to be firm. We got to make sure that we don't back down on what we want. And if they're reasonable it's only because they want to make sure we don't get anything that will hurt them. We can't hurt them physically. We know that. Anything we do that's violent they can do a hundred times worse. So forget that. But we can hurt them financially. They don't run those industries as charities for us."

The small crowd cheered. Phillips noticed Lucky Johnson standing up, his right hand clenched in a fist, his arm pumping upward, and shouting, "Right on!" He would be a good man.

"They run those industries for a profit. They've got contracts. We can't bargain with them with weapons, because they have more than we have. We can't bargain with a riot, because there's only one way that ends. And we can't bargain with them by being nice and sweet, because they love that and they won't have to do anything. The only bargaining power we have is to keep the industries shut down. That's the only thing that will bring results, and what we want is results. We want all the shit that has been going on in prisons for years, all the promises they always make—we want those down on paper and we want them delivered."

During the applause Meyers stepped to the microphone. He said that Phillips was right but that the staff wouldn't believe it unless the whole population stayed militant. There had to be total support of the strike.

In a procedure half self-appointment and half crowd reaction, the dwindling audience elected a committee to "do something." The dental lab prisoners voted as a bloc for Phillips and Jones. There was a quick shouting of approval for three Puerto Ricans to represent the Spanish population, and for Johnson, Meyers, Phillips and, with a special cheer, Irwin.

Irwin left early. The window of his door was supposed to be uncovered at all times, but Irwin had put up a piece of cardboard to give himself privacy. The cardboard hung by a single nail in the oak door. The guards liked Irwin and left the cardboard in place, merely swinging it aside to look in for counts. Irwin wasn't watching for the count. He was looking out the window, over the wall, to a dark and disturbed sky, sleet and snow slanting through the melancholy landscape, the naked trees glistening in wet blackness, bending before a bitter wind. He was tired and depressed and he didn't know what it meant.

Irwin's absence wasn't noticed in the auditorium. There was too much confusion. Men continued to argue whether to return for the four o'clock count. Some insisted that once they were locked in their cages the protest was over. Others argued that if they weren't in place for the four o'clock count the protest would fail.

A different debate on the same subject was in progress elsewhere.

Inside the warden's office, littered with empty coffee cups and full ashtrays, Alldredge, Cansler and Dodd were agonizing over a decision that had to be made in less than an hour.

Would the prisoners report for their four o'clock count? If they did not, the institution was out of control. Prisoners would be free to mass in enough numbers to take command in limited areas. They could seize hostages, start fires, trash buildings.

If the prisoners did make the four o'clock count, what was the administration's next move? Most men would be in cages or locked in dormitories. Men could be released by small units, one tier of cages at a time, one dormitory at a time, escorted under heavy security forces to the dining hall and returned and locked down before the next unit ate. That had something to be said for it. There was, after all, a communist and some of his friends up there. They might take advantage of any freedom to turn the place upside down.

But even if they answered the four o'clock count, the place would not be really secure. About 250 prisoners, most of them kitchen workers, were on duty at their stations, counted in their work areas—not locked up. Meyers was a kitchen worker and maybe he had planned a riot. If they locked down the rest of the institution, the 250 men left in the kitchen and other open work stations might consider it a double-cross after the no-reprisal promise. It wasn't hard to get out of the kitchen into the storeroom for large supplies of food. And into the slot outside to break into the industries, start fires and destroy the factories. A couple of hundred rebels could keep up a defense from the third floors against the gun towers and ground attacks, with enough food and industrial supplies to stand off for hours. They might even break out prisoners from the jungle dormitories next to the kitchen building. It would leave the place a wreck.

If the staff locked down the institution at four o'clock and somehow got the kitchen workers to report back to their housing units, what would they do the next day? Keep them locked down? The strike would succeed by the staff's own hand. The population had been told that they could present grievances to the warden, but as yet there were no grievances, so there was nothing for the warden to work on. The guards could break it up by putting a couple hundred men into segregation and sending busloads of the militants to other prisons all over the country. But the remaining population might rebel because of the no-reprisal promise. If Lewisburg had an open rebellion it would leak out to the newspapers, and the Director would be under fire.

An answer to the warden's dilemma was unfolding in the auditorium three flights above him.

Most prisoners were confused by the proceedings. People had come in and out of the auditorium, with never a stable constituency. There was jockeying for power, with Alger, Wagner and the Masons seizing initial control of the stage microphone. As a performing guitar player, Alger was familiar with the microphone. But the significance of microphone control was not lost on Meyers, a veteran of such things, and it was not long before he, Phillips and Jones were quietly taking over the microphone when Alger, Wagner or Eddie Mason paused for breath.

The radicals worried that the conservatives were getting control and feared planted informers might be among them. The conservatives were worried at the aggressiveness of the radicals and suspected them of ulterior motives.

There were loudly expressed doubts that the auditorium events represented the prison population at all, given the small and shifting attendance. Ethnic politics reared its head with the election of three on the committee to represent whites, three for the blacks and three for the Latins. And when that had all been done the committee members were not sure what came next.

In short, it was like most political meetings. Despite 200 years of American electoral democracy and 140 years of party conventions, free world politicians perform no better than the convicts in the auditorium of Lewisburg penitentiary did in the first democratic proceeding in the history of the institution. In many ways the prisoners had done better. They had existed as a representative body for only an hour and a half. They had no precise grant of power. They were asked to present a priority list of the most painful tribulations of 1491 men without talking to them in a systematic way. They did it after years stripped of personal decision-making. They woke, ate, worked, played and slept on command of whistles and bells. Now they had to make profound decisions for others in less than two hours.

It was not surprising that a request was sent to the control center for permission to hold a mass meeting in the auditorium that night. It was telephoned to the warden's office, where the answer was an immediate no.

Then the warden made his decision. He had solved the last strike in less than an hour. He had credit with prisoners. He could liberalize some rules, a concession Washington had already authorized but not announced. Reports from informers so far were not alarming. Violence talk was being put down by leaders. If the four o'clock count went well the warden would order everything normal for the rest of the day— meals, recreation, usual night lockdown. By nighttime the warden would have the grievances, the next morning he would announce that he had them under consideration and promise action on some of them at once, and release everyone for a normal workday. If the four o'clock count went well and the kitchen crew stayed on the job.

The control center called to say that John Wagner, prisoner-correspondent for *Penal Digest International,* wanted to see Cansler. Cansler left for control.

Would the associate warden reconsider a night meeting at the auditorium? A lot of the men were sore about not knowing about the afternoon election and not being able to vote. Maybe the committee that got elected wasn't representative. And the committee needed a meeting to get grievances. Wagner would consent to be the intermediary to settle differences, and he'd have more influence if he could arrange the night meeting. Cansler said he'd give an answer after the night meal.

Wagner went back to the auditorium and announced the news as everyone was leaving. Some, Jones included, were going to the four o'clock count, but reluctantly. "Once we're locked up again, man, it's all over." But the majority had prevailed.

The warden's office waited for the important returns. The four o'clock count was good. Complete in the housing units. Complete at the work stations. Preparation for evening meal proceeding normally. Good. Follow normal schedules. Be relaxed. Avoid arguments. Watch for signs of trouble. Look out for fights. Don't be careless. Be where you can communicate at all times. Act relaxed. But if prisoners seem ready to take over any location, get out and get out fast. Don't be taken hostage.

Wagner was back on the first floor of B block. His friends were calling him crazy for getting involved. John Alger, in a nearby cage, listened to the talk quietly, uncertainly. When prisoners moved aggressively he felt pulled to them. He and Wagner had been on the auditorium stage together. But neither had been elected to the committee.

A guard came by and everyone listened.

"Wagner. You're wanted at control."

As Wagner and the guard disappeared down the tier, a man called out, "I'll send you cigarettes, buddy." They assumed he was being taken to segregation. And "Hope the bus ride's comfortable, John." They assumed he would be transferred to a distant prison.

At control, Cansler was waiting for him, surrounded by ten officers. The associate warden told Wagner there would be no night meeting in the auditorium but the warden would meet with the committee on Red Top at six-thirty, after the evening meal. Wagner would be given clearance to visit committee members' housing units to pass the word.

As Wagner went through the units on both sides of Red Top he was peppered with questions he couldn't answer. He heard bitter talk that something was going on and the men didn't know about it. After chow, some men said, they were going to meet on Red Top and demand to go to the auditorium for voting and grievances.

He also heard the rumor in every part of the prison: a hundred Pennsylvania state cops with clubs, gas masks and tear gas were in the basement ready to bust heads.

The same rumor got to B block before Wagner returned. John Alger heard it and waited anxiously to see if Wagner would come back. Alger took his hand mirror and held it between the bars of his cage at an angle to scan the corridor. Remarkable for this time of day—not a single hack in sight. Maybe they, too, were down in the basement waiting.

Then the population was released en masse for its usual evening meal. The act created a sudden wave of relief among the prisoners. There was more shouting back and forth than usual, and more communication between blacks and whites than ever before. It was good-natured banter.

The release for the evening meal also resulted in one of Dr. Z's more notable performances, a performance that was a turning point.

4

FREE ELECTION

Some people at Lewisburg thought Dr. Z was crazy. He was a gaunt man with deep-set black eyes, only his wisdom and eyeteeth visible. He believed that the American Dental Association had made people obsessive about teeth in a conspiracy to protect dentists' jobs.

He did some curious things. Like bringing down the high blood pressure of a prison officer by manipulating a collarbone while the man lay on a bookcase in the prison library, where, as everyone in the prison knew, Dr. Z held office hours. Or assuming the lotus position in the prison exercise yard, not too remarkable for a man of forty-three, but not usually done in December dressed only in jockey shorts. Or insisting that the American Medical Association had promoted the false doctrine that saliva transmits germs. To demonstrate his rejection of this heresy, Dr. Z had offered a piece of his watermelon to a dozen of his doubters who spit on it and watched as he publicly ate the watermelon and urged his audience to note whether his health declined thereafter. It did not.

Bernarr Zovluck, in his own way, was more religious than Bill Irwin. He was a walking ecumenical movement, attending Jewish services Friday night and Sunday afternoon, Protestant on Sunday morning, Catholic late Sunday morning, and throughout the week a variety of evening sessions of the Gideons, Mormons, Pentecostals and Christian Scientists.

He was born an orthodox Jew on the Lower East Side in 1929, became a chiropractor and developed a vigorous practice, some of it done by mail, though his profession, like that of bishop, requires the physical laying on of hands to work its wonders. There came to pass, in his opinion, a misunderstanding with one of his clients about a

54

putative cure for disease in exchange for money, a transaction conducted, unfortunately, through the postal service, and in 1969, in the opinion of the United States District Court for the Southern District of New York, he was guilty of violating Section 1341 (2) of the United States Code and sentenced to four years of prison for mail fraud.

Dr. Z lectured young prisoners on their careless ways, fasted for alarming periods of time and did not flinch before pursuing his ethic before the most fearsome opposition, including Jimmy Hoffa.

Months before, when Hoffa was not yet the beneficiary of President Nixon's Christmas pardon, the two men had engaged in a loud and bitter controversy. Dr. Z was outraged at insults Hoffa used in reference to people who worked with their hands.

"You, Mr. Hoffa, of all people, a great national labor leader, should refer to laboring people with dignity and respect!"

Hoffa had yelled back, "Working people are like grapes on a vine— they're there to be plucked!"

Dr. Z's defense of working people had not extended to the prisoners on strike. He was not at the dock during the afternoon speechmaking. He was one of the "scabs" Meyers had talked about. He liked Joel Meyers and Ron Phillips, but he thought they were wrong to take part in the work stoppage. He went to the afternoon session in the auditorium to dissuade them.

"What do you possibly expect to get from doing this thing?"

"You know," Meyers said. "The staff told us to do it. As long as we stay peaceful, no action against us."

"Don't do it, Joel. Don't go ahead with this crazy strike."

Meyers grinned. "Hey, you're just the man to have on the committee."

"Absolutely not! I'm against the strike. Prisoners have no power. The institution will always win. Any method of fighting them except through legal channels will be self-destructive. This is all an exercise in futility. Please, Joel. Use sense about this."

Meyers and Phillips were adamant and Dr. Z left at once, sad and depressed. He wished those two were not so determined to be martyrs to their ideals.

Dr. Z's own ethical impulses were to turn events in an irreversible direction that night. His official job was in the kitchen in charge of peeling vegetables, in which capacity he remained against the strike throughout the afternoon and early evening.

The normal release for the evening meal after the four o'clock count convinced most of the population that the protest was effective and that obedience to rules, like making the four o'clock count, was the correct move. There was still the rumor of a riot squad in the basement, the rumors now describing 100 staff members and 500 Pennsylvania state police. But the announcement of resumption of normal eating had the effect Warden Alldredge had predicted. Without any dramatic move by the staff, the reassuring heartbeat of prison control, the rhythm of routine, the conforming schedule seemed to take over again, as though an airplane engine had hesitated in midflight and recovered.

Dr. Z was working his vegetables in the kitchen when Meyers came by arguing with the rest of the kitchen crew to walk off the job. Some did and some did not. Dr. Z argued with Meyers against the walkout and he argued with the rest of the kitchen crew. There was confusion in the kitchen, but out front the first units of men were eating.

In the midst of Meyers' agitation Cansler, Dodd and Lieutenant Baker walked in and asked what was going on. They called the leaders of the kitchen crew into the adjoining officers' mess and told them that the warden was going along with all reasonable requests of the inmates and if the kitchen closed down there would be no chance to work on grievances. And there would be "consequences" for people who left their jobs.

Tony DeAngelis, of the Wall Street salad oil scandal, was a prisoner working in the kitchen; he spoke against the walkout. Dr. Z said he was in sympathy with the goals of the prisoners and would offer his moral support. But he didn't think the kitchen workers should go on strike unless it was made clear to the population that there would be no food and no laundry, that the institution couldn't be expected to carry on these functions without the prisoners. Let the prisoners know this and then vote for a strike and if they voted in favor, Dr. Z would join them. The net effect was to get the kitchen crew back to work.

Dr. Z had just returned to his vegetables when he heard booing by prisoners in the dining room. He looked out at the tables. Catcalls were being directed at a young black prisoner pushing a cart full of dirty trays toward the kitchen for washing. Men at the tables were yelling at him, "Scab!" and "Quit, you motherfucker!"

Dr. Z was outraged. He walked out to the front of the dining room and addressed the tables. "Men, you should be ashamed. I don't think it's right for you to boo this man. It is his personal decision whether to work or whether to strike and you have no right to coerce him. If he didn't do his work, you would not be eating. If you are sincere, if you believe genuinely in the attitude you are expressing when you insult this man, if you sincerely believe in a strike, then you should be prepared to fast. You should leave your food on the table and go back. Stay on strike if you believe in the principle. But if you want to eat, do not insult this man."

The men at the tables had laughed when Dr. Z began but they were quiet when he finished. No one left the tables but no one booed the man with the dirty trays.

When Dr. Z returned to the kitchen, Meyers and several others were again arguing with the men to quit in the kitchen. The kitchen crew was more unified for the strike than before. Officers called kitchen workers into the staff dining room again. This time, Dr. Z recalled later, he was shocked at the language some of the officers used to describe prisoners —obscene, racist, anti-Semitic and anti-Latin. It was too much for Dr. Z.

By this time Phillips was in the dining room, tending to the demands of his appetite while hoping that the strike would be total. He was hard at work taking in maximum nutrition when he heard a large cheer break out in the dining room. He looked up. Dr. Z was marching out of the kitchen, the entire kitchen crew behind him. The kitchen had joined the strike.

Completing the evening meal was not a problem. The food was already cooked in the giant ninety-gallon stainless-steel kettles, waiting in the steam tables along the serving line. The staff could ladle it out. But a turning point had been reached. In the warden's office the startling word that the kitchen crew had just walked out reversed the warden's optimistic plans. The walkout of the kitchen crew plus the rumors of "a march on Red Top" after the evening meal for the first time gave the top command a feeling of imminent danger.

Curt phone conversations with the three guards at desks between dormitory wings on the west side of Red Top informed Cansler that hundreds of the prisoners were "milling," walking about with no particular purpose. "Milling" was ordinarily permitted during some periods, unlike some prisons where prisoners had to have a stated destination for walking inside the institution. But milling in large numbers near the control center made Cansler nervous.

Prisoners were shouting back and forth, trying to communicate down the west corridor. Sounds echoed against the concrete walls and polished floors of the endless tunnel, causing men to shout louder, creating even more echoes.

Chief source of the shouting was prisoners trying to find someone to whom to address their particular grievances. No one seemed to be certain who was on the committee. Committee members at first tried to circulate among the men for grievances, but the massed confusion made it impossible to record anything in an orderly way.

There was another source of noise. Laughter. A carnival atmosphere overrode the irritation of trying to find committee members in the crowd. One of the prisoners later described it as a picnic. Some men had gone to the inside recreation area, some of the normal evening activities had already begun, but for most of the prisoners along the corridors leading to Red Top there was laughter, shouting and easygoing wisecracks. The guards were laughing along with the prisoners.

Irwin left the dining hall and went to the commissary. Earlier in the day he had failed to buy the goods he wanted and he hoped he could get them now. He also knew that it might be wise to stock up on extra fruit in case the strike materialized. The line was especially long. Other prisoners had the same idea. An emissary from the committee found him there and asked him to attend the six-thirty meeting with Cansler at Red Top. In disgust, Irwin again left his position in the commissary line and went to Red Top. But the grille gate at the end of the corridor, sealing off the corridor from Red Top, was locked. No officers were in sight. Even more disgusted, Irwin returned to his cage on the third floor of J block and went to bed.

Other committee members found each other along the corridor and retreated out of the chaos to the steps leading to the library. John Wagner joined them. They were trying to reach agreement on what to say if they met with Cansler. At six-thirty a group of prisoners led by Jimmy Hilty and Billy Genco came to the library steps and asked the committee not to meet with the warden. They said most of the population had not even known about the afternoon meeting and the men didn't think the committee represented them. One of them said, "You gotta get another meeting so all of us can vote on a real committee."

Committee members looked at each other. No one objected. They sent Wagner to tell Cansler that the committee could not meet with the warden at six-thirty, that too many prisoners felt that there should be another meeting in the auditorium to elect a more representative committee. The committee couldn't collect and sort grievances in time for a six-thirty meeting anyway.

At this point there was a sharp difference in the interpretation of spirit in the main corridor.

Prisoners of all political shades agreed that the atmosphere was good-natured and relaxed, if noisy. They also noticed that suddenly none of the officers at corridor control desks were visible. Without prisoners noticing it, every guard seemed to have left his duty station. Prisoners noted the bewildering disappearance of the guards.

Evaporation of the visible staff might be explained by a different interpretation of events by Associate Warden Cansler. The milling of men in the corridor, the shouting, and the walkout of the kitchen crew gave him the feeling that the institution was about to go out of control. He could have been influenced by two fiery speeches made near Red Top by unpolitical prisoners expressing their accumulated grievances to anyone who would listen. One was the prisoner who umpired summer baseball games, and his voice, in the best umpire tradition, carried well.

Or the associate warden may have been influenced by the knowledge that in any large crowd, especially a crowd with compacted emotions, gaiety can turn quickly to violence. For keepers of prisons, mass laughter is not funny. They had better allow the evening meeting.

At seven o'clock the prison public address system came alive with an announcement by the associate warden. A general meeting of the entire population was approved for the auditorium for the purpose of electing a committee that would represent the whole population in presenting grievances. This was on condition that they elect a committee of twelve men satisfactory to everyone and that the meeting be over and the auditorium empty by eight-thirty.

Committee members were as surprised as the rest of the population by the announcement. Previously skeptical prisoners reassured each other that it was an officially approved meeting: Cansler was really telling them to elect a committee. Someone walked into Irwin's cage and shook him awake.

When committee members arrived the auditorium was full. Seats were jammed and men were standing in the back and sitting in the aisles. This meant more than 1100 men. Meyers and Phillips were surprised to walk in and find the microphone already in command of Wagner, Alger and a third prisoner who had not figured in the earlier events. He was Bob Wolcott, an expert on interstate stolen vehicles and prison escape, doing a three-year sentence.

Alger was telling everyone excitedly to stay calm "even though the Pennsylvania state cops right now are surrounding the prison!"

Wolcott stepped to the microphone, with Wagner, John Alger, and

Sam Mason beside him, and called for nominations to the committee. By now Phillips, Jones, Meyers, Lucky Johnson, Eddie Mason and the three Puerto Ricans were mounting the stairs to the stage and the auditorium broke out in applause.

Wolcott, alternating with Wagner in managing the proceedings, asked, "Any objections to these guys for the committee?"

There was applause again. No objections.

There was whispering among the delegation on the platform. Three men walked off the stage. Wolcott announced that three members of the afternoon committee had asked to be released. They were the three Puerto Ricans. They said their English was not fluent enough.

By prearrangement three other Latins filled the void. The three new men were popular among the large Puerto Rican population.

Wolcott introduced them: "Marcello Vivero!"

Vivero, thirty-six years old, had been at Lewisburg four years on a sentence of ten years for buying, selling and transporting narcotics. The announcement of his name was met with wild applause.

"Mike Estrada!"

Estrada was popular, too, a friend of Vivero, by coincidence in on the same kind of charge, but younger. He, too, was elected by acclamation.

"Pedro Hernandez!"

More applause. Luis Pedro Hernandez was known to everyone as editor of *The Friday Flyer,* the official prison paper. That made the original nine.

Names were yelled from the audience. Occasionally a name would evoke boos, accepted as a negative vote. Heavy applause became an affirmative vote. With each new man, Wolcott or Wagner, now both working the microphone, would ask if there were objections, and if there were none the man was added to the committee. In that manner were added Richard Moore, the older black, forty-one, mild-mannered and well-liked, who had spoken briefly that afternoon. Jimmy Hilty, who had approached the committee to enlarge the group, had a fiery personality, was a bank robber and appealed to the prisoners because of his aggressiveness. Alger was elected; nominated by a friend in his block, he was a figure seen on the stage of the auditorium that afternoon and at the start of the evening session. And then Walter Scully, fifty-four, among the oldest men in the institution, doing twenty years plus a fine of $5000 for bank robbery. As an old-timer he stood out because he was different. Most old-timers are resigned to long sojourns without hope for release and make docile peace with their keepers, but Scully was forthright with officers, knowing the line between direct talk and insolence.

One of the men elected was Ronald Tucker, a young black doing time for bank robbery. He had not been particularly noticeable but he appealed to men around him for a certain arrogance, his bulging watery eyes often intense as he repeated bitter Marxist slogans or Maoist aphorisms. He did not look the image of the militant black. His hair style was moderate compared to Jones's and Johnson's, and he wore a pencil-thin mustache. When he read he wore general issue eyeglasses with pink plastic rims that gave him a deceptively mild appearance.

That made thirteen members of the committee. Wolcott had just announced that Wagner would be the representative of *Penal Digest International* reporting on the committee and he, Wolcott, would be the secretary. Committee members looked at each other. Wolcott? Who had made him secretary? A number of them were about to move to the microphone to say something when a short olive-skinned man rose from the audience. "Wait a minute! Wait a minute!"

The men on the stage stopped moving toward the microphone and the prisoners in the auditorium quieted. The short man yelled, "Okay. You got people on that committee representing all the parts of the population. Except one. What about the Italians?"

There was loud cheering and stamping of feet.

The man yelled, "I want Billy Genco on the committee to represent the Italians!"

William Genco, escapee and counterfeiter, was voted in by acclamation.

Some of the committee members, notably Scully and Meyers, were approaching the microphone again to ask who had told Wolcott he could be their secretary, when another man stood and called out from the audience.

In a heavy accent the man said that there were a number of people of French descent in the prison and everyone but the French were represented on the committee—people of color, people of the Spanish language, people of the Italian language—but nowhere was there a person of the French language. The man wished to have as the French representative on the committee Mike Buyse. There was no objection and Michel Guy Buyse, Belgian by birth, Canadian by nationality, until recently visiting-room orderly, walked to the stage to represent the fourteen prisoners of French descent in the prison.

There was general hilarity in the audience as the ethnic vote accumulated and on the stage Phillips said to Meyers, "No one from Luxembourg?" The laughter made everyone forget that there was a man no one had voted for who said he was secretary of the committee.

The oversight of this question was further deepened by Wolcott's reading of committee members from the final list in his hand: "Phillips, Jones, Eddie Mason, Alger, Johnson, Tucker, Hilty, Vivero, Estrada, Hernandez, Scully, Moore, Genco, Buyse, and John Wagner as reporter for *PDI* and Wolcott, secretary."

The crowd applauded and committee members on the stage were smiling back, some raising their fists, when Meyers turned to Phillips. "The son of a bitch left my name off the list."

Phillips asked if Meyers was sure.

"Of course, I'm sure. He never mentioned my name and I was on the committee that was voted in again tonight."

Phillips and Meyers went to the microphone, where Wolcott and Wagner were standing. Phillips said they had left Meyers' name off the list.

Wolcott said, "Gee, the committee's pretty big already. Cansler said twelve and now there are fourteen."

"Yeah," Meyers said. "Fourteen plus Wagner here as a reporter and you as secretary that no one voted for, and me who got voted on twice not on the list. You know I was on the list."

"But the committee's too big now and the administration might use it as an excuse if we make it bigger."

Meyers said, "Okay, let me have the mike. We'll leave it to the guys."

Wagner quickly said, "No. If you want to, sure, you're on."

Meyers said, "Listen, Wagner. It's not me that wants to. It's the men. They voted for me. They never voted for you or Wolcott. So let's get it straight. This ain't your committee and who the hell are you to be trying to run things?"

Wolcott took the microphone. "Joel Meyers was on the afternoon committee. Any objection to him being on the committee?"

There were loud cheers.

Irwin had arrived after the start of the proceedings and took a seat in the audience. He moved from bench to bench to talk to friends. He was happy to be out of the limelight.

The committee was completed and now there were nominations of two men from each housing unit to collect grievances that night and turn them over to the committee in the morning. The electing process worked its own way. Someone would call out from the audience, "We want Smitty from D block." And someone else would yell, "Fuck Smitty, we want . . ." and after a loud argument across benches D block would agree on two representatives.

The election of grievance collectors was done by working from the east end of the main corridor, the "wrong side of the tracks," toward the west. A block, B block, C block, D block, across Red Top to E dormitory, F dormitory, G semi-honor block, H dormitory, I block—and then it stopped at J block, the full-honor housing unit. These were the most desirable quarters in the prison: fifty one-man cages with unlocked doors reserved for long-termers with more than five years to go, ninety-two cages for shorter-term prisoners. No one was supposed to get in who was on close custody, or who had not been at Lewisburg at least a year and had not gone for at least six months without even a minor conduct report. The waiting list was very long. Some qualified prisoners waited years for an opening. It was assumed that committee members would suffer unpredictable punishments of some kind, but even the minor role of collecting grievances, despite the permission given by the warden, could bring retaliation, and loss of desirable quarters was one of them. So there was a sudden slowing of the process when it came to the most desirable quarters in J block.

"Okay, who from J block?"

A black prisoner stood up on one of the benches and said, "Who's here from J block?" As he scanned the audience he suddenly saw Irwin.

"Hey, Irwin! What the hell are you doing down here? Why ain't you up on the committee? Why don't you represent us? We need this cat on the committee! You know him! He gave that heavy speech this afternoon on the dock!"

The audience turned, spotted Irwin and broke into ear-splitting applause.

Irwin edged out of the bench and walked toward the stage with the applause continuing, men reaching out to slap him on the back as he walked down the sloping aisle. As he was climbing up the steps to the stage he heard Wagner at the microphone: "Let's nominate Irwin chairman of the committee!"

The prisoners stood and clapped, whistled and made Texas yells.

Irwin walked to the microphone. "Okay. Thank you. If I'm chairman I guess I can say something for the whole committee. We are going to represent you. We are going to do everything we can to correct your grievances."

More applause.

"But I've got a request for you. You've got to support us. We're only as strong as the population. We represent you. If you aren't behind us we're nothing. We're just a small bunch of cons who'll get the shit kicked out of us and end up screwed as usual. But that's not the point. The same thing will happen to you. So we support you. You support us. We stick together and we win."

Applause.

"Let's not kid ourselves. It isn't going to come easy. But if we stay unified we can do something. We're not going to accept the usual sell-out. We've all been through strikes before. Most of us have had a bad fucking from them all. Let's put that behind us. Let's make sure that this time it will be different. This time no bullshit, no sell-out, no fighting among ourselves. We're not making any big-mouth claims. But we will tell you the truth, and what we promise you we will do."

The prisoners stood and yelled approval.

Irwin, ten minutes earlier genuinely happy that he was returning to obscurity, was now a charismatic leader, poised and powerful. He waited until the auditorium was silent.

"As your chairman I have another request of every single man in this institution. Walk straight with your head high. You don't have to hide anymore!"

The auditorium was quiet.

"We're going to do what's right. We can be proud of that. We're going to conduct this strike like no other strike before. We can be proud of that. No violence and no bullshit. We don't need shanks [knives] and we don't need hostages. We do need unity and we do need pride."

The population was subdued.

"We've already taken the biggest step—we just decided we're men."

Irwin stepped back from the microphone. He felt something deep inside, almost like his conversion. He was doing something open and direct. Years of learned behavior in prison survival fell off—dampened emotions, repressed ideas, diminished expectations. Now he felt capable of enduring anything. He was no longer hiding. He was fighting. It occurred to him fleetingly on the stage that he had spent much of his life in fights—fistfights. Now he was fighting peacefully and for the first time he was fighting not for a friend or for a partner but for an idea.

By now Irwin was firmly in charge. Wagner, Wolcott and Alger, formerly surrounding the microphone, were to one side.

A prisoner called for quiet. Irwin told the audience to pipe down and

let the man talk because there wasn't too much time before they had
to be out of the auditorium.

The man spoke. "Listen! I been in all kinds of fucking joints for a
long time. For the first time we got us a real committee. An elected
committee. You represent us. You stand up for us and we'll stand up
for you. But don't take any motherfucking shit. You gotta be recognized. Don't do anything until that bastard the warden and that motherfucking cunt Cansler recognize you."

Once again the auditorium broke into sustained applause.

Someone else stood up. The man called out, "Are we on strike?"

The air was filled with "Strike! Strike!" Fists shot into the air again.

Irwin said, "Okay. We're on strike. That means no work in the
industries."

Applause again.

Meyers came to Irwin's side. "Irwin, that means no work anywheres,
doesn't it?"

Irwin addressed the crowd. "If we're on strike, we're on strike. Not
just industries. Do we shut down everything?"

Shouts of "Everything!" "Stop the whole joint."

Irwin held up his hands. "You know what that means? No commissary. No kitchen. No laundry."

There was applause again.

"Nobody works?"

The crowd yelled approval.

A man stood and yelled for attention. "How about keeping the
commissary open. Then we don't get cut off from supplies."

There was a short argument, shouted from bench to bench. A prisoner yelled above the other calls, "What about laundry? We'll need
clothes."

That started another argument on the floor. Someone else called out,
"Hell, you need food more than anything else. Why not keep the
kitchen going? We'll feed ourselves. Fuck the laundry and commissary."

Irwin, now in full command, spoke over the microphone. "Either
we're on strike or we're not. Either the joint is coming down or it's not.
If we start making an exception of this place and that place, first thing
you know the administration's going to have the joint running full tilt
and telling us we can be on strike as long as we want. Now let's put
it to a vote. Industries? Kitchen? Commissary? Laundry?"

Each time the large chamber filled with the cry of "Strike!"

An older prisoner came onto the stage and pulled Irwin aside. He was an experienced convict. "I need to get it straight, Irwin. How about hospital workers? We're on strike, too, or not? I don't want no confusion."

"Why, certainly you're going to work. If there's an emergency and somebody needs medical attention I'd expect you to work."

The old con said, "It's all right with me, you understand, Irwin. But I don't want no misunderstanding. You mind clearing it with the population so we all got it straight? I don't want no problems."

Irwin went to the microphone. "I overlooked something. There's only one exception. Anyone who works in the hospital, not just X ray, but any hospital job, can work. If they want to strike, okay. But if they want to work, okay. That goes for dental clinic, too. Not the lab. Lab don't treat people. But the clinic. Is that clear? We make an exception of the hospital. We got to take care of people who need medical attention. If anyone in the hospital or dental clinic got strong feelings against working, okay, but it's all right to keep medical care open."

Applause ratified the decision.

A white prisoner stood up and yelled for attention. "One thing. If we're gonna win this strike we got to stick together. And that means whites, blacks, everybody. The screws keep us divided. But we can't fight them if we fight ourselves. We're in this together. Whites and blacks. We're all cons. We're all brothers."

There was yelling of "Right on!" It was an unusual declaration.

A black prisoner stood on a bench and called for attention. "Listen! I'm a black nationalist."

A white prisoner yelled, "Well, right on, brother!"

The black prisoner turned around toward the back of the auditorium where the white man had spoken and said, "Thank you." He turned around again. "I want to say this. We elected three guys to represent the blacks and three whites to represent the whites and three Latins to represent the Latins, and we got Italian and French. But we don't want the three whites to just represent the whites, and the three blacks just to represent the blacks and the three Latins just representing the Latins. We want this committee to represent all of us. The only reason why we have three blacks and three whites and all that bullshit is so the press on the outside can't distort it and say this is a black thing or this is a white thing or this is a Latin thing. This is plain and simple a prisoner thing!"

That, too, was an unusual declaration.

There were a few unity speeches by committee members who were given time at the microphone. They all called for nonviolence. Irwin ended the meeting with a reminder to everyone to return to their usual evening activity and the eleven o'clock count peacefully, to avoid disturbances and give no excuse for the institution to claim disorder. By eight o'clock, half an hour ahead of schedule, the auditorium was empty.

Irwin immediately called a meeting of the committee in the front rows of the auditorium. He was irritated at the self-appointment of Wolcott and Wagner and pointedly told Wagner to go to the control center and inform Cansler that the meeting was over and that Irwin would want to see him in a few minutes.

When Irwin walked down to control, Wagner was there, as was Cansler and the other associate warden for the business office, Cramer.

Irwin said, "Mr. Cansler, we finished our meeting. The men elected a committee and elected me chairman. So I'd like to let you know the results of the voting of the population. There'll be no work tomorrow."

Cansler's face darkened. "Why not?"

"Well, for one thing, we got to get the grievances together."

"You mean you don't have the grievances with you?"

It was clear that the administration had expected that reports of a peaceful meeting meant delivery of grievances and end of the strike.

"Certainly we don't have the grievances, Mr. Cansler." Irwin's tone was indignant. "There are two men who've been elected to collect grievances from every housing unit. We were elected to represent the whole population, and you can't expect us to decide what the wishes are of the whole institution in an hour and get them cleared up. As a matter of fact, I'm here to request that the committee be permitted to meet at eight-thirty tomorrow morning so we can look over the grievances and get them straightened out and deal with things as a committee."

Cansler pursed his lips. "Okay."

Wagner spoke. "I'll be glad to continue as emissary during the meetings."

Cansler asked Irwin, "Who's on the committee?"

Irwin asked Wagner if he had the list. Wagner said he didn't, that Wolcott had it.

They started reciting names as Cansler jotted notes on a folder from his jacket pocket. He said, "You got names *and* numbers?"

A prisoner is close to nonexistence without his prison register number. For one thing, in a community of 1500 there were men with the same names. There were at least three Moores, two Joneses and, of course, two Masons. The compilation of committee members went slowly.

"Which Moore? John, you know Moore's first name? I don't either. You know him, Mr. Cansler. He's the black guy, tall . . ."

Men were placed by housing unit, where they worked, whether they were white, black or Latin. It didn't work very well.

"By the way," Irwin said, "the men voted to make one exception to everything closing down, the hospital."

Cansler grunted and then said, "You realize if the men don't work that various activities will have to be curtailed?"

Irwin knew what he was talking about—eating, exercising, commissary privileges and maybe worse things. He said, "We made our decision, Mr. Cansler. Curtailing services is up to you."

The two officers left. Irwin walked toward his quarters, Wagner trailing behind. Wagner excused himself from Irwin when a group of Italians near Red Top called him over to ask what had happened in the talk with Cansler and Cramer.

Irwin kept walking, alone, tired. But when he got back to his cage on the third floor of J block it was full of other men from his floor. They listed grievances and they wrote letters. Someone brought in a typewriter, a privileged instrument. Letters were typed to newspapers, lawyers, relatives, members of Congress, announcing what was happening. They had no way of knowing whether the letters would get out of the institution, but they worked on them until four in the morning.

As the work started in Irwin's cage, similar activities were developing elsewhere. In B block Alger turned a trash barrel over, sat on it, put a pad on his lap and wrote down grievances that prisoners in B block wanted brought before the committee.

There were still hundreds of men playing cards, sitting at chess boards, watching television, reading in the library. Eleven o'clock count was normal and the penitentiary was locked down. No incidents.

The warden's office was not normal. The strike was not over. The grievances were not on paper in the hands of the warden to be taken under consideration while the men went back to work the next day, with an answer days later when emotions had cooled and ringleaders had been isolated. The warden had hoped to notify Washington that the institution would be back to normal. Instead he called the Director at his Virginia home in Washington's suburbs. The news was not all bad.

There were no incidents, the population was nonviolent. But the next day the institution would be locked down.

Then the warden instructed Cansler to draw up emergency plans, including special assignments for every employee reporting for work in the morning and an immediate call for employees now on vacation or on days off. They would need all the hands they could get.

If the prisoners weren't going to work, they would be kept locked in their cages. Massed idleness on the loose would result in violence. The lockdown could be used strategically as pressure to go back to work. But it would have to be used carefully. As the population went without normal eating, as they began to run out of cigarettes, and as they tired of sitting in their cages, there would be less enthusiasm for the strike. But there could also be enthusiasm for destruction. The timing and tactics would have to be just right.

Food preparation would be the first problem. The staff could do it but it would be hard and so would food distribution. Prisoners would have to be fed in small escorted groups. Industries would complain of lost production on contracts, but at the moment that was a secondary problem.

More immediate was the work the institution did for others. With the kitchen and laundry workers out, the prisoners weren't in much of a position to complain about short food and dirty laundry. But the Lewisburg laundry did work for 150 men in the Lewisburg farm camp, the minimum-custody prisoners who produced dairy, beef and vegetables outside the wall, and for the 350 men in the honor camp at Allenwood. But that could be put aside for now. If the strike ended with the delivery of grievances tomorrow night there would be time enough to catch up on laundry for the outside camps.

The good counts were a hopeful sign. The committee was rejecting talk of destruction. Prisoner-informers were quoting committee members at the auditorium as being against violence. They did have those commies on the committee, but it was a good thing that the night meeting enlarged the committee. Dodd agreed with Alldredge and Cansler that there were five men on the committee who might be helpful.

The prospects for the next day looked good. But the warden decided not to let women office help report for duty, except for his personal secretary.

The warden told Cansler to assign twenty of his biggest guards to form a special riot squad, to be held in reserve all day in case something went wrong and to beef up the morning watch.

There were no Pennsylvania state troopers in the institution, but the state police had been routinely notified that "an incident" was in progress.

In his cage in C block Phillips lay in the dark reviewing the wild events of the day. He felt exhausted. Like Irwin he had been in prison long enough to distrust extravagant emotions. Coolness and restraint were the keys to survival. Long sentences caused insanity unless the prisoner learned to repress emotions, to lower the temperature of sensibilities, to hibernate excitements. But Phillips had to admit, lying in the dark, that he felt alive for the first time in years. Fighting back was an exhilaration.

5

THE EDUCATION ROOM

Irwin woke up. Automatically he looked out the window. The sky was gray again. He turned back to his cage. Something was wrong. It was nothing he could put his finger on, but something was definitely strange. He became alert. He opened his door and listened. Then it came to him. There was no noise. No clangings. No whistles. No shouts echoing. No distant banging. Prisons are never quiet. But Lewisburg was quiet this morning and it all came rushing back on him, the sudden lurch in his life.

He read the Bible and prayed and then opened his AA book. He took his red ballpoint pen from the shelf and wrote in block letters, slanting across the February 15 page of the book:

THE MEN VOTED ME CHAIRMAN OF THE STRIKE COMMITTEE.

And then he read the Meditation for the Day:

I will try to be unruffled, no matter what happens. I will keep my emotions in check, although others about me are letting theirs go. I will keep calm in the face of disturbance, keep that deep, inner calm through all the experiences of the day. In the rush of work and worry the deep inner silence is necessary to keep me on an even keel. I must learn to take the calm with me into the most hurried days.

It was remarkable how that seemed to fit the moment. It could be, like fortune cookies and horoscopes, that we invest ordinary words with our own meanings and then think of them as magic in their knowledge of us. He took his pen and drew red lines carefully under each sentence.

He read the Meditation again, slowly. Then he read the Prayer for the Day printed directly below:

> I pray that I may be still and commune with God. I pray that I may learn patience, humility and peace.

He underlined that, too.

On the other side of the prison, on the east side of Red Top, Phillips, on the third floor of C block, woke up tired, his eyes swollen. It felt like the middle of the night. He reached for his watch. Ten minutes to two? Why was he waking up that early? He looked around and saw too much light. He looked at his watch again. It was upside down—seven-twenty.

Out of habit he walked, almost sleepwalked, to his wash basin and held the hot water button until the water was warm. He measured out two spoons of instant coffee into his steel cup and ran hot water into it. He sat in his wooden chair sipping the coffee, his long legs sprawled, letting the coffee wake him up, waiting for the seven-thirty work whistle. Something disturbed him. It was minutes, sitting on his chair, staring at his coffee, before he realized that the seven-thirty work whistle hadn't blown. Of course not. The place was really shut down. He realized the source of a strange feeling. It was the silence. He thought, That's what they mean when they say silence is deafening. He sat still and "listened" to the silence. It was eerie. As though he were the only human being left in the institution. Or on the planet. It didn't make much difference.

At about the time Ron Phillips was turning his watch upside down, civilian employees of Lewisburg Federal Penitentiary were walking to the front gate for work, shuffling through the sally ports and gates with their eyes down, reading sheets of paper. A lieutenant handed out assignment sheets placing each person in a new place for the emergency. At the gate there was none of the usual banter and raucous shouting. It added to the strange quiet.

Cansler assigned staff to the dining room to prepare and cook food under the direction of the civilian kitchen supervisor. He put a few men in the laundry to supply clothes and sheets for the farm and Allenwood. He made sure that he had the riot squad formed and several collections of guards to be concentrated near the dining room before he started the feeding of breakfast to the locked-up prisoners, one floor at a time. This time there would always be more guards than grouped prisoners. He also wanted another squad on the floor ready to converge on the mess hall or quarters in case anyone made a break during their breakfast release.

Then he sent a guard to get Irwin and Wagner.

Once again Irwin and Wagner began narrowing down the committee members to eliminate others with the same names. As each new name was verified, the man would be called to the control center, Irwin and Wagner would agree he was on the committee and the man would be asked if he knew the numbers of any of the other elected committee members. Cansler would then direct some of the committee members —not all—to the mess hall for breakfast, saying, "When you come out, go to the education department to start your meeting."

Irwin and Wagner were still confirming committee names with Cansler when some members of the committee—Scully, Alger, Mason, Hernandez, Buyse—were already fed and sent up to the second floor of the administration building, to Room 3 in the education department.

They sat in Room 3 waiting for others to arrive when someone—no one seems to remember who—said, "This fuckin' room must be bugged. They picked it out." This started a quick inspection of the room, along windows, inside ventilators, under tables.

At nine-thirty two guards appeared at the door of Phillips' cage. They unlocked the cage. One guard, carrying a clipboard, said, "You got a meeting," and gestured for Phillips to come out. Both guards avoided Phillips' eyes. They, too, seemed to feel strange. Perhaps at the silence. Or the broken rhythm of the prison. But perhaps at the subtly altered relationship. The prisoner was not doing what they wanted him to do but what he wanted to do. For the first time the guards' schedule depended on him. It was a new and difficult relationship to deal with.

The three walked down the stairs in silence, out to the main corridor, where Meyers was waiting with another guard in front of the opposite wing, D block. No one spoke as they walked down the echoing corridor toward the control center. Red Top was deserted. Hilty, Genco and Vivero arrived and moved ostentatiously away from Meyers, not bothering to conceal their dislike.

Irwin, Wagner and Cansler came to the Red Top side of control and Irwin said, "That's all of them," and they were escorted by guards up to Room 3.

The newcomers were informed of the fear of bugging.

"It figures," someone said. "They picked this room and had all night to fix it."

Someone looked toward the light fixture on the ceiling and called out, "All right, you motherfuckers, listen if you want to. Maybe you'll get something through your thick heads."

Irwin said, "Hell, we got nothing to hide."

Scully said they ought to demand another room.

Outside the door was T. R. Young, supervisor of education. When he saw Irwin and Scully gesture for him to enter the room, he opened the door and asked if they had the grievances to give him.

Irwin said, "Mr. Young, when we have the grievances we'll deal with the warden. We've got our own messenger, Wagner here. We want to meet in another room. This one isn't suitable."

Young withdrew. He returned in a few minutes. Cansler had approved a change of rooms. Young said he'd unlock Room 14, the "education room" down the corridor and around the corner.

Room 14 was on a corner with windows on two sides and four tables set in a hollow square. It had a blackboard and shelves of supplies. Two typewriters were on a small table in the back. When the last of the committee came in, Irwin and Scully were talking at one side of the table. Scully's friends, Genco and Hilty, kept close to him.

While Irwin and Scully talked, the others, somewhat playfully, looked underneath the table and into the backs of shelves, pretending to be calling Cansler: "Hello, hello! George, am I coming through? Testing, testing . . ."

Irwin and Scully were nodding as though in agreement. For Irwin it was a new assessment of the man. Scully was known throughout the institution as a tough man not to be fooled with. Irwin's only contact with him before had been a bad one. It was on a food line when Scully had been a few places in front of him and performed one of those acts that inspired loyalty. A prisoner had brought his tray back to men waiting in the line, saying to Scully, "Look at the shit in this tray. Just try smelling it." Scully had looked, smelled and said, "That meat's not fit to eat. It's rotten." He had stepped out of line and said loudly, "Everybody in the line stay right where you are. They've got some rotten shit up here we got to get changed." Scully had walked up to the kitchen officer, pointed to the meat in the counter. The officer smelled the meat and nodded in agreement and ordered one of the kitchen crew to replace it. Scully turned and said, "Everybody stay put until we get that meat changed."

Irwin didn't want any meat. He was a vegetarian. He hated to wait in lines, particularly stalled lines. There had been times when he had skipped an entire meal rather than wait in a line that wasn't moving. So he went to the counter past the meat and put only vegetables on his tray. It struck Scully as deliberate disunity. The two men stared at each other. But nothing came of it.

Now in Room 14 they were nodding in obvious agreement. They went to the blackboard and Scully, with Irwin watching in approval, began writing things. There were five numbered items when they got through.

Irwin turned toward the end of the table, a natural place for the chairman. Wolcott, the secretary, was there. Irwin said nothing and was about to sit along the side when Wolcott said, "Okay, guys. We might as well start. The first thing we need to do is get the grievances on paper."

Irwin stood up, red-faced. "What the hell are you doing, Wolcott? Who the hell do you think you are?"

"Well, I'm the secretary."

"Who the hell elected you anyway?"

Wolcott mumbled something inaudible.

"Get the hell out of that chair! Nobody elected you to anything! I was elected to this committee and I was elected chairman."

Wolcott quickly vacated the chair and after a reshuffle at the end of the table Irwin sat in the center chair, Scully to his left and Hilty next to Scully. On Irwin's right, when the shuffling was over, were Mason and Alger. Wolcott had taken an unobtrusive chair midway on the side of the table.

Seated at the long table to Irwin's right were Moore, Tucker, Jones, Johnson, Meyers and Phillips. Opposite them were Genco, around the corner from Hilty, then Buyse, Wolcott, Hernandez, Vivero and Estrada. Seats at the table opposite Irwin were empty.

Phillips looked around the table. The four blacks all together on one side. Also all the people he thought reliable as militants. And across from them the Latins, with Hilty and Genco making sure they were as far from Meyers and as close to Scully as possible. Wagner, the *PDI* observer, sat at the far corner of the table below Estrada.

This was a rare event, historic in a federal prison—prisoners elected by the population to present grievances to their keepers.

Prisoners organized to complain are seen in the public mind only in riots or in the prison paper as a trivial committee elected to improve Christmas entertainment.

For the federal prison bureaucracy the meeting in Room 14 was a revolutionary gesture, something new and different for the prison system that considered itself the most progressive in the country, if not the world.

Prison keepers historically had suppressed prisoner voices. Prisoners, devoid of other mechanisms, had expressed their frustrations by riot, rebellion and wrecking. Human beings, and animals for that matter, have a fundamental need to sense that their communications have been received, understood and taken seriously. Remove this mechanism, and communication descends to the remaining convincing method of the hammer and torch or threats of death to a hostage.

Societies, insisting on the need for erring citizens to develop self-reliance, learned slowly. Centuries of total repression and resulting total rebellion had produced only the faintest awareness that it is safer to let prisoners voice their complaints, sounder to let them have a share in implementing change, than to wait for the never-ending catastrophe of prison rebellions.

Ironically, the federal prison bureaucracy, traditionally run by men celebrated as humanitarians, was among the slowest to learn. The National Prison Association, predecessor to the present American Correctional Association, conservative organization of wardens and directors of corrections, at its founding meeting at Cincinnati in 1870 issued Principle No. 5:

> The prisoner's destiny should be placed measurably in his own hands; he must be put into circumstances where he will be able, through his own exertions, to continually better his condition. A regulated self-interest must be brought into play and made constantly operative.

Even that, startling as it may have seemed to prison keepers in the late nineteenth century, was not the first idea of a prisoner-run mechanism for self-government, for a peaceful mechanism to permit prisoners to speak systematically, to act rationally to resolve differences. In 1825 the New York House of Refuge, a juvenile prison, had a jury entirely of prisoners to decide on punishment for prisoners who broke rules. Three years later similar self-government in the Boston House of Reformation attracted the attention of Alexis de Tocqueville, in this country to see the new American invention of prison.

J. E. Baker has recorded the growth of the idea. Beginning in 1843, for over a hundred years in the Massachusetts State Prison at Charlestown the maximum-security adult section regularly elected six representatives to discuss prison conditions and punishments with the staff. In Elmira reformatory prisoners had self-government and their own juries for punishment in 1888. In a dozen major state institutions various forms of elected representation on substantive matters continue today. It has often been sabotaged by unsympathetic staffs, or drifted into a corrupt alliance between staffs and prisoner-racketeers. But it has been successful in many prisons. As the men gathered in the education room of Lewisburg prison there were fourteen states with prisoner-elected councils that decided on prison punishments and negotiated grievances. But not in the "progressive" Federal Bureau of Prisons, where continued voicelessness of the totally powerless is considered the way to encourage prisoner self-reliance and responsibility.

The eighteen prisoners seated around the three sides of the hollow square in Room 14 on the second floor of the administration building of Lewisburg Federal Penitentiary were not concerned with history but with some items on the blackboard. They were, by accident and an impulse of their warden, historically important in the bitter evolution of American prisondom. But for the committee they were practical necessities.

Bill Irwin was not thinking of history when he opened the session with "Let's get down to brass tacks."

But if they weren't thinking of history books, many of the men on the committee were thinking of their own histories in prison. The five items on the blackboard were preconditions before the committee would present grievances to the warden. Most of the men had been in prison strikes before and they understood many things. They wanted formal written recognition from the warden that they were the elected committee authorized to represent the population in handling the grievances with the administration. They wanted confirmation in writing that there would be no reprisals taken against the committee members or anyone else in the institution because of the work stoppage if there was no violence. They wanted the visiting room reopened. They wanted a lawyer of their choice to help them. And they wanted a member of the press present at all times.

Committee members looked at the board and expressed their opinion, item by item. The letter of recognition started their first argument. Phillips, Meyers and Scully pressed the point that the population wanted the committee to negotiate grievances, not just hand in a piece of paper and go out of existence.

Phillips would testify later, "We had seen the duplicity of the prison administrators. They ask for your grievances; you give them your grievances; they throw them in the drawer, tell you to go back to work and nothing changes. I think everybody in America is fully aware of this, that men have been asking for changes and demanding changes and nothing really happens. So we felt this had some historical significance, and we didn't want it to slip through our fingers like so many other strikes and work stoppages had."

Vivero, Estrada, Mason, Moore and Buyse were against the letter of recognition. They felt that the committee's only job was to collect grievances, present them to the administration and end the strike as soon as possible. Wolcott and Wagner, while not voting, said they thought it was a bad idea, too.

Scully argued strongly in favor of formal recognition and, following his leadership, Hilty and Genco. With the exception of Moore, the side of the table with "the militants" was solidly for it. Hernandez spoke in favor of formal bargaining. Alger agreed with the majority. The objectors conceded, making it unanimous.

No one questioned the no-reprisal promise in writing. Captain Dodd had made the promise on the platform yesterday noon. Associate Warden Cansler had made the announcement on the public address system the night before. But everyone in the room, every man in the prison, knew that promises of no reprisal are habitual in prison protests, an accepted technique for regaining total control, a standard move to persuade prisoners to come forward and reveal themselves as leaders or to give up a momentary advantage. And there was no prisoner who did not know, some from personal experience and all by knowledge of prisons, the terrible consequences that usually followed "no reprisals." There are men who have been in solitary confinement for years after a promise of no reprisals. After the rebellion in the New York City jail in the previous year, once protesting prisoners had surrendered and top officials and the press had left the institution, prisoners were forced to march naked between lines of guards who beat them with clubs. The torture of rebelling prisoners after Attica came out in court, including one prisoner who testified under oath that afterward, when he was subpoenaed to testify in court about staff abuses, he was stripped by guards and a broomstick pushed into his anus and shoved deeper and deeper until he promised to lie in court. There were, of course, milder forms of reprisal. A planted weapon on the bed of the absent prisoner, "found" by guards during a shakedown. Loss of a favored job or housing unit. Transfer to the worst job and to the most savage housing unit where the gang rapists or other sadists understood that the punished man was fair game. Or endless condemnation to solitary confinement, punitive transfer to a distant prison, loss of accumulated good time, a label that permanently made them ineligible for parole and put them into the worst parts of the worst prisons they might ever be transferred to.

The visiting-room demand had come up in conversation while changing from Room 3 to Room 14. A number of committee members had heard about it. Federal prisons have men from all over the country. Relatives, most of them poor, might come 3000 miles to visit, have to take expensive private transportation to the remote town, a cab to the isolated prison, and then find the visiting room closed. For some prisoners it meant nothing—an alarming number never have visits during years of imprisonment, some claiming they want no one in their family to see them in captivity but in truth because there isn't anyone who cares enough. But to the majority who do get visits it is vital. The committee recognized that keeping the visiting room closed was a bargaining pressure for ending the strike. Wives, mothers, brothers and sisters, some after days on Trailways buses from Atlanta, Cleveland and Denver, were paying fourteen dollars a night in nearby motels waiting to see someone on an annual visit. At some point they would have to give up and go back. If the strike ended right away the visit might not be a total loss. During a strike and its feared aftermath of retaliation, visiting relatives were one way to get word to the outside world—reassurances if all was well or calls for help if staffs were taking private revenge.

The committee wanted a lawyer to represent them in bargaining with the administration. The committee recognized, as they sifted through two hundred pieces of paper with written grievances, that some were complicated. Some might be remedied by the warden, some would require action by Washington headquarters, some were problems for the courts and Congress. A lawyer would be a channel to the outside world, restraint against maltreatment of prisoners. Irwin had been reading about constitutional cases brought in Virginia that led federal judge Robert R. Mehrige, Jr., to order drastic changes in Virginia prisons. The lawyer had been Philip J. Hirschkop, and Irwin said that would be his choice. Irwin even remembered his address. Prisoners often have unusual memories for addresses—they are their lifeline to the outside if their written materials are lost, stolen or destroyed in a shakedown.

The fifth demand was for a member of the press to be present during negotiations. There had seldom been a prison protest that did not reveal prison abuses, irrationalities or breaking of law by the staff. When it became public, there were citizen groups, news organizations, judges and public officials who found it surprising that an instrument of law enforcement, a prison, would break its own rules or violate the law or administer its duties corruptly. The institution, while under uncontrolled publicity, might be forced to make changes.

But if there was no free channel to the outside world it was the prison that managed the information, and the public heard only that the prisoners were acting with violent irresponsibility and the prison, after saintly patience, was acting with dutiful firmness. It is a rule of life that men of power, unwatched, tell lies. They lie because they believe they have responsibilities that justify it, that their lies are for good purposes. After a period of acceptance of their lies they no longer believe that they are lying but fighting bravely against bad influences. It is fashionable in politics to repeat Lord Acton's aphorism "Power corrupts and absolute power corrupts absolutely," but it is never applied to prisons, the social institution with the most absolute power known to civilization. A prisoner's ability to reach the public with firsthand observation of a professional journalist is instinctively recognized by prison keepers as a threat to their power. Rebellions can always be put down. Escape of secret information cannot.

Each item was brought up in order and a vote taken on it around the table, skipping Wolcott and Wagner, who had no votes. It was unanimous for all five. There would be no presentation of grievances until these conditions were met. They instructed Wolcott to write the conditions, addressed to the administration.

Wolcott, not strong on spelling, started each of the five preconditions, "We Whant . . ." and ended with:

> These 5 demand is priority before anything else is start, we will not start meet unless these 5 demand are receive, this demand should be isued to the population by P.A. Systhem. Open communication with Population.

The committee told Wolcott to give the paper with the five demands to Wagner and asked Wagner to get them to the warden. Wagner went to the door where Officer Young and several other guards were waiting in the corridor. Young took Wagner to an office down the corridor where Young telephoned Cansler. In a few minutes Cansler arrived in the room with Wagner and Young. He read the list. He asked Wagner what it meant. Wagner told the associate warden that the committee was pretty strong on it, that they had voted unanimously not to go any further until these conditions had been met. "They're very hard-nosed on it, Mr. Cansler."

Cansler shook his head. He said there was no way he could approve these. Then he added that he was sure that the warden would never approve of them. But he'd take them downstairs. Downstairs the warden, Cramer and Dodd waited for Cansler's return. They assumed he had the grievances and the strike was close to an end.

In Room 14, committee members looked over the sheets of paper from the housing units listing demands. Irwin, with some of the men around him, started sifting out trivial ones, saying that anyone with objections should speak up. They threw out dozens, like a request for a better brand of peanut butter in the commissary, color television instead of black and white.

At a desk in the back of the room Meyers and Phillips sat with a pad of paper making notes. They were talking earnestly.

"Look," Meyers said, "we got to stick to this very closely to keep this thing on the track. Some guys here are ready to roll over and play dead right now."

Phillips agreed. "Let's make sure that one of us answers all the talk about caving in."

Phillips looked up and saw that Vivero, at the large table, was staring at them. He stared back. "Yeah," Phillips said to Meyers, "we're going to have trouble."

Meyers grunted and then proposed a wild idea. He loved to play bureaucratic games, predict the response and gloat over how correct he was.

"We're the elected representatives of the work force of this institution, right?" he said to Phillips. "So I think we should write a letter to the National Labor Relations Board asking for certification as bargaining agent for the prisoners who work for the United States Government inside the prison."

It would be a month before a letter would reach the NLRB but Meyers was correct. In good order, four months later, the National Labor Relations Board replied:

> We do not believe that we have jurisdiction in this matter. Although as you know, we do conduct union representation elections in units of employees of private employers engaged in interstate commerce, we do not have the authority under the statute to conduct the elections you suggest. Apart from such questions as whether prisoners are employees or whether federal prisons are engaged in interstate commerce, the Board does not have jurisdiction over the federal government as an employer or over federal employees. Sincerely, John C. Truesdale, Acting Executive Secretary.

Copies to W. J. Usery, Jr., Assistant Secretary of Labor, and Vernon Gill, Executive Director, Federal Labor Relations Council. Mr. Truesdale enclosed a booklet on the benefits of orderly collective bargaining.

Inside the warden's office Alldredge, Cansler and Dodd were angry at the demands. The warden agreed that he could not grant any of them, certainly not in writing. Cansler reported that Wagner thought the committee was strong on it, but that there had been a serious split earlier on whether to hold out for these preconditions. Maybe the split would widen if they stood firm.

The warden wrote in bold letters across the top of the sheet, "Denied —NLA," and handed it back to Cansler.

On the way to the education room Cansler stopped at control to check on feeding. One floor of men at a time was being released for breakfast. The staff was serving. The food was hot but there were no seconds. Prisoners were asked to eat without delay so other tiers could eat. Breakfast would not be finished until three P.M. All was going well. Cansler continued up the stairs.

Wagner was still in the office with Young. Cansler handed him the paper. "Like I said, all denied by the warden. Better tell them to forget the stuff on this paper and get down to business on the grievances. The warden has no power to do the things you got there. Get the grievances on paper. That's what we want."

Wagner carried the paper back in the room and reported Cansler's message.

It was agreed in the committee that it was now a waiting game but they should spend the time putting the grievances in order.

Sorting of the prisoner suggestions was done at the big table. Someone suggested writing letters to ask the lawyer and the press to be present. Meyers was considered knowledgeable and grammatical. He was assigned to dictate the letter to Wolcott at one of the typewriters in the back. Meyers slowly dictated a letter to Tom Wicker of the New York *Times,* explaining the strike and asking if he would be present during negotiations. Wicker had been called for by prisoners in Attica during the prisoners' rebellion. Meyers also dictated a letter to Hirschkop in Alexandria, Virginia, asking if he would be their counsel during negotiations.

Irwin was quiet, resting his head on his arm from time to time, appearing to be in meditation.

Phillips talked with Scully and Hilty about the need for prisoners around the country to form some kind of union. It was casual talk about the idea in general. Phillips did not propose it as an object of the Lewisburg strike. He left the two men to see how the slow dictation was going when Vivero gestured for him to come over.

"Those demands you read on the platform yesterday, Phillips, they were kind of—ah—you know—radical, weren't they?"

Phillips checked his immediate response of anger. Why should he explain himself to this macho conservative? He adopted the casual tone of controlled talk in prison. "I'd call the demands necessary, Vivero. But I guess the administration would consider them radical."

Vivero said, "In my country we have many communists and they talk like you and Meyers."

"Well, good, Vivero. I'm glad to know that you have some good people in your country."

"Ah ha, Phillips! Then you admit that you're a communist!"

Phillips checked himself again. "Where's your country?"

"Chile."

"Maybe that explains why you're unable to understand the American spirit."

Phillips regretted it at once. It sounded like a Fourth of July speech. He became aware that Vivero had tensed. For a moment Phillips thought there would be blows. But suddenly Vivero smiled broadly and relaxed. Phillips smiled and relaxed.

Phillips thought to himself, I think he was putting me on. I think I like the son of a bitch.

Phillips went to watch the painful process of Wolcott typing and spelling several variants of the name Hirschkop. As he watched, Phillips became aware of something, a signal that was one of his most reliable vital life signs—his stomach was growling. He hadn't eaten for almost twenty-four hours. He said out loud, "Jesus Christ! I'm hungry!"

They looked at their watches. One o'clock.

There was a brief argument on whether they should risk going to the mess hall, being separated and put in their cages for permanent lockdown. The discussion ended with the agreement that they first had to get a definitive response directly from the warden. Maybe Cansler was taking over. Maybe he was misrepresenting their position. Wagner was told to tell Young that the committee wished to see the warden personally.

Ten minutes later the committee members heard footsteps in the outside corridor. They all took their places at the table. The chairs opposite Irwin were empty. The committee members looked at Irwin. He was sitting tall and confident. "Okay, Billy," Jones said, "it's all yours." Irwin nodded.

The warden had come to see them.

Noah Alldredge strode into the room holding his six feet in almost military bearing, his expression friendly, an impression strengthened by a slow nod toward the group. He was trim, his graying, wavy hair seeming, as always, freshly barbered, wearing a smartly fitted suit with a metallic sheen.

Behind the warden was Cansler. Cansler was not as meticulous about his fashions. He was taller than Alldredge but somehow seemed shorter. He did not nod. His eyes quickly scanned the U-shaped table where the committee members sat; his expression was one of disdain.

Trailing behind were Associate Warden Cramer, a caseworker named Calibro and Mr. Young. The warden sat in the center of the table facing Irwin, Cansler beside him.

The committee members sat still. A few shifted nervously in their chairs. Most sat stiffly, faces expressionless.

The warden, in a modulated voice that was neither hostile nor ingratiating, consistent with his tough-but-fair manner, said, "I'd like to hear what you've come up with."

Everyone turned toward Irwin. The chairman stood up, his face firm, his stance tall. He said, "Warden Alldredge . . ."

And then something happened to Irwin. He began to stammer. "Warden . . . I . . . You know I have the greatest respect for you, Warden Alldredge, and my action here represents no disrespect for you. In fact, I want to say . . . I want to say that you have always treated me with kindness and consideration . . ."

The warden nodded in sympathy. The members of the committee stared at Irwin in disbelief.

Irwin was silent for a long moment. He felt like a traitor to a friend, to a man he thought of as a father, more than he did his real father. When Irwin had quit the dental lab in disgust, after a long period of training in a good assignment, his enraged supervisor ordered Irwin punished by transfer to Leavenworth. Irwin had gone to Alldredge, and the same day his name had been taken off the bus list for Leavenworth. He recalled his gratitude every time Alldredge spoke to him on Red Top or in the mess hall, the only warden he had ever known who walked freely among the men, talking and listening. Irwin remembered his debt to the warden when, on holidays, the warden came through the dining hall with Mrs. Alldredge and their two daughters, a gesture of implicit trust in the prisoners. And Irwin remembered his debt to the warden when, as he rose to speak for the population that had elected him chairman, his eyes had met the eyes of Warden Alldredge.

As Irwin stammered, apologizing, starting to read the five demands, and apologizing again, the warden's expression changed from sympathy to discomfort.

At this point Scully stood up, his hand on Irwin's forearm, possibly in comfort, possibly in restraint. Scully spoke coldly. "Warden, we can't take any further action until we get an affirmative answer from you on our five demands."

The warden looked almost as relieved as the committee members. Scully ordered Wolcott to read the first demand: a letter from the warden recognizing the committee as the authorized body to deal with the administration on prisoner grievances.

"I cannot grant that. I don't have the power to give you any such letter. You don't need any letter to do your job. I authorized the population's meeting in the auditorium, I authorized the population to elect this committee and I authorized you to meet here for the past several hours. The fact that I'm here talking to you is recognition."

There was a moment of silence. Wolcott broke it by reading the second demand: a letter from the warden guaranteeing no reprisals against committee members and none against the rest of the population as long as things remained peaceful.

"I can't give you anything of the sort in writing. You don't need a letter from me on that, either. You have my word that there will be no reprisals."

For the first time committee members reacted spontaneously. The blacks talked about being double-crossed. One of them said, "Warden, don't give us that jive about promises."

Meyers said, "Warden, Tom Kolmeyer and I were in the strike in Allenwood a couple of years ago. I believe you remember that." Meyers could not resist his demonic grin. "And you gave your word to everyone at Allenwood that if the strike ended without a riot there'd be no reprisals. There was no riot and Tom spent the rest of his sentence in the hole and I got punitively transferred."

The warden's lips pursed briefly and he began to answer when Scully spoke. "Warden, let's put it this way. You give us your word. Your word is good. We believe you. Then you go outside the gate and a truck comes along and hits you. You're dead. How good is your word then? We'd be at the mercy of the staff."

Scully stared deliberately at Cansler. Cansler stared back.

The warden began answering Scully when Meyers spoke again. "Another thing, Warden Alldredge. There's a rumor that you're planning to retire pretty soon. If you retire and you haven't put your signature to a piece of paper representing the policy of the institution as a whole, then whoever succeeds you can go back on your word even if you yourself never go back on your word."

Scully said, "We'd want both associate wardens to initial the letter."

The warden answered: "First of all, I can't retire as long as this thing is going on, so that's no problem. If I died the day after I signed a letter my signature wouldn't mean a thing. Whoever took my place would have the authority and responsibility to do whatever he had to. There are 1500 inmates in this institution and neither you nor I can guarantee what's going to happen."

He looked around the table for reaction. The committee members were silent. The warden said slowly, "My word is my bond. There are plenty of prisoners in this institution who know that. You know and they know that I've proven my good faith. So you'll just have to accept my word for no reprisals as long as this thing is kept peaceful."

Committee reaction burst out again. Once more the blacks openly sneered at the warden. Cansler looked at them with cold contempt. One of the blacks said, "Warden, you talk as though we were stupid children. Things could happen here lots worse than happened already. We're talking about serious things, and you're asking us to act like Boy Scouts."

Tucker, his eyes bulging, accused the warden of making a "bourgeois pettifogging" statement to obscure the issue. Lucky Johnson said, "We've had lots of experience with the word of people around here, you know, Warden. We don't need any of that bullshit, you know, about word is bond. We get that every day."

Jones said bitterly, "You're showing bad faith right now, Warden. You promise us no reprisals but you won't put it in writing. What kind of good faith is that? You take us for fools? To be deceived time after time, in prison after prison, including in Lewisburg penitentiary, and then when you won't put in writing where you put your mouth, you ask us to take it on faith? Would you ask a grown white man on the outside to do that? You know you wouldn't. You just expect us to fall into that trick bag because we're nothing but cons, nothing but low-life criminals. Anything is all right for us."

The other side of the table began to defend the warden. One of them said, "Wait a minute. We aren't talking about the warden. If he gives his word in front of all of us here, we know he means it. Captain Dodd gave it and Mr. Cansler gave it. It isn't the warden . . ."

The two sides of the table began shouting at each other.

Scully pounded his fist on the table. He gestured to the blacks on his right and the Latins on his left to be quiet. "We got more business to do. Wolcott read the next one."

The next one was to reopen the visiting room.

"That won't be possible while this institution is in emergency condition. I don't have staff to supervise the visiting room because staff is doing all the cooking and all the other duties being left undone during the strike. I have responsibility for the safety of visitors and I simply can't guarantee their safety during this condition."

The next demand was for a lawyer to work with the committee.

"There is no need for a lawyer. We don't even have any grievances yet, so I can't make a judgment on whether there is a need for an attorney. I can't see that an attorney would do anything to help resolve this situation. You present the grievances and I will act on them. I promise you answers in *The Friday Flyer* within two weeks. So I will not grant you a legal representative."

At the words *"Friday Flyer"* Irwin came to life. His face was flushed. *"The Friday Flyer? The Friday Flyer?* Warden, do you mean to sit there and tell us that we're supposed to represent this whole institution, 1500 men, men who have elected us, given us a mandate to get their grievances settled, men who have voted to strike until these justified grievances are corrected, and you mean to sit there and say that all you're planning to do is give an answer in *The Friday Flyer?"*

The warden frowned. Irwin's earlier reaction had been reassuring. Now Irwin was speaking bitterly, once more fixing the attention of everyone.

"You're telling us that you'll take our sheet of paper with the grievances and give your answer in *The Friday Flyer!* That's insulting. It's no different from the slaves in the slavery days slipping up to the master's house and leaving a note on the back porch asking for a potato to keep from starving to death and waiting a couple of weeks until the master is kind enough to read the note and answer it."

The committee once more was nodding in agreement with Irwin.

"I'm simply not going to accept that. I don't want to deal that way and nobody else wants to deal that way. That's what this is all about. The master-slave. That's the way we've always been treated and we don't want it anymore."

Jones whispered passionately, "Right on! Right on!"

"We wanted to sit down and talk with each other with dignity and pride and respect for each other. And now you don't want to show us any respect. You don't want to treat us like human beings. You want to treat us like pieces of shit. We don't like that and we won't have that."

Irwin sat down. He had become visibly more restless as point by point the warden had denied the demands. Whether out of embarrassment at his original reaction, his guilt at letting down the population, or indignation, he was once more eloquent and passionate. Now he was sitting straight and angry.

Scully nodded at Wolcott to read the fifth demand.

The last demand was for the presence of a member of the press.

The warden looked pleased. "On that you'll find it interesting to see this policy statement." He unfolded some papers on the table. "Under this policy PMB has been extended to members of the press. You'll have full access to the press without hindrance, so you don't need any press representative here during your committee work."

"PMB" was Prisoners Mail Box, a special container for letters that, according to regulations, could leave the institution unopened and uncensored. Up to now this had been limited to letters to the President of the United States, members of Congress, federal judges, the Surgeon General of the United States, attorneys, and the Board of Parole.

The warden, holding the papers high, read, "This is Policy Statement 1220, Point 1A, dated February 11, 1972, which I received just yesterday. Wagner, maybe you can read it so the committee will know exactly what it guarantees about access to the press."

Irwin held his palm toward Wagner. "John, don't read that statement. We're not here to be lectured to. Warden, we're here to get your answer to our five conditions. We need a yes or a no. You're saying no and you're asking us to listen to a policy statement."

Scully stood up and agreed with Irwin. Scully said, "Wagner, give that stuff back to the warden. And Warden, we don't want you or any of the staff to bother reading it to us. You're only trying to delay us and divide us. We have one issue here. Do you agree to these five conditions or not? You've given your answer and that's all there is to it. We have nowhere to go until you can agree to those conditions. We do nothing else as a committee until we get an affirmative answer from you."

Alldredge stood up, and with him the rest of his party. The warden said, "You have one purpose as a committee—to draw up the population's grievances and submit them to me. I've given you every reasonable leeway possible. If you haven't got the grievances ready for me by three o'clock I may have to disband this committee and use some other method of getting the inmate grievances where I can act on them."

The warden turned and started to leave the room. Cansler had opened the door for him when the warden changed his mind, turned and walked back into the room, stood behind Estrada at the end of the table and began reading the policy statement.

Scully rose and interrupted. "Warden Alldredge! We're not interested in propaganda. We're interested in getting action on our demands. If you can't do that you might as well leave. And take your policy statement with you."

Alldredge turned on his heel and walked rapidly out of the door. The staff followed him. Cansler was halfway through the door when he turned, stepped back over the threshold and pointed his finger toward the head of the table. "Y'all get that?" He was spitting out the words: "I'd advise you to have those grievances by three o'clock or else!" He looked over the whole room coldly and walked out without shutting the door.

The table was silent for a second. Then curses came from every side. "Motherfucking bastard!" "Dirty low-life screw!"

Vivero, Estrada and Hernandez seemed particularly offended by the associate warden's manner. They had been vociferous in defending the warden and had led the argument for accepting the warden's verbal guarantee of recognition and no reprisals. But now they were more angry than Scully or Irwin. The associate warden had managed to unify the committee.

Irwin and Scully called for a vote. Does the committee stand on its statement—no grievances until the demands are met? The committee voted unanimously to stick to the preconditions. As usual Wagner and Wolcott did not vote.

There was about an hour to go before the three o'clock deadline. Irwin said they might as well keep going on sorting out the grievances and working out some language, "just in case he changes his mind." Each of the grievances having to do with the major complaints—parole, minimum wage, prisoner punishments—was handed to a committee member, beginning with Genco at one end of the table. The committee member would read the rough note, recorded by hand by Wolcott, and say whether he agreed or disagreed, and if he disagreed how he wanted it changed.

They had hardly noticed the passage of time when at three-ten the door opened again. It was Cansler. He closed the door behind him. "Y'all got those grievances?"

Irwin said, "Mr. Cansler, you know our position. No agreement on the five conditions, no grievances."

Cansler reached behind him with his right hand, opened the door and with his left hand made a sweeping gesture toward the corridor. "Clear the room!"

Scully said, "Wait a minute, Mr. Cansler. You're locking us up again. We were elected by the population. You can't disband us without letting us explain what happened. I think it's going to be better for everyone if there's some explanation on the PA system. Otherwise there's no telling what the reaction of the men will be."

Cansler said he would inform the population.

Scully said, "Mr. Cansler, I don't think they'll be very impressed by that. I think there could be trouble unless they hear it direct from someone on the committee."

The associate warden thought for a moment and then said, "All right. The rest of you'll be escorted back to your quarters. Scully, you come with me to control."

The men were being led through the empty corridors, two guards with each committee member, when they heard the PA system. It was Scully, introducing himself and explaining that he was spokesman for the committee, that the committee the population had elected was being disbanded by the warden because the committee had five preconditions before presenting grievances and the warden refused to accept the conditions. The account was slow and orderly. Scully was saying, "So your committee asks you not to consider going back to work . . ." when his voice stopped and there were banging sounds over the PA system. The next voice was Cansler's saying that the old committee had failed to do what the prisoners wanted, which was to present their grievances to the warden, so each housing unit was asked to submit names for a new committee to their cellhouse guard. Cansler had snatched the microphone out of Scully's hand.

Cages and corridors all over the prison echoed with boos and curses.

By that time the committee members were back in their cages, uncertain what came next. Meyers, in D-7, went to his outside window that looked out on the outer cages of the next building, B block. Men were crowded at the windows of all three floors of B block.

Meyers yelled out an account of the afternoon's proceedings, the argument for insisting on the five preconditions. When he said the warden had promised only that the grievances would be answered in two weeks in *The Friday Flyer,* B block became an edifice of multilingual profanity.

Meyers, indefatigable, then went to the narrow slit in the door of his cage and repeated his account for the benefit of the cages on the first floor of his own block.

As he talked, he could hear men, their ears to the slits in their cages, calling out, "Good fucking man." "Don't let them put you in their trick bag!" And "Right on, man." "We been fucked too many times before."

In cages all over the prison the process was being repeated. Where cages had windows to the outside, men from the committee were calling out an account of the demands and the disbanding of the committee to prisoners crowded at the outside windows of adjacent blocks. Then they turned to the openings of their own cage doors and called out to the waiting audience in their own tier. In dormitories men full of questions gathered around returned committee members.

At about four-thirty P.M., not long after the mass grapevine had completed its passage of information, a contingent of guards came to the first floor of D block to take its occupants to breakfast, among the last in the day-long string of the "morning" meals served by the prison staff. Breakfast was navy beans and eggs, no seconds.

When Meyers got to the mess hall there were about a hundred men seated or waiting in line. He stood at the line and made a speech to the mess hall. He said that the warden had threatened to disband the committee if it didn't come up with grievances before the preconditions.

"It's possible there'll be a new committee. But it won't be your committee. It's going to be the warden's committee. It won't represent you. It's going to represent Alldredge and Cansler."

Guards heard the talk but did not interfere. Meyers went from table to table getting reactions. They were positive, urging the committee to stand fast.

D block men, including Meyers, were escorted back to their quarters.

At about that time a prisoner from the committee was writing a letter. He put it in an envelope, sealed it carefully and wrote on the envelope, "The Warden—Private." Quietly he handed it to a guard. The guard looked at it, put it quickly in his pocket. The guard knew what to do with it. He took it to the block officer, who personally rushed it to the warden's office.

The warden's office was a battle station. Reports were being sifted and strategy mapped. There had been a debriefing of Mr. Young, the supervisor of education who had stood outside the committee's meeting room. Young had written a memo:

Scully . . . took the floor and it became apparent rather quickly that he was the actual leader of not only the group but the population as well.

They had found the ringleader at last. Scully had to be watched and worked on as the key man.

The officer arrived with the letter addressed to "The Warden— Private."

The letter told what had happened inside the committee room in the absence of the warden, who was on the side of the warden's position, the names of "the radicals" keeping the committee on a hard line, and said that Joel Meyers was probably their leader. The word went out from the warden's office to watch Meyers and arrest him at first opportunity.

By the time word got to the guards on Red Top, Meyers was back in his cage from breakfast.

At ten P.M. D block was called out for "lunch." This time Meyers didn't make a speech but instead began at once going from table to table to explain the situation and get a reaction.

A guard came to him. "Meyers, you going to talk or you going to eat?"

Meyers grinned. "Well, if you're giving me a choice, I'd rather talk."

"I ain't giving you a choice. Either get a tray or leave the dining room."

Meyers got a tray, put some food on it and went to a table, talked for a short time and then, tray in hand, went to another table.

The guard came to him again. "Turn in your tray, Meyers, and leave the mess hall."

"I haven't eaten yet."

"Never mind. Just put your tray down and leave. Right now."

Meyers put down his tray and started to walk. He felt someone grab each of his arms and turn him toward Red Top. He looked around. Two guards were holding his arms. When they got to Red Top about forty guards were waiting to accompany him. He was obviously being arrested. He didn't know what the charge was. He wondered why, if they were going to arrest him, they didn't do it when he made his speech before the whole mess hall at five o'clock but did it at ten o'clock. He said nothing. The guards said nothing.

At the end of the east corridor they went down steps to the basement. The guards stood while the segregation officer told him to empty his pockets. He was told to take his clothes off. He went through the skin search: "Hold out your hands, wiggle your fingers . . . brush your hands through your hair . . . lift up your balls . . . bend over, spread your cheeks . . . lift up your left foot . . ."

He went through it automatically. They had him do it every time he went to the visiting room and returned from it. He usually made wisecracks. He made none now. He waited to see which level of segregation he was going in—the less severe S-2 or even the least severe S-5, or to the worst one there in the basement, S-1, "the hole," where you got no socks, no shoes, no transparent window, no personal effects, no reading, and where some neighboring cages held prisoners already demented from solitary confinement. They gave him underwear, khaki trousers and shower clogs. That meant the hole.

6

IRON HOUSE, INCORPORATED

Lewisburg penitentiary remained eerily quiet, its population locked in their cages twenty-four hours a day except for two meals when they shuffled in small groups under heavy escort to a subdued mess hall.

Of all the unnatural silences the most complete was in Eddie Mason's "iron house," Chairman Irwin's place of employment, the factories.

In his daily confidential report to the Director in Washington, Warden Alldredge wrote, ". . . the institution is still operating at minimal efficiency."

"Minimal efficiency" to describe the most important financial function of the prison was an understatement. It was not operating at all. The five three-story buildings that housed the industries no longer emanated the whine of fork lifts, the crash of metal presses, the choral clack of commercial sewing machines marching up endless seams. Outside on the railroad siding, freight cars collected undisturbed dustings of snow, their interiors cavernous and silent.

It was strange even for that strange creation FPI, Inc., an American corporation whose proper name is Federal Prison Industries, Incorporated, an entity with headquarters in Washington, D.C., with fifty factories throughout the United States, its board of directors a collection of prominent Americans who annually declare an impressive profit and who draw their labor force from men, women and youths turned over by the Attorney General of the United States to the Federal Bureau of Prisons. It is not often that a national corporation is brought to a standstill by captive labor.

Directors of FPI, Inc., are appointed by the President of the United States, serve without pay and undoubtedly count their time a contribution to the rehabilitation of the American criminal. They are not alone in their delusion.

FPI, Inc., has its parallel in most state prisons and many county jails, where factories are run for the benefit of the state or local jailers or private entrepreneurs or favored politicians, but do little or nothing to prepare the prisoner for the free world. The typical state prison conducts vocational training in making the state automobile license plates, not an industry found in the free world. But no state or county institution clothes itself with the elaborate pretense of pure benefit for the prisoner that suffuses the propaganda of Federal Prison Industries, Inc.

Whatever the cruelty of past practices, pretentiousness was dispensed with. Prisoners of war and slaves have usually been pressed into the worst work. Shackled to oars, they propelled ships, sometimes until they died. In the seventeenth century the French instructed jailers to reduce their killing and maiming of prisoners because they needed able-bodied men to propel a growing navy. The practice ended in the eighteenth century not out of any kindly regard for human life but because fabric sails for ocean-going vessels had produced the only motive power cheaper than disposable human bodies—the wind.

Prisoners were moved to land-locked workhouses, often contracted out to private enterprises. Imperial countries dumped convicts onto unexplored shores of new colonies to hack out communities in a desperate struggle to survive. Some of the "first families" of America, not a few of whose descendants now insist that criminality is inexorably genetic, were fathered by despised British criminals exiled to North America.

The Industrial Revolution put convicts into factories, with widespread brutality and corruption by prison keepers and their friends. In the United States, convict labor produced the first manufactured work shirts and ironware cooking utensils.

Labor union growth constricted prison labor, recognizing that the philosophy of a decent day's wage for a fair day's work could not grow if slave labor were widely available. Or if convicts were used to break strikes, as they once were.

Private businessmen began to oppose prison labor because only a favored few entrepreneurs had political connections that gave them access to the slave labor, making competition by others impossible.

Like so many vexing contradictions in society, this one descended upon the outcasts, including the most rejected—prisoners. A coalition of unions and management developed the present doctrine: No prisoner work could compete either with union labor or free enterprise.

That is why the most famous member of FPI's board of directors is George Meany, president of the AFL-CIO, the most powerful spokesman in America for the philosophy of high wages for working people, but who twice a year approves at FPI board meetings wage rates of nineteen cents to forty-six cents an hour, the rate in effect before the Lewisburg strike, or the most recent rate of twenty-six cents to fifty-one cents an hour. During the Lewisburg strike Mr. Meany was not heard from on the subject of men protesting work at nineteen cents an hour.

The operational commissioner of FPI is the Director of the Federal Bureau of Prisons. His board of directors includes prestigious business executives: James Lindley Palmer, retired president of Marshall Field Company department stores, "representing retailers and consumers"; John Marshall Briley, senior vice president of Owens-Corning Fiberglas Corporation, "representing the Secretary of Defense"; Berry N. Beaman, senior partner of Universal Vise and Tool Company, "representing industry"; William E. Morgan, president emeritus of Colorado State University, "representing agriculture"; Peter B. Bensinger, of the Chicago Crime Commission, "representing the Attorney General"; and Mr. Meany.

The corporation's fifty factories in twenty-one prisons are guarded by walls, chain-link fences and gun towers. They make a variety of goods used by government agencies. Five of their factories make electrical wires and simple electronic circuits. Eleven factories make plastic and wood furniture. Ten manufacture textile products, from wiping cloths to cotton gloves. Eleven turn out desks, footlockers and brooms. Six produce desk calendar pads, print government reports and turn out traffic signs for federal highways. Three factories manufacture military shoes, boots and dust brushes. Four places have prisoners punching data-processing cards for the Department of Agriculture.

The corporation provides a basic need for some prisoners: an opportunity for selected prisoners to avoid total idleness. The corrosive effects of idleness are obvious, from catatonic depression to violent frustration, and are endemic even in the busiest prisons. The federal corporation helps relieve the idleness of some convicts.

The additional argument is sometimes made that many men and women are in prison because they never learned "good work habits." This is probably true. It is also true that, for most, "good work habits" failed to develop because the only work in their future was hateful labor that other members of society refuse, furnacelike laundry shops at subsistence wages with no chance for improvement or day labor with dead-end work forces. With few exceptions, that is what most prisoners also do in prison.

Some FPI, Inc., jobs are promising for future employment of the prisoner when released. But they are a pitiful percentage of the whole. Some FPI money is put into vocational training for jobs needed on the outside. That is an even more pitiful percentage of the whole.

The 1975 Manpower Report to the President lists certain white-collar jobs that are available for trained workers, despite a recession—service workers of a technical kind like dishwasher repairmen and auto mechanics, and retail trade workers. A negligible number of FPI jobs provide training for these jobs. The jobs worst hit by unemployment are the majority of jobs for which FPI, Inc., uses prisoners.

The basic motivation of FPI, Inc., is to grow for its own sake, to make work for its salaried bureaucracy and for the convenience of the institution. In that sense it is following the corporate ethic of the free enterprise world. But it has ironies peculiar to itself.

Most prisoners are politically conservative. But one can speculate on the irony of nationalistic prisoners in Leavenworth, for example, where military boots and paintbrushes are made. The nails for boots to be worn by American soldiers fighting in Vietnam "against communism" were made with nails imported to Leavenworth from the Soviet Union. Brushes used to paint American naval vessels "containing communism" in Asian waters were manufactured with bristles that came from China. Part of the Cold War rhetoric justifying American military pressure against communist states was to protect "free labor" and to come to the rescue of "slave labor" trapped in the totalitarian states. It will never be known whether the Russian worker who made the nails for the American military boots manufactured in Leavenworth was paid more than the assembly-line boot nailer in the Kansas prison whose weekly wage was $7.60. Some men were in prison for refusing to join the United States armed services in their "fight against communism" and they were asked to use communist-produced goods for the United States military services.

Most FPI workers are more conscious of a different irony. They make storage cabinets used by the FBI, an agency involved in all of their prosecutions, they produce the desks of the U.S. attorneys who prosecuted them, and they fashion the black leather thrones used by the United States District Court judges who sentenced them. Women prisoners in the federal prison in Alderson, West Virginia, make by hand the personal flag that stands behind the desk of each new Attorney General of the United States, who is their chief prosecutor and prison keeper.

All FPI prisoners are conscious of the difference between their wages and their supervisors'. The factory bosses work for the corporation, not the prison where their factory is located. They have a remarkable boss-to-worker ratio: one administrator for every six workers. Average pay for the work supervisors is $12,500 a year. Average pay for the prisoner-workers, counting bonuses for extra production during rush orders, is $838.54 a year.

There is another irony. FPI, Inc., helps finance the addiction of prisoners to hard drugs and medical experiments on federal prisoners. Prisoners in the federal system are solicited to submit to pharmaceutical company experiments conducted at the government hospital at Lexington, Kentucky. Former addicts are asked to let themselves be readdicted and then tested with new chemicals, and to let themselves be infected with dangerous diseases so that drug companies can test experimental compounds. They are promised private rooms, good food, a few days off their sentences—and up to forty dollars a month in "Meritorious Service Awards" if they are used for especially hazardous experiments. Under the law, Meritorious Service Awards can be drawn only from profits of Federal Prison Industries, Inc. Readdicting cured addicts and infecting prisoners with dangerous diseases are not listed in the FPI catalogue of paid occupations for the "rehabilitation" of federal prisoners.

There is an ultimate irony that few if any prisoners realize. The corporation, an integral part of the federal penal system punishing criminals, is itself in violation of the U.S. Criminal Code.

The corporation was created by Congress under Title 18 of the United States Code, Section 4122 (b) which states, "Its board of directors shall provide employment for all physically fit inmates in the United States penal and correctional institutions . . ."

A strict constructionist, a devotee of obedience to law, might assume that when the board of directors is ordered to "provide employment for all physically fit inmates in the United States penal and correctional institutions," that, as a group gathered to prevent crime and return criminals to useful life, they might take the law seriously.

Their industry has never provided work for all physically fit federal prisoners. It gives work to no more than 25 per cent of them. At the time of the Lewisburg strike only 382 of the 1491 prisoners had FPI jobs. The corporation has never operated in all the federal penal institutions. There are now more than fifty such institutions and FPI has work in only twenty-one.

It might be argued that it is unreasonable to provide work for all prisoners in all federal institutions. Some prisoners might not want to work. Many would prefer to take academic courses. Others are assigned to cook, do laundry, clean officers' quarters and scrub floors for no pay. But that is not what the law says.

The violation of law by FPI goes further.

Section 4123 of the U.S. Criminal Code says:

> Such forms of employment shall be provided as will give the inmates of all Federal penal and correctional institutions a maximum opportunity to acquire a knowledge and skill in trades and occupations which will provide them with a means of earning a livelihood upon release.

Most FPI jobs are unskilled dead-end jobs. On assembly lines men pound nails into shoe heels, sand arms of chairs, spend years sewing the inside right inseam of a khaki trouser using an obsolete sewing machine, making brooms—in short, the menial dead-end jobs they held before prison and to which FPI sends them back.

The result of this shows in the jobs ex-prisoners get. In 1970 FPI used some of its profits to hire job-placement officers to find work for its ex-employees. After their release, 15 per cent could get no job of any kind; 70 per cent got low-paying bottom-of-the-barrel unskilled jobs like dishwashers in restaurants, laundry workers, janitors. The industrially skilled jobs, centerpiece of FPI's propaganda, went to 7.9 per cent. The job-placement function of FPI has since been discontinued.

While the aura of public service surrounds prison industries as it does prison itself, the real limitations are to protect private corporations. The FPI law states:

> Its board of directors shall . . . so operate the prison shops that no single private industry shall be forced to bear an undue burden of competition from the products of the prison workshops and to reduce to a minimum competition with private industry or free labor . . .

It is a contradiction that flaws FPI at its heart. It cannot train prisoners in good, marketable vocations at decent wages as long as it is limited in making good, marketable products. It can never pay decent wages without penalizing workers in the free world.

In South Carolina the state prison keeper, William Leeke, a progressive jailer, has built open, twenty-man dormitories near major cities of his state. The head of the dormitory is known in the community and helps each man find a job that pays a good current wage. The prisoner leaves the dormitory in the morning and is completely on his own until the end of work in the evening. After a month he has weekends at home, since the dormitories are in his home city. He pays room and board for the dormitory, removing the cost from the taxpayer. He supports his family with his regular working wages, taking families off welfare or family-destroying poverty. At work he has noncriminal friends and colleagues. He saves money. By the time he has served his sentence he has a job that is well developed, friends who are working at similar jobs, and he is an accepted, productive member of the community. There is no bureaucracy, no expense to the taxpayer, no pretentiousness; there is real involvement of the prisoner with normal life and economics, and less crime.

This cannot work with federal prisons, because their prisoners come from all over the country, most far from home. The federal system is dedicated, despite its periodic declarations, to huge buildings housing several hundred prisoners in isolated locations far from jobs in cities.

Despite its crippling contradictions, FPI, Inc., is one of the most profitable manufacturing corporations in the United States, sustained by the requirement that government agencies must give the corporation first bid on all products it makes. Its returns on sales have seldom dropped below 20 per cent, making it one of the ten most profitable industrial corporations in the country.

The corporation was started by Congress in 1934 with an initial investment of $4,176,040. By 1972 FPI, Inc., had returned a clear profit to the Treasury of $82 million, or over $2 million a year, a rate of return that few government investments, or any other, could yield. Now its profits are turned to building new factories and increasing its civilian payroll while keeping steady the low number of inmates employed. It began in 1934 with $2,719,694 in assets—buildings and equipment. Today its assets are worth more than $70 million.

The corporation moves by mindless momentum, using its profits neither for the training of most prisoners in profitable occupations nor for the direct benefit of its workers. Until embarrassed in 1972, it turned its profits back to the United States Treasury.

The factories are an integral gear in the engine of federal prisons, the facade for "rehabilitation," sustaining the rationale for isolated fortresses.

FPI, Inc., has not reduced the crime rate or substantially improved its prisoner-employees' access to good jobs after release. The corporation's boasts of sophisticated vocational training continue to appear in slick four-color brochures, printed, of course, by prisoners in the most oppressive maximum-security penitentiary in the system, at Marion, Illinois, where they dutifully set in type such bitter deceptions as:

> The Federal Prison Industries, Inc., provides employment and training for inmates of Federal correctional institutions through . . . the search for and development of new training-oriented industries utilizing skills in demand in the labor market.

The prisoners who set this in type then march back to their cages to continue their punishment for violating the federal law. A different federal law. The products of Federal Prison Industries, Inc., those desks in the White House, the U.S. embassy chairs, the circuitry for missiles at Redstone arsenal, the boots worn by Marines, the flag behind the desk of the Attorney General of the United States, the leather thrones of judges, thousands of highway signs on the interstate system, the hospital gowns worn by wounded soldiers, the wooden chocks that go under parked Air Force planes—might better conform to standards of honest labeling if each bore a tag:

> This is the product of a corporation of the United States Government that is acting in violation of Section 4122 (b) of Title 18 of the United States Criminal Code, an item manufactured by captive labor receiving an average of 37½ cents an hour and serving sentences in federal prisons because they, too, acted in violation of Title 18 of the United States Criminal Code.

PART TWO

On solitary confinement:

"I believe it, in its effects, to be cruel and wrong. In its intention, I am well convinced that it is . . . meant for reformation; but I am persuaded that those who devised this system of prison discipline . . . do not know what it is that they are doing. I believe that very few men are capable of estimating the immense amount of torture and agony which this dreadful punishment . . . inflicts upon the sufferers. . . . I hold this slow and daily tampering with the mysteries of the brain to be immeasurably worse than any torture of the body."

CHARLES DICKENS
American Notes, 1842

7

THE SECRET OF SANITY

On February 17, 1972, Lewisburg Federal Penitentiary attracted the attention of press and public because Ralph Ginzburg, the maverick publisher, started his first day of a three-year sentence for "use of the mails for non-mailable material." He had mailed his erotic magazines from United States post offices that happened to have real names, like Intercourse, Pennsylvania (Zip Code, 17534), and Blue Ball, Pennsylvania (Zip Code, 17506). His case had been years on appeal, the Supreme Court had upheld the conviction five to four, and he surrendered to U.S. marshals, but only after he had dropped a copy of the Bill of Rights into a trash can in front of the United States Courthouse on Market Street, Lewisburg, Pennsylvania (Zip Code, 17837). As of that moment the drugstore across the street was selling *Playboy* and other sex magazines more explicit than anything Ginzburg had mailed from Intercourse and making sales to, among others, prison officers who would guard Ginzburg at the nearby honor camp, Allenwood.

Warden Alldredge, as was his custom, issued a press release on the receipt of a prominent prisoner, and added, "There has been little or no change in the work stoppage situation."

As with so many of the warden's press releases on the subject, this was true or false depending on the point of view.

From the warden's point of view nothing much had happened, because the prison was still on strike and the industries were idle.

From the point of view of committee members a lot had changed. Twelve of them had been arrested and placed in segregation.

Early on the morning of the 17th, Warden Alldredge announced on the public address system that the first committee had been disbanded for failure to present grievances. He was entertaining volunteers for a second committee of sixteen. Not many housing units responded, so he added prisoners of his own, gathered them in the chapel and had them meet with Cansler, Cramer, and Greenlee. The associate warden let them read the new policies coming from Washington on liberalized rules for correspondence and a slight raise in the industrial pay scale. They were instructed to go to their housing units, report this to their fellow prisoners and come back with prisoner responses the warden could act upon.

The result, from the warden's point of view, was disastrous. The new committee members received overwhelming verbal abuse from their units. Angry prisoners insisted on dealing only with the committee they had elected. Accusations of snitching and strike-breaking were thrown at new committee members. In a number of units new committee members started to walk down the tier of cages and after the bitter shouting quickly turned back, banging the grille gate to be released to the corridor and safety. They returned to the control center and said they had to meet with the original committee, because that was the sentiment of the population. The warden agreed. He sent the second committee to Room 14 and ordered the original committee members called to control. Only Phillips, Scully, and Wolcott appeared. When they heard that they were supposed to turn over their material to the second committee, Phillips and Scully refused. Wolcott said he would go up.

Inside Room 14 the new committee asked Wolcott to read the five preconditions. As he was reading the third one Scully came into the room. The appearance had an explosive effect. Immediately most of the second committee stood and shouted loyalty to the first committee. They said they didn't want to be there, that they had been ordered by the warden and that the population was solidly behind the original committee.

Scully told them there was no need for them to stay, that the original committee would win its five demands and win the strike if it continued to have the support of the population. The second committee left.

Officer Young asked Scully what he thought he was doing.

"Mr. Young, there's no use you and I having anything to say at this moment, because I represent the committee and I only can talk to the men and the institution. I have no authority now."

Only Wolcott remained behind, writing something on notepaper. As Scully walked out of the room, Young tried to talk. Scully kept walking down the corridor, Young constantly asking him for an explanation.

Finally Scully turned around. "Look, I don't want to be rude. But there's nothing we can say. I represent the committee and the committee has to deal with the warden."

The warden's reply came two hours later. Two guards were sent to a committee member's cage. The prisoner was told that the original committee was meeting in the chapel. He was escorted in silence to the chapel. The chapel was dark and locked but about a dozen officers were at the door. The prisoner was ordered to spread-eagle, feet wide apart, arms spread with palms against the wall, while a guard frisked him for weapons. Then ten guards escorted him to segregation.

The arrest of Lucky Johnson was typical. As he was led to the basement, he asked, "Am I arrested?"

"Yeah."

"What for?"

"Cansler will tell you."

In the basement each arrested committee member went through the standard routine: Give name and number, empty your pockets, undress. Skin search: "Lower your head and run your fingers through your hair, open your mouth, stretch out your arms, palms down, wiggle your fingers, palms up, wiggle your fingers . . ."

As the prisoner followed instructions he tried to detect the level of physical threat from the guards. And signs of the level of segregation he was headed for.

After the skin search he was given back his clothes. Relief. It would not be S-1, the worst level, where the punished prisoner is permitted only partial clothing. The smokers were given back their cigarettes. Something akin to joy. That meant S-5, the least severe segregation, the only one where smoking is allowed.

The squad of guards ordered each prisoner up the stairs to the hospital on the first floor and up a second flight of stairs to the S-5 cages on the second floor, down a long concrete aisle past steel-encased doors, accompanied by the guards from S-5, who unlocked an empty cage, put the prisoner inside, slammed and double-locked the door.

Most of the men had never been in segregation before. Most of the cages were filthy, with dirt and paper on the floor, scum on the toilet and washbowl. The cage was fourteen feet long and six feet wide at the far end, where a steel casement window could be opened. The front of the cage was narrow, containing only the door, most of the rest of the corner cut off by a slanting wall that enclosed plumbing. Next to the door was a steel sink with its two push-button controls for hot and cold water. Around the corner of the slanted wall was the seatless steel toilet.

In the far corner near the window was a locker for personal effects, except that when the committee member was put into the punishment cage he was permitted no personal effects, books or toilet goods. Near the locker was a wooden classroom chair with a writing arm. The bed was a thin mattress on a steel slab anchored by pipes to the concrete floor. An orderly had given the prisoner two sheets and a blanket. No pillow. At the head of the bed, on the wall, was the earphone connected to the prison's AM radio circuit.

The door was special. It was encased in steel. In the upper half was a small opening whose importance surprised prisoners in the days that followed. The window at the other end was larger and, for one row of cages, overlooked the prison exercise yard, with, ironically, the miniature golf course directly below. The S-5 windows could be opened, but the punished prisoner was forbidden to call out or speak to anyone on the ground, two floors below. If he did he would be sent to the more severe S-2, S-3 or S-4 cages on the third floor or to the S-1 cages in the basement. If a prisoner on the ground was caught communicating with a man in segregation he would himself be arrested and placed in segregation. So the window, while admitting light and air, provided little human communication, except, under the right conditions, the ability to stretch an arm and touch the outstretched hand of the prisoner in the next cage.

The small opening in the steel door was the real contact with other human beings. Through it the prisoner could look out on the five-foot concrete aisle separating the parallel rows of segregation cages and see part of the faces of other prisoners directly across who might be looking out at the same time. Through the hole a prisoner could call out to unseen prisoners in neighboring cages. The opening provided cross-ventilation from the window, relief in winter from heating of the cage from the single pipe running through a corner.

Partway down the door was another opening, eighteen inches wide and five inches high, where food trays were pushed into the cage.

The openings could be closed for punishment by a sliding steel plate on the outside, a "wicket." The wicket was usually up halfway to keep the food slot closed.

A sixty-watt bulb burned from six A.M. to eleven P.M.

After a time each S-5 prisoner was given a toothbrush with the handle cut off, a two-inch pencil sharpened or replaced only once a day, and a razor with the blade locked in, limitations to prevent creation of weapons.

In that way eleven members of the committee were placed in segregation: Alger, Buyse, Estrada, Irwin, Johnson, Mason, Moore, Phillips, Scully, Tucker and Vivero. Meyers had been sent to S-1 the night before. Two days of confusion in paperwork among the many Joneses in the prison delayed the delivery of Clarence Jones to S-5. Others would be added later.

The sense of isolation was heightened by knowledge that their mail was intercepted or destroyed. Later, prisoners would report seeing guards tearing up letters. Some letters were opened by the FBI and by prison authorities, who decided how much pressure to put on a prisoner on the basis of what they read in his letters. One man sent a letter to his wife the first day he was put in the hole and three weeks later received a letter from her asking why he hadn't written for three weeks. Meyers had been receiving mail daily from his wife, mother and members of his party, but in his first three weeks of segregation he received one letter. He mailed a letter to his parents on February 16; they had not received it by early March.

At the earlier meeting of the committee Warden Alldredge had attempted to read a new policy statement of the Federal Bureau of Prisons allowing privileged mail to newspapers through Prisoners Mail Box, the presumably unopened and uncensored letters sent by prisoners. One such letter was written to me from Lewisburg on February 17 and arrived in Washington March 15.

Prisoners had other circumstantial evidence that their "privileged" mail was being read. A medical technical assistant (MTA) was supposed to visit segregation every day. Prisoners never seemed to see one. Tucker became ill, vomited and became unconscious, but no MTA could be summoned. Mason became sick. One of the prisoners mailed a PMB "unopened and uncensored" letter to a federal judge complaining of the lack of access to medical care. A few hours after he handed the letter to a guard an MTA reported to the cage.

Interrupted mail increased the psychological pressure of isolation. The men were not told why they had been arrested or what would happen to them, only that they would be isolated indefinitely.

Solitary confinement makes most people psychotic. A normal person deliberately imprisoned in an austere room no larger than a bathroom soon becomes disoriented and desperate. Charles Dickens noted in 1842 that prison segregation drives men mad. *The Encyclopaedia of Human Behavior* says, "So far the experiments have indicated beyond much doubt that the human being cannot continue to function in a normal way if he is deprived of sensory impressions from the external world."

Yet, some prisoners survive and become stronger.

Sanity under deliberate attack can be lost by any human being, but prisoners in American institutions may hold on to their sanity in the oppressiveness of prison better than the average citizen. Most prisoners are poor and grew up in threatening neighborhoods and schools. They have learned to survive like soldiers in combat. Prison deepens the same threats and stimulates the same defense mechanism of hatred for the enemy. The most deliberate assault upon their sanity—indefinite segregation—does not always break them, because they have already been conditioned by life to adopt a hatred of the enemy—their prison keepers and the society that supports the prisons. In their isolation this provides a marshaling of thought and emotion that prevents collapse of the person.

Each of the men had his private mechanisms for survival. Meyers could mentally compose finely constructed analyses of how this treatment was a preparative technique for control and destruction by a fascistic regime. Irwin, at first forbidden to have his AA book and Bible, thought of all his actions in the face of treachery by officials he had trusted in the prison and then worked at trying to forgive them. Later he tried reconstructing in his mind in the greatest possible detail the most exciting moments in his life. The first items were attempts to re-create in specific detail every time he had made love. Eventually he tired even of this.

John Alger, an absorber of whatever environment surrounded him, reacted in his own way to defy his punishers. He became a radical. Alger, inclined to bravado, had written to his parents just before the strike, "Harpers Mag wrote another article about my fight with the U.S. Parole Board." The article was by Dr. Willard Gaylin and, unfortunately, had no reference to Alger.

With his election to the strike committee his letters took on a grandeur. "I personally feel that I have 1360 men behind me . . ." He wrote his parents that he might testify in Washington about the parole system. "It's an honor to society to be asked to come before the House and Senate to speak." There was never any question of his testifying or addressing the House or Senate.

By March 3 he was saying there would be a "thousand-person demonstration in front of the Bureau of Prisons in Washington." A few days later he said it would be "2000 demonstrators." It was a reference to the Prisoners Solidarity Committee, an adjunct to Joel Meyers' Workers World Party. They did demonstrate before the Bureau headquarters in Washington, though their numbers did not exceed twenty-five.

Before long he wrote to his parents, "I've become rather politically aware in the last few months, I've some ideals." A few weeks after that he was quoting Mao to his parents. "I've read Marx and Lenin. . . . It was an experience that has shown me that I'm a tool of the businessman."

The survival of all the men was aided by a feeling of involvement in a larger struggle.

For Lumumba Jones it was a continuing fight, with a fervor and power that would remain unbroken. While he was in prison both his mother and stepfather died. He could have visited them on their deathbeds or, taking a choice, gone to their funerals. But only if he had $300 to pay for the traveling and lodging expenses for himself and two accompanying guards. He did not have the $300. It confirmed for him the universality, in and out of prison, of humanity defined by money. Later, he wrote me from his isolation cage:

> I have been made to repress all my natural instincts of fully expressing myself as a human being. I've been thrown into this bedlam, this microcosm of madness called prison mainly because of my "class and color," to be decomposed both physically and mentally. I, Lumumba, refuse to be dehumanized. I will resist and resist and resist.

Ronald Phillips had been in solitary confinement before. He knew the dangers of disorientation in isolation, the slow drifting from reality as the same walls and simple images burned into the mind day after unnumbered day, the hopelessness that grows out of the blur of unpunctuated time. After he obtained his first two-inch pencil and sheet of lined paper, he drew a calendar, seven squares across, five rows down. He had been put in segregation on the 17th, a Thursday. From that he filled in the numbers, remembering that 1972 was a leap year, to 29. He began in his head, "Thirty days hath September, April . . ." and then he stopped. April! He would rather face that later if it lasted that long.

The committeemen in segregation discovered later that they had separately shared three experiences that changed their view of the struggle and of themselves.

First, they reviewed their lives. After the recollection of favorite scenes of the past—childhood games, excitement of their crimes, sex episodes, thoughts of distant people now out of touch—they began looking, most in puzzlement, at the sweep of their whole lives, to find some connection with this unexpected present. For most, there emerged explanations of their careers that were new. It was the contemplation that Quakers 200 years ago had hoped would happen in penitentiaries. Except that none of the men was penitent.

They felt group pride and personal fulfillment. For most of them this was the first time they had knowingly and willingly suffered for something called "the general good," the most significant unselfish act in their lives. They had bitter differences on proper strategy and they would show individual frailties in withstanding their punishment. But they discovered that no one doubted the rightness of the cause. The prison system acting badly had achieved something it had never been able to do acting properly—instilled self-esteem and self-control in the punished prisoner.

The third emotion they experienced in their separate cages, a feeling that gave them strength in adversity, was contempt for their punishers. Long afterward Phillips, sitting in a penitentiary visiting room, would describe how he could survive the hostile isolation that breaks ordinary individuals:

"I reject them and their judgment of me. The first time I really decided, consciously, that these people were hypocrites was after I'd come to know Warren Camp.

"Warren was a draft resister, a really nonviolent man. He was so opposed to violence that he was a vegetarian so that he would not be responsible for the killing of animals. He'd come from New York City, gone to San Francisco State, and when he was ordered to report for induction into the armed forces he refused to take his physical, he refused alternative service and was sentenced to three years.

"I met Warren the day that we were transferred to Lewisburg together. Although we had been at McNeil Island together, Warren was assigned to the farm outside, and the only time he'd come inside the wall where I was, was when he was arrested and sent to segregation for refusing to slaughter hogs. His charge would read 'disobeying a direct order.'

"When we were transferred we were shackled, legs and wrists to the waist, for two months in the back seats of some U.S. marshal's car, going across the country, stopping every night at some county jail, then waiting for some marshal who was headed to the next stop. During that two months we argued and talked and argued. At first I wasn't so sure that I liked him. I identified with the 'regulars'—the hip and tough guys —as I had all my life, for survival. I was completely apolitical at the time. But we became real friends. He was the first person I knew well who was educated, had real convictions about society and was totally nonviolent.

"When we got to Lewisburg he went to Allenwood and I went to the wall. I'd see him when he would be sent to segregation. I used to hear the guards and other officials talking about Warren. They hated him.

"After he got out he wrote regularly. He lives with a woman, a schoolteacher, and they've been together for years. They tried to get on my visiting list but they were not allowed. She tried to visit me and got as far as the Lewisburg visiting room, where she was turned back when they discovered that she lived with Warren.

"I asked why they couldn't visit. They said Warren was not a proper person. That's when I knew, in 1970, that if they considered Warren a bad person, they could be dismissed as people whose values are to be taken seriously. From that time on there was no way that they could reach me. I had contempt for them and their whole system. I suppose it made me feel superior in the sense that I knew how stupid and hypocritical they are. Who am I to feel superior? No one. But I knew that I was superior to them. This contempt for them, this confidence in my values over theirs, made it possible to stay sane."

8

"WE ARE NOT ANIMALS. . . ."

Warden Alldredge and his director in Washington were coming to the reluctant conclusion that the strike was more than the work of a few troublemakers. They believed there were special villains—the hard-nosed Scully, the communist Meyers—but they had misjudged reaction to the committee's arrest. "The warden's committee" had reported almost unanimous anger at the administration. With few exceptions the second committee had no appetite for replacing the men sent to segregation.

Here and there prisoners offered passive resistance. In K dormitory, a basement living unit on the east side of Red Top, men refused to line up for eleven o'clock count and had to be separated by a special squad. Some men from K were sent to segregation.

By Friday, the third day after the start of the strike, Warden Alldredge was assuring the Director that "the general population appear to be in a good frame of mind." He continued to fill his report with praise for his staff, noting their quick adaptation to cooking and serving meals.

But on the same day, the warden ordered a shakedown of the institution, looking for weapons. From an inspection of every prisoner and every cage the guards could find only 150 items the warden classified as weapons. Later he would report this as a sign of imminent rebellion. It was, however, a remarkably small number for a penitentiary with 1491 prisoners; in most institutions prisoners regard a "shank," a homemade knife, as normal equipment for personal self-defense. In his later grim description of the "weapons" shakedown the warden would not note that over half the implements were the short lengths of broom-sticks used by prisoners to prop against the push-button faucets of their sinks to keep water flowing.

On Saturday the warden and the Director were disturbed by plans for a demonstration outside the penitentiary in support of the strikers. All government officials tended toward hysteria at the thought of demonstrations. It was especially true of prison officials, who by nature were unused to public pressure. The demonstration was planned by the Prisoners Solidarity Committee, an arm of Joel Meyers' Workers World Party, by anti-war radicals encamped in Harrisburg sixty miles away for the trial of Philip Berrigan and others, and by students and faculty from Bucknell University on the other side of the city. The thought of a demonstration attacking the prison was serious enough, but if there were "incidents" the resulting publicity would bring attention to the strike. So far the Bureau had managed to keep word of the strike strictly local.

The warden sent his public relations man to officials of Bucknell University. The man urged them not to permit outside demonstrators to use the campus as a staging area and not to let students and faculty take part. University administrators expressed sympathy but told the warden's representative that, unlike the warden's institution, Bucknell could not order its community what to do.

Saturday dawned another gray day. The warden held his defense plans in readiness. The day wore on. The expected demonstration never materialized.

Warden Alldredge's relaxation from the nondemonstration was marred by a blizzard. It stopped traffic along Interstate 80 and blocked Route 15 to the penitentiary. Some of his staff couldn't get to work for the evening shift and some of the morning shift couldn't get home.

The storm was a mixed blessing. It probably discouraged the demonstration, but it irritated the staff. They were stranded in prison on the first day of a three-day holiday declared in the new pattern of making Washington's Birthday always fall on the third Monday in February. On the other hand the holiday gave the warden some comfort. Monday would not be a normal weekday, which meant that it would not count against days of lost production in the Federal Prison Industries.

The demonstration took place on Sunday in eight inches of snow. Security at the entry to the reservation would have been appropriate for a military attack. FBI agents were present, photographs were taken. The worst casualty was a break in the unofficial quarantine of information about the strike; news began to leak out beyond the surrounding towns. Otherwise the demonstration was uneventful.

Director Carlson was worried. He had begun reminding the warden that any time outside help was needed the Director could get staffs from

Danbury and other prisons plus a force of marshals. The warden assured the Director that he needed no outside help, that the mood of the prisoners was good, that there was no sign of violence and by next week production would be resumed in the shops. He had a plan.

On Monday afternoon, Washington's birthday, the warden transmitted his daily confidential report to the Director:

> Tomorrow could possibly be our moment of truth as it will be the first work day since the long holiday weekend. Staff have been circulating through all areas in an attempt to "feel the pulse" of the population regarding the possibility of their returning to work. I have requested all on duty members of the staff to submit written reports to my office in an attempt to gain some insight into their thinking.

"The moment of truth" passed without drama. The warden, reporting to the Director in his next daily transmission, did not use the phrase.

> Following the close of my previous report at 2:30 P.M., Monday, February 21, 1972, the institution continues to operate at minimal efficiency. Today the work stoppage is seven (7) days old, however I feel several inroads have been made. As an example, the general population continues to approach the problem with an excellent attitude and one of cooperation toward everything with the exception of reporting to their assigned details.
>
> Yesterday I requested all on duty staff members to solicit those inmates they knew well in an attempt to gain some insight into their thinking. This program continued throughout the nighttime hours and I feel the largest portion of the population are almost ready to return to productive situation. I am playing the entire situation in a low key with the hope the population will make up their own minds regarding to work. I do not feel we are in a position to afford them an "either/or" choice . . .

The warden could not afford an "either/or" ultimatum, because the staff had returned saying it would not work.

On Wednesday the warden told the Director:

> The meals continue to be of excellent quality and are well accepted by the population. Very few of the inmates have missed any meals, therefore there can be no doubt they are satisfied with the food. . . . All Caseworkers interviewed the residents of I & J housing units in an attempt to gain some insight into the general thinking of the population. There are indications most of the population prefer to return to work in order to return the institution to normal.

At one o'clock Wednesday, the ninth day of the strike, the warden created another "moment of truth." He issued an order for all prisoners to report for work, to do the kitchen, laundry and other details so that officers could reopen the shops and let FPI prisoners earn money again. Only 350 men out of the 1491 agreed to work.

The warden ordered close questioning of prisoners in J block, the honor quarters, prisoners with unblemished records, with most to lose by protest. Returns were dismaying. Almost every prisoner in J block refused to go back to work. They supported the punished committee and were angry at the broken promise of no reprisals. It was clear that the same sentiments existed in other housing units. Bitterness was deepening throughout the penitentiary.

A prisoner previously uninvolved, unpolitical and uninterested managed to have his letter reach me during this period:

> They have aroused men, like myself, who were otherwise disinterested, because of the heavy-handed way in which they showed their complete lack of good faith.
>
> Meanwhile, the inmates are remaining absolutely calm and non-violent, following orders, and being courteous to the officers.
>
> I felt that the administration would prefer that we take hostages, riot and burn so they can depict us as animals. We are not animals, we are men, and want to act like men so that we can be treated as men.

Anger mounted when the prison grapevine reported the punishment of their strongest committee members, Scully sent to S-5, Irwin and Meyers to S-1. The Irwin incident especially enraged the population.

Like most of the committee, Irwin had been placed in the least harsh segregation. At first the S-5 food trays were better than normal. Irwin, a vegetarian, had requested that his tray have no meat products. Since the advent of strong religious and racial protests over sacrilegious food by prisoners from certain sects, prisons had offered alternatives in order to avoid hunger strikes and court orders. But each time Irwin's tray was pushed through the cage's food slot there was a standard portion of meat. Usually he threw the meat onto his windowsill or down into the yard and watched the birds eat it. He loved birds and worried about their survival in cold and snow. Occasionally the trays would appear with every part mixed, a meat gravy sloshed over salad, rice and jello. Irwin, irritated but uncomplaining, would throw the entire contents of the tray into the yard and watch sparrows and starlings feast.

One day the segregation orderly yelled through the feeding slot, as usual, "Wanna eat?" The tray came through with a T-bone steak. Irwin threw the steak out the window and watched a flock of sparrows tear it apart. He ate the small portion of salad on the tray and placed the empty container back in the slot.

A guard lowered the wicket. "Irwin, where's your steak bone?"

All bones had to be returned as potential weapons. Irwin said the birds had it. He was rearrested and taken to S-1 for failure to return a meat bone.

By Wednesday both Meyers and Irwin were returned to S-5, but the population knew about their treatment. Prisoners placed in the S-1 cages are issued only underwear, khaki trousers, shower clogs, a towel and a blanket. S-1 windows are painted over to prevent a view and are welded shut.

Like other cages, Irwin's was heated solely by a pipe running from floor to ceiling, sometimes too hot and sometimes cold. S-1 cages were in the basement, five feet below ground level, the cold compounded by frozen earth against the lower half of the wall and freezing winds against the windows. As a Bureau of Prisons official critique put it blandly, years before, "It is hard to get equable temperature and good ventilation in basements."

Irwin could not get "equable temperature and good ventilation." He was freezing. When he was placed in the cage he noticed that S-1 guards that night included two notorious for hurting prisoners in the hole. But he was very cold. He knocked on the steel door for attention. One of the sadistic guards lowered the wicket. "What's all this fucking racket, Irwin!"

"There's no heat in this fucking place. I'm freezing."

"You make any more noise in here, Irwin, and I'll fix you so won't never make no noise again."

The guard slammed the wicket shut. It cut off communication and any heat that might have leaked in from the corridor. Irwin spent the night shivering on the bed, listening to the wind shrieking around the welded window.

On Wednesday the warden announced the reopening of the visiting room. There was relief, with cynicism. The warden's reason for canceling visits had been lack of staff because of the strike; the strike still continued and the blizzard made manpower problems worse. It intensified the population's feeling that no official word could be trusted and that Washington was desperate to resume production in the factories. Communication between prisoners and guards became worse.

The warden and his aides were bitter at the unified resistance. Daily assurances to Washington that the strike was ending were wearing thin. Alldredge and Dodd talked about the possibility of letting the original committee out of segregation to take up its listing of grievances. They, with Cansler objecting, had decided the move had to be made when they received a request from a prisoner that let them release the committee and save face.

John Wagner, peacemaker and representative of *Penal Digest International,* was conscious of growing tension and eager to resolve it. For one thing, it would help strengthen the role of *PDI* in representing prisoners. At the end of his evening meal on Wednesday he asked a guard for permission to see the warden. The guard returned from a telephone to say Wagner could go to Captain Dodd's office, where Lieutenant O'Brien would see him.

Wagner told the lieutenant that the population was solidly behind the first committee and tension was rising. He had offered his services as a go-between at the start of the strike and he wanted the warden to know that he was still available. Would the warden let Wagner visit each member of the committee to urge work toward a settlement? Less than an hour later a guard came to Wagner's cage in B block. The warden would let the committee out of segregation the next day to resume its meetings.

Wagner was excited. He had always been in favor of a careful sifting of grievances and their quick delivery to the warden. No clerical problems should delay the process. Wolcott was secretary of the committee, but Wagner, more skilled in typing and note-taking, had a complete list of the grievances as they had been approved by the committee. As correspondent for *PDI* he was one of the few prisoners at Lewisburg with a typewriter and supplies in his cage.

The committee wanted to circulate the grievances by mimeographed copies, so he typed stencils. He arranged the grievances in order at his desk. It was ten-thirty P.M. when he typed the start of the first stencil:

PRISONER-GRIEVANCES
at the
U.S. Penitentiary
Lewisburg, Pennsylvania

There was no question what came first—parole. The prison system does not tell a prisoner how long he will remain locked in a cage. The indeterminate sentence assumes he is "sick," and therefore someone— guards, social workers, a distant parole examiner, the board in Washington who has never seen him—decides when he is "well." But the parole system never commits itself to what will make the sick person well. It may hint at a prescription one year—more schooling, work in the industry, group therapy—and the next year when the prisoner has completed their prescription shrug it off with a different prescription. There was the mechanism of "good time," days off for good behavior that once earned could be taken away for an infraction of a rule, sometimes of a rule the prisoner had never been told of. If any good time was taken back, a man was not eligible for parole.

Parole was one of the ideas that seemed progressive and humane, keeping a prisoner caged no longer than usual. But it had resulted in maddening uncertainty over whether a prisoner might stay in a penitentiary for three months or twenty years. He might fulfill all the recommendations of his prison keepers, his guards, his case managers, and his parole examiner, and then, after a five-minute interview with a man who had never seen him before, receive, six months later, Form H-7 from the United States Board of Parole with a form:

> The case of the above-named has come to the attention of the United States Board of Parole [or its Youth Correction Division] on the basis of:

There would follow six multiple-choice boxes, with an x opposite "an application for parole," and under that another standard printed form:

> The Board in its office in Washington, D.C., has carefully examined all the information and evidence at its disposal in relation to the above-named. On the date shown below, the following action with regard to parole, parole status, or mandatory release status was ordered:

Then would come, usually, the typed line continuing the case for another year or denying parole until expiration of the full sentence.

The impersonality, the impossibility of knowing standards by which the prisoner is judged, the fact that the answer is, with the exception of a dozen words, a printed form, added to a bitterness that suffuses every prison system and makes the United States Board of Parole a machine for driving prisoners to rage.

John Wagner began typing on the stencil:

> In the matter of procedures and regulations of the United States Board of Parole we hereby request the implementation of the following recommendations to eliminate the flagrant inequities which exist in the current federal parole system:

He typed eight requests. There should be a separate parole board at each institution with hearings on a monthly basis with people who have had daily experience with the prisoner.

There should be a review of each prisoner's case within ninety days of his beginning a sentence.

The board should establish a positive program for each prisoner at his first hearing and grant parole if the program is followed successfully.

The prisoner should have the right to see the contents of the institution's records presented at the parole hearing, have the right to a lawyer and the right to produce witnesses on his behalf.

Decisions of the board should be given immediately after the hearing and, if the prisoner asks for them, should include reasons for denial.

All prisoners shall be subject to parole after one-third of their sentence.

Any portion of a sentence served by a prisoner while on parole should be credited toward his full term if his parole is later revoked.

It would take Wagner over an hour to type out each item, with care for both the language and the typing.

There was no question about the second most important item on men's minds: the industries. Wagner typed, "II. In the matter of policies and procedures of Federal Prison Industries, Incorporated, we hereby request . . ."

The federal minimum wage for workers in FPI.

Full pay for national holidays.

Coverage by workmen's compensation for injuries received at FPI work and pay while disabled from a work injury.

FPI workers with satisfactory work records should get a week's vacation with pay regardless of disciplinary actions unrelated to their work.

No payroll deductions for suspended work due to staff meetings not initiated by prisoners.

FPI workers enrolled in educational and vocational training should not have pay deductions for time spent on courses.

Net profits of FPI should be used in the institution for improvement of buildings and programs for prisoners.

Prisoners assigned to the central dental laboratory should get pay similar to FPI employees.

It was now after midnight, but Wagner continued typing stencils. He had batches of individual grievances the committee had put in rough order and he began under Roman numeral III:

Non-FPI workers in other institutional work, like laundry and kitchen, should get at least twenty-five dollars a month. These inmates should get the same extra good time for satisfactory work as FPI workers. If a prisoner wishes not to work because of illness or age he should be permitted to remain idle without compensation or extra good time.

Inmates should have the right to practice their political and religious beliefs.

Inmates of legal age and meeting normal requirements should have the right to vote in federal elections.

A certified doctor should be on call at the prison hospital twenty-four hours a day.

An inmate who becomes sick should be able to go to the infirmary at any time of day, regardless of regular hours of sick call.

All segregation should end because it is cruel and unusual punishment.

Thirteen other items listed grievances like overcrowded quarters that did not meet the prison's own standards, open gym and arts and crafts during evening leisure hours, food prepared by a trained staff with prisoners assigned to kitchens being taught "meaningful" skills usable in the food industry after release, an end to disruption of visits with prisoners and permission for conjugal visits.

Visiting room rules in federal penitentiaries are rigid. Visitors—wife, mother, father, sister, brother—might see this card in the antechamber while awaiting admission to the electronically double-gated passage into the visiting room. They might not be told by their family member in prison that before he entered the visiting room he was stripped and his mouth and anus inspected, and that after he left them he would be stripped and his mouth and anus inspected. But the card they see states:

VISITING INSTRUCTIONS

Visiting hours are 8:00 A.M. to 3:30 P.M. Daily.

Each inmate is permitted 7 hours of visiting time each month. Extra visiting time must be arranged for in advance with the Caseworker.

You may embrace and kiss at the beginning and the end of the visit, within the bounds of good taste.

Please keep the coffee table between you during the visit and avoid physical contact.

You may show photographs to the inmate, but first ask the officer's approval. Note taking is not permitted in the Visiting Room. . . .

Any fraction of an hour is counted as a full hour. The seven hours a month is total for all visitors.

Children must be kept quiet.

No more than three persons at a time may visit with the prisoner.

Only visitors previously approved by the prison may visit. Sometimes a visitor is disapproved because the visitor knew the prisoner before his incarceration and sometimes because the visitor did not know him before incarceration. Any married woman visiting a prisoner must have the signed approval of her husband. In the Marion prison, visitors speak through faulty telephones on opposite sides of a glass wall.

In fact, visiting-room behavior is flexible, depending on the guard present and the attitude of the warden. I have seen visiting rooms where a man and wife, after their first approved embrace, sat opposite each other with the coffee table between them, their fingertips touching, and a guard came by and warned them to not touch fingertips. But most of the time the guards are not rigid and there is kissing and embracing forbidden by the rules. Sometimes four people, including children running around, are permitted to visit. Sometimes a man may have more than seven hours a month. But it is all arbitrary. If, for some reason, the guard on duty, or the institution itself, wishes to harass a prisoner, the strict rules may be invoked, the visit ended, the visitor taken off the approval list and the prisoner punished.

The stenciled grievances continued: Caseworkers required to have professional standards equivalent to those in private agencies; Spanish-speaking prisoners should have Spanish-speaking caseworkers, hiring of black and Spanish-speaking staff; an inmate welfare fund maintained by contributions from prisoners for helping prisoners making deathbed or funeral trips if the prisoner does not have money of his own; furloughs for nondisciplinary prisoners; and "An inmate-comprised committee shall be established permanently to receive, evaluate and forward other grievances to the Warden and his staff at bi-weekly meetings to be attended by the Warden."

Wagner carefully read over his stencils, holding them to a hallway light to read the typed letters cut on the green waxy surface. The committee had asked for a mimeograph machine but been denied one.

He doubted that anyone could object to these reasonable requests. The parole requests were those made by congressional and other study groups over the years.

The minimum federal wage for workers was unlikely but it was a bargaining start for sensible wages for work that profited the FPI corporation. Lack of full injury payments and care from FPI injuries was a major cause for bitterness.

If a prisoner was taking high school or college courses, or special vocational training, he had to choose between his FPI job and improving his education. Profits made by the corporation were sent back to Washington, while the penitentiary vocational training and other help for prisoners remained minimal. It was beyond the comprehension of prisoners and contrary to the literature issued by FPI and the Bureau of Prisons.

In fact, many of the demands were those that the Bureau of Prisons already claimed to be policy but were universally ignored. The idea of rural Anglo-Saxon guards acting as caseworkers for Latin prisoners who did not speak English was common. The Bureau claimed increased standards for its workers, but it was a sham.

The Federal Bureau of Prisons, with few exceptions, was filled with guards who gradually had their titles changed without commensurate training. A guard was promoted to correctional officer and then to caseworker and then to case manager, and then as an experienced case manager, never having had substantial professional or administrative training beyond his high school–or–less education, would get transferred to Washington headquarters, where he became a divisional head, still, in viewpoint and background, a guard.

Psychiatric evidence was that indefinite segregation tended to produce psychosis in healthy human beings, yet it remained the standard punishment. Every experienced prisoner knew someone he had come to like as a normal person who was sent to indefinite segregation and had become a madman, forever lost to rationality.

The prisoner-supported fund for visits to deathbeds or funerals was an attempt to let prisoners themselves compensate for cruelties in the system. In federal prisons if a prisoner's immediate family member is about to die he must make a choice. He can make a deathbed visit, that is, on certification by the doctor back home and confirmation by a local federal probation officer that the mother or father or sister or brother or son or daughter is indeed about to die, the prisoner may either visit at once, before the death, or wait until after death and attend the funeral. However, the prisoner must pay his own way, and if he is under close custody must also pay for the expenses of two guards to accompany him at all times. Since federal prisons had inmates from all over the country these costs were sometimes prohibitive, especially since most prisoners made no money and FPI workers made about eight dollars a week. A prisoner under close custody—having served, for example, only one year of a ten-year sentence, or with an escape record —whose wife was dying in Chicago would have to choose whether to see her before death or only at the funeral. In either case he would need almost $1000 to pay for the travel, food and lodging expenses of himself and two traveling guards.

Wagner finished the five stencils, some of them redone several times to make them typographically perfect. He looked at his watch. It was three A.M. He typed at the bottom of the last stencil, "Dated this 24th day of February, 1972. Submitted by (signed by Committee)"

He lay down, exhausted.

Wagner woke with daylight. The grapevine informed the whole prison that the committee was coming out of segregation to meet again. Wagner waited for a guard to open his cage for the meeting, and for mimeographing of the stencils. He would never attend another meeting of the committee and the stencils would never be run off inside the prison. By eleven o'clock he realized that for reasons he didn't know and was never told he was no longer included in committee deliberations. He slid the box of stencils over to Alger's cage and told him to make sure they got to the committee.

9

"AROUND THE CLOCK"

In midmorning of Thursday, the 24th, a guard lowered the wickets of particular cages in S-5 to say, "You're going to a meeting."

It was noon before committee members were released and escorted down stairs lined with guards to the main corridor of the prison. It was an exhilarating experience. They had not been out of their cages for more than a week, and walking, while uncertain at first, was exciting. Even the view of Red Top seemed like homecoming. It was good to see companions and grasp arms, though the fact that they had not changed clothes or bathed for over a week was detectable.

The mood was exuberant: "We won. The population stayed unified behind us."

At control center they met the five committee members who had been allowed to stay in population. Committee members were asking each other about health and food when they noticed four new prisoners walking with them, saying they were going to Room 14 with them.

"What do you mean, you're coming to Room Fourteen with us?" Irwin asked. "What the hell are you?"

One of the four said, "We're observers."

"Observers for who?"

"The rest of the population."

Irwin looked at Scully and other committee members but all shrugged and went upstairs. As they climbed the familiar steps to Room 14 in small groups, the original committee members, they discovered later, had each, independently, decided that the "observers" were very strange. They took their places at the tables, with the observers at the end where the warden and his staff had been on the first day.

Irwin was about to announce that the observers were invited to leave when Luis Pedro Hernandez asked to speak. There was a warm feeling among original committee members, and Hernandez, always likable, was urged on. He looked intensely uneasy. "Fellas, I didn't mention this before. But, you know, I've got a bad heart."

Immediately everyone knew. Hernandez was going to withdraw from the committee. It was true that he had suffered a serious heart attack months earlier.

"I just don't think I can take the strain of these committee meetings. I had a talk with the warden and he said I should ask your permission to resign. I'd like to stay with you, but, you understand, I mean, I have to consider my health."

He looked desperately around the table. "You understand?"

Most of the committee members went to his side. They told him they understood and held nothing against him. Phillips, Meyers and Johnson remained in their seats.

As he got to the door, Hernandez turned, raised a clenched fist and called out, "Hang in there, fellas!"

As soon as the door closed, Scully turned to the observers. "Okay, 'observers' . . ."

The leader of the observers spoke. He was Anthony L. DiLorenzo, an interesting man. Anthony DiLorenzo was reputed to be many things, among them a leader in the mafia or, at least, a worker in good standing. Whether or not this was true, he lived a privileged life in Lewisburg, having been given the best honor quarters without the usual waiting period, even though he was considered dangerous. He was also said to be leader of the freight-theft rackets at JFK Airport in New York.

Whether or not this was all true, he had been described by the FBI in 1969 as heir apparent to the mafia family of the late Vito Genovese. He was forty-four, husky, dark, with a wide face and grim mouth. He had participated in labor racketeering with Johnny Dio and Harry Davidoff of the Teamsters, in which capacity he was once arrested for aggravated assault with a baseball bat. He had superior resources compared to his fellow prisoners sitting around the table in Room 14. These went beyond the trivial matter of his neatly washed and precisely ironed shirts and trousers. He was serving a ten-year sentence at Lewisburg for interstate transportation of stolen property and conspiracy, part of the government's attempt to break the ring that had stolen millions of dollars' worth of stocks and bonds from Wall Street firms. On the day of his original arrest on the charge, DiLorenzo had friends who posted

$200,000 for his release within four hours.

Anthony DiLorenzo, observer appointed by Warden Alldredge, now spoke. His diction was not perfect. It had strong traces of New Jersey street inflections, but he had no trouble making himself clear. "Youse guys is taking the wrong approach. I was a union organizer and I know how these things work. Youse should hand in the grievances. Give 'em. Take my advice. It's what the guys out there want. I was a union organizer. I know. Take what you can get. Don't push so hard you end up with nuttin'."

"Who sent you up here?" Phillips asked.

"The guys in J. They don't like the way things is going. They think you guys is stalling and throwing away everything. They want youse to turn in them grievances. I tell ya, when I was organizing—"

Irwin said, "Listen, we got a lot of work to do. This strike is serious and we got no time for bullshit."

DiLorenzo looked aggrieved. "Believe me, Irwin"—he pronounced it "Oiwin"—"you gotta understand. I'm behind you guys a thousand per cent."

Irwin looked at him with disgust. "Yeah? Well, a hundred per cent is good enough."

Scully interrupted. "Look," he said to the whole group, "we're all pretty funky. We been in seg for over a week, and our clothes are filthy, we haven't shaved, and we stink. Let's ask Cansler for a shower and shave. While we're getting ourselves cleaned up you guys who aren't in the hole can make the rounds of the cellhouses and find out what the population wants us to do."

The twelve segregated members were taken to the maximum-security block on the east side of Red Top for showers, shaves and clean clothing. It was a feeling of incredible luxury.

On the way to the shower room they talked with prisoners in the first-floor tier of cages. There was shouting: Stand firm on the five preconditions, do nothing until there's formal recognition, and "no reprisals" in writing. Back in Room 14 the five committee members who had surveyed other housing units came back with the same response. One said, "It's incredible. They're one hundred per cent."

Phillips turned to DiLorenzo. "Well, tell us where you get this word that the population wants us to quit?"

"Well, I tell yuh. They don't understand. I was a union organizer and I can tell youse right now that this approach of yours ain't gonna work. We just ain't in a position to do hard bargaining."

He seemed to have regained composure. He put his feet on the table and slowly lit a cigar. "Take it from me, fellas, the smart thing to do is to turn those grievances over right now."

The three other observers sitting beside DiLorenzo twisted nervously in their chairs. Irwin recognized one of them as one of the two prisoners he had seen walking through the shops the morning of the 15th urging men to stay away from their work that afternoon.

"Hey, you," Irwin said. "I been meaning to ask you something. None of us started this strike. Right? I was in the shop Tuesday minding my own fucking business and I see you and this other guy going around starting a strike. You didn't even have the decency to come to my machine and ask me about it. So you and this other guy start the strike. But I never seen you at the dock, or up there on the stage at the auditorium, or volunteering to collect grievances. You never come out front. How come? How come you work so fucking hard to start this strike and then disappear and now you're up here telling us to give up?"

The man squirmed and said he was strong for the strike and he was just there to let the population know what was going on. As he talked, DiLorenzo moved his hand with the cigar in front of the man as a wordless order to stop talking.

"I gotta tell you guys something. This joint is crawling with cops. They got goon squads all over. The state cops and National Guard are in the basement and they're ready to take this place like Attica."

As DiLorenzo talked, Scully motioned for Irwin to walk to a corner of the room. They gestured for Hilty, Genco, and Phillips to join them. Scully said, "These bastards are just snitches and finks and they're here to break up the strike and break up this committee. They got to go."

Everyone agreed.

They went back to their seats. Scully said, "All right. You guys get the fuck out of here. All you're doing is preventing us from working."

DiLorenzo said, "Listen, fella, we're the ones got youse guys out of the hole."

Lumumba Jones stood up. As usual, he made a striking impact, with his high butterfly Afro, and his granny glasses giving him the look of a black Ben Franklin, but his face was hard. "We said go!"

DiLorenzo persisted. "You guys gotta face facts. They're gonna attack this place any minute now."

By now Irwin's face had begun to redden. At the same time his bulk seemed to swell. He rose like an avenging Old Testament angel. "Can't you hear? Don't you understand English? Get the hell out of here! Right now!"

DiLorenzo was the last out the door. Guards in the outside corridor had been watching, fascinated, through the window in the door, but now they could hear, and DiLorenzo shouted back, "Don't say I didn't warn you. Turn 'em over! Turn 'em over!"

Meyers said, "Great exit speech for the benefit of the hacks."

The committee was momentarily exhausted from the exchange.

Someone said, "Listen, with those guys working for Cansler, there's no telling what lies they'll tell. We got to have some way of letting the population know what's happening."

But the committee was divided. Some wished to do what DiLorenzo suggested, to turn over the grievances to the warden and disband the committee. But Scully, Jones, Hilty, Phillips, Meyers and Genco were fiercely in favor of first getting recognition as a committee to discuss the grievances with the warden and a written promise of no reprisals for anyone not committing violence. They were beginning to hear disturbing stories from the cages in S-1.

Their first attempt at compromise was a sealed message to Cansler at five o'clock asking to circulate among housing units to get opinions on an important issue and to be released from segregation. Both were denied.

So the basic issue came to a point: Should this be another ordinary prison strike with a request for changes, or should the committee ask to negotiate the changes face to face? Should they stress specific changes or a mechanism for discussing problems on a continuing basis? The divisions on the committee were deep and sincere. The committee was at an impasse. Its five preconditions had not been met. It could not agree on whether to submit grievances and retire or hold out for creation of a continuing body of discussion with prison officials.

Some of the committee were opposed to anything like a permanent council. It was a new idea and most prisoners had little background in normal channels of free-world communication and negotiation. Some were shaken by DiLorenzo's statement that they were about to be attacked "like Attica."

Others were adamant about the need to create a continuing body. Their recall from segregation was a sign of the population's solidarity. They had known other strikes in other prisons, recurring semi-annually because there was no continuing channel for negotiating grievances. And for some it was a philosophical imperative that the powerless gain some measure of responsibility over their lives.

Phillips tried to break the impasse by painting a parallel with industrial workers on the outside. Prisoners today, he said, are like industrial workers fifty years ago when there was no legal basis for unions, when the idea of a union to negotiate with management was considered subversive, when management always promised to deal with individuals fairly and then dismissed individual complaints because the individual had no power against an organized company. But now unions are taken for granted. The government says it is a good thing. There is a department in Washington doing nothing but dealing with union contracts. Workers bargain as a normal thing. So what seems radical today in prisons could become normal.

"We know what's wrong and what's unfair in prison," he said. "But no individual prisoner can change anything. As an organized group we can deal with the kind of work done in the industries to make sure it is real training for really good jobs on the outside. Maybe we can even affiliate with regular unions on the outside, make contacts with companies on the outside to help get jobs after release instead of wandering alone like most ex-cons begging for jobs and hoping their past won't be discovered."

His argument seemed to convince nobody.

It was getting late and they had no way of knowing when they would be dismissed again. So Vivero asked for the floor. "I think we can make a good compromise. Why don't we do this? Why don't we tell the warden that we'll ask the men to go back to work if he'll give us the recognition we want?"

The initial response was joyous. In their fatigue it seemed the perfect answer. The warden wanted to get the industries working and the institution back to normal. The prisoners wanted the right to deal with the administration face to face to argue their points for change.

Meyers, Phillips, Jones, Johnson, and Tucker argued against it. They said if the men went back to work there would be no reason for the warden or Washington to pay attention to the committee or the grievances.

The argument raged, men against other men, groups against groups. They hardly noticed that it had become dark outside, that they hadn't eaten for a long time, that the prison waited in suspense for a decision.

Mason argued strongly for asking the men to go back to work. It would convince the warden that they were sincere and they would get the recognition they wanted. Phillips said the minute the men agreed to go back to work they would lose their bargaining power.

"Tell me what reason we have to believe they'll bargain in good faith? Just tell me, Eddie? Didn't they tell us to go to the auditorium and elect a committee and didn't they tell us there'd be no reprisals and didn't most of us get sent to seg? Is that good faith? We're not in church praying. We're in prison and we're representing 1500 prisoners. I think your idea that we'll convince them we're sincere is absurd. They know very well we're sincere in wanting to get some changes. And we know very well they're sincere in not wanting any changes. Nothing's going to change, nothing has ever changed, by our doing what they tell us."

Irwin took over. "We can't go on doing this forever. Why doesn't each side pick a spokesman for its argument. Let the spokesman make his case for back to work and a spokesman make his case for holding out. Then we'll vote."

The back-to-work forces picked Eddie Mason, the holdouts, Joel Meyers.

Mason said the heart of the situation was that nothing was happening. There was no movement. "We're at dead center. If we don't get off our ass you know what's going to happen. They're going to move in on us. Sooner or later they're going to do some shit—they're going to attack, they're going to strong-arm, they're going to punish. I don't know what they're going to do, but they're going to do something and then it's all over. In the meantime, they're telling lies about us. We heard it on the radio, right? They'll convince the population that we aren't really trying to help them, that we're just trying to save our own skins. So while we got some clout, let's make our move. Let's make our offer. Dig? You give us a letter of recognition as a committee that can bargain and we'll tell the guys to go back to work.

"That way the guys know, the administration knows we're not just fronting for the militants in the population, but we're representing everyone, including the guys who want to go back to work. It'll show everyone we're reasonable. The longer we wait the weaker we get. All the administration has to do is hold out and hold out and pretty soon the population will turn against us. We got to make our move while we have some clout."

Most of the heads around the table nodded in agreement.

Meyers stood up. "Number one. The administration seems to be the one feeling the most pressure from the strike. They're backing down. Our people went on strike realizing it would require a certain amount of sacrifice. Men out there aren't urging the population to go back to work. There isn't any pressure by the men to reopen the shops. The warden called us back because the strike is holding up. Are we going to be the only group in this prison to fold?

"Number two. The men support us on the five grievances, the pre-conditions. These haven't been met. So there's no change. If we go out there and ask the men to go back to work before we get our preconditions they'll feel that we're selling them out. Our strongest support comes from the militant prisoners but if we tell them to go back to work we'd have the most militant prisoners against us. We will have isolated them, we'd expose them to trouble and punishment and those who would refuse to go to work would be in real trouble and it would be our fault.

"Our job is not to weaken the militants but to support them. It's always true in any situation that there are leaders who see the issues and take risks. The population understands that. If we lose the militants and they turn against us, the whole population will turn against us. If we're not recognized yet as the men's bargaining agent we have no right to ask them to go back to work.

"You were in the housing units today. You know what the guys are saying. They're saying, 'We don't want to go back to work without an agreement.' Eddie, you know you heard that and all of us did.

"We have a responsibility. We were elected by the population. Over and over they let us know that they're behind us, that they don't want this to be just another prison strike with some grievances and some sweet talk and then extra ice cream on Sunday. If we fail them they'll think we're traitors, and if we don't hold fast then it may be the last time we can get the Federal Bureau of Prisons to accept the rights of prisoners to make legitimate complaints and negotiate on them. We're not just a bunch of cons up here in a room like a debating society. The whole prison is depending on us. Every federal prisoner in the country is depending on us. Prisoners have always been powerless. They've always been exploited. They've always been destroyed. For the first time we have some power. We have the power of unity. We have the power of nonviolence. If we throw away that power, if we tell the prisoners to go back to work before we get satisfaction we'll be nothing but a bunch of traitors."

Some men applauded. Some booed. Phillips quickly asked for a vote.

Irwin said, "Okay. Let's go around the table. Do we submit the grievances and ask the men to go back to work?" Irwin pointed at Meyers at the end of the table on his right and said, "Each guy say yes or no."

The vote was ten to five against turning in the grievances and against asking the population to end the strike. Moore, Mason, Buyse, Estrada and Vivero voted for ending the strike.

Vivero leaped to his feet and pounded the table. "I protest that vote. We're acting like a bunch of jackasses. One man makes a speech and you let him change your minds." By now he was yelling. "We can't let communists control our minds!"

The room was deadly quiet except for Vivero.

"Most of you agreed with me a minute ago! Why have you let yourself be tricked by Meyers?" He looked around the table angrily. Then he said softly, "If you don't go along with me, I'll pull all the Spanish prisoners out of the strike! They'll listen to me! I warn you. If you don't change your votes, we'll break the strike!"

Meyers whispered to Phillips, "The rotten traitor!"

Vivero did not speak idly. Without the Spanish-speaking prisoners the strike would collapse. What Phillips had done for Meyers, call for a vote while the committee was still excited by his arguments, Vivero did for himself. He called for an immediate vote on his proposal to tell the warden they would ask the men to go back to work tomorrow if the warden would give the committee official recognition. He won thirteen to two. Only Meyers and Phillips voted against Vivero.

Irwin and Jones looked uncomfortable as they voted for the Vivero proposal and afterward Irwin approached Phillips. "Ron, you know we need the Puerto Ricans. If they pull out we're finished."

Phillips only shook his head.

"Ron, listen. Do you think the warden's going to accept the proposal?"

"No, I don't."

"Then why not make it just to show him up?"

In fact, Phillips thought the warden would be crazy not to accept the proposal. Once the men were back to work there would be nothing to bargain with.

Scully told Wolcott to tell a guard outside the door that they needed Cansler because they had a proposal to make. They waited, each man with his own thoughts. Many of them imagined the next day with the work whistles once more blowing, the shops at full speed, the kitchen and laundry at work.

The guard came back. "The warden and the associate warden are not available and you'll have to wait until tomorrow."

The warden, the associate warden and the Director in Washington had just lost their chance to win the strike.

The guards escorted the committee members back to their segregation cages.

On Friday the work whistles did not blow. The committee did not ask the prisoners to go back to work. Instead they were escorted to Room 14 to await the time when they would tell the warden they were ready to end the strike. When they reached the control center, on the way to Room 14, Mike Estrada pulled Marcello Vivero aside and spoke to him softly in Spanish. Phillips understood Spanish, but Estrada was speaking too softly for him to hear. But whatever he was saying had a profound effect on Vivero, who first looked troubled, then seemed almost to tremble.

As they mounted the stairs Genco moved next to Phillips, nodded toward Vivero and said, "Don't worry about Marcello. We fixed his ass."

Once seated around the table, Genco stood and asked for attention. He reported that the population was upset about the suggestion that they go back to work. In fact, the strongest feelings were among the Latins, who regarded the suggestion as a sell-out. Genco unfolded a note and handed it to Marcello Vivero.

Vivero read it silently. His face darkened. He whispered for a long time with Estrada and then rose. "I must read this note from the Spanish population." He paused. It was difficult for him to speak. But he read from the note. " 'Marcello, we are too ashamed of you to call you our brother. What made you think that we would ever consider breaking the strike? We will be the last to return to work. Did you think us cowards? It is you who is the coward. If you cannot represent us with honor we ask you to resign.' "

Vivero put the note on the table. His eyes filled with tears, his voice cracked. "I hope you will forgive me for my selfishness last night. I confess I was weak. I regret it. I remain with you to the end."

Irwin's eyes also filled with tears and he went to Vivero and hugged him. Other men did the same, and there were half a dozen men, watched in amazement by guards looking through the door windows at troublemakers, who had tears on their cheeks.

After the emotional scene subsided a guard stuck his head in the door and said that Cansler would be up shortly.

One of the committee, not one active in the argument the day before, said, "When that bastard comes up here I think we better grab him. This nonviolent stuff ain't going anywhere. As long as we hold him, they'll listen to us."

Irwin, Scully, Meyers, Phillips and half a dozen others jumped up in a chorus of disapproval. Irwin said, "Yeah? And after we grab him what the hell are we supposed to do with him?"

The man said with a sneer, "Cut the fucking bastard's head off."

Irwin said, "That's exactly what they'd love. That's exactly how we'd throw away every bit of power we have now. I don't want to hear any more of this hostage or violence shit and if anyone in this room has any ideas about that we'll all keep it to ourselves but I want that person to walk out of here right now."

No one moved. He turned to the man. "You with us? No grabbing, no nothing?"

The man nodded agreement.

It was the first and last mention of violence in the committee.

Shortly afterward Cansler appeared. He read a long memorandum "To All Concerned," dated February 25, 1972, that day, and signed by the warden. It said:

> You have almost convinced me that as a group you do not and never did intend to present the grievances of the inmate population for me and other unnamed officials to consider. . . . I have permitted you to assemble the population on at least two occasions to develop grievances, use the Public Address System to report to the population and permitted you to circulate among the population for their views, all without success.
>
> I then chose and permitted selection of another inmate group with whom you refused to meet. Four well-known inmates were then selected, two at the request of the population, two by selection. . . . All of this has produced nothing but the same preconditions using different words. However, this committee will be allowed to continue to meet on a daily round-the-clock basis as you desire until you are able to produce some grievances representing the general population.

Cansler put the signed memorandum on the table and left.

Now at least they knew they could meet as long as they wanted. Perhaps they could resolve their basic dispute.

But the argument resumed. Someone said the memorandum promising they could meet round-the-clock as long as they wanted was signed by Alldredge and that constituted written recognition. Meyers and Phillips opposed the idea, saying they should get specific written recognition of the committee as a negotiating committee and written promise of no reprisals, plus presence of an attorney and a representative of the press.

Mason, Vivero, Estrada and Moore pressed for handing over the grievances. By now the stencils cut by the absent Wagner had been read and approved.

The argument swung back and forth. Finally Hilty had a compromise: Turn in the stencils with the grievances on them with an attached cover letter that would have to be signed by Alldredge before the grievances would be officially received, the cover letter to have some clauses that would commit him to cooperation in negotiating the grievances.

The idea was another relief from the impasse and passed twelve to three, Irwin, Meyers, and Phillips objecting.

But since Meyers was the most articulate and familiar with legal concepts he was assigned to compose the cover letter.

Wolcott was told to get word to Cansler that the grievances would be turned over shortly but not to say anything about the cover letter. Wolcott left the room briefly and then returned. Wolcott spoke at some length with one of the guards, who went at once to the warden's office.

Meyers started dictating the cover letter.

He dictated the start of one letter and enough members disapproved to discard it and start again.

At four o'clock Cansler came to the room. Meyers was still dictating the letter and asked for a little more time.

The letter was headed "February 25, 1972. From the First Inmate Committee to Warden Alldredge, Administrative Officials, General Population and the Press."

It said, legalistically among other things:

> We express our willingness to engage in serious discussions to come to terms on the grievances listed at the end of this document. . . . I, Noah Alldredge, Warden of the United States North-Eastern Penitentiary at Lewisburg, Pennsylvania, do as spokesman of the Administration of this Prison, hereby recognize the committee, which was elected at the insistence of my administration under conditions provided by said administration on February 15, 1972, as the Legal Bargaining Agent of the inmate population at this institution. Furthermore, said administration will parley with said committee to redress and/or relieve grievances and disputed conditions as expressed by the inmate population through said committee which shall represent the inmate population.
>
> In the name of said administration, I hereby promise to the limit of my powers to prevent any punitive acts against any inmates for any acts undertaken in connection with the Work Stoppage which began on February 15, 1972, or in connection with the formation of said representative committee.
>
> I finally agree, in the name of said administration, that qualified legal counsel shall be present to witness and observe any and all substantial parleying which shall take place.

There was a place for the warden's signature.

It was awkwardly phrased but it was essentially the preconditions of February 15.

The letter was finished when Cansler came in again. He said he had to have the grievances at once. Irwin said they had been promised round-the-clock meetings. Cansler said that couldn't be done now because Washington headquarters closed at five P.M. for the weekend and they had to have the grievances in Washington before that time.

What about the promise of round-the-clock meetings?

Cansler said, "I'll be back in five minutes. You have the grievances ready. If they are, prisoners will be unlocked for work on Monday and the grievances will get answered in *The Friday Flyer* in two weeks."

The committee was in disarray. Suddenly everything had returned to the start. The strike would be lost. Irwin, Meyers and Phillips did not want to turn over the grievances under those circumstances. If they could delay until after five P.M. it would be the weekend and the strike would go another two days, adding pressure to resolve the grievances and get the industries back to production. They were willing to stall, even though the grievances were cut in stencil form and the cover letter completed. Most of the other members genuinely believed that the letter and grievances were not truly complete since they had not signed the stencils.

Something new had to be devised to prevent the sudden loss.

In ten minutes Cansler opened the door. Behind him the corridors were lined with more guards than they had seen before. "You got those grievances?"

Irwin said, "Mr. Cansler, we need more time."

"All right! Clear the room!"

Meyers and Phillips went to the small table in back of the room where the grievances were in the box of stencils. Meyers put the box under his arm while he tore the first, unfinished cover letter into small pieces and put it in the wastebasket.

Cansler yelled, "Did you hear what I said?"

Phillips, his back to Cansler, watching Meyers shred the cover letter, said quietly, "No, I didn't hear you, Warden. What did you say?"

"Ah said, 'Rack 'em up, buddy!' "

The warden had made a stunning reversal. He had changed his mind three hours earlier, two hours after he gave the committee his signed promise to let them meet round-the-clock.

He was having trouble with his staff. As the strike continued, the hard-nosed officers spoke more openly of cracking heads. With prisoners perpetually locked in their cages, conversations between staff members became less cautious. Remarks like "Only one thing those fuckin' commies need is a little pick-axe therapy," and he heard reports of talk in the officers' mess about "fucking niggers" and "black bastards." Cansler reminded him daily that prisoners in their cages were running out of cigarettes and coffee and this meant eventual rioting.

Secret letters from within the committee tempted him to move. Two letters had arrived in his office the morning of the 25th, one from Wolcott telling him the committee was split and the radicals taking over, followed by a message Wolcott whispered to a guard in the corridor in early afternoon saying the committee was planning a trick on the warden with the cover letter.

Michel Buyse, representative of the French, wrote a letter to the warden two days after the meeting of the 16th offering to give the warden the grievances despite the committee's decision on the five preconditions. He sent another on the 25th, the last day of the committee meetings, saying the same thing. Before the meeting of the 25th he had communicated to Cansler privately to say that only five of the committee members were sincere but were outvoted by "the other eleven radical people," Scully, Irwin, Genco, Hilty, Meyers, Jones, Phillips, Johnson, Tucker, Mason and Alger. The committee members, suspicious of Wolcott, did not know about Buyse's communications.

But the most powerful pressure on the warden to renege on his promise crystallized with a call from Washington shortly after he sent his round-the-clock memo to the committee: Unless the institution was back in production by Monday, the Director will send a contingent of guards from other institutions to take over the prison and make the prisoners go back to work.

If the Director sent in an outside force, it would mean that Noah Alldredge had lost control of his institution. He had worked 30 years to build a reputation. He did not have much time. It was already early Friday afternoon and Washington headquarters would close at five P.M. For all he knew, the Director would put his plan for outside forces in action by the end of the day. The warden determined to tell Washington before closing time that he had taken tough action to guarantee the institution back at work on Monday.

The prison system had responded as it always does when confronted with subtleties of human behavior.

Lumumba Jones had told the prisoners from the kitchen dock,

"These motherfuckers don't believe that we are men, that we have brains, that we think for ourselves, that we can understand a situation and be intelligent about it. *That,* brothers, *that* they don't know how to deal with." Now, ten days later, he was proven right. He had been right about something else that day: "They *want* us to do something violent. They're gonna try to make us do something violent. They *know* how to deal with violence."

That night the prison, over the warden's signature, issued a press release:

> This committee had been constituted for the sole purpose of presenting to the administration grievances which led to the work stoppage which began February 15th. Eleven days of activity on their part failed to accomplish that purpose, and as of 5 P.M., February 25th, they were disbanded. The committee members were then moved to our administrative segregation unit.

Prisoners heard the press release reported on their radios. It was, to put it mildly, untrue. The warden told the public that "eleven days of activity on their part failed to accomplish" their purpose. He did not say that on eight of those days, on his orders, they were locked in punishment cages, forbidden to speak, to meet, or to do anything to accomplish their purpose.

The prisoners had tried to settle differences by peaceful negotiation. Their grievances were what students of prisons had been calling essential for over a hundred years. In one of the more astounding acts in prison history, a committee of elected prisoners, with 1400 other prisoners unified behind them, had conducted negotiations, had been lied to by their prison keepers, but during the entire episode of ten days the prisoners had not committed a single act of violence.

The real punishments were about to begin, in the tradition of the Bureau of Prisons, out of sight. About that there would be no press releases, truthful or false.

10

ANOTHER "FREE ELECTION"

It would damage the image of the Federal Bureau of Prisons if it openly tortured prisoners in order to produce profits. Both physical and psychological torture have always been denied by the Bureau.

But the Bureau had problems. It wished to maintain its public appearance of a progressive correctional system, a model for the rest of the country, able to lead its prisoners to a state of respect for law and rejection of violence. Only violent aggression by prisoners would justify spoiling this image by official violence. In twelve days of attempting to create a peaceful mechanism for discussing grievances, the Lewisburg prisoners had not committed a single act of violence. The warden had confirmed this in his confidential daily reports to the Director and in his press releases. That was one problem.

A more pressing problem was the warden's fear that Washington would take over his institution unless prisoners were back in the factories by the following week.

The factories were not academic parts of his problem. The day prisoners went on strike the Lewisburg factories had over $1 million in contracts to fulfill. Penitentiaries were rated on their production and profits. A loss could provoke politically awkward audit or transfers and demotions for FPI supervisors. Penitentiaries competed with each other for contracts and one prison's loss could be another's gain.

Two weeks before the strike began Lewisburg won a highly profitable contract for almost a third of a million dollars. Delighted officials at Lewisburg had signed the agreement on February 1:

> LOCKER, CLOTHING. Gray single-tier steel clothing locker. With hooks, coat rod, towel bar, and hat shelf. Four (4) removable shelves.

Sanitary leg base. Semi-louvered doors, designed for padlock. Knocked down . . . 7125–753–6238 . . . estimated annual purchase, 7,272 at $40.85 each. Total contract: $297,061.20.

Lewisburg was supposed to ship 606 of these a month from its Reading Railroad siding. A penalty could be assessed if it fell behind. The strike had already cost half a month's production.

The strike could even hurt the $98,000 contract for X-ray film cabinets that Irwin and Eddie Mason had worked on. The Lewisburg factory was in competition with one in the federal prison at Milan, Michigan, which had the contract for 1600 slightly smaller ones, while Lewisburg got the order for 880 large ones. Production delayed too long might be captured by Milan.

Lewisburg and Milan already were in production races on a contract for 201,214 steel desk trays, each prison supposed to produce half the total. If Lewisburg fell too far behind, Milan's share could be increased, even though FPI favored the big penitentiaries with older prisoners. The younger prisoners in medium- and minimum-security prisons felt less pressure to volunteer to work in the factories, or if they did they were slower workers.

The warden's dilemma was to get men back to the machines by Monday to avoid the Director's taking over his prison and still maintain the public image of a prison system that did not torture.

The answer to the dilemma was Lewisburg's second venture into democracy since election of the prisoner committee. This exercise in free choice began at eight A.M. Saturday. The warden addressed the population over his public address system:

"Late yesterday afternoon I decided to disband the inmates' committee. They are in administrative segregation and will not be meeting again. At no time did they present a grievance to the administration, so there can be no response from me or anyone else on this subject."

Thus the prison population learned that discussion of grievances and promises of no reprisal were over.

The warden added another announcement. Today every prisoner would be interviewed by two members of the staff about returning to work. They should consider their answer very carefully, the warden announced, because their reply could have "very serious consequences."

And so the second "free election" in Lewisburg history began. Each prisoner was called out to meet a pair of staff members. The prisoner was shown a form headed by the prisoner's name and number. The first paragraph repeated what the warden had announced about the elected committee. Then it said:

> We know that it is in the best interest of the inmates and the administration not to continue the present situation indefinitely.
>
> (1) We are therefore requesting that you now make a decision whether you will return to work at an assigned job.
>
> (2) Before making the decision you should know that a negative answer may be cause for disciplinary action which will become part of your record and which can result in loss of good time, loss of present housing and possible transfer.
>
> (3) After thinking all these things over carefully, indicate your decision here.
>
> YES, I will return to work.
>
> NO, I will not return to work.

And so each prisoner chose whether to extend his years in a cage under harsher conditions or vote "freely" to give up the strike without the promised consideration of grievances.

William McAllister, a Canadian serving time for bank robbery, lived in I block, an honor dormitory. The day the strike began he stayed away from the dock, he refused to take part in the afternoon meeting of the auditorium and he did not attend the evening meeting in the auditorium. In short, he refused to be active in the work stoppage and continued to do his official work as orderly in his dormitory. He testified later, "I felt that four years of imprisonment had taught me to mind my business and I didn't attend the meeting in the auditorium."

He was asked if he felt the elected committee represented his views. He answered that he couldn't say because the committee had been locked in segregation, had been forbidden to speak to the other inmates, and that he, like the rest of the population, had been locked in his quarters, thus preventing any communication between the committee and the general population. He said, "I can't honestly answer your question."

When asked his answer to the work questionnaire, he said he preferred to remain mute. "I felt this was a psychological thing which should not have been asked many inmates in the institution. I felt that these questions would strip a man of his dignity and his self-respect if he had to take sides between the institution and the inmate committee. I chose not to take sides. I asked to remain mute."

He was told he could not remain mute.

The next morning an officer came to his quarters. "McAllister, let's go." He obeyed. He was taken to the harshest segregation, S-1 in Cage 103. By the next day there were five men in the cage. The cage was six by twelve and had one slab for a bed and one mattress. The lights were on twenty-four hours a day. He was issued the usual boxer shorts, khaki pants, T-shirt, shower clogs, blanket and towel. When he entered the cage there was another prisoner who had refused to sign the statement, James Spencer. The cage was cold. Spencer was bare from the waist up. He was shivering, his lips an alarming blue. McAllister asked him what was wrong. Spencer said he had suffered a heart attack a few months earlier and couldn't stop shaking in the cold. McAllister gave Spencer his blanket and towel to try to warm him. Three more men entered the cell. The next day four mattresses were added to the cell but they could be used only by covering every part of the floor and overlapping.

Spencer had been put in the hole the night before. His answer to the questionnaire was "When everyone else goes back to work, yes, I'm willing at that time to go back to work." As he was being led down the stairs to the basement an officer told him, "I want to warn you not to open your mouth to say anything. Just do as you're told and go, because if you don't you're going to be sorry for it."

He was told to strip and be searched. He started to ask for the nitroglycerin pills for his heart disease but was told to shut up. He was put into the cell naked. Several hours later a guard threw in a pair of shorts and trousers. By this time Spencer's lips were blue and he had begun his shivering. His left side was numb and his left leg felt asleep with a pins-and-needles sensation. His first meal, pushed through the feeding slot on a paper plate, was a small square of grilled cheese sandwich and a paper cup with an inch of coffee. The wicket was kept closed by the guards. When other men pressed into the crowded cage they feared for Spencer's life and banged on the door for help. An officer lowered the wicket and said if they knocked on the door again the guard would fix them so they'd never knock on anything else the rest of their lives. Spencer begged his cagemates not to do anything else, because he feared spraying of Mace or beatings would kill him.

Men came and went in that cage. Later Lucky Johnson was put in Spencer's cage and saw bruises that Spencer told him came from officers' punches on the way to segregation.

Thomas Bullock, another prisoner who declined to sign the work statement, had a different story. He was called out of his quarters on the west side of Red Top on Sunday night. In the main corridor guards told him to strip naked. When he was naked an officer twisted his arm behind his back and marched him down the full length of the main corridor, across Red Top, to the segregation basement. On the way, he said, they punched him, calling him "nigger" and "instigator." As they approached the doorway to the stairs going to the segregation basement, the officer said, "Watch out for the doorway," and then gave Bullock a body block, smashing his naked body against the side of the doorway. He was put into an S-1 cage naked. Inside, another prisoner had shorts, khaki pants and a blanket, so he let Bullock have his khaki trousers. The cage was cold but not freezing. The light was on twenty-four hours a day. Food on the paper trays often consisted of a spoonful of peas and a swallow of coffee. Air in the cage was foul. Like most of the rest in S-1 he was there eight days without leaving the cage, without a view of the outside, without washing.

Walter Battle was another prisoner marched naked down the main corridor to the segregation basement. He was put in naked but given a blanket. He was fourth man in the one-man cage. This, too, was Sunday night, a favorite time for segregation guards to take private vengeance on prisoners. Regular officers were gone and there were few witnesses.

Felix Rosario, Puerto Rican, had become a serious orthodox follower of the Islamic religion, different from many other prisoners who were members of the Black Muslims. He, too, was called out late Sunday night. He had just finished a shower and evening prayers facing Mecca when a group of guards called him out. Rosario put on his clothes, picked up his Koran and went down the stairs of F dormitory to the main corridor, which was lined with more than thirty guards. He could see down the tunnel to Red Top, where there were guards wearing tear gas masks. He saw another prisoner walking down Red Top naked, between the guards. Rosario was frightened. He stood against the wall waiting to see what would happen to him. A lieutenant strode over, grabbed the Koran from his hand and threw the book on the floor. Rosario knew this was part of the standard technique to provoke a prisoner to anger, justifying a beating to be reported later as controlling a prisoner attempting assault upon guards. The learned response of experienced prisoners is to remain silent and unmoving, to give no excuse for a beating by massed guards. But Rosario was a serious religionist, and against all his experience in prisons he said in astonishment, "You know what you just did? You threw a holy Koran out!"

There was a tense moment. A younger guard appeared to disapprove of what was about to happen. The young guard picked up the Koran and said, "Rosario, have it." Rosario in surprise and gratitude said, "Thank you very much." It apparently had stopped a beating. But Rosario was told to strip and was marched naked down the main corridor to the segregation basement.

Four or five other naked prisoners were there, waiting to be put in S-1 cages. Rosario asked one of the guards if there wasn't something they could have "to cover ourselves." The guard said, "We don't have anything." Rosario had once worked in the basement, in "receiving and discharge," and he knew there was always an oversupply of underwear, shirts and trousers. But he decided to remain silent. They put him in a cage with three other men who were already asleep, sharing one mattress on the floor. They wore the standard segregation khaki pants and T-shirts. Later other mattresses were thrown in. He tried to ask for something pork-free because of his religion. But no one paid attention. He would try to eat one meal a day retrieving whatever was free of pork or pork products. He was there nine days. He was sometimes able to retrieve only one spoonful for a whole meal.

One of Rosario's cagemates, a prisoner named Hewlett, was particularly bitter about the food being pushed through the slots the first days they were in segregation. As soon as he could, he wrote down the precise contents of the meals. He recorded that four men shared one "10-in-one" hamburger, which meant ten hamburgers from one pound of meat. This one tenth of a pound would be cut into four pieces and one quarter of one hamburger assigned to each of the four men in the cage. On Hewlett's plate there were also nine peas, a slice of bread and an inch of coffee in a cup.

Another prisoner, living on the privileged third floor of the honor dormitory in J block, was Burrell Baskim. He was called out on the weekend, told not to bother dressing, was marched in shorts down the stairs to the main corridor and the 750 feet to the segregation basement. He was put in an S-1 cage naked. Twenty minutes later guards put in another prisoner naked. A short time later a third naked prisoner was shoved in. Slowly—it was hard to count time in the basement, jammed into the tiny four-walled cage—a blanket would be thrown in, or a pair of trousers. The lights were on twenty-four hours. That cage was hot and despite the lack of clothing the four prisoners were sweating. Baskim was there fourteen days. One of the other men in the cage, Joseph Evans, counted three beans on one of his paper plates.

James Miller, another prisoner put in S-1 for declining to sign the back-to-work agreement, was in the midst of a legal appeal. He was not permitted to bring his papers with him. A Federal Bureau of Prisons policy issued in June 1971 had "guaranteed" the right of a prisoner to legal materials. It became "the law of the land" on November 8, 1971, when the United States Supreme Court issued a decision making access to legal materials mandatory for all prisoners in the United States. Miller had no idea how long he would be kept in the hole. There was no way even to slip a note out of the cage. The window was welded shut and painted over. The only other possible openings were in the steel door—the feeding slot and small window—but both were shut off by the wicket. Shouting at the door was futile because no one ever answered, if, in fact, anyone heard. The only possible communication, as Spencer and his cage mates discovered, was to knock or kick on the door. Miller knocked on the door until a guard lowered the wicket. The prisoner began asking how he could get his legal materials. Just as Miller opened his mouth the guard sprayed a Mace-like chemical, Federal Streamer, into his mouth, face and eyes, paralyzing them for over an hour.

Floyd Gunderson was called out of his quarters and put into a segregation cage naked for an hour before he was given trousers. Eventually five men were pushed into the cage. He had a different problem. He had been diabetic for thirty years and received regular insulin shots adjusted to normal food intake in the prison mess hall. He had eaten "breakfast" at three P.M. on the Saturday of the questionnaires. That night he was taken to segregation. His next meal was Sunday morning, two sandwiches on a paper plate, but the filling, believed to be cheese, smelled so foul that he dared not eat it. If he vomited he would lose whatever slight nutrition he had.

He drank some black coffee. No sugar in coffee is permitted in S-1. Unlike most of the men in segregation who tried to get medical attention and could not, Gunderson got some. Each day a guard would open the wicket, order Gunderson to stick his arm out, and a medical technical assistant would give him a hypodermic shot of forty-three units of insulin, his normal amount when eating normally.

By Sunday afternoon Gunderson was dizzy and confused, which he recognized as early stages of insulin shock. He needed either more food or less insulin. He went into shock on Sunday night and again on Monday. Each day he and his cagemates begged for the prison doctor to see him, but nothing happened. On March 1 they helped Gunderson write a letter to the prison doctor:

> I've . . . gone into an insulin reaction twice, but both times the meal came in time to pull me out of it. The meals have gotten increasingly smaller lately and I realize if I go into reaction at night and have to wait for breakfast I might not live.

The letter, addressed to Dr. Budin of the hospital staff, was received and placed in Gunderson's medical file. Dr. Joel Aryeh Budin later testified that he had been notified by the medical technician and by the Gunderson letter that Gunderson was having insulin shock in segregation but he testified that he did not bother to visit Gunderson.

Dr. Budin also testified that it was true that if Spencer, the heart victim, was denied nitroglycerin pills and if he was kept in a cold room he had a high risk of a fatal heart attack. He did not visit Spencer, either.

There are fourteen cages in S-1, three of them tiled, with only a sink-toilet combination of steel. The rest have a single slab for a bed. During the weekend fifty-six men were jammed into the fourteen cages built for one person each. When no more could be pushed into S-1, the other men refusing to sign the back-to-work agreement were placed in E and F dormitories, transformed into punishment quarters. Food was sparse, crowding stifling.

It did not take long for events in S-1 and E and F dormitories to circulate through the population. On Monday, February 28, work call was sounded. Though threatened with extended time in prison, loss of housing and jobs within the institution and transfer to other penitentiaries thousands of miles away, 25 per cent of the population, now risen by new prisoners to 1259, refused to work.

The warden's press release for the day pictured a population eager to return to work at first opportunity, offering their services in gestures of voluntary assistance to the staff. It was not a model of reportorial accuracy:

> Beginning Saturday a volunteer force of 150 inmates began to assume duties involved in their own care. By Sunday the force had grown to 250 and at 8 A.M. Monday the remainder of the population returned to their assignments.

If the Sunday force of workers was 250 men and on Monday "the remainder . . . returned to their assignments" it would mean 1259 prisoners at work. The truth was that only 942 reported, and the other 317 were held in punishment quarters with inadequate food and denied medical care.

The press release ended on a happy note:

The work stoppage was without serious incident and no violence or property damage occurred.

11

"I'M NO LONGER AFRAID
OF FREEDOM. . . ."

She was calling from an outdoor phone booth. I could hear the noise of trucks and cars in the background. The prisoner's mother had traveled to Lewisburg from a small town outside of New York City for a scheduled visit and found, as she put it, "the prison is locked." She had not received a letter from her son for a week and the town was full of rumors about a strike.

Shortly afterward I got a call from a lawyer who had seen his client inside the penitentiary. The place was on strike and there were rumors of a sympathy strike at Danbury prison, of men being jammed into the hole with Macings and beatings. He had called because at the time I, as an assistant managing editor of the Washington *Post,* had written about prisons.

The letters began to trickle out of Lewisburg, one from the wife of a committee member who sent me a letter her husband wanted to be sure the paper received:

> I feel very strongly that my safety is in great danger. With this letter I'm begging you to please send someone to inquire about my safety and the safety of other members of the committee. Please hear us out! Please! The information that they are giving out is false, just like the officials did at Attica. . . . If by chance anything happens to me, I would appreciate if you let my family know. My mother's address is . . .

Another envelope arrived with a sheet inside bearing the simple message "Help!"

A series of telephone calls to the Bureau of Prisons and to Warden Alldredge confirmed that there was a strike in both prisons. The officials said the strikes were ended and they denied that there had been beatings, Macings, withholding of medicines or any other of the punishments rumored.

It became clear from conflicting accounts that only an interview with both sides, with a chance to test specific incidents with times, places and eyewitnesses, could produce a sound picture of what had happened. Arguments with Director Carlson and Warden Alldredge over days had no effect: the Federal Bureau of Prisons had a rule against journalist interviews with willing prisoners. I wrote a formal letter to Director Carlson requesting interviews with the segregated committee members and he wrote a formal letter denying permission. The Washington *Post* and I, as co-plaintiffs, asked the U.S. District Court in Washington for a restraining order against the Bureau interview rule.

Judge Gerhard Gesell at first denied our petition. He read the same Bureau policy statement that Warden Alldredge had attempted to read at the first meeting of the Lewisburg prisoners committee. He was interested in one section:

> Representatives of the press are encouraged to visit Bureau of Prisons institutions, to learn about and report on correctional facilities, activities, and programs.

The judge asked the Bureau attorneys if that language did not permit what the newspaper was asking. The Bureau lawyers answered ambiguously and the judge told the newspaper he thought there was no issue. Reporters could visit Danbury and Lewisburg to get facts about the strikes.

As soon as court was over I tested the policy. I went to Danbury and asked to interview in private the strike committee prisoners, including Arthur Burkhardt Banks, from whom I had received a letter. John J. Norton, the warden, said that was not permitted, that the policy on press visits meant that a reporter could tour the prison with a guard, speak casually—meaning four or five minutes—with a prisoner he met at random, so long as the conversation was limited to educational, sports and other "helpful programs of the institution." Could I talk about the strike? No. I toured the prison, engaged a prisoner in conversation. The guard heard it all, the prisoner preferred not to say anything about the strike.

I went to Lewisburg to the warden's office, as I had months earlier on a different kind of visit. Warden Alldredge was cordial, as he had been on my earlier visit. With him were Associate Wardens Cansler and Cramer. I told him I would like to speak confidentially to committee members in segregation. Warden Alldredge said in almost the same words used the day before by Warden Norton that if I wanted a truly balanced picture of the institution I could tour the institution in the presence of an officer and speak to any prisoner I met at random, if the conversation was casual—meaning four or five minutes—and if we spoke only of recreational and educational programs.

I thanked the warden but said that was not the purpose of my visit nor was it the most immediate public issue at the moment. I told him that Bureau attorneys had given Judge Gesell the impression that the Bureau policy would permit me to conduct interviews with willing prisoners by name.

"I know nothing about that. I do know that such interviews, alone, with individual prisoners, preselected by you, are not allowed under Bureau policy."

We talked informally about the rationality of the policy. What was his personal feeling about the harm of interviews with prisoners?

"If the press comes here to interview anyone they want, they'll get a one-sided, biased picture of the institution. You'd end up with interviews with radical revolutionaries."

I asked him what better way of learning the truth could there be than listening to a prisoner who claims mistreatment, having him put his name to his accusation, do the same with alleged eyewitnesses, and then permit the authorities to give their side.

"For example, Warden, I'm told there were beatings and Macings of men placed in the hole during the early days of the strike. If prisoners are willing to stand behind those claims in public and you have evidence they are wrong and I print that, isn't that the safest way to get a balanced picture?"

Warden Alldredge stiffened. "Mace is not used in this institution!"

It was typical of Noah Alldredge that he wanted to be seen as a reasonable man and in the end he suggested a compromise. He would let me pick fifteen prisoners at random from the file of the population and I could speak to them in a group without an officer present. I had our legal case in mind. I doubted that much would come from it, since prisoners are fearful of talking in groups to an outsider. Or if they do it is often standard bravado. On the other hand I didn't want to appear uninterested in cross-section attitudes of the prisoners. The warden asked his secretary, Betty Smith, to bring in two drawers of 1800 file cards. He said there was a card there for every prisoner in the place, in the penitentiary, on the farm and at Allenwood.

"Are the cards for committee members and everyone in segregation in there?"

"Yes."

"If I'm lucky and pick one of them will you let him join the group?"

The three officials looked at each other. The warden said, "You go ahead and pick your cards while I make a phone call."

He called Director Carlson in Washington and after a quiet conversation got approval for his offer to me.

The only clue to the cards was the alphabetical separator. I tried to remember all the names of the committee members. There were a couple of J's—Jones and Johnson, a couple of M's—Mason and Moore. I dipped into the card file as often as I could into the initials of committee members. I got half a dozen of the right initials but none of the committee members. Two of my selections had been transferred, two were in Allenwood and one was in the hospital.

I was taken to Room 14, where the committee had met. Ten prisoners were brought in, bewildered and hostile. I explained the situation and said no one was obliged to stay. Three men left at once. In a few minutes, without explanation, three more prisoners took their place. The group was nervous, perhaps because officers were peering in from the door window. One prisoner said he had personally watched an officer tear up prisoner letters during the strike and a different officer read another letter and remove one page of it. Another prisoner said he saw an officer read a letter from a committee member and put it under his necktie, held by its clasp.

Four of the group did not know there was a Bureau policy of uncensored letters to the press. Six of them knew about it but didn't believe that the letters were really unopened.

I asked about beatings and Macings. Some men remained expressionless and others shrugged. "You know, lots of rumors," one said. One man said quietly, "I saw an officer throw away medication supposed to go to a sick prisoner and laugh. 'No workee, no pillee.' "

If they had a choice would they rather speak to a reporter individually or in a group?

After a short silence one prisoner said, "Look, we're all in a position of being prisoners. Every man in this place wants to get out. Any one of us here might do anything to get out of here and could be turned into an informer. Look at Boyd Douglas down there in Harrisburg. He got out of prison and got money and everything he wanted because he informed on another inmate. If we talk in a group we don't know who's going to inform on us, or be a government witness, or who may repeat what he heard to a second prisoner in front of a guard who gets it distorted. That's why no one likes to talk in a group like this."

There was a knock on the door. Through it I saw a gaunt, dark-eyed prisoner. I opened the door and he shook my hand.

"Sir, the word is out in this institution that you are here. And I wish personally to congratulate you on your work and on your necktie."

I was wearing my "prison tie," bright red. Prisons are places of dull colors.

It was my introduction to Dr. Z. He spoke eloquently about the injustice of punishing men who had followed officers' instructions to form a committee, men who had been hurt because they acted nonviolently on behalf of their fellow prisoners. As he spoke an officer entered and ordered him out.

I told the group to let me know if they had any trouble as a result of this interview and left.

There was now evidence for a full hearing before Judge Gesell. It was plain that the Bureau prohibited private interviews with willing prisoners. The Bureau argued that doing that would create a "Big Wheel" problem, notoriety for prisoners who used press attention to make trouble in the institution. Norman Carlson testified under oath that the Bureau had studied all the states that permit press interviews, with the conclusion that they caused serious problems. Judge Gesell reserved decision.

A routine news story giving both sides of the testimony ran in the paper. Four days later I received an anonymous letter from a prisoner in a federal penitentiary. Enclosed was a memorandum from Director Carlson to all his wardens only a few months earlier stating that pressure and court decisions pointed to a forced change in press interview policies so it would be better for the Bureau to come up with a plan of its own. The plan did not interest me particularly. It was merely ridiculous: the interview between reporter and prisoner would be held in the presence of a prison officer who would tape-record the conversation, and the prison would retain possession of the tape. What did interest me was the last paragraph of the memorandum in which Director Carlson said that undoubtedly there would be some associate wardens and officers disturbed by a change in the policy but the wardens could tell them that the Bureau had studied all states that have interview policies and had found only minor difficulties. The memorandum, after confirmation of its authenticity, was entered in the court record.

Judge Gesell issued an order permitting press interviews with willing federal prisoners. It was a short victory. The Bureau obtained a suspension of his order until appeals had been completed. We won in the Court of Appeals but more than two years later lost in the U.S. Supreme Court, five to four. But during the few days before the Bureau obtained a suspension of Judge Gesell's order I went to Lewisburg to interview as many of the segregated committee members as possible.

This time when I made my courtesy call to the warden's office he was chilly and I was taken directly to the visiting room. The officer told me to fill out a pink card for each prisoner I wished to see. I put down the committeemen still in segregation—Phillips, Meyers, Jones, Irwin, Johnson, Mason, Alger and Tucker. I added one other name of a prisoner, unconnected with the committee, who I had heard was badly hurt from beatings by guards. As the officer called the names into his phone I looked around the familiar visiting room.

Behind the visiting-room officer's desk was the triad of rest rooms with the signs over their doors: "Ladies," "Men" and "Inmates."

At the other end were the soft drink and cigarette machines. There was a scattering of couples and four children. That was good. Each time I had been there earlier the officers had been proud to say that if the visiting room was not crowded they let the time run to three-thirty instead of the official three. Two of the couples were holding hands. Two women waiting for prisoners stared at a spot behind the visiting-room desk. They were looking at a red bulb over a steel-grated door. When the red bulb flashed it meant that a prisoner was on the other side waiting to see his visitor. The guard would unlock the door and a visiting-room scene would follow: sometimes an ecstatic rush into each other's arms, sometimes a slow, cool but excited walk, but other times a cold deliberate approach with hostile greeting between man and wife.

None of the committee members appeared for a long time. It was almost two o'clock. Would I be permitted to interview after three? The officer said, "Three o'clock sharp is end of visiting hours." He added about the man allegedly beaten by guards, "He won't be available. He's aggressive-assaultive and not safe."

Whatever else caused the delay, it gave the committee members a shower, shave and clean clothing for a visit.

Eventually the red light flashed, the grilled gate folded back and Phillips, lanky and smiling, moved out. It was two o'clock. I picked a far corner and we began talking at once.

"None of us knows how long we'll stay in solitary. We could spend the rest of our time there, never seeing anyone, never getting into the rest of the prison population. It's possible I could spend thirteen years . . . and never get outdoors. There's no way of knowing."

He was excited, looking around the large room at ordinary people in street clothes. "Of course, we're all afraid of 'the tour.' That's prison jargon for the government moving a man from prison to prison around the country, always keeping him in solitary. We all know of some men, nonviolent men, especially political or draft cases, who have spent their whole time in solitary, doing the tour."

He described the S-5 cages, the pressure of endless confinement and how small things became magnified. Like the two-inch-long sawed-off toothbrushes.

"It's one of those things that sounds unimportant on the outside. But if you're in prison and especially in solitary such a thing really forces you to hold on to your sanity. Why do they do it? To keep us from making it into a weapon to kill ourselves or someone else. But we've a steel locker in there we could make a weapon from. And there's that clear glass in the window that would make a beautiful weapon."

How was he holding up?

"You get a feeling of hopelessness. You become convinced that you're never going to get out, never going to leave that empty space."

He paused, trying to get across his feeling, and then held his hands up in simple exasperation. "We have a need for human contact."

When Meyers came out under the flashing red light he had his typical flat-footed walk and broad grin.

"My own opinion is that they never intend to let us out of segregation. This morning they transferred thirty-two men to Atlanta. Most of them were involved in the work stoppage one way or another. Who knows? Maybe they sent them out knowing you were coming up here under a court order and might want to talk to them.

"We were worried about Springfield. That's the Federal Bureau of Prisons nuthouse in Missouri. But I think that danger's past. The real danger is that we're going to be in solitary as long as they have control over us."

Clarence Jones was next, erect and smiling. I was his first visitor in twenty months. His parents had died while he was in Lewisburg and he had been unable to attend their funerals for lack of money.

"They're punishing us for what they told us to do. Then they trumped up charges that no one ever heard of before. I got into this place in 1969 and I was never given any instruction on the rules, and was never given a book about the rights and wrongs of this place."

Being in segregation had given him time to think about his own life and why it had brought him so much grief. American society had puzzled him and now he thought he had found an explanation for himself, for blacks and others.

"I'm a student of scientific socialism and this experience has a strong bearing on it. While we've been in the hole we heard a speech by Nixon. It had an impact on all of us. I can't describe in words the feeling it gave us. It was like a shock, as though we prisoners are not the only people lied to but all of the American people are lied to, that in a way everyone is a prisoner of these people."

Had all committee members come to this conclusion?

No, he said, they had different politics but they all saw the corruption in the country's institutions, they saw that the prison did what people wanted done. Irwin was not political, he said, but that was something else.

"Will is really amazing. Here was a guy who all his prison life really believed that the prison system was just, that if he did everything they wanted him to do they'd treat him straight. He really was what the staff wanted, the 'model prisoner.' I can't tell you what a shock it was to this man when they did this to him, when they said, 'Go ahead and elect a committee,' and then threw us all into solitary. He couldn't believe it. It had a really deep effect on him."

Time was running out. We said goodbye. Irwin came out. I described him in a newspaper story as looking like a neighborhood bartender, not knowing he was a reformed alcoholic.

I told him I had already talked to Meyers and Jones.

He interrupted. "I'll tell you, what they do to inmates whose politics they don't like is horrible. I don't believe the same way as some of the other guys I'm with, but I don't believe anyone has a right to tell another man what to think as long as he doesn't hurt anyone. There's no question. If you're political, if you have beliefs they don't like in prison, you get extra punishment and bad treatment."

Irwin described a change that many committeemen later put in other words. "After all my troubles in the past, for the first time I've come to realize why I was so violent whenever I got out of prison before.

"I'm ashamed of it now. Why, I'd be a wild man. I'd get out and beat people, I mean really hurt them, people I never met before, and I always thought it was because I hated people because of what happened to me in prison.

"Now I understand something. I did all those terrible things to other people because I hated myself. All my prison life I've played their game, I've been the 'model prisoner.' I've conned them, I played the rehabilitation game, I treated the staff with humble respect and I always did whatever was expected no matter how humiliating and—you know?— I always got parole! Always!

"I'd get out and beat someone, maybe in my own family, almost senseless— Jesus, I'm lucky I never killed anyone. Back I'd go to prison, and I'd do the same thing—play the con game, be bowing and scraping, accept everything. I really hated myself because I had no self-respect. I accepted irrational and dehumanizing things and said, 'Thank you.'

"Now I realize that I have self-respect. I'm doing what I feel is right and I'm not hurting anyone in the process. So now I'm in solitary and I suppose now I'll never get parole. But I don't hate myself anymore.

"For the first time I realize that it wasn't what the prison people did to me, it was what I did to myself. That's all over now. I'm no longer afraid of freedom, because I'm no longer afraid of myself. I know that in a crisis I have the moral courage to do what's right."

A bell rang. It was three o'clock.

PART THREE

Eight men now lived in cages a few feet from
each other. They did not begin this way. They
began in scattered corners of their country, in
a New Hampshire farm, a Harlem flat, a Los
Angeles barrio. They left life trails everywhere
—Florida, South Carolina, Delaware, New
Jersey, Pennsylvania, Ohio, New York, Massachusetts, Rhode Island, Canada, Kansas,
South Dakota, Colorado, Wyoming, Texas,
Missouri, California; trails in the memories of
parents, relatives, friends, enemies, lawyers,
victims; trails in school records, diaries, hundreds of letters, thousands of documents in
official files. The memories of those they
touched poured into my tape recorders and
notebooks, in small New England cottages, in
West Coast ranch houses, in Pittsburgh business offices. The scenes of the search had wild
contrasts: judges' chambers lined with red-
and-gold-bound books, dark places in central
cities with waiting figures suspicious of a
stranger asking questions, newspaper morgues
with clippings of crimes no longer common-
place, bureaucratic cubicles of probation officers whose hands sometimes concealed portions
of reports prosecutors preferred kept secret,
banks through which I walked mentally reconstructing crimes, knowing ahead of time each
detail I would see, a dozen visiting rooms of
jails and prisons. Tape cartridges in the mail
spirited from behind bars with disembodied
voices from distant places. Questions, cross-
checking, new questions, renewed memories,

deep friendships strained by more bitter questions, all of it the detritus of earlier disintegrating lives, the fragments left behind in the multiple paths that finally led to Union County, Pennsylvania, to Lewisburg Federal Penitentiary, to the last cageblock on the east end of the tile tunnel, on the second floor of the north wing, and the eight cages where the occupants, their life trails now converging in one place, lived more closely in spirit than most blood brothers.

12

PRISONER NO. 23429–145

Joel Meyers was a soldier. Not in the United States Army. That's why he was in prison. He was a soldier in the cause of communism, as eager to do battle by argument and propaganda as any Marine by screams and guns.

He marched—or rather, planned, talked, joked, dissembled, organized, manipulated, argued, cajoled, needled, conspired, dreamed— toward a vision. The vision was of a world of defeated imperialists, capitalists, colonialists, liberals, fascists, and racists, replaced by the rule of the common people expressed through communal power vigilant against the forces of oppression and counterrevolution.

Like all good fundamentalists, he believed in a Day of Judgment when "sinners shall be cast into Hell and the righteous shall rise in Heaven." In his case the Day of Judgment was the World Revolution, which would cast into hell capitalists who did not embrace the faith, and heaven would open to the workers of the world.

Like any dedicated missionary, he worked day and night to convert the faithless, to fight the iniquitous, to hasten the Day of Judgment.

He was a happy warrior in his cause. He had a humorous turn of expression, he liked the absurdities of life, his eyes sparkled most when he was in verbal combat with the enemy.

Like Paul's on the road to Damascus, Joel Meyers' conversion came in a public place, at the Hillel Gate of Brooklyn College.

He was an unpolitical math and physics major in his sophomore year. The Indochina war had impressed him mostly from a television scene of the torturing of a South Vietnamese woman suspected of being a Viet Cong. His parents were liberal Democrats who voted for John Kennedy in 1960. They, too, saw the torture scene on television. When Joel, then nineteen, said it was like Nazi Germany, his parents said America couldn't be compared with the Nazis.

On April 4, 1964, when he walked through the gate at Hillel Place, young people were handing out leaflets: "STOP THE SLAUGHTER IN VIETNAM!" It was the work of Youth Against War and Fascism, an organization he had never heard of. There is nothing Joel Meyers loves more than a debate, so he argued in favor of the war. "Don't you believe in defending this country against its enemies?"

People on the sidewalk argued back. The war was not defending the American people. The war was defending financial investments of a handful of Americans. The war was letting the capitalists make gigantic war profits at the risk of engulfing the world in war.

The leaflets they handed him announced a demonstration against profiteering on human life, to be held near a Marine procurement office at 527 Fifth Avenue. Meyers went to the demonstration and helped carry placards while walking in a circle on the sidewalk across the street.

His memory of demonstrations is precise, marked by the slogans carried on placards and in leaflets, slogans remembered in the way veterans of shooting wars remember great battles—Austerlitz, Waterloo, Concord and Lexington, Bull Run, Verdun, Bastogne, Okinawa. The placard battle of April 5, 1964, was "Stop the War in Vietnam," "Bring the Troops Home," "No More Koreas," "Vietnam for the Vietnamese," and "No American Algerias."

Meyers had argued in favor of the war the day before, so the party people were suspicious. He might be an infiltrator for the FBI, CIA or New York City police, or an *agent provocateur* urging them to commit an illegal act to trap them. Key Martin, national chairman of the Youth Against War and Fascism, asked him to join them at a nearby Automat after the demonstration.

Meyers was accepted as genuine. Martin explained that the organization had grown out of a group called the Anti-Fascist Youth Committee, a splinter off the communists who remained loyal to Leon Trotsky, who fought with Lenin and Stalin after the Russian Revolution. The "Trots" were bitter at Stalin's concentration on Russia instead of world revolution. The main Trotskyist group in the United States, the Socialist Workers Party, regarded as enemies the communist leaders of the Soviet Union, the Communist Party of the United States and regular Communists elsewhere. Youth Against War and Fascism was yet another split from the Socialist Workers Party, which the YAWF regarded as also going soft, of drifting from the goal of pure communism to something akin to democratic socialism with emphasis on individual rights. The group, like all fervent religionists, was sure that it had retrieved from weaker hands the only pure formula for the future.

Meyers learned that the group began in the early 1960s with demonstrations against George Lincoln Rockwell, leader of the American Nazi Party. In late 1962 and early 1963 they had demonstrated on three issues, which are recorded in Meyers' old-soldier memory as "Hands Off Cuba," "No War Over Berlin," and "Bring the Troops Home from Vietnam."

The current campaign of the YAWF, in addition to demonstrating against the war in Vietnam, was to support Robert F. Williams, the black ex-Marine, from Monroe, North Carolina, who had formed a defense committee against the active Ku Klux Klan, was accused of kidnapping a white couple, and who had left the United States for Cuba and China.

Meyers had never heard of the Williams case before or the Monroe Defense Committee. He was told that only the YAWF was giving the cause support. He was excited. He had been mildly interested in the civil rights movement, but he had always considered futile the nonviolent approach being used by Martin Luther King, Jr., and the Student Nonviolent Coordinating Committee.

"Nonviolence just didn't go with my experience with the way things work. The federal government, the New York State government, the Army and everything else was based to a very large degree on racism. When you were confronted with these racist brainwashed people from the South who had been terrorizing black people, I didn't see how they would just be charmed by nonviolence. Sometimes nonviolence as a tactic is all right, in a situation when the violence that can be used against you is overwhelming or when nonviolence can be used in order to make a certain moral point. But as a general policy to announce that even if you are attacked and spat upon and insulted, and that no matter what is done to you, that you are not going to return violence, that you are not going to defend yourself with violence is only to encourage them to do more."

Meyers is at his best when baited, challenged to defend his doctrines against Marxist heresies. After his release from prison we met many times, sometimes over coffee near Grand Central Station, or in the Algonquin Hotel with his bicycle chained to a tree on the sidewalk, or in my home talking into a tape recorder far into the night as he munched his beloved raw fruits and vegetables.

So I told him that his attitude toward nonviolence sounded remarkably like the basis for American foreign policy, peace through strength, deterrence through power, massive retaliation to convince enemies that the American government would meet force with greater force. Did he approve then of American international military policies?

The American government was like the white racists terrorizing powerless blacks. He was not in favor of that; he was in favor of the blacks not accepting it passively.

Did he disagree with Gandhi, who preached victory through patient pacifism?

"I didn't know much about Gandhi, but I was much more impressed with the results of the Chinese revolution than I was with anything that had taken place in India."

The YAWF had decided not to fight nonviolent protesters. It supported the Deacons, the black self-defense group that said it would meet violence with counterviolence, but it also supported the Student Nonviolent Coordinating Committee. It supported Malcolm X and the Black Panthers.

The YAWF absorbed Meyers completely. He began demonstrating, which was the primary activity of the group. Arrests at demonstrations are taken for granted, welcomed as having provoked the system and proving the heroism of party members. Meyers' first arrest was at a demonstration at the offices of Local 2 of the AFL-CIO plumbers' union, George Meany's original union, which had excluded blacks from membership. A plumber trying to get into the office claimed that a demonstrator had slammed the office door on his arm. The police arrested everyone near the scene.

Meyers was charged with assault and was acquitted. In the next few years he was arrested seven times, with either acquittal or charges dropped. It was a standard tactic of police to make arrests to end demonstrations and then dismiss charges.

Physics and mathematics became less interesting. Meyers attended classes but did little work. He took off whole semesters to do organizing and placard-painting for the YAWF. His parents were distressed at his lessening interest in college and his involvement in radical politics. His father was a cab driver and fender and auto body repair mechanic; the family lived in a white working-class neighborhood in Brooklyn of Jews, Italians and Irish. There was no sharp hostility to blacks at that time, and Jews especially tended to be sympathetic to civil rights.

Surrounding neighborhoods were upper class, with some class resentment.

When Meyers was twelve he and friends would play on the Long Island Railroad tracks, climbing a forbidden fence. A boy who was caught would be put in a police cruiser, his jacket pulled over his head, and he would be pummeled by policemen in the back seat, the jacket concealing identities and reducing visible bruises. Children of the neighborhood assumed that police were their enemy.

His parents never questioned his interest in civil rights. But they remembered the anti-communist hysteria of the Joseph McCarthy era and feared their son would get in trouble that would spoil a promising career in physics. In the fall of 1965 Meyers decided to go to Buffalo, where YAWF had started.

On February 12, 1962, exactly one month after his eighteenth birthday, Joel Meyers had received a questionnaire from the chief clerk of Local Board 35, Selective Service. As a full-time student at Brooklyn College he was classified 2-S, a student deferment, until June 1, 1965, when he might be expected to graduate.

In November of 1965 he was notified that he was reclassified 1-A, eligible for immediate induction into the armed services, on the grounds that he had left Brooklyn College. So he enrolled in four courses at the University of Buffalo and on the basis of that received his student deferment again. He almost never attended classes and flunked all four courses. It was inconceivable to him that he would ever actually be called to the Army. Besides, he was far more interested in other things in Buffalo.

While he was technically enrolled in the university he was, among other things, working in a rubber factory, testing samples of plastic cases for radios. Three activities—the job at the rubber factory that supported him at two dollars an hour, his political work, and college studies—were too much. There was no question in his mind that college had to be dropped.

His political work was organizing demonstrations, including on the Buffalo campus. Martin Sostre, later to become one of the best-known American prisoners engaged in warfare with the prison system, operated a bookstore in Buffalo, and Meyers spent hours of debate in Sostre's store.

From 1962, Meyers had conducted a seven-year war with the Selective Service Administration. In September 1966 he was ordered to report for physical examination on October 6. He did not report. The board clerk called his mother, who said she would tell Joel to send the board his address in Buffalo. In December Meyers went to the board and said he had never received the September notice to report. On the form he wrote, "The reason I did not respond to correspondence from this draft board is that I never received it." He wrote that he had applied to Millard Fillmore College in Buffalo. He was ordered to take his physical ten days later. He passed. He also complied with the rule to keep the board informed of his changes of address. He wrote, "Joel Meyers, c/o Partisan and Workers World . . ."

On April 20, 1967, he received Form SSS-252, a message received by several million Americans of his generation:

The President of the United States to:
Mr. Joel Simon Meyers, 484 Fourth Avenue, Buffalo, New York.
　Greetings:
You are hereby ordered for induction into the Armed Forces Examining and Entrance Station, Building No. 116, Ft. Hamilton, Brooklyn, N.Y., on May 4, 1967, at 7:30 A.M. for forwarding to an Armed Forces induction station.

This is usually the end of anyone's joust with the United States Army. But Meyers sees life not as a single battle with victory or defeat but as a continuing struggle with merely temporary ups and downs. Two days before the deadline he reappeared before the draft board clerk. "I lost the forms that were sent to me last week. I need some duplicates." He was given a full set, including Form DD-398, a statement of personal history.

He filled it out.

Question 16: Past and/or present membership in organizations.
Answer: This is a general question which pries into an individual's private affairs and violates his freedom of speech and which I refuse to answer on principle.
Question 17: Are you now or have you ever been a member of the Communist Party, USA, or any Communist organization anywhere?
Are you now or have you ever been a member of a Fascist organization?
Are you now or have you ever been a member of any organization, association, movement, group or combination of persons which advocated the overthrow of our Constitutional form of government . . . or which seeks to alter the form of government of the United States by unconstitutional means?
Are you now associated with, or have you associated with any individuals, including relatives, who you know or have reason to believe are or have

been members of any of the organizations identified above?

Have you ever engaged in any of the following activities of any organization of the type described above . . . ?

Answer: This is a question which pries into an individual's private affairs to an even greater degree than the preceding items. . . . I refuse to answer.

Question 18: Have you ever been detained, held, arrested, indicted, or summoned into court . . . ?

Answer: Arrested on trumped up charge of simple assault while participating in a Civil Rights demonstration in May, 1964. Acquitted in 1965.

Question 19: Any incidents in your life . . . which might reflect upon your loyalty to the United States . . . ?

Answer: No.

He added an explanation:

I refuse to participate in the genocidal war being waged by the U.S. Government against the Vietnamese people. It is a bonanza for the war corporations by a slaughter of the American youth. The American bankers want to use us as tools to protect their investments all over the world. The American military is both a brutal murder crew used against the world's oppressed and a cruel trick to dupe hundreds of thousands of American youths into sacrificing their lives to the interest of Wall Street's financial oligarchy. . . .

The draft is an instrument of slave labor. To submit to the draft is to risk one's life and to offer to serve as an accomplice to war crimes defined in the Nuremberg Agreements, which hold the individual responsible to refuse to cooperate in any way with such atrocious acts. Joel Meyers, May 3, 1967.

The wheels of induction bureaucracy ground on, not having read Meyers' answers to Form DD-398.

On the morning of May 4, 1967, Joel Meyers reported to the induction examination center at Fort Hamilton, Brooklyn. Two party friends went with him as observers for what they knew would be an unorthodox proceeding.

About a hundred young men were crowded into Room 108, the "control room."

The Army routine had been followed for numberless days. Joseph J. Weber had spent two years in charge of "flow of men and the paper work" for the special procedure by which youths enter as civilians and exit as soldiers. He had done it hundreds of times.

Sometime between seven and seven-thirty, when between fifty and one hundred men are in the room, he "orients" them. He has two desks in front of the room and seats the men in the 110 plastic chairs set closely in rows. He explains what they will do that day, when they will eat lunch, whether they will fly to their new base or take trains. Any questions?

Then he takes roll call from his clipboard list of men ordered to report that morning and hands out forms. The men are then sent for a quick medical examination to be sure nothing catastrophic has occurred between the original physical and induction day.

After lunch the men file into the "oath room," where they are asked to step forward and take their oath. If it is a heavy load, the oath-room ceremony is not until four-thirty. If it is light, it might be as early as three. When the induction ceremony is over the men are fed dinner and taken to the airport or train station.

Daniel M. Smith, specialist fourth class, was the enlisted man ordered to handle the first step for this particular batch of a hundred men on the morning of May 4. The room seemed especially unsettled, so it was 7:45 before the men were seated on the plastic chairs. He was already fifteen minutes behind schedule and he had not even handed out forms. He noticed that most of them already had a paper in their hands. He looked at a sheet being read by an inductee. It was not an official form of the United States Army. It was dated Thursday, May 4, 1967:

> Like you, I have been ordered to report today for induction into the Armed Forces.
>
> We may be sent to Vietnam this summer, sent to spill blood in the war against the peasant guerillas. But the millionaires who own the huge corporations raking in lush profits from war contracts will be living it up.
>
> While they laugh and sing on the Riviera, they will be forcing us to leave our friends and families, ordering us to muddy deaths in jungles half-way around the world, in order to defend *their* far-flung properties and investments.
>
> While those of us who get crippled in the war spend the prime of our lives watching ourselves rot in Veterans' hospitals, they will have made their pile over what's left of our bodies. . . .
>
> It is an imperialist war of aggression . . . we will be ordered to commit atrocities as hideous as those of the *NAZIS* and to use genocidal weapons such as anti-personnel bombs, poison gas and napalm. . . . According to the Nuremberg Agreements we are personally responsible to refuse to carry out such orders . . . we should identify with the victims of the war—the Vietnamese people. . . . All who do will refuse to step forward today, saying NO!!
>
> *I WILL NOT TAKE UP ARMS AGAINST MY BROTHERS!!*

It was signed, in mimeograph, "Joel Meyers, member, Youth Against War and Fascism, Tel: 242-9225."

Specialist Fourth Class Smith quickly took the literature out of the hands of the men. "Who's passing this stuff out?"

The short, plump fellow with brown hair said, "I am!"

Specialist Smith told him to stop.

Meyers said he would not. "I'm an American civilian exercising my freedom of speech."

The inductees by now were staring at the scene and murmuring.

Meyers stood on a chair. "Just because you are in the military doesn't mean you can prevent me from exercising my constitutional right to free speech. In fact, because you're in the military it's your duty to protect that right."

The murmurs of the seated men got louder.

"Don't go through with induction. They just want you as cannon fodder for the bankers' war, for Johnson's war."

Meyers started handing out more flyers. "Don't let them railroad you into the Army! Don't go to Vietnam to murder innocent people!"

One inductee let out a strangled sound. "You son of a bitch, I got a brother over there!"

The man stood up. He was trapped by the closely packed men in the plastic chairs. He stood on a chair and started climbing over the backs, knocking the chairs to the floor in his eagerness to get to Meyers.

Meyers moved out of his aisle of chairs, knocking over some more.

Specialist Fourth Class Smith left the room hurriedly and came back with a lieutenant.

The lieutenant demanded to know what was going on.

"I'm handing out this literature as an exercise of my constitutional rights as a citizen of the United States and it's your duty as an officer in the Army to defend those rights."

"Stop handing out that paper as long as you're on this base!"

The men in the room watched as the shouting went from the officer in the front of the room and Meyers in the middle of the room.

Meyers shouted, "Why are you afraid of people saying these things about the war? You don't want us to know what this is all about. You just want us to function as ignorant puppets and robots. And get killed so that these other people can get rich off the war. Is that why they pay you, to prevent us from expressing our opinion that's supposed to be our right?"

Some of the inductees were listening and watching silently. Others were shouting at Meyers, "Shut up! Sit down!"

The lieutenant said, "You'd better stop distributing that literature or I'll have to call the MP's."

"I'm going to continue to exercise my constitutional right to distribute this literature and if you want to interfere with my rights, go ahead and call the MP's."

The lieutenant went out and came back with an elderly sergeant with multiple service stripes on his sleeve and a slow, unruffled air. The sergeant walked calmly to Meyers and said in a soft voice, "Son, you're just going to have to stop handing out those things. The provost marshal wants you to come with me to his office. He wants you to tell him why you feel you have to disrupt this induction ceremony."

Meyers did not move. "I was ordered to report to this room for induction by the draft board and you have no right to countermand that order. I'm not going to be tricked into leaving this room so you can say I disobeyed that order. If the provost marshal has anything to ask me, then let him come here. I'd like to have everybody else you're trying to send over to Vietnam hear what this provost marshal has to say. Tell your boss that."

More of the men in the room were yelling angrily at Meyers. He was yelling back at them that they were being tricked. Some of the inductees were arguing with each other.

Two MP's entered the room and surveyed the scene with distaste. One asked Meyers for the leaflets. Meyers carefully handed one each to the MP's. One of the MP's put his hand on Meyers' shoulder and told him to sit down and cooperate. Meyers brushed the MP's hand off his shoulder. The inductees surrounded the three men. The noise level in the room was getting higher. The MP's each took one of Meyers' arms and led him forcefully to the back of the room.

Meyers shouted at them, "Take your hands off me! I'm a civilian and you have no authority over me!"

"You're on a federal reservation now and an MP has authority over civilians on this reservation. It's on the sign at the gate."

"I'm standing on my constitutional rights!"

By this time, one inductee, shouting curses at Meyers, ran over chairs, knocking them over, desperate to get his hands on him.

The MP's saw the approaching man. "If you don't come quietly we'll have to carry you out."

They started to take him by the arms. Meyers broke away and moved to the other side of the room from the MP's and the inductee who was trying to reach him. The three headed down an aisle of chairs to the other side of the room. The MP's divided to block off both ends of the row of chairs with Meyers in the center, so Meyers jumped over two rows and ran down that row to the side of the room. One of the MP's reached him and pushed him down into a chair, but Meyers twisted away and ran down the row again. Several of the inductees were joining in the chase, shouting and cursing, while Meyers shouted back a running commentary:

"I was ordered to this room and I'm staying here! I didn't ask to come here! Your superiors ordered me to!"

People were running in and out among the chairs, which were toppling to the floor like dominoes.

Four more MP's ran into the room and cornered Meyers. They put handcuffs on his wrists behind his back, dragged him out of the room and threw him into the back seat of an MP car. Someone pulled his jacket over his head and through it he felt fists pummeling him, the same technique of the Brooklyn police with kids playing on the railroad tracks. The MP's took him into the provost marshal's office.

The provost marshal was at his desk, busy with a telephone call. Meyers waited awkwardly, his hands handcuffed behind him. It seemed to Meyers that the officer was on the telephone for half an hour, but finally he hung up and said to one of the MP's, "Is this the one?"

The provost marshal turned angrily to Meyers. "Okay, I want you to leave these premises and I'm warning you never to return to this reservation. You'll be hearing from your draft board. Escort him to the gate."

They took off the handcuffs at the gate and repeated the warning not to come back.

It was all over by eight-thirty. Meyers' friends were waiting for him at the gate and they left, congratulating themselves.

Meyers had accomplished his purpose. He was a hero of the Youth Against War and Fascism. Their paper, *Workers World,* carrying the slogan at the top of page one, "Workers and Oppressed Peoples of the World Unite!," had a long story with the headline:

YOUTH DEFIES INDUCTION
TELLS DRAFTEES "DON'T GO"

Fort Hamilton Army Base, N.Y., May 4—Armed with anti-war leaflets and accompanied by several fellow members of Youth Against War and Fascism, Joel Meyers reported for induction into the Armed Forces early this morning.

It said that he had no intention of being inducted but distributed leaflets to others urging them not to go. The story repeated the language on the flyer Meyers had distributed in the control room. The story reported statements said to have been shouted by Meyers to the officials: "No!! I will not take up arms against my brothers!! Bring all the GIs home now!!"

Meyers was not worried. As usual, he had done his homework on resistance.

When inductees for some reason failed to appear or offered an impediment to induction they were sent a second notice to report. If that failed they often received a third notice to report but were ordered to a private induction where they could not agitate before an audience. If that failed they would then be charged with evasion of the draft.

He was living in Buffalo at the time and within two days of the episode at Fort Hamilton returned to Buffalo. The Buffalo ghetto was in turmoil, like ghettos all over the United States. The Sostre bookstore was a haven where blacks could run off leaflets and read radical and revolutionary literature. When a rebellion broke out in the city's ghetto, law enforcement authorities moved against sources they speculated might have contributed to the outbreak. Among the arrests was that of Martin Sostre on the charge of possession of narcotics. Some people were convinced the charge was false, the narcotics planted as part of a police campaign to imprison radicals. Meyers said he, too, was convinced, since he had spent dozens of hours with Sostre in the bookstore and saw no sign of narcotics or narcotics trade.

The arrest of Sostre and other retaliations against suspected radicals confirmed Meyers' conviction in the rightness of his party's rigid doctrine. The YAWF had attacked the Socialist Workers Party for approving the use of federal troops to prevent violence against integrating blacks in the South. The YAWF believed that eventually the government would turn against any genuine acquisition of power by the black community, that a sympathetic intervention in early stages would only provide a public smokescreen for later reversal. The YAWF argued that oppressed communities like black ghettos ought to arm in self-defense against police and troops who try to occupy their neighborhoods. The YAWF, like the National Rifle Association, was firmly against gun control.

In Buffalo Meyers helped organize the Martin Sostre Defense Committee. On the morning of July 19 he worked long after midnight, putting together a leaflet. At three A.M. he got on his three-speed bicycle and rode to his apartment in the Lakeview public housing project on the lower west side of Buffalo. He set his alarm clock for six A.M. in order to make the morning shift at the rubber factory.

He had just fallen asleep when he became aware of a flashlight shining in his eyes. He could make out the figure of a man holding out a card and two other men holding pistols. The man with the flashlight said, "Federal agents. Let's go."

Meyers assumed that it was the start of what every radical fears, the roundup of all radicals and revolutionaries in a nationwide move to concentration camps. He was sure it was related to his work on the Sostre Defense Committee.

"What's this all about?"

"You'll find out."

The three men in civilian clothes watched him dress, handcuffed his wrists and attached them to a chain they had locked around his waist.

"Do you have a warrant?"

One of the men grabbed him by the seat of his pants and his collar and pushed him against the wall. "That's our warrant."

On the way out Meyers saw his apartment door lying on the floor. He is still curious about it, because he is not ordinarily a good sleeper, is sensitive to small noises, and never heard the door coming down.

When he emerged, handcuffed, from his apartment it was dawn. A man across the street was repeatedly polishing the same spot on the roof of his car. Another man was walking a poodle, watching everything silently. Both men had highly polished shoes. Meyers had never noticed a poodle before in the poor municipal housing block.

He discovered for certain that it was the FBI when he asked and was told inside the car. They took him to the FBI office in the post office building. A picture and story appeared in the Buffalo paper that day but the picture was one Meyers had never seen before. He claims it was retouched to make him look ferocious, that during his political organizing he always looked and dressed very straight, stayed clean-shaven with a Marine brush haircut, to make it easier to communicate with people without rousing hostility.

Inside the FBI office the agents made small talk, expressing the hope that Muhammad Ali would be beaten in his next boxing match. Meyers was convinced that it was all part of a science of getting people to relax and say incriminating things. He remained silent. He was also profoundly frightened. He had visions of a great national roundup, wide-scale hysteria, concentration camps, torture to reveal friends and associates. He remained silent and stonefaced until he was taken later that morning before a United States commissioner and charged with violation of T-50, X United States Code, Section 462 (a)—the Selective Service Act. He sighed in relief.

He was taken to the Erie County Jail and the next day released under $2500 bail.

He returned to Brooklyn, where his parents were supportive but terrified.

Between the time of his arrest and his final imprisonment Joel Meyers got married.

Early in 1965, while living in Buffalo, he attended a meeting of the Young Socialist Alliance in Detroit. Pamela lived with her divorced mother, a politically active progressive in Milwaukee. She and Meyers met and talked politics—Meyers is more comfortable with impersonal subjects. Three years later, after Meyers' disrupted induction and arrest, Pamela attended a New York convention of the Youth Against War and Fascism. This time they went out on a Saturday night date. She came back to New York to visit Meyers two or three times and then in October of 1968 began to live with him. She was at his trial with a contingent of other YAWF members.

Meyers was indicted on two counts: failing to report for induction and interfering with administration of the Military Training and Service Act. He liked to describe it, "I got indicted on two counts. One was failing to report for induction. The other one was for disrupting the induction that I failed to report for."

Meyers was represented by two lawyers from the American Civil Liberties Union. The trial began April 3, 1968. The clerk made the conventional announcement: "The United States of America against Joel Simon Meyers . . ."

The clerk of his local draft board read Meyers' previously unnoticed attack upon the draft and the Indochina war in his form DD-398, part of the prosecution assertion that he never had a sincere intention of being inducted. When she read his words "The draft is an instrument of slave labor," his friends in the courtroom burst into applause.

Judge Walter Bruchhausen said, "You stop that! If this occurs again, you are all going out of this courtroom!"

Scenes at the induction center were testified to by government witnesses.

The defense presented no witnesses. One of Meyers' lawyers, Thomas H. Baer, summed up to the jury: "There is absolutely nothing wrong with giving out leaflets in this country. . . . It has never been a crime in this country to be unhappy about going in the Army or to retain ideas that you might think are right while you are in the Army. . . . Now, I say to you, if the Army can't deal with a man giving out leaflets . . . there is something wrong."

Michael Rosen, Assistant United States Attorney prosecuting the case, told the jury, "What about a man's obligation to serve his country? . . . If you leave Mr. Meyers . . . what happens to the other hundred men? . . . Did he report for induction? Sure, after he was removed, by coincidence, his friends were waiting outside of the gate. Nice job! . . . We ask that you don't say, 'Okay, Mr. Meyers. You beat it. Nice job.' "

The jury went out at eleven-forty in the morning. During the deliberations a marshal carried a note on a yellow pad to the judge. It said, "Count I and II Hopelessly Deadlocked; Vote—11 guilty, 1 not guilty. The one dissenter . . ." Someone has obliterated a phrase after "dissenter" on the note in the official files.

At four-ten P.M. the jury came back to say they couldn't reach a decision. The judge told them that deducting their time out for lunch they had deliberated only two hours and he read them the Allen Charge, sometimes called the "Dynamite Charge," to urge a deadlocked jury to resolve their differences and come to a verdict.

". . . jurors should examine the questions . . . with a proper regard and deference to the opinions of each other. . . . You should listen to each other's arguments with a disposition to be convinced." It puts pressure on the minority in a jury. Half an hour later they returned, finding Meyers guilty on count one, failing to appear for induction, and not guilty of interfering with induction.

At ten A.M. of May 17, 1968, Judge Bruchhausen prepared for sentencing. He noted that the courtroom once again was packed by Meyers' friends.

Attorney Baer told the judge, "I am surprised to find that those people are sitting here, because I have advised the defendant that it is to his benefit that they should not be here. . . . He has indicated to me that he wants them to be here."

Baer turned to the sentencing. "I think he is a person who can and will make a contribution to society. He is not a criminal. He is not a criminal type. He is twenty-four years old, he has a sister who is nineteen years old. His folks are hard-working people. His dad is a cab driver. If Your Honor imposes a jail sentence here, Joel Meyers may not come back from the institution . . . the same man he is today."

The judge asked Meyers if he wanted to say anything before sentencing. Asking that question of Meyers at a dramatic moment before the full state apparatus with an audience of friends was like asking him if he wanted to breathe.

"I would just like to say the sentence should not be passed, because I didn't have a fair trial. It is true the jury was not of my peers and it is true that prejudices were made by both the prosecution and the court. But what is more important is the fact whoever the judge, whoever the prosecutor, and whoever the jury, the courts are organized as tools of those same money-interest people who profit extensively from the blood of good people. He is an instrument to induce violence for the benefit of hungry bankers whose properties are scattered around the world. The court exists within the framework of imperialism which causes unconstitutional laws to be enforced for the use of the country to complete a war against the Vietnamese people and also to complete a war against the black people over here. Both wars, of course, are frame-ups.

"Finally, I would like to take this occasion to declare my solidarity with all the other anti-imperialists around the world, at home and abroad and particularly the National Liberation Front of South Vietnam."

Applause broke out again. The audience was admonished again.

The judge then sentenced Joel Meyers to four years in prison.

Meyers was released on bail while his lawyers appealed.

He and Pam were living in a $100-a-month single-room apartment on East Third Street on the Lower East Side of Manhattan. He needed a job. He found one loading trucks at a Brooklyn warehouse. He filled out an employment application asking if he had ever been arrested and he answered no. After a couple of weeks the firm got around to its regular fingerprinting for warehousemen. The fingerprint check showed that Meyers had lied about never being arrested, and he was fired.

There was no crisis. In a few days Meyers found another job, doing silk-screening in a Jamaica printing plant. He was skilled in silk-screening—YAWF slogans and catchwords are emblazoned in Meyers' memory partly because he silk-screened them so many times.

The couple did well economically given their modest demands in living standards. He made a hundred dollars a week and Pam, working in a temple of capitalism, a brokerage house on Wall Street, made eighty.

The bond that originally attracted them continued in their intense activity. They had an unending schedule of meetings and were occupied almost every night until at least ten P.M., sometimes planning demonstrations, inventing slogans, printing banners and leaflets. The rest of their available time was devoted to the ritual agony of the left, debates on proper policy, politically correct analysis of world events, microscopic examination of ideological purity.

YAWF and the Workers World Party had started a new magazine, *Partisan*. Meyers wrote articles, edited, laid out photos and pages, often until four or five in the morning. One night he worked until five A.M., reported late at his silk-screening job and was fired.

He looked in the New York *Times* classified ads and noticed that there was a constant demand for bookkeepers. He picked an ad for an office easy to reach on his bus route and telephoned. The job was still open and he made an appointment for an hour later. He had never done any bookkeeping. He put on a proper shirt and tie and went to the Barnes and Noble bookstore on Fifth Avenue and Eighteenth Street, where he found a paperbound book on accounting. He boarded the Houston Street crosstown bus and studied the book. He memorized chapter titles. "Accounts Payable," "Accounts Receivable," "Bank Reconciliation," "Justification," "Trial Balances." He relied on his inherent chutzpah to get him through the interview on chapter titles, and if he got the job he could read the book that night.

Before he went into the office he put the book inside the pocket of his raincoat. He gave as a former place of employment a printing company and the telephone number of a friend who would know how to reply to inquiries. He told the office manager he had served in the Army at Fort Sill. The man asked what kind of bookkeeping he could do.

"Well, the usual things. Accounts payable, accounts receivable, bank reconciliation, justification, trial balances."

The man told him to come in the next day and a supervisor would break him in.

That night he read enough of the accounting book to see that each office had its own way of keeping books, so he didn't bother finishing the book. He did very well as a bookkeeper and was paid $170 a week.

Meyers' venture into the clerical base of free enterprise ended with a demonstration. On October 15, 1969, there was a nationwide call by peace activists for a moratorium on the war. Meyers had discovered that among the thirty people in the office some were strongly against the war and others neutral, but no one dared ask for time off for the moratorium march because it was a work day. Meyers told the other workers that he would get the day off for the moratorium. The office staff didn't believe he could do it. A few days before the moratorium Meyers asked the boss, a liberal against the war, if he could have Wednesday off "for personal reasons." The boss said he could if he would make up the missed work. Coming out of the office, Meyers told the other bookkeepers, "It's okay. He said I could go to the moratorium." A half dozen others walked instantly into the office.

Soon the boss came storming out. "What's the idea of telling these people that I said it's okay to go to the moratorium?"

"You told me I could take that day off and I'm not a privileged character here. If I can go, they can go."

On the day of the moratorium much of the staff called in "sick" and the office had to close. A few days later the boss called in Meyers and said that he lacked the skills needed, that he was being let go and that it had nothing to do with the moratorium.

Meyers' Selective Service conviction had been going through the courts. The Court of Appeals had upheld the conviction two to one, the dissenting judge saying that Meyers had not been given a chance to take the oath and that the Allen Charge had been unjustified, presumably because the judge knew there was only one juror holding out.

It went to the Supreme Court.

Two weeks after he was fired as a bookkeeper he was riding the F train in the subway, reading a New York *Daily News* he found on the seat beside him. As he scanned the tabloid he saw a news item. His appeal to the Supreme Court had failed. He got off the train and called his lawyer, who confirmed the news and said it was all over. Meyers would have to prepare for prison and surrender at nine A.M., November 24.

Prison had been taken for granted when Meyers and Pam were married. The formality of their legal marriage meant nothing but had been performed because they knew that communications with a prisoner would be difficult for an unmarried woman. They exchanged rings made, they told friends, of metal from an American bomber shot down in Vietnam.

For the next two weeks they prepared for the event of his surrender. Naturally it would be an occasion for a demonstration by the party. At least 200 members were mobilized. The surrender placards were silk-screened and banners hand-painted the night before. The placards read

"Big Firms Get Rich, GIs Die." Meyers personally painted the banner designed to be carried by two members: "Free Joel Meyers, Anti-Imperialist Draft Evader!"

Inside the courtroom his lawyers asked for a reduction of sentence. Judge Bruchhausen reduced the four years to three and a half. Without much said or done, Joel Meyers went with marshals through one door and his wife and friends went out through another. At first he was taken to the West Street Federal Detention Center and then by bus to the medium-security prison at Danbury, Connecticut, as Prisoner No. 23429–145.

After a few months Meyers was transferred to the minimum-security camp outside of Lewisburg—Allenwood. He had been at Allenwood three months when there was a strike at "the wall," Lewisburg. Mysteriously there appeared everywhere in Allenwood an announcement that "The National Convicts Council"—a spontaneous invention of Meyers and his friends—had called a strike at Allenwood in support of the strikers at Lewisburg. Prisoners kept telling Meyers and his friends that the radio said the Lewisburg strike was over. Meyers told them the radio was lying. But the radio report was true. Warden Alldredge sent a message saying he would consider the grievances of the strikers at Allenwood and if they committed no violence there would be no reprisals. The strikers went back to work. The Lewisburg strike had been over in forty-five minutes. Allenwood had stayed out two days in support of it.

Within two weeks most of the inner group that had organized the strike had been arrested for other things. One for malingering on the job. Meyers had made a figure out of wet paper and a sock and stuck pins in it. An associate warden saw the figure on Meyers' locker and asked what it was. Meyers said it was a voodoo doll. The officer asked Meyers how it worked. Meyers said that if you stick pins in it the person it represents gets sick or has trouble.

"Does it work, Meyers?"

"If you have faith in it."

The next day Meyers was arrested. He was told that he might be prosecuted for conspiring to bring harm to a federal officer or under an old law against practicing witchcraft on a federal reservation. After two weeks he was brought before the adjustment committee and charged with the less exotic offense of strike agitation. He was found guilty, withdrawn from the honor camp and transferred back to Danbury. Within days he was arrested with a leaflet in his pocket calling for a strike in Danbury. He was transferred to Lewisburg Federal Penitentiary, where he became a regular prisoner in the wall on February 4, 1970. He had been in federal custody less than fifteen months, and on his prison record he already had two strikes against him.

13

PRISONER NO. 36218–133

His first memories were of a railroad flat near Third Avenue and 127th Street in Harlem, called "railroad" because the rooms were in a row, like freight cars, and to go from one end of the tenement to the other required passing through the intervening rooms.

It was not the worst poverty of Harlem. He lived in an atmosphere poor but proud, puritanical and churchgoing, stern discipline mixed with love. His mother loved him and his stepfather was friendly. His grandmother loved him and her husband liked him. One day he would rise from rags to riches. In the playbook of the American dream Clarence Jones's childhood had the foundation of a great success, and, indeed, if he had been born a hundred years earlier, in a different skin, he might have been celebrated for his business acumen, his fortune sanitized and multiplied by the passage of time and, here and there, perhaps, a Clarence Jones Memorial Library. That he became a criminal imprisoned in the worst incarceration his government possessed was, in a sense, a cultural-historical accident.

During his earliest years his mother traveled with her common-law husband. So Clarence lived with his grandmother and her common-law husband in a household that included an aunt and uncle and a younger brother and sister. His grandmother taught him numbers, addition and the letters of the alphabet when Clarence was three. She and her husband were puritans who didn't drink, didn't smoke and attended church at least twice a week.

His mother's husband was a roving labor contractor who supplied workers for growers, including for potato fields around Bridgehampton on eastern Long Island. When the grandfather received a large settlement from a construction work accident, they bought an old house in the black neighborhood of Bridgehampton.

In 1952, when Clarence was almost six, his mother made one of her periodic stopovers in Bridgehampton and registered him in school. The principal wanted to put him in kindergarten, but Clarence was tall for his age and even then walked tall. His mother asked that he be placed in the first grade. After two weeks the first grade teacher said he was ready for second grade and his mother left on her next trip happy that her favorite son was well started in school.

The second grade class was a joy. Clarence especially liked the model community they built on a tabletop. Children were asked to bring model cars and homes and people for it. Clarence had no toys, but a white friend in his class brought a jeep that Clarence fell in love with. One afternoon Clarence quietly put the jeep in his lunchbox. The teacher reported it to his grandmother.

That night his grandmother and grandfather called him into the kitchen. They were standing together, expressionless. His grandmother told him to lower his pants and lean over the seat of a chair. He looked behind and saw her pick up the wide leather strap his grandfather used for sharpening his straight razor. She struck him on the naked buttocks three times. He shrieked. Then she handed the strap to her husband, who began hitting him like a machine. Clarence couldn't cry anymore. His grandfather didn't stop. His grandmother said, "That's enough!" But the strap kept rising and falling. She repeated twice more, "That's enough!" Finally she grabbed her husband's hand and forced the strap from his fingers. Clarence had never been struck by an adult before.

In December when his mother visited he insisted on leaving his grandparents and traveling with her. His mother was a tall, warm, pretty woman, a romantic who read *True Confessions* and *Ebony*. She gave her children affection and now she took Clarence and his younger brother and sister.

The next scene in Clarence's memory is of Florida, where he saw his first palm trees and remembers his stepfather sinking an old bathtub into a back yard for the children to play in. And then he remembers South Carolina.

His mother's husband, Rip, supplied migrant workers in old buses and stake trucks to growers along the Eastern Seaboard. He was a flashy dude who drove a Hudson with a raccoon tail, whitewalls and a spotlight with a handle inside the car. He won Clarence's loyalty early in their travels by performing the shell game and then quietly disclosing its secret to the six-year-old boy. He would put half a walnut shell over a pea and then shift that shell with another like it in circles and mixed movements on the tabletop until it was impossible to remember which was the original shell. No matter how many times he did it, Clarence never picked the shell with the pea under it. One afternoon when they were alone, Rip went through the game very slowly. At the moment that he seemed to be placing the pea under the original shell he passed his hand, palm down, toward the pea as though pushing it under the shell, but actually glided over the pea and smoothly caught it between the folds of his palm. The pea was never under either shell. It was always in Rip's palm. Rip could spread his fingers and appear to be empty-handed. Clarence practiced by the hour until he was perfect. Then he tried it with stones, pennies and dice until he could fool sophisticated adults.

The tomato-picking stop in South Carolina was long enough so that his mother registered Clarence in the local school. It was the first time he had attended a school where all the students and all the teachers were black. On his first day the teacher told him she could tell he was from the North and said, disapprovingly, that he had better mind his manners. The children sat with their hands folded on their desks. She asked a question. Clarence, as he had in the New York school, called out the answer spontaneously. The teacher told him to come to her desk at the front of the class. She asked why he didn't raise his hand before speaking. He mumbled in confusion. She told him to hold out his hands, palms up. She reached into her desk drawer, pulled out a rubber strap and slammed it down twice on his palms. The next day the teacher called him to the front of the class again for an infraction he can't remember. This time she kept beating his palms without stopping. The memory of his grandfather's strap flashed through him. He grabbed at the strap to stop it, the teacher grabbed back, he pulled it and the teacher tripped and fell to the floor.

The principal made him wait until his mother arrived and then without preamble began yelling at both of them. From the disjointed admonition, his mother pieced together the fact that Clarence had been hit with a strap not only today but yesterday. She chastised her son for not telling her about it the night before. Then she asked what it was for. When told, she denounced the principal, his teachers and his school, took Clarence in hand and never returned.

It was in South Carolina that Clarence first came into close contact with the migrant workers herded by his stepfather. His family lived in an apartment at one end of a barrackslike building next to the tomato fields. The migrant workers lived in a dormitory at the other end, territory forbidden to the children. So they spent hours peering at life at the other end. When the workers came in from the fields there was always excitement, cardplaying, drinking wine, smoking odd-looking cigarettes the men called "reefers," and occasionally a man staggering out of the latrine with a spoon and needle in his hand and collapsing loosely on a bed.

Most fascinating of all was the visit every other weekend of cars full of women who distributed themselves among the dormitories. His stepfather seemed to be in charge. Clarence was seven years old, but he felt instinctively that something exciting was happening. One Saturday while his mother was outside, he sneaked down to the other end of the building. He opened a door. On the bed was one of the visiting women, naked, and on top of her one of the men workers, naked. The man looked at Clarence over his shoulder, grunted in recognition, and then turned back to continue his sexual intercourse. Clarence watched transfixed while the two continued. After a while the man put on his clothes and walked past him out the door. Another migrant worker came in, pushed Clarence outside and closed the door.

When he got back to his end of the building, his mother and some of the women workers were sitting inside their living room. One of the women joked that the building would "collapse with all the fucking goin' on."

His mother bristled. "Don't use that language in front of the child."

One of the women cackled. "What you mean, don't use that language in front of the chile? He down there watching it!"

His mother asked him if it was true. He nodded. She told the women to go outside and took Clarence into the bedroom. What did he do at the other end of the building?

"I watched them doing it."

"Doing what?"

"Fucking."

"Don't use that word!"

"Well, you asked me."

She chastised him for breaking the rule about going to the other end of the building. She said nothing about what he saw.

They spent the next five years moving up and down the East Coast —Florida in the dead of winter, Middle Atlantic states in spring and early summer, New Jersey and New York in late summer and fall— like migratory birds following paths on an Audubon map. He was never in one school for more than three months at a time.

In December of 1958 they were driving to New York to spend Christmas with the rest of the family and stayed overnight near the empty South Carolina camp. December 2 was Clarence Jones's twelfth birthday and his father drove Clarence and his younger brother into Charleston. He parked the car in front of a large house. Inside, his father was greeted by a motherly woman. The two adults disappeared for a time and then returned, his father laughing. He said to the boys, "I've got some business to do in town. She'll take care of you."

After Rip left, the woman said, "Are you Clarence?" He nodded.

"Come with me, Clarence."

They went upstairs. The woman opened a door. He saw a room with a chair, a night table with an ashtray, and a bed. On the bed a woman in a robe was sitting, smoking a cigarette. She looked old to him. Later he guessed that she was twenty years old. She looked at him coolly. "Well, do you smoke?"

"No, ma'am."

"Do you drink?"

"Not real drinks."

"What do you want to do?"

"I don't know."

"Do you want to fuck?"

He stood frozen and excited. He had never done it before but he had seen it.

"Take your clothes off, boy."

She stubbed out her cigarette and took off her robe. She was naked underneath. He stripped off his clothes. She was patient with him and he spent fifteen minutes at his first adult sex. By the time he had dressed and was walking down the stairs his father was coming in the front door. The motherly woman said, "How was it, Clarence?" Clarence grinned and nodded enthusiastically. His father patted him on the shoulder. His brother, two years younger, asked what it was. His father patted the brother on the shoulder and said, "On your twelfth birthday it'll be your turn."

When they got back to New York his mother went to the doctor with Clarence's younger sister. Clarence and his sister had always been close and he stayed up with her many nights on the road when she cried until dawn with headaches. Each time his mother would take her to a local doctor, and each time the doctor would prescribe aspirin and tell her to relax and get plenty of fresh air. The headaches were more frequent and she called for Clarence more and more. When they got to New York this time the doctor sent her to the hospital. Her headache was diagnosed. It was a brain tumor. Two weeks later she was dead.

That winter Clarence decided to stop traveling with his mother. He moved to Bridgehampton with his grandmother. This would let him attend a Northern school—and hitch rides to the lights of Manhattan and Harlem, a hundred miles away.

One day a good-looking older girl he had noticed hanging around the schoolyard asked him if he wanted to smoke. They went to her home and sat in her parents' car in the driveway. She said, "I've got some joints. You want some?" He didn't know what she was talking about, but she was a desirable, older girl and he wanted to be cool, so he said sure. When she took two out of her bag he recognized them as "reefers." He had never smoked any and now he did it too quickly. He felt dizzy and said so. She laughed and said she'd take him to the "clubhouse."

The clubhouse was an abandoned apartment nearby. The only furnishings were an old mattress and several blankets. Thus began afternoons of marijuana and sex. Another girl and her boy friend shared the mattress with them one afternoon and afterward the girl asked Clarence, "Want to go to a party tonight and get high?" Clarence said he didn't have any joints. The girl laughed and said, "Oh, I've got something better than that."

Clarence was appalled when he appeared for the party. The girl's apartment was more squalid than any he had ever seen. The kitchen was a devastated battlefield of half-filled pans on the stove, dirty dishes stacked crazily in a sink, roaches scurrying over everything. The living-room rug was a tattered square with holes, the furniture disemboweled and broken. Newspapers and magazines were shoved like foothills into the corners. When they sat on a broken divan they created a cloud of dust with disagreeable odors.

The girl tore the cardboard off a book of matches, folded it into a trough, tapped some white powder into it and sniffed it into her nostril. She tapped more powder into it and handed it to Clarence. He sniffed. It was his first dose of heroin. After a time the apartment was transformed. He felt totally different. The surroundings looked beautiful, with soft shapes and colors. He floated on a cloud of euphoria and relaxation, the most profound serenity he had ever experienced. He was thirteen years old.

Weeks later he was injecting heroin, consciously holding back on quantities and frequency, remembering the collapsing men in the migrant camp. But the self-restraint soon dissolved as the anxiety and pain after the euphoria became intolerable. The girl no longer had enough to supply him but she knew someone who did. For a price. Clarence did not have the price.

Another boy he met in the apartment found himself in need of heroin and money. He had skills Clarence never knew. They could steal clothes in Harlem. Clarence said he didn't know how. His friend said it was easy.

Standing on the corner of 123rd and Lenox Avenue, the friend explained. You take a suit off the rack, fold it on your arm crossways, then fold it lengthways as you walk. By this time it is a compact square. You tuck it under your jacket beneath your arm and walk out slowly.

They entered a store. Clarence was frightened and repelled. He couldn't do it. His friend, disgusted, grabbed four suits and without trying to conceal them ran outside. Clarence ran after him and a few blocks away stood on a corner and sold two of the suits for five dollars each and two for ten dollars each.

Clarence disliked stealing from stores and was never good at it. Besides, the profits hardly paid for a fix a day. So the friend said they ought to rob liquor stores. Clarence said he didn't know how. The friend said that he would demonstrate.

The friend picked Brooklyn as their stage. He gave Clarence a long-barreled .22 pistol. Clarence had never handled a gun before. He asked, What should I do with it? Put it in your belt, button your jacket, and when I go inside you stand at the door until I pull out my gun, and then you pull out yours and cover me.

Clarence's first robbery was of an old man who ran a liquor store with his wife. His friend walked to the counter, pulled out a .38 and said, "Put all the money in this bag." Clarence gingerly pulled out his pistol and watched. The wife began to complain. The husband quickly opened the cash register and put all the currency into the paper bag. Clarence's friend demonstrated his coolness by saying, "Put in the change, too." The wife said in frustration, "Not the change." The husband said, "Give it to them! Give it to them! Don't make no trouble!" The two ran down the street into a subway entrance. They got out at a random station and went to a coffee shop and counted their loot. It was eighty-two dollars.

Clarence Jones was fourteen years old.

School was irrelevant and Clarence dropped out. His mother argued with him but he refused to go back.

By this time he was injecting heroin in his bedroom. He'd shut the door, tie the rubber tube around his arm to raise the blood vessel, heat the heroin and water in a spoon, draw the mixture into the hypodermic and put the needle into his arm. One day he injected himself and went to the bathroom. When he got back to his room the works—tube, spoon and needle—were nowhere in sight. He was feeling euphoric and assumed he had hidden them before he went to the bathroom. The next day when he came home his mother put them on the kitchen table. He admitted he was addicted.

"If I try to help, will you do something about it?"

He agreed.

They went to Bellevue Hospital in Manhattan. A doctor asked her to stay outside while he talked to Clarence. Clarence told him everything about his habit. The doctor asked him to wait outside while he talked to Clarence's mother. After a long time on the bench outside an attendant asked, "Are you Clarence Jones?" He nodded. The man said, "Please come with me."

In another room the man said, "Are you ready?"

"Ready for what?"

"To come with me."

"What do you mean, 'Come with me'?"

"You're coming with me to be admitted to the hospital."

At that moment his mother appeared at the door of the room. He could tell from the fear on her face that she had planned what would happen. She had deceived him. They said he could not leave without a discharge from the doctors or a demand by his family. He looked at his mother coldly. He never blamed her for arranging treatment but he never forgave her for tricking him.

After five days he was transferred to a hospital in Central Islip, Long Island. He was told it was for only thirty days. After the third month he began to be desperate, sure he would never be released. Each day was the same. He could remain in his pajamas and look at television or play pool. Or he could dress for part of the day and exercise in a fenced yard.

The only question he remembers being asked about his addiction was "Were you on heavy dosage?" They didn't ask how much heroin or how often he took it. He did not know what "heavy dosage" meant but he assumed that if he was committed to a hospital he must have had it. So he said yes. They put him on three heavy doses of methadone a day.

He had never been so high. He stayed constantly high for a month. Then they began lowering the dosage but kept him at the lower level. He asked to end it but they said he still needed it. He asked how long he would have to take it and they said it couldn't be predicted. He decided to escape.

A Puerto Rican friend, Carlos, shared his suspicion that they would never get out and agreed to escape with him. Friends started a fight in the exercise yard to draw the attention of guards while Clarence and Carlos climbed over the chain-link fence and hitched a ride on the Long Island Expressway into Manhattan.

Three hours later they were at a party in Spanish Harlem, with lots of drinking, marijuana and pretty girls. Late that night they took a subway to Carlos' mother's house on the Lower East Side. She came to the door in her bathrobe, stared at her son, dragged them inside, started yelling in Spanish, pulled a paper out of her pocketbook and stuck it under Carlos' nose. They had escaped on a Saturday. The letter notified Carlos' mother that Carlos was scheduled for release on Monday.

On Monday, before settling the mess, Carlos agreed to cash a check for his mother at a Greenwich Village check-cashing office. Inside the cubicle Carlos suddenly turned white. The teller said to Clarence, "Hey, your friend looks sick. I think he's having a heart attack. Better call an ambulance."

Clarence rode in the ambulance and watched with relief as Carlos breathed in oxygen and color returned to his face and hands. The ambulance backed onto the dock and they wheeled out the stretcher. Inside the accident room a nurse asked Clarence his and Carlos' names and the circumstances of the heart attack. She was filling out a form with the words across the top, "Bellevue Hospital."

Half an hour later Clarence was still sitting in the accident room waiting for word about Carlos when an attendant appeared.

"Did you come with the guy we just took in?"

"Yeah."

"Your name Clarence?"

"Yeah."

"You two just escaped from Islip."

That night he was back in Central Islip. This time Clarence was on the fourth floor of a special building. Nothing in his life—living in Harlem, watching migrant workers fight with knives, robbing stores—prepared him for the terror of the special ward. Ninety people on the floor ranged in age from fourteen to seventy-five. Some were addicts and some seemed to be psychotics who had no place else to go.

From a corner where Clarence tried to remain as invisible and as untouched as possible he watched the daily scenes with horror.

An elderly man in a bathrobe walked all day through the ward, ramrod stiff, saluting everybody who passed. "General Douglas MacArthur, sir, at the front!"

A younger man constantly admonished someone unseen, in violent Spanish.

A boy and a man committed homosexual acts in daylight while a small audience watched. Some of their audience sat impassively as though not seeing and others made strange noises. Two of the spectators masturbated.

A man raised his hospital gown, had a bowel movement on the floor and carefully began eating his own feces. Clarence turned away, about to be sick, when he heard a violent argument. An adolescent at the end of the ward was defying an attendant who had started to walk through the ward. The attendant came back with two others. They grabbed the boy, who started to struggle and bite the hands that held him. The original attendant, holding the strait jacket in one hand, used the other hand to strike the boy on the mouth. The mouth began to bleed. They forced the hands into the strait jacket and tied the arms around the back. They dragged the boy to a corner, lifted him off the floor and in a swinging motion threw him into a corner. The blood ran down the corners of the boy's mouth. He spit and cried. He stayed there all night. In the morning he said he had to urinate but the attendant refused to loosen his hands. The boy started to cry and Clarence could tell that he had urinated as he lay on the floor. A little later he knew that the boy had a bowel movement, also in his clothes. The next day when the food cart came around the boy could eat only if someone decided to feed him. Most of the patients didn't feel like feeding him, but one old man did. The boy was there for four days before he was released from the strait jacket. When he was untied he neither spoke nor moved but was led like a comatose robot toward the showers by an attendant who turned his head in disgust.

Weeks passed. Clarence knew that he had to get out or something drastic would happen to him. Out of the ninety people only five or six seemed rational, young addicts who long ago had gone through withdrawal symptoms and were not yet psychotic. He felt that his own sanity could not survive this forever. No one told him how long he would stay or what was planned for him.

Then, at his most desperate, deliverance appeared. An attendant told him that his father was here to see him. His heart raced. Rip was going to take him home.

Clarence was told to wash and put on the street clothes he had come in. He was escorted by two attendants to a visiting room with barred doors and windows. He waited for his father to appear. The visitors' door opened. A strange man stepped in. Without knowing how, Clarence recognized his real father, Harry Jones.

Harry had left the family soon after Clarence was born. Clarence had seen him only once before, when he was six. He had been playing in the house at Bridgehampton when his mother walked in and said, "Clarence, this is your father, Harry Jones." Harry had talked to the boy and taken him to a local beach for three hours. Clarence called his father Harry. That day Harry took him back home and then disappeared again. Clarence knew only that he ran some kind of business in a Long Island community. Somehow, after all these years, Clarence knew who the man was. They embraced each other.

They spent the whole day talking. Clarence described what went on in the madhouse. Harry was shaken. "How would you like to come live with me?"

"Yes, yes." Clarence was overjoyed.

"Okay. I'll get a lawyer and get you out of here and I'll leave some money for you on my way out."

They shook hands and embraced warmly.

Harry didn't leave any money. He didn't get a lawyer. Clarence never has seen or heard from him since that day.

Clarence Jones was fifteen years old.

A week later, when it was clear that there was no deliverance from Harry, Clarence plotted with four other ex-addicts to escape. This time it would take violence to overcome the attendants. Someone in the conspiracy told the authorities. The authorities took him to juvenile court in Hauppauge, Long Island. Once before the judge, Clarence described what was happening to him and the judge transferred him from the New York bureaucracy handling "mental health" to the one handling juvenile crime.

The Otisville School for Boys was for teen-age boys but it had more hardened criminals than Clarence had ever met before. But it was an escape from Central Islip and it had organized recreation and schooling that Clarence took until the eleventh grade. Through a friend it led to another person after he got out, Mayberry, also an alumnus of Otisville.

Within a week after his release from reform school, Clarence was on heroin again, supplied by his new friend, Mayberry. Mayberry knew techniques for a more refined form of robbery than Clarence had ever attempted before—banks. Banks paid much more per hour of robbery than liquor stores. So they robbed several savings and loan associations with individual takes of from $400 to $1000. But divided between them it was not enough to support two heroin habits and entertainment. So they took an after-hours job as lookouts for a big Harlem crap game on Lenox Avenue.

They watched a lot of dice-playing, began eying the money piled on the table and mentally transformed it into bags of heroin. They decided to share in the wealth. Through a friend he had met in Otisville Clarence knew about "Deuce," a genius at marking cards and loading dice.

A tiny notch at a particular place along the edge of a card could tell the informed player's thumbnail which card lay face down in the pack. A delicate mark on the colored design on the back could be seen only with the correct shade of tinted glasses, available from Deuce.

Deuce also loaded dice. He drilled tiny holes through the dots, filled the holes with mercury and replaced the dot. One pair of dice landed 90 per cent of the time with three or eight or nine up. With a third die exchanged for one of the loaded pair, 90 per cent of the throws were ten or eleven.

In serious gambling men are killed or badly beaten for using marked cards and loaded dice. So Clarence and Mayberry took pains. Clarence would wander into the dice game and casually drift into a position at one end of the table, playing with the table dice as they came around to him. He used the skill learned with the shell game. When it was his turn to throw the dice he would palm the table dice off the table and replace them unseen with his loaded pair. After a long run of winning, he would palm the loaded dice off the table and flick into his hand the original table pair to be handed to the next player.

After a time Mayberry would come in, not showing recognition of Clarence, and stand at the other end of the table. By the time the play went the length of the table to his partner, the other players would not associate the unusual run of wins by Mayberry with a winning streak by a different player half an hour earlier.

Crap games and card tables in Harlem raised Clarence and Mayberry's income by $250 a night. This seemed fabulous at first but it led merely to higher quality heroin taken more often, and soon even that extra money was not enough. They looked for broader horizons and found them.

Mayberry's uncle ran a thriving business in Long Island and agreed to put the two young men into the firm.

In dozens of little businesses—restaurants, liquor stores, garages—a bookie collects money from his friends and neighbors who hope to win hundreds of dollars with bets each day of fifty cents or a few dollars. The customers are among the millions of Americans who live in a world of numerological religion, a devout belief in certain three-digit numbers. Some play the same number all the time—the numerals of their birthday or their street address, or the initials of their wives translated into numbers. Or a number flashes in front of them before noontime—the first digits of a license plate that catches their attention, or the prefix of a new girl friend's telephone number. They go to the bookie and put a fifty-cent or a dollar or five-dollar bet on the number, depending on their cash flow for the moment and the strength of their inspiration for the day. If the number wins, the gambler gets $600 for every dollar bet.

Except for the odds, most illegal lotteries are relatively honest. In a less sensitive time the numbers game was universally called the "nigger pool" on the mistaken assumption that addiction to gambling on numbers was peculiar to blacks. In fact, most players were white and the pool was run by whites, usually Italian. As ethnic sensitivities increased, the name was changed and even the all-white syndicates became equal-opportunity employers.

In more grandiose moods the lottery is called the "people's stock exchange," and like the stock market breaks its own rules only for extraordinary profits or the avoidance of extraordinary loss. The winning number has to be chosen in an ostensibly incorruptible way. The more sedate lotteries use the last three digits in the daily balance of the United States Treasury as published in daily papers. From time to time there is a large concentration of bets on a particular three-digit number, some invisible mental wave that strikes numbers players in different places or some publicized number like a championship golf score or a baseball star's new historic batting average. If the last digits of the Treasury balance for that day by great misfortune for the syndicate (and great good fortune for the gamblers) should come out to that number, it is not unknown that a cooperative compositor in each of the composing rooms of the major newspapers will make a "typographical error" that day and the heavily bet number will be slightly altered in print.

To prevent this regrettable lapse, the syndicate run by Mayberry's uncle used a different system, choosing its winning number on the basis of payoffs at a race track. At a race track selected according to season and known throughout the bookie system, the digit to the left of the dollars-and-cents decimal point in the amount paid winning tickets in the first race provides the first digit of the three-digit winning lottery number. The second digit in the lottery comes from the second race, the third from the third race. This is considered an incorruptible system, though here, too, sadly, it is not unknown that when the first three races are in and the numbers represent an extremely heavily bet number for the day, a cooperative operator at the race track will make an error in reporting the payoffs to radio and newspapers.

In some cities the numbers players pick up their newspapers and turn to the U.S. Treasury balance. Or they listen to a local radio station that reports races. And at a certain moment a small number of these students of finance will be seen leaping up with an ecstatic cry: "I hit! I hit! I hit!" He or, increasingly, she will run to the telephone and shout the message to a loved one, dash into the streets bringing the glad tidings to the newsstand operator, the liquor store clerk, and the cop on traffic duty, all of whom pull out their own slip of paper to see how close they came.

To congratulators the bettor is often heard to say something like "I knew it the minute I woke up this morning—this is the lucky number!"

The word soon passes to neighboring establishments. "Did you hear? Sal hit the number today right on the nose. Had five dollars on it—three thousand bucks!"

The enterprise, like all successful ones, was operated on a basically simple plan. But it had administrative complications. The neighborhood bookies were humble people, unable to finance the lucky payoffs. Their job was to collect bets from friends and neighbors, their reward 25 per cent of every bet collected and 10 per cent of a winning number held by any customer. The remaining money went to the "front office," a businesslike operation behind steel doors that paid generous insurance to law-enforcement authorities who made sure that vice squads plied their trade elsewhere. This insurance also permitted their runners to park cars in no-parking zones during the crucial hours of the day when bets had to be collected from the network of neighborhood bookies.

But there are internal security problems. The front office needs to collect from dozens of bookies thousands of slips of paper bearing the numbers bet each morning. It also must collect the money bet on each slip. It is sad to report but it has been the experience of the front office that despite the meticulous mathematics of the business the traveling agents, or runners, who collect both the betting slips and the money that goes with them at the same time will fail to turn both over to the front office. Instead, such deviants will withhold a certain percentage of the betting slips and the money that accompanied them. The odds are very good that the withheld numbers will not win and the runner keeps the money bet, the front office never knowing that the bets were ever made. If by chance the withheld number hits, then the prudent runner conducting this variation will have conserved enough of his profits in a contingency fund to pay off the bookie who will pay off the customer. Runners who fail to maintain such a contingency fund and therefore default on payments are believed to have greatly depressed life expectancies.

Most well-managed numbers games do not depend solely on the morbid threat of death to deviating runners. Instead they hire two people like Clarence and Mayberry in a fail-safe system. Clarence collected only the betting slips from bookies every morning and delivered them to a set of offices in a city on Long Island by a certain time each day. There women with calculators at rows of desks recorded each bet from each bookie. They then calculated how much money each bookie had collected on the bets, subtracted the 25 per cent commission to be kept by the bookie and listed the 75 per cent that should be turned in. This was reported to a dispatcher, who then called Mayberry, who was waiting word at bars or apartments or coffee shops. He was told to start his rounds. The dispatcher did not tell Mayberry how much money was due. Mayberry traced Clarence's steps and collected the money bet with the bookies on his beat. He, too, would go to the front office and turn in the money. The dispatcher knew how much was to be expected from each bookie, so neither Clarence nor Mayberry could withhold anything without fear of fatal detection.

On an average day Mayberry would collect about $25,000 and deliver it to the front office. For their work Clarence and Mayberry each received $1000 a week. It was a spectacular salary and they enjoyed it. But like all good businessmen they hated to see money slipping through their hands, possibly to unworthy recipients. They evolved an inspired plan.

One of their jobs was to report changes in bookies, and as it must to all bookies, there came an occasional arrest as some policeman made a mistake or decided to retaliate against his captain who didn't share the bribes, or a new syndicate offered higher insurance fees, or the local newspaper started a campaign against illegal gambling. As a consequence some small operator had to be offered up as a sacrifice to stern law enforcement. The unfortunate small businessman would have to be replaced by someone new. Soon the new bookie's slips and bets would be added to the daily tide washing, uninterrupted, into the front office.

What would happen if Clarence and Mayberry quietly established themselves as the replacement bookie? And their friends made bets with them directly? They could then deduct the 25 per cent commission for themselves and turn in the slips and remaining 75 per cent to the front office. The weekly commissions came to $250. With that investment money, obtained out of sheer ingenuity, they could make fifty-cent bets on 500 numbers. There are only 999 possible winning numbers a day, or about 5000 a week. Ordinary single-number bets have a one thousand-to-one chance of winning, the odds that most lottery players don't like to think about. But with a hundred bets a day—with "free" money —the odds for the new enterprise became a hundred to one, or ten times better than the average for a direct hit. Before long they were netting an additional $5000 a week.

For the first time in his life, Clarence Jones had enough money to support his heroin habit with first-rate powder, with plenty of cash left over. Periodically he would visit his mother and give her money, usually half of every big hit made on his under-the-counter bets. She built a large house in Bridgehampton, in eastern Long Island.

When he looked to this territory it did not occur to Jones that he was in the hunting grounds occupied generations before by earlier builders of personal fortunes.

The flat and exclusive reaches of the eastern end of Long Island had been the playground for generations of Astors, Vanderbilts, Tiltons and Whitneys, many of whose descendants are found in history books under the title "robber barons," on grounds that they obtained railroads, real estate, shipping firms, industries and monopolies on food for astronomical tax-free profits by obscure means.

There were some resemblances in the way they and Jones looked upon the problem of accumulating money. They both had gambled on fluctuations of the market place, they did it largely with other people's money, and they did it with the superior knowledge of the insider.

Not a few of Clarence Jones's Long Island neighbors inherited fortunes also acquired illegally.

John Jacob Astor started poor. Like Jones he was shrewd and ambitious. He became a successful fur trader partly by cheating and killing Indians. But it was another event that catapulted him to a different status. In 1807 Congress passed the Embargo Act forbidding American ships to carry cargo to foreign ports, an attempt to counter the British and French embargo strangling the new country. John Jacob Astor had one of his minor clerks write a letter to President Thomas Jefferson claiming to be "The Honorable Punqua Wongchong," an influential Mandarin who wished to charter a ship in order to do the proper "funeral obsequies" for his dear departed grandfather. Jefferson asked Albert Gallatin, his Secretary of the Treasury, for advice. Gallatin knew Astor and knew about the fraud but he kept a straight face and advised President Jefferson to grant the exemption, saying it would help relations with China. The Honorable Punqua sailed with a shipload of merchandise and $45,000 for trading at a time when those who obeyed the law were out of the China trade. Astor made a financial killing. It made him a major financier who invested money in many things, including much New York City real estate. He died with $30 million. His name is engraved on the New York Public Library, and his descendants built comfortable Long Island summer mansions not far from the place where Clarence Jones had settled. In Washington, D.C., where Jones's imprisonment is managed, there is a heroic statue of Gallatin in front of the Department of the Treasury.

If Clarence Jones, like Astor, intelligent, acquisitive and ruthless, had been born a hundred years earlier in a different skin, his early ingeniousness at acquiring surplus cash might have been viewed as a pioneering enterprise. His well-placed friends in government and business would have found private ways to multiply the tax-free profits. If he had bought real estate and politicians instead of heroin and gifts for his mother, he would have long ago replaced such ugly instruments as the gun with more genteel persuaders like law firms and compliant politicians. He could have contributed his unusable surplus to build museums and universities, made speeches proclaiming the sanctity of uninhibited moneymaking and been declared a scholar and a gentleman.

The children of Society with an upper case S grew up with their career models, in elite academies, on the escalators to the hierarchy of banks and industries. Clarence Jones, born black in 1946 in Harlem, had his career models, the only people who were great financial successes—pimps, narcotics dealers and lottery operators.

People in both societies have been responsible for killing others, Society by hired thugs killing and maiming union organizers at their industries, forming monopolies to close mines and factories, voting laws that guarantee institutionalized poverty. Clarence Jones never killed anyone, though his constant use of guns made that a possibility. For victims looking into the muzzles of his weapons, death was terribly imminent. He and John Jacob Astor made up their own rules as they went along and deprived others of more money than either could constructively use. That does not excuse Astor or Jones; it only describes them.

In his framework of life, Clarence Jones became a big success. He bought a new 1967 car, a big black Lincoln Continental, from a special dealer in New Jersey. The dealer was special because he sold only stolen cars, repainted and bearing new serial numbers. His clientele was almost entirely people who would have trouble filling out a credit application blank where it asked source of income. The car was sold to Clarence at full price, with monthly installments. This transaction had the unusual provision that a missed monthly payment of even one day placed an obligation on the buyer to return the car at once for repossession by the dealer. If the buyer failed to meet this obligation the dealer would send a special pair of large men to do bodily damage to the delinquent buyer and seize the car.

Clarence bought the most expensive clothes he could find—custom suits, silk shirts, hand-made shoes—all in large quantities and varying designs. He moved into a luxurious apartment in the better part of Harlem. He had the pick of women, some of whom moved in with him if they met his fancy, and he entertained them with the best restaurants, expensive shows, and clothes. After a few weeks he might tell his girl of the moment that it was all over because he had someone else.

He was now nineteen years old.

Late one summer, during an argument in a bar, a man pulled a gun on Mayberry. Clarence fired and nicked the man. The police arrived almost instantly and Clarence was sentenced to a year and a day. He was still under the jurisdiction of the juvenile courts.

Clarence got out of juvenile prison in eight months, having accumulated time off for good behavior. But in that period his financial world had collapsed. Something went wrong with the arrangement between the front office and the police, systematic raids broke up the bookie system and runner jobs disappeared.

Clarence still had a heavy heroin habit and neither visible nor invisible means of support. So he and Mayberry turned to the unemployment compensation of dope addicts and other desperate members of the netherworld, bank robbery.

It was during this period that politics entered the life of Clarence Jones. He had heard Malcolm X preach on street corners, the first time he felt any stirring of racial pride and bitterness. Now and then he would visit a Black Muslim mosque in Harlem. He couldn't accept their religion, puritanism and discipline, but he was introduced to some of the writings of Marcus Garvey, Eldridge Cleaver and W. E. B. DuBois.

He and Mayberry had robbed a number of Manhattan banks successfully when they met a group that consisted of six black men and four white women who called themselves a unit of the Revolutionary Action Movement. They preached violent guerrilla activity against established society and robbed for the ostensible purpose of weakening the existing social structure and providing funds for the movement. The politics didn't interest Jones but their techniques did. A different mix of sexes and races was used in each bank robbery to delay identification of them as a single group. And the standard technique of abandoning a stolen getaway car and transferring to their own car was refined by having the getaway car seen at the bank, for example, contain three black men, while the transfer car would have three white women in it, confusing police on the lookout for three black men.

The group made several hauls in New England. They were done in the spirit of revolutionary fervor, but Clarence observed that after the individuals completed their split of the loot very little seemed to be left over for any cause.

Clarence and Mayberry tired of this. The large robberies were infrequent and the split twelve ways not enough to support the high level of heroin that both were injecting. Nor did it help their rapidly declining life style. Clarence had a common-law wife and two sons established in a house at East Hampton and now he spent more time with them, partly because his high life in Harlem was curtailed.

Around noon of October 15, 1968, Jones, Mayberry and two accomplices drove to woods near Bridgehampton to saw the barrels off two shotguns. One would fit under Mayberry's belt and be concealed with his jacket, and the other fit into a paper bag carried by Jones. They drove six miles toward Montauk Point, to East Hampton. At ten minutes to three they entered the First National Bank of East Hampton. One of the accomplices scribbled on a deposit slip and took it to a teller. Jones pulled the sawed-off shotgun out of his paper bag and yelled, "This is a holdup!" Mayberry pulled his gun from under his belt and climbed over the counter and ordered a woman and two men to lie on the floor. Jones handed the empty bag to the accomplice and told him to get all the cash from every window. Then Jones told teller Beth

Lester, "Come here!" He stretched her arm across the counter and leveled the shotgun at her right temple. Two of the men scooping up the money yelled from time to time, "Shoot her! Shoot her!" and "Kill her!" Jones kept her arm pinned to the counter, the gun pointed steadily at her head. Quietly, the woman on the floor crept toward a side door. Someone yelled, "Watch her," but she was out the door. Jones said, "Let's get out of here."

Inside Jones's house they counted out $23,088.04.

Nine days later at six A.M. FBI special agent William Quinn stationed two other agents at a front door, one at a back door and one at the head of some cellar stairs in a small house in Jamaica, Queens. Quinn, carrying a shotgun, and special agent Kenneth Rommel, carrying a pistol, tiptoed down the stairs toward a sleeping figure on a cot. When Quinn had quietly gone to the man's head and Rommel to his feet, Quinn announced sharply, "Mayberry! FBI! Get up! You're under arrest!"

Mayberry screamed and jumped out of bed.

Quinn raised his gun and said, "Stand still! Don't move!" Mayberry was trembling. In his bureau they found a sawed-off shotgun with two shells, one of them in the chamber ready for firing. In the drawer they counted $5071.

At the same moment FBI special agent Arthur J. Achenback knocked on the door of the home of Clarence Jones in East Hampton. Jones himself let him in. Agent Achenback pronounced Jones under arrest and found in Jones's wallet currency worth fifty-two dollars, of which three five-dollar bills carried serial numbers identical with some stolen from the First National Bank of East Hampton.

At 7:45 that morning the finger and palm prints of Clarence Jones were taken in the East Hampton police station. The prints matched the ones found on the roof of an abandoned stolen Volvo station wagon used as the getaway car for the robbery.

One of the accomplices later was escorted into the Manhattan headquarters of the FBI. The agents had found $4500 behind the pillow of a chair in the man's flat, some of the money carrying serial numbers of currency taken from the East Hampton bank. At his home, the FBI agent had shown him the mass of money. "You're under arrest for bank robbery."

"I don't know what you're talking about."

"Where did you get all this money if you didn't rob a bank?"

No answer.

When the man was taken into the FBI offices in New York it was not by accident that he went by a room with a door ajar, through which he saw Mayberry.

Moments later the agent said to the man, "We've got you. We've got the other men. We've got the money. We've got the serial numbers on the money that was taken from the bank that matches the money we found on you and the others. And we've got fingerprints. So whatever you tell us will help you."

The man decided to be a witness for the government.

No money beyond the fifty-two dollars was ever recovered from Jones. He was held under a $100,000 bond. He had a full trial of five days before a jury, with a private lawyer. After deliberating four hours the jury found the men guilty of robbing a bank, guilty of using a dangerous weapon while robbing a bank, and conspiracy to rob a bank.

The men got fifteen years. The cooperative accomplice got six years.

On May 19, 1969, Jones was brought before Judge John F. Dooling for sentencing. The judge asked if he had anything to say first. Jones said he didn't. Judge Dooling asked him to stand before the bench: "You must be sentenced to—I fear—a fearful term of imprisonment.

"Anything could have happened in that bank that day. If someone had made the wrong move, if one of you had got upset someone could have been killed, and that is the horrifying part of it. . . .

"I am under no illusion that you had the best chance in the world to be an ideal fellow. I don't have any illusions about that at all. Your life has been a hard one, no doubt. But the law can't take account for those things beyond a certain point.

"Now, I mean to sentence you to an indeterminate sentence. That's a sentence under Section 4208 (a) (2)."

Section 4208, subsection (a), paragraph 2, of the United States Code follows a long line of impulses to do good in criminal justice that ends as a perversion, making prison sentences in the United States the longest in the Western World.

The judge continued. "Now, I am sure that you will be told at West Street, you will be told at whatever prison you are confined to that any (a) (2) in a bank robbery case where a gun was used doesn't mean a thing, they will keep you in for the maximum."

"West Street" in Manhattan is where federal convicts are held to await permanent assignment to a prison.

"Now don't you believe it; 4208 (a) (2) is a real sentence, and it is particularly so in the case of a man as young as you are," Judge Dooling said.

"You can work your way out of jail—and believe me, Mr. Jones, it's worth the effort. Don't lose heart about it and don't listen to these old wags that try to tell you there is no use in trying, because there is. It would be my hope that you can work your way out of jail just as quick as possible."

Clarence Jones had not heard the old wags' tales because he had never before been in federal custody.

The judge continued. "Now then, I am afraid, Mr. Jones, that is all I can do for you. It is the worst day of your life."

The judge looked down at a paper. "On the jury's verdict on counts one, two and three of the indictment, you, Clarence Jones, are committed to the custody of the Attorney General of the United States or his duly authorized representative, who shall designate the place of confinement for the term of twenty years on counts one and two and five years on count three . . . to become eligible for parole at such time as the Board of Parole may determine, the sentences to run concurrently."

When Clarence Jones had been arrested the Attorney General of the United States was Ramsey Clark. Three months later, by the time of his final sentencing, the Attorney General was John Mitchell. The duly authorized representative in charge of assigning prisons was the Director of the Federal Bureau of Prisons, Norman A. Carlson, and in the routine of such cases his subordinates decided to send Clarence Jones to Lewisburg Federal Penitentiary.

Six months later Jones wrote a letter to Judge Dooling:

> I beg you, Honorable Judge Dooling, to search your heart and find some leniency. Your sentence imposed on me is just the same as giving me life. . . .
>
> At least give me a chance to re-enter society before this dreadful penitentiary instills me with hate and scorn for everything good in this country of ours. . . . My entire life is in your hands.

Letters like these are common on judges' desks. Federal judges have 120 days after passing sentence during which they have the power to change their minds but after which the case passes entirely to the parole board, barring some spectacular exceptions. Some prisoners don't know this and later discover bitterly that during their first four months in their new prison they could have asked for leniency. But they have not lost much. Judges are inundated with letters. Some letters are recognizable examples of a prison art form, composed with the help of skilled inmates who know the judges' sensibilities and who do it as a favor or for pay, such as several cartons of cigarettes. Some are sincere expressions from desperate human beings. Some judges look at each letter individually or have their clerks screen out the ones that seem to be unusual. Others hardly read them at all. One judge in the District of Columbia has his clerk routinely type out a denial form for every such letter received and shingle the forms on his desk every Tuesday morning, leaving only the signature line exposed, and then he signs them en masse. Whatever their source and whatever the practice of the judge who gets them, the letters are pieces of jetsam that flood across judicial desks in an almost indistinguishable flood.

Jones received a standard form denying his plea.

More than a year later Jones wrote another letter to Judge Dooling:

> Dear Sir, Again I humbly submit another request for a reduction of sentence or at least your personal recommendation for early release due to new social factors in my case.

He noted that his stepfather had died two weeks earlier, and his mother had been in and out of the hospital five times recently, and his brother was away in the United States Air Force.

> I've been in jail now two years and three months. . . . You can check with the authorities here at Lewisburg and also at West Street on my conduct record which is clean. I've tried my best to adjust to the rules and regulations laid down by the Administration which you probably know can be difficult at times, yet I have had no disciplinary report thus far.
>
> I know the crime I was convicted of was quite serious. . . . The biggest mistake of my life. But must I pay for it forever?

The judge wrote back to Jones:

> The time period in which the court is authorized to reduce sentence expired long ago. It is accordingly ordered that the attached motion to reduce sentence is denied.

In the United States Courthouse in Brooklyn the file marked "United States of America versus Clarence Jones" was stamped "Closed."

14

PRISONER NO. 36234–133

The sound began, a high, chilling monotone of primal terror from a constricted throat no longer able to utter words.

Bill Irwin steeled himself. He listened as the victim in the next cage struggled. He heard the sound of a body being thrown onto the rubber mattress, the stifling gurgles as someone inserted a rubber mouthpiece to prevent smashing of teeth when the electric shock sent the jaws into spasm. Then the buzzing sound and silence as the man in the next cage became instantly unconscious.

By now Irwin's body was trembling beyond his control. He tried to stop the shaking by pressing against a concrete wall of his cage. He fought against the sound in his throat that wanted to screech. An instinct told him that he must protect his brain—the storehouse of the good, the bad, the sweet, the bitter, the only identity, the only memory he had. . . .

His earliest recollection was of standing on a chair by the big bay windows. Through the white curtains shimmering in brilliant sunshine he could see three oak trees towering above the sixth-floor tenement. His mother was wiping his face with a damp cloth.

"Don't!"

"Ah, come on, Willy, you've got to be clean if you're going to get your picture taken, now don't you?"

The picture taken that day in Yonkers, New York, was long lost, but the warmth of the sunlit curtains, the three oak trees, the lilting voice of his mother remained with him, a scene suspended in brilliant sunshine and sweet serenity.

Everybody loved Mrs. Irwin, especially her youngest child, Billy. She believed in leprechauns and was full of Irish folklore, curious for a

German Protestant from Pennsylvania.

Bill's adoration of his mother survived a periodic ritual. His mother and his sister knew they could frighten him by adopting solemn faces and singing:

> The judge said, "Stand up, boy
> And dry your tears.
> You're sentenced to prison
> For twenty long years.
> For twenty long years, boy,
> Is a mighty long time.
> Yes, twenty long years, boy,
> Is a mighty long time."

He would run into his room crying. His brother John, five years older, would comfort the child and tell him funny stories.

Mr. Irwin was a bitter and taciturn man, a sandhog digging the new Lincoln Tunnel under the Hudson River. Relatives had put him in a Catholic orphanage in the West and he never forgave either the Church or most of the human race. His wife seemed to be the only person he accepted fully. He insisted on her full attention.

Bill was four when he noticed that if his mother was fondling him in her lap and she heard her husband's footsteps she would spill the child onto the floor and tell him to get out of sight. She turned away instantly from all the children the moment her husband arrived.

His father often yelled at his sons, "I'll knock you down and kick you for falling, you son of a bitch!" Bill was still four when he watched in horror as his father knocked John down with his fist and then stomped on him as the boy curled on the floor.

Bill Irwin was in prison twenty years later when he received word that his father had died. His first reaction was "I've been cheated. I wanted to beat the bastard to death." As the years passed, Bill Irwin would change his mind about his father, would find, to his shock, that he had some of his father inside him.

His other brother, Dick, also tormented him. Dick joined neighbor boys in beating his baby brother. Bill remained small for his age until his late teens and had the nickname "Mousie." Once when Dick had Bill on the ground a woman shouted, "You get off that poor little boy!"

Dick kept his elbow on Bill's neck and reassured her, "It's okay, lady. This is my brother."

When Bill was ten they moved to Rockaway, New Jersey. He hated to leave Yonkers. Rockaway turned out to be a small town embedded in the suburban sediment that leaks westward out of Newark and Paterson.

Easter morning of 1944 began as many others had for Bill and Dick. They slept together in a double bed and began the day by trading punches as they stood on the bouncing mattress. To Bill's surprise he hit Dick solidly in the chest, Dick flew through the air backward and struck his head on the edge of the open closet door. Bill jumped on him and shook him by the throat. When he let go of Dick's head it landed on the floor like a stone.

Bill stared at the lifeless form. The words came into his head: "I just killed my brother."

He felt a profound calm. He dressed slowly and carefully, stepped over his brother, closed the door behind him and went to the kitchen. His mother's relatives from Buffalo were visiting and they laughed and gossiped around the breakfast table. Bill joined them silently.

Without panic or excitement he waited for what he knew would happen. Someone would come into the kitchen and announce, "Dick is dead!"

Everyone would stop talking. His mother and sisters would scream. His father would stand up and stare at Bill. And Bill would say without hesitation, "I did it."

He heard steps coming downstairs. The door opened. It was Dick.

Bill ran outdoors. He stayed away all day. At nightfall he returned, resigned to the worst beating of his life. But everyone was sitting at the dinner table in good humor and his mother asked mildly why he was late. Dick looked unexceptional. It was the last time Dick would ever hit Bill in anger. Later they would become good friends.

Sex, like everything else, was competitive, usually violent and in groups. When Bill was nine, still in Yonkers, his first sex competition was with Dick. An older girl lived below them on the fifth floor. She would wait on the landing of her apartment while Dick and Bill raced up the five flights of stairs. Whoever won could kiss the girl and put his hand inside her panties. When he was eleven Bill, a perpetual troublemaker in school, was often banished to the cloakroom, where he struggled with the girls sent in to get the sponge for cleaning the blackboard.

Theft, like sex, was a game. Irwin could not remember a time of real privation in his family but neither could he remember when it was not standard childhood practice to steal. In Yonkers it was taking ice cream from the street vendor or grabbing dollar bills out of the pocket of "the Mayor," the ragged man who liked little girls. One of his best friends, Bony, introduced Bill to robbery, grabbing money from cash registers of shops while Bony distracted the storekeeper.

It was his other close friend, Mick Muldoon, who worked most closely with Bill on the great warehouse heist. It was 1943, during World War II, and a warehouse in town loaded with shoes for lend-lease caught fire. During the war good shoes were scarce and the town volunteer firemen and policemen were seen loading their cars, trunk lids wide open, with boxes containing a hundred pairs of shoes each. Children and their parents joined the enterprise. For a long time citizens of Rockaway wore remarkably similar footwear. The boys returned after the fire for more shoes, to sell at a dollar a pair, and were caught. They went to court and were given probation. It was William Irwin's first appearance in court. He was thirteen. Mrs. Irwin was angry because some of the policemen who escorted Bill to court were the ones who had stolen shoes the night of the fire.

Shortly afterward Bill and Bony stole a bottle of whiskey and, while drunk, stole a car, drove to Delaware, and were arrested. They were put on probation.

That fall Bill entered school and at first sight of an old enemy, the big fat principal, defied him, punched him and was expelled. He waited until summer and went with Mick Muldoon to Mick's grandmother's in Pennsylvania. They loaded their belongings in Mick's old car. Mick had an ancient .32 revolver, so they planned a holdup. In a tailor shop Bill demanded the proprietor's wallet while Mick pointed the revolver. The tailor resisted. Bill shouted, "Shoot him, Mick! Shoot the son of a bitch! Kill the bastard!" The tailor's dog snapped at Bill's heels. They ran out empty-handed and drove away. Bill denounced Mick for not shooting the tailor.

Mick threw the gun into Bill's lap. "Okay, bigshot. We'll pick out another spot. You're such a bigtime killer, you can show me."

They drove to a tavern. Bill put the gun in his jacket pocket. He and Mick took two seats at the end of the bar near the door. The bar was empty except for two men playing checkers at a table at the other end and the bartender, a large man with a broken nose.

"What'll you have, boys?"

Bill used his toughest New York accent. "Give us two fuckin' beers."

"I'll give you the beers, but watch your language."

As the man started drawing the beers, Bill pulled the gun from his pocket. "Okay, buddy, this is a stickup. Just turn around and bring me the dough out of the till."

The bartender slowly pushed the tap handle back, put the two glasses of beer on the bartop in front of him and without looking at Bill and Mick walked around the end of the bar to the customer side, walking calmly toward Bill and Mick. Bill felt paralyzed. He thought of pulling the trigger but something told him the old pistol wouldn't fire. He stood up and watched hypnotized as the bartender approached. The bartender walked slowly into a phone booth and started dialing a call.

"Mousie, let's get the hell out of here!"

They escaped, stole a small amount of money from Mick's grandmother and drove home again.

Bill went to Dover High School, five miles from Rockaway. He was expelled for fighting. Under New Jersey law he had to attend school until he was sixteen. He was only fourteen, and if no regular school would take him he would have to go to reform school. His mother sent him to live with her husband's cousin in New York. The nearest school was a Catholic one, St. Barnabas, but it was a grade school. Since Bill's aim was to attend school solely for legal purposes—a Protestant with no religious, racial or academic prejudices—he became a student at St. Barnabas parochial grade school. His teacher was a kind nun who knew his past history but never used it against him. He fell in love with her and obeyed her. When he started to fight in the schoolyard she hurried out and prevented it. She seemed to appear like magic every time he was about to get into trouble, take him to the rectory and talk to him for a long time.

"She convinced me that I was a good person and she made me feel embarrassed for acting bad. That's the first time that had ever happened."

A few weeks later he got into a fight with his father's cousin where he was staying. Somehow Sister Julia found him a foster home in the neighborhood. There were two other children from an orphanage in the same household. One was nine years old and told the foster mother everything that Bill did wrong. Despite threats by Bill the boy continued to tell tales.

Bill waited for an afternoon when no one else was home, tied the boy to a bedpost and whipped him with a belt. The foster mother discovered it.

Back in New Jersey, his mother felt that the parochial school had been a good experience, so she entered him in a parochial school in

Morristown, ten miles away. It lasted half a day—he had a fistfight with one of the teaching brothers. His mother found another parochial school, where a few days later Bill was expelled again for fighting.

Bill Irwin was only fourteen years old but he had been under supervision for four years, under a probation officer, Emeline P. Flanigan, remembered by Irwin as a kind, firm and understanding woman. In retrospect he cannot comprehend where she got the patience to work with him. The territory where he was known as a holy terror was expanding. But she tried to keep him out of reform school and did it now. She was willing to make a deal with the public school in Madison, thirteen miles away. The only condition was: Absolutely no trouble. The principal would instruct Bill's teachers that they were to leave him alone; he did not have to open a book or lift a pencil, take any tests or participate in classroom activities.

Birthdays were not a big thing in the Irwin household. At the end of the evening meal his mother might bring out a cake and say whose birthday it was. No presents, usually. But September 5, 1946, was the biggest birthday in Bill's life so far. It had a significance he could not yet see—of his next twenty-eight birthdays, only nine would be spent, like this one, in the free world. But that was not the special quality of his birthday in 1946. He was sixteen and it meant he didn't have to go to school anymore, not to the fat principal's, not to St. Barnabas, not to all the schools he'd been kicked out of, and not to Madison thirteen miles away, where he had spent all his time, by mutual agreement, doing nothing. He had now completed the legal requirement of compulsory "education" until the age of sixteen.

While he was still in Madison High he had had his first alcoholic blackout. In the Irwin neighborhood enlisting in the armed services was an opening to a larger world, not unlike a middle-class family sending a son to a university. When one of the gang joined up, there was a celebration. One such night they collected three pints of whiskey and six bottles of wine and went to a movie to drink. The next thing he remembered was getting out of the car in front of his house, feeling a little high and a little tired but otherwise normal.

His mother was waiting for him inside the door. "Where the hell have you been?"

"To the movies, Ma."

"And just what time do you think it is now?"

She took him by the ear and pushed him into the kitchen and demanded that he tell her the time. Four-thirty. He was stunned. That was when he usually got up to dress, eat and take the bus and train to Madison High. His mother slapped him and told him to take a bath and get to school. The next night he was sent directly to his room, but he climbed out a window and down a porch post to Mick Muldoon's to find out what happened. Mick told him a story of drinking, breaking up taverns, vomiting and fighting. Bill felt strange that he had gone through hours of wild activity without any memory of it. He was a fifteen-year-old alcoholic but he didn't know it.

Bony suggested hitching to Florida. He had been getting letters from Peg, a girl who had lived in the neighborhood but had moved recently. This interested them both. Peg loved sex, individually and in groups. That afternoon they were in Philadelphia and on their way south.

The two boys hitchhiked, hopped freight cars and were beaten and kicked by railroad police in Atlanta. They burglarized some place every day for food and drinks, and finally landed in Tampa. Peg's father had a good job in an aerospace industry and her mother, believing that Bony was a serious fiancé, took in the boys. A few months later they were kicked out.

The night Bill arrived back in Rockaway he was walking from the bus stop toward the Irwin house when he met his brother Dick. Dick offered to buy him a drink in a local tavern. After the first drink Dick said, "Bill, the family doesn't want you to come home. Ma thinks it'll be better if you live someplace else and so do your sisters."

Bill didn't believe him. They kept drinking and he decided to go home, though by that time he was drunk.

When he entered the house, his father said, "What did you come back for? Nobody else would put up with you?"

Bill stumbled toward his old bedroom.

His father said, "You drunken son of a bitch! Come back here!"

But Bill kept stumbling and fell asleep on his bed.

Thus ended the childhood of Bill Irwin, age sixteen.

By the time he was seventeen breaking into bars and liquor stores had become a habit, as routine a way of getting money as cutting lawns is for other boys. Finally he was caught for breaking into a tavern and stealing money, cigarettes and whiskey. Emeline Flanigan had to admit defeat.

Bill Irwin at age seventeen was committed to his first imprisonment under sentence, the reform school at Annandale, New Jersey, the beginning of Bill Irwin's life under control of the state. Fifteen months after being sentenced to Annandale he was paroled. Two months after that he was caught burglarizing a liquor store and this time sent to the tougher juvenile prison in Bordentown. Two years later he was paroled from Bordentown.

Bill Irwin's emergence from a prison was merely an explosive interlude, like a bronco released in a rodeo, trying to prove his virility by shaking off respectability and drowning himself in liquor. He continued to be arrested for stealing, for drunkenness, for fighting. His family wanted no more to do with him. Some of his brothers and most of his friends were in the same kind of trouble, passing in and out of jails. The circle of his rejection grew steadily wider from Rockaway as he moved from roominghouse to roominghouse in towns ever more distant from his family. He decided to hitchhike to the West.

Relatives of his father in South Dakota took him in but he was bored with their placid life and chilled by the bleak landscape. He went to Cheyenne. His record there: Arrested for drunkenness on March 6, 1953; married April 16, 1953; separated October 2, 1953.

In Denver he worked eighteen months in the manufacturing plant of Western Electric. It was the longest single stretch of work in the free world he would have. Drunkenness and surly behavior ended that job.

Bill Irwin finally landed in a genuine state penitentiary. The language of his indictment gave it a criminal grandeur:

> On or about September 8, 1954, William Ryan Joseph Irwin, then and there feloniously, burglariously, willfully, maliciously and forcibly did break and enter, and feloniously and burglariously, willfully and maliciously without force did enter with intent to steal the moneys, goods and chattels of the said John A. Peras and Peter N. Peras doing business as Stilwell's Cafe in the said office and storehouse . . . contrary to the form of the statute in such case made and provided, against the peace and dignity of the people of the State of Colorado.

It was, in fact, an act of drunken stupidity. Irwin put it more plainly to the police:

"About eleven-thirty P.M. Hanks and I bought a bottle of whiskey and went to my apartment, where we finished the bottle. The other fellows came up about one-thirty A.M. and we sat around and talked for a while. . . . When they went to sleep, I decided to get another drink. When I found that the bars had closed, I decided to break into one of them. I went around to the back . . . and broke in through a window. Inside I picked up a couple of quarts of whiskey, then went home. I woke up . . . and we had a few drinks. We decided to go back to

Stilwell's and unload the joint. We got into the alley and I decided not to let the other guy go in with us because he was drunk. Hanks and I went in and carried out a diamond ring, whiskey, meat, coffee, canned goods and $11.50. When Hanks and I came out, the other guy had passed out in the alley. We woke him up and he helped us carry the stuff to the apartment. Then we got drunk all over again."

In the morning the police walked in and arrested them. Irwin immediately confessed and offered to make restitution if they would put him on probation. The police told him to tell it to the judge and recorded his physical appearance at the time: "White, weight 175, height 6 feet, brown hair, fair complexion, hazel eyes, scar ¾ of an inch on left side of forehead, tattoos, a woman on lower left calf. Mother, dead. Father, defendant does not know address."

In court the judge read the confidential social history.

> He has been a problem to his parents, juvenile and adult authorities since he was quite young. At this time he is separated from his wife and claims he cannot locate her in Denver and he has never seen his child. During interviews at the county jail he expressed little remorse for his past and present anti-social behavior.

The report said his adjustment at Annandale reformatory had been satisfactory. Bordentown, adjustment poor. The New Jersey parole board records showed that an official told him, "You go around with an attitude that makes it almost impossible for anyone to know you, in the first place. And in the second place, your work record in the institution so far has been very poor."

His Bordentown report said:

> Subject rationalizes his delinquency as due to his inability to gain satisfactory recognition legitimately. However, as subject gradually realized the basic dilemma presented by his personality structure . . . he appeared to show a disinterest in further grappling with the problem. . . . Retreats from any further effort to restructure an inadequately oriented personality with the aid of professional personnel."

The judge read Emeline Flanigan's report from New Jersey:

> William has always appeared very much attached to his mother who has been ill with cancer for many years. She died within the last year. Mrs. Irwin protected William from his older siblings and his father. Mr. Irwin was a hard-working man without as many cultural interests as Mrs. Irwin . . .

The social report of the Denver court said that Irwin's associates were mostly bad, all heavy drinkers and robbers. He had been arrested at least fifteen times for drunkenness in Denver.

Judge William A. Black sentenced him to from two to ten years in the Colorado State Penitentiary in Canon City for burglary and conspiracy to commit burglary.

Canon City was a violent penitentiary. He saw murders and beatings unlike even the rough life in Bordentown. But by now he was a big, aggressive man, and that protected him from other prisoners. He learned how to make friends with strong associates. He never stopped drinking, and eighteen months later he was paroled on condition that he remain in Denver.

Two months later he was back in New Jersey, working in an iron mine near Dover, where he met Madeline. Madeline, five years older than Bill, separated from her husband, was pretty, witty and made everyone feel happy. She had three children, one a boy thirteen, whom Irwin liked. They moved into a duplex apartment, with two elderly ladies living next door.

The ladies next door were terrified. Sober or drunk, Bill was loud. And he was often drunk. The police started visiting Irwin's side of the house. It did not dawn on Irwin that the ladies next door were calling the police until the day he opened the kitchen door leading to their common cellar and discovered one of the ladies on the top step with her ear to the door. He roared at her and she left, shaking. The police started calling four or five times a week. It didn't help that the chief of police lived at the other end of the block.

One day the chief of police came to the apartment to investigate the usual complaint. The chief, a potbelly flowing over his belt, reminded Irwin of the principal, who had beaten him in the school cellar. Irwin poked his finger into the chief's chest, told him to get the hell out of the house. Irwin, by now out on the sidewalk, was yelling obscenities at the chief as neighbors watched dumbstruck. This was Thursday. On Friday night Irwin and Madeline had visitors they frequently put up. "Stewart" was a married man who lived a few blocks away, "Rosalie" a seventeen-year-old girl having an affair with him. Periodically they would spend the night in an upstairs bedroom. On Saturday morning the police car pulled up. Irwin ran upstairs and told Stewart and Rosalie to get dressed, and got to the door in time to let the police in himself. It was the chief and a woman he had never seen before.

The chief asked, "Mind if I look around?"

Irwin assumed that by now the couple upstairs would be up and dressed.

"I don't mind. I'll take you around."

They went upstairs. The bedroom was empty. They opened the bathroom door. Stewart was putting on his shorts. The chief grunted and headed back downstairs. As he went by the closet door he opened it. Rosalie was getting into her brassiere.

Downstairs the chief said he wanted Irwin to come with him to the police station. "If you refuse, then I'll go back to court and get a warrant for both you and Madeline."

Irwin could see no charge the chief could bring against him. He had been worried about Stewart and Rosalie being caught in bed, especially because Rosalie was under the age of consent and Stewart could be charged with statutory rape and Irwin and Madeline as accessories. But the chief did not catch them in the act.

Nevertheless, the chief's threat bothered Irwin because he had come to care for Madeline and her children. The idea of her being arrested was disturbing, an act that he felt responsible for. He remembered his humiliating the chief, his drunkenness, his loud talk heard through the wall of the house, his terrorizing the old ladies. Madeline had never been in trouble with the police before. His short time with her had convinced Irwin that she was genuinely devoted to him and to her children. After the first visit of the chief, Irwin had warned her not to be trapped into anything incriminating. They maintained separate bedrooms, with Irwin's clothes in one and Madeline's in the other, and by prearrangement Madeline was to say that Irwin was only a roomer, paying board and room plus providing money for her doing his laundry, income to help support her children adequately. As the chief stood there waiting for his reply, Irwin considered the situation well in hand and no threat to either of them. He said he would go with the chief.

The chief placed him in a cage and left. Irwin found later that they had gone directly back to the house and brought Madeline to the station, threatened to have her declared an unfit mother and take away her children. If she signed a statement saying that she and Irwin had sexual relations knowing that they were not married to each other, they would bring no charges against her and nothing serious would happen to Bill. She signed and they let her go home. They charged Irwin with adultery, took him to the county jail and held him under $500 bail for sentencing.

The $500 bail was not a serious problem. His pay at the iron mine was good and he arranged for bond. But the day he was to be released a Teletype from Colorado said he had jumped parole. He had been ordered not to leave Denver without permission and owed Colorado eight years' imprisonment. His release on bail was canceled and preparation made to send him to Colorado. The local police made no secret that they wanted him out of their jurisdiction. Some of them had spent too much of their law enforcement careers hearing about Bill Irwin, the rough, tough drunken brawler. But Colorado disappointed them. The Western authorities said they would let New Jersey punish him first.

Irwin was released on bail. Madeline was frightened. He took a hotel room and put some clothes there. Then he and Madeline rented another apartment in Dover, where they lived together.

For nine months life went on, less boisterously than before. Irwin tired of fights, not wanting his troubles to hurt Madeline and the children. His work in the mines paid for a lawyer to defend him against the adultery charge. Adultery committed within the State of New Jersey did not strike either client or attorney as something to worry about. The lawyer said neither he nor the prosecutor had ever known of anyone in the state going to prison for adultery. The law was dormant. The courts granted thousands of divorces every year to citizens who insisted under oath that they had committed adultery. Besides, the only real evidence they had was a statement taken from Madeline under threats.

But in the fall the lawyer had bad news. The police were going to press the charge anyway. They were sick of dealing with Irwin. If he fought the charge and beat it, then they would have Madeline declared an unfit mother and take away her children.

The prosecutor had a deal to offer. If Irwin would plead guilty, without a trial or a defense, they would see that he got only a year's sentence, probably suspended, and Madeline would be left alone.

For weeks Bill Irwin thought about the deal. He loved living with Madeline. They had a powerful sexual attraction for each other, more than he had ever felt for another woman. But that was not the real difference. For the first time in his life since preschool years with his mother he felt a delight to be in another person's presence. Madeline was warm, loving and smart. It was a surprise to him the first time he realized as he quit work that he was looking forward to going home to Madeline. And, even more surprisingly, to the kids. The thirteen-year-old boy was devoted to Irwin. Madeline had a job on the assembly line of a nearby electronics plant. Irwin had a good job at the mines. He was even beginning to have religious feelings and discovering that he didn't yell as much, that his temper did not take over, that he and Madeline could talk without shouting. He hated the thought that the police would end it all.

The idea of the children being taken from Madeline and put in an orphanage—like his father!—was intolerable. It paralyzed Madeline when she thought of it. If he got a year sentence, suspended, there would be no problem and Madeline and the kids would be safe. Even if he got a year of actual prison, he'd be out in nine months with good behavior. One of his best friends, Mick Muldoon's brother Jock, was doing a long stretch in Trenton State Prison and he wouldn't mind seeing him again. At least four other guys he had grown up with were also doing time at Trenton State and it would be good to see them again. Madeline's job at the electronics plant would keep her going until he got out and then they'd be back together again. He pleaded guilty.

The judge gave him two to three years in Trenton State Prison.

In Trenton State he met Jock and his old friends. Prison life didn't bother him.

But he couldn't get Madeline off his mind. It was hard for her to travel to Trenton, so he requested a transfer to Rahway State Prison, which was easier for her to visit and was more open.

When he saw Madeline across the visiting room his blood would race, from the sexual stimulation and the memory of her warmth. They kissed passionately during the visits and told each other about every remembered minute since the last visit. They wrote to each other every day.

After a few visits she told him that his friend Stewart, who had been in the upstairs bedroom with Rosalie, was driving her to the supermarket and the laundromat. Irwin was worried but Madeline was so honest that he knew she was not holding anything back. Stewart had lots of girl friends and was loyal to Bill and Madeline. On his birthday Stewart had asked Madeline for a kiss and she gave him one and told Irwin. Irwin wanted to warn her that the relationship would grow into something more intimate but he didn't want to sound distrustful or plant an idea that might not have existed before.

The fear of separation from Madeline increased. Irwin became more religious. He signed up in prison as a Jew. He told Jock it was only to get special food. But he was reading the Bible steadily and was impressed with the Jews' ability to sustain suffering and still be special to the deity. He was circumcised in the prison hospital.

One visiting day Madeline was not smiling. As soon as they embraced she burst into tears. The local paper had run a story about Irwin and her. The story hinted that they had been running a whorehouse and Madeline was the madam. It had caused a sensation in the small town where she had grown up and everyone knew her. Now no one would talk to her, even her oldest friends. At work girls next to her on the assembly line had stopped work until the foreman moved her away from them and she was fired.

He never felt so helpless. If he were on the outside he would walk into the newspaper office and make them run a correction. And if he were walking on the street with Madeline and a former friend turned her head, he would confront the friend and make her say why she was doing it and get it out in the open. But he was totally frustrated.

At that crucial point he was transferred back to Trenton. She did not visit him for a long time. He was within a short time of discharge and was made an orderly. He was increasingly religious but this did not prevent him from accepting a job, through his status as an orderly, as a lieutenant of another prisoner who was the biggest heroin dealer inside the wall. He helped distribute the bags of heroin to paying prisoners. Irwin didn't use the stuff himself. His dealer, a rich man from his trade, was treated with respect by the staff and some of that status gave Irwin a feeling of security.

He alternated between delivery of heroin packets for the prison pusher and religious despair in the darkness of his cage.

More and more he read his Bible and prayed. He bargained out loud: "God. Listen to me. Man, you let me out of here, you help me straighten out this trouble Madeline's having, and I'll be good, really good. Anything you want me to do. I'm all yours. I'm not jiving you. I'm serious. Help me just this once and I'll do anything."

He searched his Bible for guidance, for penance, sacrifice. He read of sackcloth and ashes. In the last book of the Old Testament it was written, "And now entreat the favor of God . . . Behold, I will rebuke your offspring, and spread dung upon your faces . . ."

One night a guard found Irwin naked in his cage, rubbing feces over his face.

The next night, ten days before his release date, two huge guards came to his cage. He asked if he was arrested and they said he was. Irwin knew there were eleven packets of heroin taped under his bunk and assumed he had been caught. The guards took him through the basement to a medieval dungeon. It was reached by curving stone steps. The door was inches-thick oak. As they opened the door he could see that there were no windows and no artificial light. The dim light from the corridor illuminated walls of great stone blocks that were moist. Before he could survey the entire cell they slammed the door. He was in total darkness. Groping along the walls, he ascertained that there was a large can that seemed to be a toilet—there was no sink or conventional toilet—and another can with water in it. The only other feature in the cell was an indentation in the wall with a concrete slab on the bottom. It was the only thing that could be interpreted as a bed. He crawled into it and worried. He knew that he could be severely punished for running heroin inside the institution. He concentrated on what might happen and how he should react to it.

The next morning a squad of guards opened his door. They put handcuffs on him, leg irons, a chain around his waist and shackled his handcuffs to the chain. He asked, "We going to court?"

One of the guards said, "We got orders to take you to the Vroom Building."

Irwin almost screamed involuntarily. Inside his head the words "God! God! God!" ricocheted endlessly. He had an instinct to run, to fight, to bite. But another instinct warned him not to lose control. He must not behave in a way that would make him seem crazy. He repeated to himself as he shuffled toward the transfer van, It's all right, Bill. It's all right, Bill. You've got only ten days more and you'll be able to talk to the doctors and let them know you're all right. Everything is going to work out. Just be calm. Just be calm. Don't argue. Be calm.

The van drove to the Trenton State Hospital for the Criminally Insane. It was built like a prison with a special refinement—a doctor, not a warden, was in charge. Irwin was taken to what he learned later was called "Shit Row." He was undressed, given a hospital gown and put in a cage that contained only a toilet bowl and a rubber mattress on the floor. He said to the guard, "I want to see a doctor."

The guard said he would.

"But I want to see him now. There's something I have to tell him right away."

The guard said he'd see a doctor soon enough and slammed the barred door.

Irwin looked around the cage, looked through the bars at the tier of cages and thought, Oh, my God. What am I doing here? I don't belong here.

Bill Irwin saw a doctor soon enough. The doctor came to his cage door. With him was a squad of heavy guards. One guard pushed a wheeled machine with wires and dials into the entryway of the cage while four others grabbed Irwin and wrestled him to the floor.

"Doctor! Doctor! Listen to me! Before you do anything, listen to me! Please!"

The guards held him down while the man who had been pushing the machine rubbed a greaselike substance on his forehead and temples.

"Doctor, will you listen to me!"

One of the guards put a rubber form in his mouth, the doctor leaned over, placed two electrodes on Bill Irwin's temples, and Bill Irwin received the first electroshock to his brain.

When he woke up after the shock he couldn't remember what had happened. But from sounds he heard the next day he discovered the routine. The goon squad—four or five large guards—accompanied a technician who rolled the mobile electroshock machine along the tier. They came on Mondays, Wednesdays and Fridays. Each course of treatments consisted of twenty shocks. Irwin doesn't remember ever being told how many he was scheduled to get nor does he remember ever talking to a psychiatrist or psychologist during the course of his "treatment."

Each time the first thing he heard was the rumble of the machine being pushed along the steel tier, the sound echoing off the steel, concrete and tile. He would deliberately try to remain unexcited. The doctor had to be convinced that he was not insane. Irwin was practicing constant self-discipline to be calm during it all. A guard would call out, "Trip One." Somewhere another guard would push a switch to open the electrical lock on cage No. 1. Then the sounds would begin.

"No! No! Please! Someone! Not today! Please! Please! God, please! Mama! Mama! Please! I'm all right! Mama! Please . . ."

Irwin would remain lying on his rubber mattress, his face impassive. He could hear the murmur of the doctor in a Germanic accent. There would be a muffled sound, a buzz of the electrical machine and then silence.

A cell door would close. The next call: "Trip Two."

It was then that the "sound" would usually begin, the wordless screech.

Bill Irwin steeled himself.

"Trip Three."

The mass screech resumed. The man in No. 3 began struggling and gurgling.

By his twelfth shock Bill Irwin could no longer repress the screech. Later he would tell me, "I felt shame at my giving in to terror. I've been afraid all my life. You can't get into as many fights as I've been in without having fear, but I was always able to overcome this fear. In a way that's what my fights were about, to see if I could overcome my fear. I was always able to control it and use it to my advantage. But now I was succumbing to this fear and going into panic and terror. It was one of the most humiliating things that has ever happened to me. It was degrading and I was filled with shame that I should be so frightened."

He does not remember ever receiving an explanation of what the shock treatments were for. He does know that if two prisoners in another part of the institution had a fight over a weekend, the next Monday both were given electroshocks "to calm them." It did have a momentary calming effect. He walked around almost semiconscious, sometimes guided by an attendant.

He was given a second full set of shocks for a total of forty. They started on the third series of twenty. Irwin's lifetime temper began to surface as the shock treatments went on. Docility did not convince the doctor that he was sane. He saw only endless shock treatments until, he feared, he would have no brain at all. One day, he stood by his cage door as the machine was rolled down the tier. He acted with docility. The guard called out, "Trip Four," the barred door opened, and Irwin came out like a wild animal. He picked up guards and threw them to the floor, he knocked the machine on its side, he went for the doctor's throat. One of the guards, a man Irwin had become friendly with, was not exempted. Irwin broke his finger. The squad finally subdued him, gave him a hypodermic injection that knocked him out. Then they gave him his shock. Later the friendly guard, after exhibiting his splinted finger, said the doctor had turned the machine current higher than they had ever seen it before, and after Irwin was unconscious from the first shock, gave him a second.

Much of the sequence of events during this period is hazy in Irwin's memory. No one knows what happens during an electroshock treatment except that it rearranges the electrical relations of the brain cells, with unpredictable effects. No one knows, including doctors who administer it for a conglomeration of ailments. Ernest Hemingway and Sylvia Plath were given electroshock treatments for "depression." Both committed suicide shortly thereafter.

Sometime during the shocks he was taken to see visitors. He was groggy and had to be led by two guards. He was wearing a white hospital gown and handcuffs chained to waist shackles. He sat in a booth with a thick glass panel. He saw in a booth on the other side Madeline and Stewart. The booths and the glass window between them seemed to be soundproof. They had to talk through a telephone that didn't work well. Nothing of the content of the conversation remains with Irwin.

He remembers that after his first twenty electroshocks they took him to a less restricted part of the hospital, but he was heavily drugged. His recollection is that he was given two hypodermic shots of liquid Thorazine a day. It kept him so groggy that he couldn't stand up. He remembers the first time during this condition that he needed to urinate. He could see his toilet bowl across the cage. He crawled on the floor to the bowl. In a long, painful set of motions he struggled to get to his feet. Once on his feet he began to fall over.

"I started to fall. I willed my hands to come up, you know, to protect me. And my hands wouldn't move from the side of my body. I didn't have any muscle control. I couldn't move my hands. I saw the floor coming up to my face but I was able to just barely move my face to the side so I didn't break my nose. Of course, I smashed the side of my cheek open.

"My mind was working so groggy, so slow, I didn't know what happened. I tried again and I fell again, just the same way. Then I realized that I had to change something and I crawled up on that toilet and I squatted like a woman and I remember thinking, as groggy as I was, feeling a bit silly about it—they had finally made a woman out of me."

Then he was taken for his second set of twenty shocks. Once more he would resolve not to succumb to terror. But as each of the patients began screaming in terror, the animal screech caused trembling beyond control and Irwin would find himself making the same wordless sound as the rumbling machine approached, the guards throwing him onto the floor, the attendant rubbing the electrolytic grease on his temples, pushing the boxer's rubber mouthpiece between Bill's crushed teeth, the doctor appearing overhead, the electrodes in his hand, murmuring in his guttural accent, "That's all right. Be a good boy. Nobody is going to hurt you. You won't feel a thing. That's a good boy." Then blackness.

The second set of twenty shocks was completed. The third series started.

Whatever the shocks did to Irwin's brain, they did not remove his instinct for survival. He knew that unless he did something he could never escape from the nightmare. He was no longer on massive Thorazine. On the days between shocks he asked questions and discovered the name of the psychiatrist on his case. He didn't know if he had ever seen the psychiatrist but he was determined to meet him. He walked out of the ward. Irwin said he was going to find his doctor and went from ward to ward, quietly asking for the doctor by name. After what seemed like hours, someone told him the doctor he was looking for was in an office at the end of the ward. He entered the office. There was an attractive woman. He asked where the doctor was. She said she was the doctor.

He had carefully rehearsed what he would say. It would have to be calm, factual, rational. He told who he was, what his record was, and how many shocks he had received. He said that he didn't want any more shocks and he was not insane.

"If you didn't need these shocks, they wouldn't have given them to you," she said.

He insisted that he didn't need them.

"Well, I have to accept that the people who put you on these shocks knew what they were doing and I have to go along with their diagnosis until I know you better."

Irwin begged her to stop the shocks until she was convinced from her own knowledge that he needed them. He said things were happening to him that might not ever change if they continued. "Even my teeth!"

He showed her the crumbled front teeth.

"Look," he told her. "It isn't as though I'm asking you to pardon a life sentence. All I'm asking you, I'm begging you, is to watch me, study me, do anything you want, look at me for as long as you want, but make up your own mind about my taking those shocks. You've got the power to do whatever you want with me. If you look at me for a while and then decide I need the shocks, you know that the next day I'll be on shocks. You're the boss. And I don't mind telling you, I'm scared. I'm terrified of those shocks. Maybe if I was crazy it wouldn't make any difference to me."

Irwin could sense a change in her. She said she would take him off the shocks temporarily and make up her mind after she studied the results. He never had another shock.

Suddenly he was in a minimum-custody building, free to walk on the grounds, to have visitors and letters. One day he got a letter from Madeline. She really needed a change, Stewart had been wonderful to her, she loved Bill but she didn't know when he'd get out or how he'd be. She was desperate, so she and Stewart were going to California together. Goodbye and good luck. She didn't say where in California she was going.

She was dropping him. He began to feel himself getting dizzy but he reasserted his self-control. Two weeks afterward he received a letter from Jock Muldoon, who told him more. Madeline had left with Stewart, but they had taken everything that Bill owned—his clothes, his books, his ID cards, and they had cashed an income tax refund check he had waiting for him. His two best friends had run off and now they had taken everything he owned. At first he had forgiven Madeline out of pity for her desperation. Now she was malicious and Stewart worse.

He put his feeling on a tape cartridge he was able to spirit to me: "I had a strong desire to kill. It was real but I was afraid to show it. At this time I believed that a psychiatrist could tell everything you were thinking even if you concealed it. So I was afraid to show this but I was even afraid to feel it. I was afraid the psychiatrist would pick it up and put me back on shocks and never let me out of the nuthouse. If they felt I wanted to kill someone they'd never let me out.

"So I began praying to God to forgive Madeline. I wanted to be able to forgive her. Not for her sake. I didn't care about that. I thought she needed to get killed, both her and Stewart. But for my sake. I was scared for my life, scared I'd never be released from that place if they suspected what was going on in my mind. Rather than try to fool them, I decided they were too smart for me to fool. I'd have to be sincere. I'd have to have a sincere desire to love and to forgive and everything. So I was determined to make myself think that way. I made up my mind, I prayed to God, that I was going to love her in spite of everything. I prayed that I could make myself think that way. I made up my mind I was going to love her in spite of everything. I used to make up letters to her every day saying I loved her. I'm writing letters still."

Suddenly Bill Irwin was free. He was asked on a Monday if he thought he was ready to meet the staff for an evaluation. The next day he met a panel of ten people. That afternoon he was given a pair of slacks, a short-sleeved shirt and a summer jacket. It was a bitter cold winter day. A guard took him to the bus station, bought a ticket to Rockaway for $4.75 and gave Bill the twenty-five cents change from his five dollars release money.

Within an hour Bill was drinking. On the bus he met two men and a young woman, blacks. He showed them his discharge papers, told them about his experience; they opened a bottle of whiskey and shared it with him.

By nightfall he was in Rockaway. He got change for his quarter and called a sister on the telephone. Her husband answered and greeted him warmly. His wife grabbed the phone from him and demanded, "What are you doing back in town?"

Irwin apologized for the shame he had brought the family and begged her to let him stay just overnight.

"No. I can't do a damn thing for you."

Irwin hung up. He had fifteen cents. He had only one hope. Mrs. Muldoon lived on Hunky Row, a rundown section of poor Irish, Hungarians, Poles, Germans and blacks. He knocked on her door. He didn't know what he would do if she was not home or turned him away.

The door opened. She looked at the figure in the dark and then said, "Billy! I'm happy to see you. Bring yourself in and let me see you better."

She hugged him and wept.

He remembered later: "I was never so happy in all my life. I've always thought of her as my mother since that day. She's a big fat woman who has an alcoholic problem and at times her children have been very embarrassed by her, but to me she's my mother."

Mr. Muldoon greeted Bill warmly. They sat him down and made him supper.

During his incarceration the iron mines had closed. Unemployment in Rockaway was high. Mr. Muldoon worked on a night shift but after a night's work he would drive Irwin all over the area to factories, warehouses, lumber yards and construction projects. There was no work. As Bill walked around town people he had known turned away or crossed the street as he approached. Even kids he raised hell with a few years earlier would smile wanly and rush off. He was convinced he had to leave town. One night Rosalie called him long distance to say she had heard that Stewart and Madeline had been married and that Stewart had killed his new bride. He didn't believe it. But someone said they remembered a headline like "Shortest Marriage in History," in California or Nevada or somewhere like that.

Irwin left, first for Denver, where he burglarized enough money to get to California, where he went to the public libraries in San Francisco, Los Angeles and San Diego looking at old newspapers for an account of a bride's murder on her wedding day. He never found it. He went back to Denver.

In Denver he met an old drinking pal, Tommy, a seventy-year-old ex-con. Under the old man's tutelage they did armed robberies. Tommy was arrested and Irwin taken to the station. Tommy drew Irwin aside and told him he was already stuck with a mandatory life term so he would take the rap for them both and Irwin should deny everything. It worked and it was only a matter of hours before they would release Irwin. A plainclothesman came to Irwin's cage. It was a parole officer. They had just discovered that he had skipped his Colorado parole and owed them more time. He was shipped to Canon City penitentiary. A year later he was paroled to Denver again. Thirteen months later, after uncounted arrests for drunkenness—one in Los Angeles, which proved that again he had left Denver without permission—he was sent to Canon City penitentiary for the third time.

William Ryan Joseph Irwin was a living monument to the curative effects of the criminal justice system and brain therapy. He was, by his own description, an alcoholic who when drunk was obnoxious, assaultive and larcenous. The state's treatment for this was night after night in filthy drunk tanks, endless lectures by tired magistrates, curses from cops who had to handle big unpleasant drunks, and a reputation guaranteeing that every transgression was a prophecy fulfilled.

Convicts often claim, "There is no justice." Most convicts are guilty of the crime they were charged with. But most of them know that if "justice" means the even-handed application of the law, they have not received justice. Bill Irwin was a drunk. He fought. He lied. He stole. But he knew many people, including policemen and judges, who were drunks, who fought, who lied and stole, but were never subject to criminal prosecution.

He also knew that millions of citizens commit adultery but, as far as anyone knows, William Irwin was the only person in his time to be sent to the New Jersey State Penitentiary for adultery. There are millions of people who are anti-social, filled with self-flagellating despair and carried away in irrational religious trances, who believe in the literal interpretation of the Bible, but they are not subjected to electroshock treatments against their will, and do not have imposed on them, by a stranger signing a piece of paper, an unpredictable rearrangement of their brains.

In Colorado William Irwin, still an alcoholic, in a stupid impulse for more liquor after store hours, had stolen goods valued at $370.62 from a saloon and was sentenced to ten years in prison. He had been an alcoholic since he was fifteen years old. He would be almost continuously in the hands of the state for over twenty-five years. It would cost society a quarter of a million dollars to punish William Irwin during the course of his career and much of it would be listed in budgets as "treatment." For a man with native intelligence, Irwin acted stupidly. He might be excused if he thought society was more stupid than he. A quarter of a million dollars might have been spent more intelligently and with greater peace for both William Irwin and society.

The Colorado parole board committed Irwin back to Canon City because he still owed thirty-two months on his ten-year sentence.

In Canon City his best friend passed the time by creating exciting rumors. When that palled his friend answered a call for prisoners to volunteer donation of a kidney in the new kidney transplant operations in Denver. In the boredom that followed Irwin tried his hand at creating rumors. Two spectacles in crime excited the prison population. One was the kidnapping from a Lake Tahoe hotel room of Frank Sinatra, Jr., the nineteen-year-old son of the pop singer, and his release three days later after payment of $240,000 ransom. The other was the courtroom spilling of mafia secrets from a former mafioso, Joseph Valachi. One day Irwin created an uproar by inventing a radio news report that the mafia had assassinated Valachi in the courtroom. It was discovered by nightfall and Irwin laughed at them all.

A few days later a friend, Butch, called down from his cage directly above Irwin's: "Hey, Bill, you got a brother named John?"

"Yeah."

"Well, he's the guy who kidnapped the Sinatra kid."

Irwin began laughing. He knew Butch was desperate to retaliate for the Valachi rumor.

"Yeah, sure," Irwin said, laughing.

"No shit, Bill, honest to Christ. I ain't shitting you. It's right here in the paper."

"Yeah, okay," Irwin yelled back, chuckling.

"Listen for Christ sake, Bill, I ain't shitting. Look, does he live at—wait a minute—at . . ." and he yelled down a Los Angeles address.

Irwin thought for a moment and yelled back, "You stupid son of a bitch, you seen my letters addressed to him. Who you think you're kidding?"

"Jesus, Irwin. Look."

Butch dropped a newspaper from his cage to where Irwin could pull it inside his cage. Butch was right. There was a story, a picture of his brother John, and an account that said John had done the telephoning for the ransom but had confessed to police. The authorities had recovered $233,855 of the $240,000.

Irwin was stunned. He had always had special affection for his brother. From his earliest childhood, John had been Bill's protector from his brother Dick. And now the paper said he was talking to the police. Even the brother of someone allegedly talking to the police could be in trouble.

He was relieved when he was ordered to the local Veterans Hospital for a series of tests to confirm that his kidney was eligible for donation. What impressed him was the freedom of the hospital, good food, and the chance to talk to someone other than prisoners. A private guard was at his door twenty-four hours a day, but most would take a walk when Bill had a sexual visit from a Denver girl friend. For him it was fair exchange for a kidney.

Within days he was sent to Colorado General Hospital, where a woman from Los Angeles had been flown to receive his kidney.

Irwin was told the woman's name but forgot it. He never saw her. But her brother came in to thank him. Irwin's response was "Man, look at you. You big, strong brute. Why don't you donate your kidney?"

The man retreated in embarrassment.

"When I look back," Irwin said years later, "I can see that I was a louse. I was boisterous, loud and aggressive, all the things I don't respect in people today. I was all of those things. And what I did to that woman's brother! I cringe when I think of it."

Apparently the transplant was a success but Irwin knows little about it, even if the woman is alive today. For a year he had pains in his back as his body adjusted to the loss of a kidney.

He applied for parole and was denied it, even though the state psychiatrist disagreed with the Trenton diagnosis and said that anyone with Irwin's childhood would be anti-social. But he was sent to an open minimum-security honor camp at Pueblo.

The last year of his imprisonment was strange. He joined Alcoholics Anonymous in order to get higher quality vodka and to share control of the illicit liquor traffic inside the camp. He earned substantial amounts of money by running the camp poker game, taking 10 per cent of every pot. Guards helped smuggle in commercial liquor but they charged so much it was more profitable for Irwin and his partner to walk into town between counts and drag cases of liquor across the fields. He was drunk most of the time. He also started taking a variety of pills to get new sensations. Thirty days before his release he had to beg to be sent to the more disciplined prerelease center because he wanted to be sober when he hit the street.

Once back in Denver, he worked at day labor again, at $1.25 an hour, if the weather was good. He began living with a woman. His drinking increased and so did the pills. The woman kicked him out. He took a room in a flophouse near the State Capitol in downtown Denver. The first night he bought cheap wine and some pills and fell asleep trying to read the Gideon Bible. His first mystical experience came in the middle of the night, during a drunken, doped sleep. In a dream a man appeared whom he knew to be Jesus Christ, not because of the conventional prayerbook picture but because the figure wore garments of a weave he had never seen before. Irwin was frightened and watched as the figure circled over him in a tightening spiral until, almost smothering him, the figure lay on top of him and entered his chest. Irwin trembled and fell into a deep sleep.

When he woke he felt that something profound had happened to him but he didn't know what. The next night after he had earned a day's wages at Manpower, Inc., he was on his way to visit a friend in the hospital with a gift carton of cigarettes and some magazines when he realized that it was the first conscious gesture of thoughtfulness he had ever committed without labored consideration or ulterior purpose. He was so impressed, and so suspicious that it was a sign of the phenomenon the night before, that he stepped inside a Pentecostal church. He watched people sighing, crying and moving spasmodically in a kind of ecstasy. He began attending the church Wednesday nights. He watched the loud praying and calling out, attracted by it but detached. One night the preacher reached him powerfully and Irwin found himself at the altar weeping uncontrollably. The minister beseeched him to give up his sins, to give himself to Christ. Irwin wept without understanding what it all meant.

The next two years were spent ricocheting between drinking, drugs and religion, Madeline still on his mind. He went to Los Angeles, where an old friend from Trenton State Prison finally explained the mystery of Madeline's "murder." Stewart had left Madeline for another woman, whom he married. At the drunken wedding reception the bride and an usher disappeared for three hours and upon their return Stewart shot and killed his bride. That accounted for the newspaper story about "The Shortest Wedding." It meant that Madeline was still alive. Irwin was wildly excited.

Another excitement stimulated Irwin at the same time. Out of the blue, William Irwin, smalltime drunk and burglar, suddenly had an urge to rob banks. It could have been the need for money to find Madeline. Or the symbolism of the bars of a teller's window like bars of a prison, but this time with a respectable member of society under his control on the other side. Or the impact of thousands of bank-robbing legends that fill prison bull sessions. Or simply the higher rate of return compared to burglaries. Whatever the reason, "cracking a jug" became an emotional urge other bank robbers have described.

Irwin and his penitentiary friend held up two banks in a single day, despite some disabilities of Irwin in his new trade. He did not know how to drive a car, so he did the dangerous gun-toting while his partner did the easier driving for the same pay. Irwin was also filled with false lore about bank-robbing, like the idea that zinc oxide on the face blurs features on photographs from the automatic cameras that record bank holdups. And he disliked robbing women, not a rare instinct among robbers, though a chivalry that disappears with experience.

His face shiny with zinc oxide, Irwin held up a check-cashing office and got $1000. Then he turned to his first real bank job, in Long Beach.

He put his pistol in his belt, a folded paper bag in his pocket and walked into the bank, his face still shiny. Two teller windows were available, one with a male teller busy with a customer, the other with a woman teller with no waiting. Irwin got into the line in front of the male teller.

The woman called out pleasantly, "May I help you?"

"No, thanks. I want to speak to this man."

Irwin stepped to the man's window and pulled out the pistol and paper bag. "Now I don't want to hurt nobody. You won't get hurt if you just put all the money in this bag."

The teller began sweeping piles of money into the bag and emptying packets of bills from his drawer.

The woman teller approached the man's window.

Irwin said, "What are you doing?"

"I'm giving you the money from my window."

"I don't want the money from your window!"

Irwin refused to touch the money she had piled up on her counter. He walked out of the bank. The car was soon on a freeway and heading north to Culver City, near the MGM studios. They counted the loot: $7200 from the bank plus the $1000. They split it evenly. They went to the nearest bar to toast their success and Irwin announced that he was flying back to New Jersey immediately to find Madeline. He didn't know it but at that moment he was within several blocks of Madeline.

The next morning he was in Rockaway. Ten years had softened the faces of people who saw him. He could enter a bar and old friends would talk. They confirmed that Stewart was in prison for murder. One friend made a phone call for Madeline's address—back in Los Angeles. Irwin flew back to California.

He took a cab direct to Madeline's Los Angeles address. She was shocked to see him. She let him in cautiously. Some of the old feeling came back. She looked different to him but he was happy to see her. For the first time he told her he had pleaded guilty to adultery and as a result undergone shock treatments only because he didn't want her to lose her children. They talked for hours and in the end she was contrite and asked him to move in. She had a job in a Santa Monica plant making underwater equipment.

As the days wore on the joy he felt in her presence disappeared. She disliked California and nagged him about returning to New Jersey. He was conscious that she had lost her figure, her wit and spontaneity and was now fat, haggard and depressed. Jobless and morose, he went back to bank-robbing.

Women tellers and zinc oxide no longer interfered with Irwin's proficiency in robbing banks. His lack of a driving license did and he picked up a series of old prison pals to do the getaway driving.

His bank-robbing career ended on October 30, 1967. It was a Monday and he needed money. A romantic young man from Venice, California, never before involved in crime, offered to drive the car, saying it was like a TV series. Irwin put an old .38 revolver in his belt, the folded supermarket bag into the pocket of a flashy sports jacket with black and white checks, and told his young friend to drive around until things felt right.

"Drive up Washington Boulevard."

When they got to the corner of Centinela Avenue he said, "Stop here. That looks like a nice Bank of America."

The holdup went quickly although his pistol stuck in his belt when he first pulled it out, attracting the attention of a customer behind him. As he left the bank Irwin had the feeling that his departure was observed. He told the driver to zoom around blocks making sudden turns until Irwin felt they had shaken any followers. He stopped at a liquor store for a six-pack of beer and a bottle of vodka.

Inside the driver's apartment Irwin draped his sports jacket over a living-room chair and went into the kitchen to count the loot: only $1745. It was split two ways and he paid the driver $400 additional to buy Madeline the old secondhand car he had used in the holdup. Irwin cursed when he realized his net for the morning was only $472.

They were drinking in the kitchen about an hour later when someone knocked. Irwin, now relaxed and expansive, unlocked the front door.

"FBI!"

Irwin coolly let in three men, one who identified himself as a Los

Angeles city detective. Irwin disclaimed any knowledge of the car they said had been used to rob a bank that morning. As they talked in the kitchen the city detective seemed to be staring at the living room. Irwin followed the detective's gaze. They were both looking at the loud black and white sports coat. Irwin was sure that no other jacket like it existed in California. Later he would speculate that some invitation to punishment moved him to wear it in the first place and leave it in plain sight afterward.

The detective said, "Mr. Irwin, whose coat is that?"

"That's my coat. Why?"

"Where were you earlier this morning, Mr. Irwin?"

"Over at my apartment."

"Stand up. I'm going to frisk you."

They found a roll of bills in his pocket.

"Hold out your hands and don't fuck around! You're under arrest."

The detectives put Irwin and his partner, both in handcuffs, into a squad car and drove them to the Santa Monica police station. (By coincidence, that same day I was sitting in an office doing research on Main Street, Santa Monica, directly across from the entry to the Santa Monica police station. Unable to erase habits from police-reporting days, I watched every police car entering the drive. I probably saw the car bearing Irwin, four and a half years before I would meet him.)

The agents put Irwin and his partner in separate rooms.

Irwin told the FBI agent, "Look, you know I'm busted and I know I'm busted. But if I tell you now in this room I'm going to go to prison, that guy in the other room will go to prison, too. When we get to prison for our fifteen or twenty or whatever the hell it is, he's going to tell everybody in the joint that I ratted him off. And you know I can't do that. I can't stay alive that way. You give me ten minutes alone with this guy, to explain to him that we don't stand a chance, we're better off copping out, and then I'll tell you what you want to know."

The FBI agent agreed. Irwin went to the other room, where he spoke alone to the driver. The driver, never involved with the police before, was bewildered and frightened.

Irwin told him, "Don't snitch. Don't tell them nothing. I'm busted and I know it. They got witnesses. Everybody and his brother seen me in that bank. And that fuckin' jacket. But they don't know a thing about you. As far as anybody is concerned, you were just selling me a car. You don't know anything about a bank being robbed. This is a Monday morning. We talked Sunday about my buying that car. So tell them we took the car for a test run because there was something wrong with one of the brakes and I asked you to stop at the bank so I could cash a check and pay you for the car. We stop at the bank, a few minutes later I come out with the money and we drive off. Back at the house I give you the money for the car and that's all you know. Got it? Now stick to that story. You got to choose. Right now. You either tell that story and stick to it, or else you cop out right now. It's your decision. I don't want to see you go to prison. I been in prison and with my record I'm going again for a long time. But there's no sense in both of us going. If you want to stick to that story, I'll back you up. That's the best I can do for you."

Irwin walked back to the room with the FBI agent. In the meantime, on the basis of Irwin's promise to confess, a stenographer had been brought in. The FBI agent said to him, "Ready to start?"

Irwin said, "Just a minute." He pointed to the stenographer. "Is that my lawyer?"

"No, this is your stenographer."

"Well, you certainly don't expect me to do anything like this without a lawyer, do you?"

The agent glared at Irwin. He knew he had been deceived. He said coldly, "That's not what you told me, Irwin."

"Well, I'm willing to cooperate the way I said. But I'm going to cooperate only in the presence of my lawyer. I know you wouldn't want to violate my constitutional rights."

The other agent came in and said about the driver, grimly, "He won't talk."

The tension and three beers began to have their effect on Irwin. He had to urinate urgently. But his hands were still shackled behind his back. "I got to take a leak," he said.

The agents looked at him with disgust and kept on talking quietly to each other.

Irwin feared that he would wet his pants. "Okay, damn it. Let me go to the can and I might talk to you."

They unlocked the handcuffs and accompanied him into the bathroom. Then they put the handcuffs on again and took him to the stenographer.

"Ready?"

"Soon as my lawyer gets here."

"Take the son of a bitch to the county jail."

Los Angeles County Jail. There are hundreds of thousands of people alive for whom those words evoke something unspeakable. Some are no longer alive because of it. Technically, it is, like all jails, primarily for the holding of persons who have been arrested or detained or found wandering or otherwise of uncertain legal status. Most of those who pass through are found innocent. Some are innocent but go to insane asylums. Others eventually are found guilty and go to prisons. Or if they come from Los Angeles County and are sentenced to less than one year for a minor crime, they serve it in Los Angeles County Jail. But all of them, the innocent and the guilty, the sane and the insane, the sick and the well, the drunk and the sober, enter a bedlam that punishes more harshly than any judge.

Over 200,000 persons go through its maddening gates each year.

Irwin had done it once before. As he sat on his shackled hands, cuffed behind him once more, in the police van, he remembered the time he spent there waiting for Colorado to take him back.

In May of 1963 he had entered the first tank, where unidentified, unbooked and uncounted men are crowded into a concrete chamber fifty by seventy-five feet. Irwin remembered that he came to the tank exhausted from days and nights without sleep. But there were so many men in the chamber that he couldn't lie down. He leaned against a wall. Getting to the two urinals was torture, pushing bodies pressed together as they stood, and stepping on those lucky enough to occupy enough space to lie or sit. Waiting in line for the urinals and watching men vomiting, sometimes in the urinals and sometimes before they got there. And men sleeping under the porcelain of the urinals, catching the spray.

After three days they took away his watch, his belt, cigarettes, matches and anything else in his pockets and he was "booked," an act that is routine in clerical systems but in Los Angeles County Jail means that you have passed from the first anonymous madhouse into a madhouse where you had identity. Irwin in his first detention waited three days for the guard at the grille to shout his name. While waiting he learned to grab a sitting space on the floor when men left to be booked.

The second night he was puzzled by a young guard. It was hot and sweaty but the guard wore leather gloves. He paced outside the barred door smacking one leathered hand into the palm of the other. He heard a yell from down the corridor and turned to the detention tank, screaming, "Aw right! On your feet! On your feet! Move to the back! Move it! Get to the back!"

The men in the tank were puzzled. There were only fifty and no need to pack together in the back.

"God damn it! I said move it to the back! We got a hundred guys waiting to come in there, so move it! Against the wall! Against the wall!"

Irwin moved toward the back, muttering to the man next to him, "Who's he think he's bullshitting? You couldn't move a hundred more people in here with a shoehorn."

But from the back wall he watched a hundred more men, pushed, half-carried, shouldered into the tank. Irwin was taller than most and watched the scene unbelieving. After the new crowd was jammed in, the noise of 150 voices was deafening. When an officer came to the door and called a name to be booked nobody could hear it. Added to the undefined noise was the shout "Quiet! Everyone quiet! No talking! Stop talking! No noise! No talking! Quiet! Quiet!"

Soon the prisoners whispered, "Hey, quiet." Their names might be called for booking—deliverance—and they might not hear. The level of noise subsided until only one voice could be heard.

The voice belonged to an old drunk hanging on to the front bars. He was so intoxicated that he was swaying even in the crush of supporting bodies. He kept calling to the young guard, "Hey, buddy. How about a smoke, huh? You got a cigarette, ol' buddy? They took away my cigarettes. How about it?"

The guard told him to shut up.

"Aw, come on, ol' buddy. I really need a drag."

"I told you to shut up. You can't smoke in there and you can't have any matches. Now shut up."

"Aw, please, pal. Be a buddy. Give an old man a couple of drags."

The guard turned to him and said, "This is the last time I'm warning you. Shut up."

"Jeez, all I want is a cigarette. What d'ya say, buddy?"

Finally, the guard turned to him with a smile. "Oh, all right." The guard turned toward the end of the corridor and called to a control room, "Trip the door for one man out."

The barred door opened, the guard reached in, extricated the old wino from the crowd and closed the barred door behind him. The wino was happy.

"I knew you'd be a buddy to an old man. You're okay, pal."

The guard gave him a cigarette. The old man put it in his mouth and held his mouth forward as the guard lit the cigarette with a lighter. The guard put the lighter in his pocket. The old man had just pulled in a full chestful of smoke when the guard's gloved fist, coming from behind his shoulder, hit him square in the teeth. The man's whole body lifted slightly in the air and then sank against the wall like an empty sack, teeth and blood drooling out of a mass of red that was the bottom of his face. Now Irwin understood why the guard wore leather gloves on a hot night.

At the end of the third night, at about four-thirty A.M., a guard yelled, "Irwin, William R." The act that a week ago would have seemed like catastrophe was now blessedly welcome. He was being "booked" after arrest. He could sleep. He was taken to another chamber, where he was fingerprinted, photographed, told to undress and get into a shower stall. When he came out of the shower a man with a bucket and paintbrush told him to turn around and bend over. He felt the paintbrush over his buttocks and bristled into his anus. He was told to turn around. "Lift up your prick." The paintbrush rolled through his groin. It left a pink color and smelled like strong kerosene. He was given his clothes back, given a thin mattress rolled small enough to put under his arm and was told to follow a prisoner-trusty to his cage.

Irwin was shuffling with exhaustion. He had slept only fitfully for three nights and he knew as soon as he got to his cage he would unroll the mattress and fall into a deep sleep. He followed the trusty up steel stairs to an upper tier of cages. Where they walked was a puzzling sight that Irwin in his sleepiness did not try to analyze. On the six-foot steel grid walkway along the cages were men sleeping on mattresses scattered haphazardly, like ghetto residents sleeping on their fire escapes on hot nights. The trusty showed him a barred door. "That's your house. You sleep on the freeway." He pointed to the steel walkway. In jails and prisons each man's cage is called, ironically, "my house."

He was assigned to a seven-man cage. But the cage was small, with only two bunks, steel slabs, one above the other, welded to the steel wall. The most senior or the most strong prisoners had the bunks and could put their mattresses on them. The next two most senior or strong prisoners could lay their mattresses on the floor underneath the first bunk. The other three men unrolled their mattresses outside, on the freeway.

Irwin did not question it. He unrolled his mattress on the nearest bare steel space he could find and lay down. He had just crawled onto the mattress when the place exploded with sound. Whistles were blown and guards shouted, "Wake call! Everybody up! Get your asses out of the sack!"

Irwin sat up and watched. Along the freeway awkward forms rose in the dim light and rolled their mattresses. Cage doors were unlocked. During the day all mattresses of men not occupying a bunk had to be rolled up and stored underneath the lower bunk. Otherwise there was no room in the cage or on the freeway. Nine o'clock at night was the earliest a man without a bunk could unroll his mattress.

Later that morning Irwin was sitting on the concrete floor of the cage, leaning against the steel wall in the back corner, groggy, maintaining a minimum conversation, sizing up his cagemates to see who was a threat, who would make trouble, who would be a friend, when a new man was put in the cage. He looked like a creature out of the forest. His hair was long and tangled, his beard straggly. He stank. Someone said he had been in the hole for two weeks and explained that in the hole there was no shaving or showering. The man asked who would lend him some shaving stuff. Irwin remained silent, unsure whether the man was sane. Someone lent him a tube of shaving cream, a shaving brush and a razor. The man put his hands into the toilet bowl and splashed water on his face. Irwin said nothing but scanned the faces of other prisoners. Conversations continued without a break. Quietly he watched the man put shaving cream on his face, cup water from the toilet bowl in his hand and pat the cream into his beard. He dipped the brush into the water, worked up a lather and wetting the razor periodically in the bowl, slowly shaved himself, looking closely into a small polished metal mirror propped at the back of the toilet bowl.

Irwin watched as unobtrusively as possible. He was sure the man was mad. But he knew better than to intrude in a prison scene he did not know yet. None of the other prisoners paid attention to the kneeling man. Irwin kept quiet. The man from the hole returned the shaving material, curled up in a corner and fell asleep. Half an hour later a call was heard on the freeway.

"All right, men, come and get it. Got apple pies. Milk. Lots of goodies."

It was a peddler with the concession to sell food and toilet goods, cage to cage. Two of the prisoners bought cartons of milk. They put the cartons inside the toilet bowl.

Irwin couldn't stay quiet any longer. He said to the prisoner sitting on the floor next to him, "What the fuck is that with the toilet bowl?"

The drains of sinks were leaking. Water dripped on the floor and made it messy when men unrolled their mattresses to sleep. So the water was shut off on sinks, and the toilets were converted to water basins and refrigerators. If a prisoner had to use the toilet for conventional functions he walked along the tier until he found a cage where the sink did not leak and the toilet was used as a toilet. This meant that the occupants of that cage were unpleasant because of the almost constant line of men using their toilet. Anyone wanting to use a toilet at night had to disturb a dozen men, including some sleeping next to the toilet.

That was in 1963. Now, four years later, he found a new county jail. Detention tanks were cleaner and less crowded. Cages built for one man contained only five men instead of seven. But there was the same mixture of sane and insane, drunk and sober, strong and weak, the same madness and terror.

Everything was run in a military manner. Tiers of men marched to the mess hall. But so many people ate in the mess hall that there was less than three minutes to eat. Sometimes the shifting in line and squeezing in at a table took most of the time and unless food was wolfed down unchewed it was lost to the garbage barrel. Some prisoners had sent appeals to the courts on the cruel and unusual treatment of being given food but not being permitted to chew it. All personal watches are removed at booking so they noted the exact time by the dining hall clock that they had to collect their food, ingest it and dump the remainder into the swill barrels. Consequently all clocks in the mess hall had been stopped so no one could time the abbreviated period permitted for chewing.

The detention tanks were clean. But cockroaches still ruled the cages. Periodically a spraying squad wearing gas masks came through to kill cockroaches, filling the cages with mist. The prisoners had no gas masks and coughed, gasped and breathed through moist towels. But that night as they sat in the cage playing cards, cockroaches once more fell off the ceiling into their hair, or on their faces as they slept. After lights were out some prisoner invariably became so maddened by roaches that he slammed his shoe against them on the steel wall, making noises like an echoing artillery shot. Other prisoners yelled, "Fuck off, for Christ sake!" "The fuckers'll just come back by the millions!" Or, "Will the idiot banging the roaches cut it out, for Christ sake. We got them, too."

The last time Irwin was in for only ten days before being shipped to Colorado. This time he was in for five months. He had to adapt to the culture.

He learned, for example, when to put his money inside his mouth. Prisoners were permitted a limit of six dollars in cash. But many, like Bill, had more because they could play cards skillfully or had a racket. There was no place for personal property except pockets of the county clothes. Prisoners would be marched to the showers, a long stall with fifty shower heads. As they approached, a large guard in charge screamed constantly, "Aw right! Hurry it up! Strip and get under the shower! What's the matter with you guys? Get those clothes off! You got exactly ninety seconds by the clock! Come on, move! Move! Move!"

Showers were important. Men stripped, left their old clothes in a pile, to be picked up afterward and exchanged for new clothes. They rushed to the shower heads, the huge guard shouting all the time to hurry. Five men under each shower head would try to get wet enough to soap up and wash down before being ordered out with soap still on them. And while they were doing this two men assigned by the guards went through the pockets of all clothes left at the entry to the shower. Anything of value disappeared. If a man under the shower saw it happening and shouted, "Hey, that's my six bucks," he was told to keep moving to the other end of the shower room. So old hands, like Irwin, who had learned to become old hands quickly, prepared for their weekly shower by folding their money tightly and putting it in their mouths.

After the shower there was a body search every prisoner learns like a standard military manual of arms. "Raise your arms, palms down, wiggle your fingers, palms up, wiggle your fingers, let's look into the right ear, left ear, open your mouth, stick out your tongue, lift up your left foot, wiggle your toes, lift up your right foot, wiggle your toes, bend over, spread your cheeks, stand up, lift your balls." Prisoners hate it. Some guards also hate it.

At night, playing cards sitting on the steel freeway, there might be a sudden rush of guards screaming, "All right, everybody! Grab the bars! Grab the bars! Hey, you, don't go in there! Out here, grab the bars! You, get out here! Off the crapper and grab the bars! Get a hold of the bars!"

When everyone was standing with hands held high holding the bars on the outside of the cages, the guards told the first five prisoners to get into the cage in front of them.

"But I don't live there!"

"Don't give a damn. Get your ass in there! Hey, you, get inside!"

When all the prisoners were locked in cages, the guards went to one of the cages, had the door tripped open and had each prisoner come out, one at a time, naked.

"Aw right! Arms out, palms down, wiggle your fingers . . ."

After all five prisoners had been strip-searched and were standing naked on the outside holding the bars, the guards would shake down the cage. Bedding was torn off bunks and thrown on the floor, the five stacks of personal property were lifted up high and let fall item by item onto the floor, pockets of clothes were turned out and letters and wallets dropped, magazines, books, newspapers, candy bars, notebooks, milk from cartons would be emptied onto the mound and pies dumped on top of that. Then they would be gone, a tornado leaving as quickly as it had come, looking for contraband. The naked prisoners would walk back into the cage and stare at the soggy mess in the middle of the floor.

In his five months Irwin saw rapes, murders and beatings, listened to calm conversations on whether to kill a man who was listening to the decision. If the verdict was against an informer his head would be held in the toilet bowl until he drowned.

Irwin was big and tough and made friends with the right people. But it took all his skill to stay out of the crossfire of the hatred, including between whites and blacks.

He watched white guards in numbers goading lone blacks. One night he saw a black prisoner held by two white guards. The prisoner was told to lean against the wall with his arms and feet spread apart. Then the guards poked him with their billy clubs in the ribs, in the anus, in the groin, in the belly.

"What's the matter, nigger boy, no fight in ya?"

Jab.

"This the way your whore mother likes it?"

Jab.

At any moment they might kick one of his feet out from under him and he would go down onto the concrete with two billy clubs and booted shoes hitting him.

The worst tension was between prisoners. Blacks and Chicanos organized when there was a fight; whites did not. Guards usually picked the meanest, ugliest, and most perverted prisoner to be tier tender, the prisoner in charge in the absence of the guards. And as long as trouble did not reach the outside, the tier tender and his friends could do what they wished.

Irwin watched across the tiers one night. A black tier tender made a specialty of beating and raping white hippies, especially white hippie peace workers. He was boasting loudly. "Yeh, they moved me down from there. They got pissed 'cause I broke his damn jaw. Some white kid with long hair, said he wasn't going to be fucked. Man, I fuck anything I want to fuck. I knocked this son of a bitch down and fuck him and this screw tried to stop me. I told the screw to beat it 'cause I wasn't gonna be stopped fuckin' by no goddamn screw. I'm just waitin' for some piece of white meat to come into this tier I can fuck. I'm ready, man."

A young white man, perhaps nineteen, came in. He was beaten and homosexually raped by the tier tender and four of his friends. Everyone on the tiers watched and heard, helplessly.

This is known in American jurisprudence as "pretrial detention."

The legal trial of William Irwin finally took place months later. The driver of the car pleaded innocent and asked for a jury trial.

Irwin was indicted for violating the United States Code that makes it a federal felony to steal money from a bank insured by the Federal Deposit Insurance Corporation, an agency of the United States Government, and another felony to do it with a dangerous weapon. The indictment was signed by the United States Attorney for the district, Matthew Byrne, Jr., who was, unknown to Irwin, to sign the same indictment in the case of Ronald Phillips and, later, to be a federal judge who heard the Daniel Ellsberg case.

Judge Andrew Hauk refused to accept Irwin's guilty plea. Irwin's appointed lawyer raised the issue of mental health. The judge signed a standard form ordering a psychiatric examination by an appointed psychiatrist, Dr. Eric Marcus:

> The question of mental competency and legal responsibility of William Ryan Irwin having been raised and the court being advised that there is reasonable cause to believe said defendant may be presently insane or otherwise so mentally incompetent as to be unable to understand the proceedings against him. . . .

On January 8, 1968, the judge announced,

"The court finds defendant sane, able to assist in his own defense and able to understand the proceedings against him."

One month later William Ryan Irwin was sentenced to twenty years in federal prison.

> The judge said, "Stand up, boy
> And dry your tears.
> You're sentenced to prison
> For twenty long years.
> For twenty long years, boy,
> Is a mighty long time.
> Yes, twenty long years, boy,
> Is a mighty long time."

A few days later Judge Hauk wrote a letter to the U.S. Board of Parole, noting that he had given Irwin an (a) (2) sentence permitting almost instant parole and urging the board to release Irwin "on parole at the earliest moment the Board of Parole feels proper." Judge Hauk reduced the sentence to twelve years.

Irwin wrote him, "For the first time in my life I was before a man of authority that I felt it would be wrong to lie to."

A year later, from Leavenworth, Irwin asked Judge Hauk for help in getting vocational training, which had been denied him because he was too old and because he had too much time to serve. He asked the judge, if they didn't permit him "to better myself, to improve my condition, why should I expect to act any differently when I'm released? Your Honor, I'm desperate. I've got to learn something."

But the 120 days from sentencing had passed and now William Irwin's life was entirely in the hands of the Federal Bureau of Prisons.

15

PRISONER NO. 36791–133

It may have been bad luck to call the baby "Lucky." The mother had an earlier child when she was seventeen and named him after her husband, a guitar player who had left North Carolina to work as a laborer in New York City. Things did not go well, so when the second son was born a year later they thought it might change the family fortunes to give him the formal, legal name of Lucky.

It didn't work for the father. Four years later he was killed in a fight over borrowed money.

It didn't work for the mother. She was twenty-two years old with four small children when her husband was killed. She moved to Philadelphia to be near her parents and within a year remarried, had three more children with a man named Johnson, who often beat her in front of the children and soon before her seventh child was born deserted the family.

And it didn't work for Lucky. He was born in Bedford-Stuyvesant, even then, in 1947, on the way to becoming the grimmest ghetto in America. The killing of his father left his mother unsteady, so he and the other children spent most of the next year in North Carolina with their father's relatives. At the age of five he was reunited with the family in Philadelphia and told that his mother had remarried in his absence and that all of them were now named Johnson. When Lucky Johnson was nine his stepfather disappeared and was never again seen by Lucky.

"I have been unlucky all my life."

Lucky Johnson was fathered and schooled by a typical American ghetto.

At Blaine Elementary School, Lucky, at age seven, had to prove himself. Not with skill in the alphabet, numbers, colors, forms and intellectual puzzles—survival skills in the world of conventional work and middle-class culture. But by street shrewdness and survival by individual violence.

In his first entry into the neighborhood he was chased and beaten almost every day by the resident gang. Inevitably this led to the ritual confrontation with a gang member selected to challenge the new kid one-to-one. It was in the schoolyard and Lucky, bloody, gouged, knocked down and kicked, kept fighting back until his willingness to fight qualified him for acceptance.

The fight gave him membership in the only group that had significance in his world. It transformed his neighborhood from a place of humiliation and terror to a territory where he had safe passage, where he could move with confidence and respect.

The outside world thinks it sees similarities between them and the residents of poor districts. Ghetto dwellers are counted as residents of the same city, citizens of the same nation, speakers of the same root language. They both watch television, shop in stores, attend school. But the similarity is an illusion. The citizens of the poor districts belong to another culture, another country, another world that they do not control.

Trapped inside ghetto walls, the compacted residents turn against themselves in their competition for the inadequate supply of space, safety and goods. It is an escalating struggle destructive of harmony, gentleness, selflessness and family cohesion.

When the outside world preaches peace and quiet it is heard by citizens of this other world as it would be heard by soldiers in combat, surrounded by violence they cannot ignore. If the call to quietude fails, the police go in, demonstrating yet again the importance of physical power.

Brutalizing of the young is the norm in the streets of North Philadelphia and thousands of other islands of malignant neglect. It is visible to the eye in squalid homes, dirty streets, abandoned buildings, deadly schools, defeated human beings. But it is also visible in the unsentimental statistics of the United States Bureau of the Census for the neighborhood that nurtured Lucky Allen Johnson.

There is less than a square mile in the part of the North Philadelphia ghetto bounded by Thirty-third Street, Susquehanna Avenue, Nineteenth Street and Montgomery Avenue. People live there four times more closely packed than Philadelphians as a whole. There were 34,000 people there when Lucky's family moved in, and the same number in

1960, by which time Lucky was thirteen and had been arrested twice and seen homosexual rapes and stabbings in a reform school. In those ten years the population of his ghetto, 97 per cent black, had to live in 10 per cent fewer homes, while in the same period the country as a whole was enjoying new housing that expanded 5 per cent faster than population. It is interesting to speculate what would happen to social order in a middle-class neighborhood if every tenth house was destroyed and its residents required to find living space in the same neighborhood, without cars to travel, vacations, hope in school, confidence in work and income.

In Lucky's ghetto neighborhood his friends and enemies had little to give them hope or escape. More adults had never been to any school than had finished college. Eighty per cent had never finished high school. The 7600 families averaged incomes of seventy-two dollars a week. A fifth of the families earned less than thirty-two dollars a week. When national unemployment reaches 6 per cent it is in alarming headlines; double the national rate is normal in the ghetto.

Despite the comforting myth of a Cadillac at every ghetto door, in Lucky's neighborhood in his teen years there were cars available to 31 per cent of the households. In the United States as a whole there are cars available to 74 per cent of households, cars considered a necessity for finding and keeping jobs, shopping economically, and maintaining contact with a changing world.

Crowded into this morass was a concentration of the pool from which most crime is drawn, males between the ages of ten and twenty-four, in Lucky's ghetto enough of them to form the entire population of twice his area in the average suburb—1800 youths, 40 per cent of the ones under eighteen living in a household without two parents.

Lucky lived much of his early childhood with his grandmother and his stepgrandfather, the man she had married after her divorce from Mrs. Johnson's father, reputed to be Irish. When his mother felt overwhelmed she would send Lucky down the street to live with his grandparents, who were strict Baptists, who attended church and took Lucky with them. His grandparents had stern codes of conduct. They withheld their love if a child transgressed. His grandmother was so condemning of people who got in trouble with the police that she would never visit or write Lucky while he was incarcerated. She welcomed him back only when he was released.

Like most parents in the ghetto, his grandmother did not spare the rod.

His first confrontation with the police was relatively mild, his grand-parents' reaction unexceptional. In third grade, after he had been accepted in the neighborhood, Lucky took lunch money away from another boy. The boy told his mother and the mother called the police.

In the ghettos of Philadelphia every child grew up aware of the "Cisco Kid," a tough police officer who boasted of walking into a ghetto scene and routinely knocking heads with his knuckles and his night-stick. He was believed to shoot gang members accused of stealing and to create internecine war among black youths so they would kill each other. The Cisco Kid, Frank Rizzo, rose to become commissioner of police and then mayor of Philadelphia on the reputation of being brutal with blacks. In Lucky's ghetto they knew him well. He represented the police, which is to say the enemy in a violent war.

The policeman who picked up Lucky at his third-grade class hit him on the head a few times, kicked him into the police cruiser and turned him over to his grandparents. His grandmother beat him with a strap. He was eight.

One day when he was nine and on the way to school he stole a piggy bank from the back window of a neighbor. Someone saw him and reported it. He used the forty-seven cents to buy candy but by the time he reached school, late for class, the police were waiting for him. They banged him on the head and kicked him as he got into the police car and again when he got out at the police station. Inside the stationhouse they hit him some more and took him to the youth center for juvenile delinquents. He was there for three days with no word from anyone—family, court or police. On the fourth day he was taken to a hearing where he was charged with breaking, entering, larceny and truancy. No one from his family was present, so the hearing was postponed. He went back to the youth center for three more days without word from the outside. Then he was returned to court, where his mother had been subpoenaed.

The juvenile counselor asked Lucky's mother why she had not come to the youth center after Lucky's arrest or to the earlier hearing, though she was notified of both. She said her son was a bad boy, that he needed to be kept in jail to teach him a lesson and that it was good for him to know that if he ever got in trouble his mother would not show up.

The counselor responded angrily, "Maybe you're the one who should be in jail, not him. Something has gone wrong somewhere. A nine-year-old boy steals a piggy bank and goes to jail. Something's gone wrong somewhere."

Lucky feels that whatever warmth there had been in the relationship with his mother disappeared with that episode.

When he was ten Lucky saw his brother-in-law murder his common-law wife. The couple lived in the flat below the Johnsons. One evening he heard shouts on Twenty-ninth Street and pushed through the crowd. His brother-in-law was beating his wife for going out with another man. Family fights were common and Lucky watched as he had dozens of other physical fights. His brother-in-law pulled a razor out of his pocket and cut the woman's throat completely through the front, slashed her on the head, on the arms and on the breasts until she fell dead on the bloody sidewalk.

Six months later he was on a corner of Diamond Street when he saw a woman hitting a man with her fists. The man tried to swing back but the woman was too strong and ferocious. The crowd laughed. One of the bystanders was a boy with a baseball bat. The man lunged for the bat and, while Lucky watched, beat the woman to the ground with the bat and hit her on the head until she was dead.

Violence was everywhere. The school was patrolled by police. Boys competed in taunting the police, and throwing stones at the cruiser cars from hidden corners. The police retaliated by beating almost every boy they questioned.

Lucky's older brother had already been arrested and had spent time in reform school. After Lucky's first arrest the two brothers entered a period of two years of regular burglary for spending money. For two years between his ninth and eleventh birthdays Lucky and his older brother stayed away from home as much as possible. His stepfather had regularly beaten their mother and the children; after he disappeared the boys were already more at home in the street. Lucky was skinny, so when the gang broke into the small back windows of supermarkets, drugstores and garages, Lucky would crawl inside and open the back door. They did it once or twice a week. They were caught, arrested for truancy and sentenced to two and a half years in a former military academy, now a reform school at Glen Mills, twenty miles west of the city.

Glen Mills was a mixed experience. For the first time in his life he was stimulated by a teacher and learned quickly what he had never learned at school—to be a good reader, how to write and how to do mathematics. He was learning in the classroom and excited by it, devoted to a teacher, a white woman, who was later replaced by her daughter, from whom Lucky also learned a great deal.

But elsewhere in the "reform" school Lucky was learning something else. Fighting and violence, always part of his environment, helped him survive in reform school. But he had never had contact with homosexuality before.

The juvenile population ranged in age from seven to seventeen. Boys were assigned to cottages according to age, but within cottages violence was the basic relationship.

Within each cottage the new boy had to box the strongest old boy. The boys who lost, or lost without hurting the opponent, were regularly beaten and often gang-raped—sodomized and forced into multiple oral intercourse by the ruling gang in the cottage. Even if a boy fought hard and beat his opponent, if it appealed to the gang they would still gang-rape him. In the prisons as in the ghettos the worst treachery is to cooperate with the hated authorities, so the boy who was weak or who feared constant fighting had only one choice: to be injured fighting off gang rapes and gang beatings, or to submit without fighting.

Fortunately, Lucky had been prepared for reform school by a life of juvenile violence, so he was able to demonstrate toughness and fighting spirit. Even so, he has a sensitive face and soft brown eyes. Lucky is not certain what would have happened to him if his older brother had not been ruler of the cottage next door. The brothers watched out for each other.

The "reform" school was supposed to be preparing them for a life of constructive nonviolence. He saw a gang rape or a gang beating at least once a week for the 130 weeks he lived in the reformatory.

Lucky spent his twelfth, thirteenth and fourteenth birthdays in the Glen Mills reformatory. He came out at fourteen and a half, having completed the prep school of the poor.

He returned to his mother's home, to school and to breaking into stores. Eight months later he was arrested for breaking and entering. The contest with the law continued.

He and two other boys broke down the back door of a local radio shop and stole miniature battery-operated radios and a secondhand television set. Lucky's part of the loot was three portable radios. Two days later he was walking home from school with his girl friend and two other classmates, one of the stolen radios to his ear as he walked. He heard a voice from a cruiser say, "Hey, boy, come here!"

Inside the police station they released the three others immediately. They wanted Lucky. They took him into a room. He was fourteen and not yet tall. The two policemen were husky.

"Where'd you get that radio?"

"I bought it."

"You're lying, you little black bastard. Come out here."

In a corridor the policeman grabbed Lucky by the shoulder, spun him around and kicked him in the pants.

Lucky got up off the floor. The policeman punched him in the ribs. "You're lying, you little punk."

"I ain't."

The policeman twisted Lucky's arm behind him. Lucky turned in pain, the cop brought the edge of his palm against the side of Lucky's neck as he kicked him in the ankles and Lucky went sprawling down the corridor, dizzy.

Lucky and another boy were charged with breaking and entering. He was locked up six months before he came before a judge. Once in court, he confessed that he had broken into the shop and stolen the radio. He also said that the others had not been involved. The other boy was released. Lucky spent his fifteenth birthday behind bars.

In the courtroom there was a discussion of what to do with Lucky. His mother said she couldn't handle him and sent him to live with her father in Buffalo, New York. Lucky became involved in the youth activities of the ghetto in Buffalo, gang warfare more vicious than he had known in Philadelphia. Lucky had to prove himself again, as he had when he was seven.

But he had graduated. He had to prove himself with guns. His gang was the Ballbearing Kings and they fought other gangs with chains, pistols and shotguns. Every full member with status had to have his "piece." Lucky stole a shotgun.

Lucky needed the gun for a retaliation raid against a rival gang. The two gangs met late on the night of February 26, 1962. Shots were exchanged, including one by Lucky that hit a rival gang member, though not fatally. The police arrived and Lucky was caught.

It was the next morning by the time Lucky was fingerprinted, photographed and booked. Age? Lucky thought a minute. Today was his birthday. He said, "Sixteen."

In New York State this made him subject to an adult charge for a serious crime. He was booked for assault with intent to kill.

In court the judge looked at the short slender defendant. "How old are you?"

"I'm sixteen today."

"Exactly sixteen today?"

Lucky nodded.

The judge asked the arraigning officer what they showed as the defendant's birthdate.

"We have it as February 27, 1947, Your Honor."

"When was this fight?"

"Last night, Your Honor."

"Before midnight?"

"Yes, Your Honor."

"That means that when the offense was committed with which this defendant is being charged, he was fifteen years old. Is that right?"

"It looks that way, according to this record, Your Honor."

The judge turned to Lucky. "Is that right? Did you turn sixteen just today?"

"Yes, Your Honor."

The judge turned, irritated, to the prosecutor. "Get him out of here. He's a juvenile and doesn't belong in this court."

Lucky was taken out, feeling saved from an adult prison by the freakish timing of the battle. If it had been two hours later he might have gone before the adult court and been sent to an adult prison with bigger, more frightening people than he had known before.

Only after the judge sentenced him to eighteen months in a juvenile institution did his relief change to horror. He would go back to a place like Glen Mills, with beatings and rapes—and his older brother would not be with him this time. As he was being led from the courtroom for delivery to the reformatory, he broke away. He slithered past the bailiff, opened a door and ran down a stairway. At the bottom of the stairs he opened a door to the lobby and freedom and ran into the arms of a waiting policeman.

Because of the attempted escape, half an hour later his eighteen-month sentence was increased to three years. He was sent to the Elmira reception center for classification. Eight weeks later he was committed to the New York State Vocational Institution at West Coxsackie, which has older youths and young adults convicted of serious crimes.

Most of the prisoners in Coxsackie were from eighteen to twenty-five, tough and hostile. It was the first time Lucky had encountered segregation that was officially reinforced and encouraged. Prisoners divided into three camps, blacks, whites and Latins, and they warred on each other. In the yard they stood along opposite walls. In the center were the "creeps," white inmates who had not proven their toughness, who were preyed upon homosexually or beaten regularly or made to run errands for the dominant prisoners. A creep could shed his humiliating role by picking a fight with a tough black. He would then be welcomed to the "white" wall.

One day in the yard a creep saw Lucky walking along the wall and yelled, "Get the hell back where you belong, black boy."

Later, the creep walked toward Lucky's open cage door. Lucky knew there was going to be a fight. Lucky hit him hard in the face, knocked him down and jumped on him. Guards separated them.

Lucky went to the hole. He was stripped of all his clothes and put naked into the barren cage. There was no mattress and no blanket on the slab bed. After three days he was given clothes, a mattress and a blanket. He considered himself fortunate. It was warm weather, so he did not get the "cold shoulder"—a custom that forced the naked prisoner to open the window in winter on pain of being beaten.

Lucky was in Coxsackie for two years and four months. He had spent his sixteenth birthday in the holding cage in Buffalo and his seventeenth, eighteenth and nineteenth birthdays in Coxsackie prison.

He was released in June of 1965 with eight months more of parole. Back in North Philadelphia Lucky moved in with his mother. His stepgrandfather got him a job as mechanic's helper at $1.25 an hour. Lucky spent all his money on sharp clothes and making an impression on the neighborhood. When his mother reminded him that it was about time he began paying room and board, Lucky slapped a five-dollar bill on the kitchen table and walked down the stairs. His mother threw the five-dollar bill after him. After about a year he was fired for coming to work late.

In March, while awaiting sentence for stealing a car, he was arrested for stealing a second car. He was sentenced to Holmesburg prison in Philadelphia, eleven months for the first car and twenty-three months for the second car.

In Holmesburg prison two new experiences changed his life. One was his first experimentation with drugs—pills sold through the prisoner-guard rackets. The other seemed paradoxical—his initiation into the puritanical Black Muslims. In Coxsackie he had heard prisoners from New York City talk about Malcolm X preaching black radicalism on the street corners and in barrooms and pool halls.

Until that moment in Lucky's life, attacks on the racial caste system had been a distant battle. In the 1950s there were rumblings in the courts. In the late 1950s and early 1960s there were televised clashes between civil rights workers and Southern white resisters. It was a phenomenon of Martin Luther King, Jr., and other nonviolent leaders.

These movements sensitized the nation to the pressure for change. But as in any social movement, most people were spectators, the activists white or religious or middle-class-oriented blacks.

To young blacks in the urban ghettos there was not much appeal in a campaign to enter middle-class white society and certainly not by offering one's body passively to the tender mercies of the attacking police. Urban youth and the police knew each other too well.

But the Muslims touched ghetto youths. Elijah Muhammad, leader of the Black Muslims, reached the lowest social levels of urban blacks with shrewdly effective doctrines. He attributed to the white race all the worst characteristics that for centuries white bigots had claimed to be true of blacks: whites were dirty, decadent, drunken, diseased, whoring, raping, cultureless animals whose society was in the last stages of disintegration. The judgment extended to white law enforcement officers, who hated the Muslims but respected their force and unity. In prisons for the first time blacks stood together around the Muslims, who walked in militarylike formation. White guards treated them with unprecedented caution.

There were millions of blacks who could not accept the puritanical life and rigid discipline but who identified with the Muslims, felt the pull of unity when confronting white society, who adopted the rhetoric and attitudes of the faithful, and who were excited by hearing the Muslims hurl open insults against whites that up to now they had only heard whites saying about blacks. Black pride and contempt for whites became something to be expressed openly, insistently, belligerently.

The most celebrated figure in the Muslims was Malcolm X, born Malcolm Little, once "Big Red," former hustler, dope peddler, numbers runner, bootlegger, pimp, the most brilliant and articulate Muslim in America. He spoke on streetcorners of Harlem and soon by invitation all over the world. He knew the ghetto toughs and they recognized him as one of their own. By 1964 he had fallen out with Elijah Muhammad, had become less insistent on immediate black separatism and maintained some white friendships. He was assassinated in February 1965, reputedly by rival Muslims. He and, later, George Jackson were to become the strongest inspirations to black prisoners throughout the United States.

Some of Lucky's friends had joined the Muslim unit in Holmesburg prison. It had an enormous appeal to Lucky. It rejected religion as he had known it, the puritanical, condemning, otherworldly Baptist practice of his grandparents. It rejected whites and white police. It rejected the economic system of the United States. It challenged police and prisons and offered unified protection against them. It reached deep into the ghetto where other movements had not. Increasing numbers of blacks saw prisons as a natural extension of the ghetto. Muslims had found a raw nerve at the center of impoverished blacks' life experience in America.

Lucky read *The Autobiography of Malcolm X* and began his entry not only into the Muslim movement but into thinking about the larger world and his place in it. This was in 1966. The fact that Malcolm had been killed by rival gunfire was something convicts and ghetto veterans understood.

He also understood for the first time the meaning of serious organization. The guards at Holmesburg, ordinarily tough and ruthless, treated the Muslims with respect. For once guards exhibited fear, a reversal of the roles behind bars. He discovered something else: for the first time in his life he was respected, or at least feared, for his blackness.

Lucky was paroled on his twentieth birthday. Back in his neighborhood he found no local Muslim unit. He was uncertain about his next step. His brother had signed up for a second hitch with the Marines in Vietnam. A relative showed Lucky how to use speed, injecting amphetamine directly into his blood vessels. Lucky began using drugs heavily.

For a time he worked at the Benjamin Franklin Hotel as a valet earning sixty-five dollars a week plus tips, using the tailoring skills he had learned at Coxsackie. He left this to take a job at a hundred a week as a tailor's assistant in a downtown haberdashery, doing alterations of men's suits. He was laid off a few months later, his work habits unsatisfactory.

His work was interspersed with burglaries to support his drug habit. He was arrested once for possession of dangerous narcotics but beat the charge. A few months later he was arrested for burglary and larceny. He had unexplained gunshot wounds but the charge was dismissed.

Five days after his twenty-first birthday he married. His wife, according to relatives, was a heavy user of drugs and had two children born out of wedlock when Lucky met and married her. Twelve days after their marriage Lucky was arrested again, this time for illegal possession and use of narcotics. He got out on bail.

Seven months after that Lucky was arrested for burglary, larceny, conspiracy and receiving stolen goods. He was found guilty of receiving stolen goods and sentenced back to Holmesburg for from six to twenty-three months.

His first weeks in Holmesburg were a fog of pain and depression as he experienced cold turkey, the withdrawal symptoms from drugs without medical assistance. He survived it but made connections inside the prison to become a drug customer inside the wall.

Drugs passed easily through the walls of Holmesburg, as they do at most prisons. Usually guards are the chief smugglers. A bundle of heroin that cost $120 on the street was worth $240 inside the wall, a comfortable extra income for guard-entrepreneurs. The prisoner makes arrangements for someone outside to pay the guard, keeping the financial part of the transaction outside the prison. Inside the prison the passage of smuggled drugs from guards to prisoner-racketeer is not difficult.

Lucky underwent a double development that was common. He resumed his interest in black nationalism and political ideas but not so deeply that he dropped the narcotic life. The Muslims in prison had evolved since the last time Lucky was there. Now they tended less toward puritanism and more toward urban guerrilla activity. Black belligerence was exciting as an expression of racial pride. But dependence on drugs hemorrhaged personal pride.

In May of 1969 Lucky was paroled again. The Vietnam war had suspended a national commitment to racial equality and economic justice. Richard Nixon was President of the United States, preaching law and order, feeding public fear of the poor and of the nonwhite.

The assassinations of John Kennedy, Robert Kennedy, Martin Luther King, Jr., and Malcolm X had wiped out the most powerful American figures in social action and national unity. As predicted by the earlier Commission on Civil Disorders, the American people were dividing into a white nation and a black one, into an affluent part fearful of losing its economic advantage and a poor one bitter at its abandonment. Peaceful demonstrations and the philosophy of nonviolence had been shattered. The country moved toward violence, in the Indochina war, at home in the fragmented movements. Lucky Johnson joined the Black Panthers.

The symbol of the Black Panther, lithe and powerful, walking toward the observer with arrogant grace, first used by the Lowndes County, Alabama, Freedom Party in 1965, struck a sympathetic chord in hundreds of black groups around the country. Two students at Merritt Junior College in California, Huey P. Newton and Bobby G. Seale, read Malcolm X, Frantz Fanon, Engels, Marx, Lenin, Mao Tse-tung, Ho Chi Minh, Che Guevara. These told them that, historically, revolutions against powerful opponents did not come peacefully.

A hierarchy of leadership imposed stern rules on all local Panther units. Narcotics, marijuana and drinking on party duty were forbidden. No one could use a firearm unnecessarily. Members could not belong to anything except the military unit of the Black Liberation Army. No member could steal or commit crimes against any other black. Arrested members would give only name and address.

Rules for members' behavior were directly from Mao: Speak politely, pay fairly for what they buy, return everything borrowed, pay for anything damaged, do not hit or swear at people, do not damage property or crops of the poor, do not take liberties with women, and if anyone is captured by the Party they will not be ill-treated.

Discipline was to be inflexible: Obey all orders, take nothing from the poor masses, and turn in everything captured in attacks on the enemy.

Like the Muslims, the Panthers appealed to ghetto youths untouched by official, traditional programs. But unlike the Muslims, the Panthers had no concern with religion, theology or rigid segregation. They were willing to work with white revolutionaries who accepted their leadership and program, at least during early phases of the struggle. For ghetto youths who had grown up at war with the police, the Panthers gave sacred purpose to the life style of fighting and robbery.

Lucky was typical of Panther-oriented young men. He identified himself as a soldier in the movement but he continued to live as he did before. Panther expression of black belligerence appealed to the victims of ghetto life but the rules of personal conduct did not. He could not think of any adolescent friend who had gone to college but all his acquaintances were alumni of reform schools and prisons. Like the graduates of Groton and Harvard, he associated with institutional comrades with whom he had moved toward adulthood.

After his parole Lucky was simultaneously more politically active and more addicted to drugs. He attended Panther Party meetings, organized door to door, assisted in the party program of serving hot breakfasts to ghetto children. These activities required money, and rent was running out on the storefront headquarters of the North Philadelphia chapter.

Lucky had other financial problems to worry about. His heroin habit was costing him more all the time.

The night before the Fourth of July in 1969 a solution to this dual problem seemed at hand. Lucky and two friends, "George" and "Leon," met at the corner of Twenty-ninth Street and Ridge Avenue to discuss a crucial piece of intelligence. While they talked on the streetcorner, another friend, Bruce, sauntered up with a portable radio, wanting to pawn it for some heroin. The original three asked him if he wanted to share in their enterprise. He accepted.

The Container Corporation of America has a large industrial plant on an elongated island in the Schuylkill River, along the northwestern edge of Philadelphia, separated from the village of Manayunk by bridges.

An employees' credit union on the plant grounds received $40,000 in small denominations every Thursday morning in preparation for cashing paychecks. The security in the office was very informal. There were no cameras. And hundred-dollar bills were the largest denomination.

The informant, who cashed checks at the credit union himself, was able, for a price, to draw a diagram of the office and of the road leading off the plant grounds. The four men made plans to do it the next week. Leon would wait in a parking lot outside the plant "gate," a single yellow-striped wooden bar. George, Bruce and Lucky would walk inside as though regular workers during the busy lunch hour. George would stand outside the office as a lookout along the corridor of the credit union in the small one-story building on the company street. And Bruce and Lucky would go inside and get the money.

It had the earmarks of a perfect set-up.

What they didn't know was that a woman unknown to them, Rosemary Dooner, at about the time they were talking on the corner of Twenty-ninth and Ridge Avenue, was falling down the steps of her home and spraining her right elbow. This would change everything.

The next Thursday morning Lucky and his partner Bruce shot up with heroin, but not enough to fog their reflexes. They drove to the parking lot of the plant and Leon waited in the car outside the gate. George lounged outside the door of the credit union office looking as anonymous as possible.

Lucky, wearing a bright yellow jersey, and Bruce, in dark glasses and wearing a blue hat, went inside and sat down to wait for a customer to finish at a window. The manager, Charles Moetsch, asked the man in the yellow shirt if he could help him.

"I'm waiting for my buddy."

"Well, you'll have to wait outside."

The two men went outside.

The other person in the office, cashier, bookkeeper and assistant treasurer of the Concora Federal Credit Union, was Rosemary Dooner.

With her sprained elbow she couldn't run the coin-counting machine. Mr. Moetsch asked her to stack the money in batches to confirm delivery of the right amount from the First Pennsylvania Company. Most of the paychecks were for $100 or $140, so she decided it would be easier for Mr. Moetsch to work quickly if she stacked the packs of hundred-dollar bills in crisscross fashion.

Miss Dooner was stacking the packs of hundreds when she heard a thump on the counter. She looked up and saw a dull silver pistol pointed at her face. The pistol was shaking. A man in a yellow jersey had leaped on top of the counter and was still getting his balance, his gun hand moving up and down to establish equilibrium. He said, "Don't move!"

She screamed.

The man in the dark glasses and blue hat ran around the end of the counter with a knife in his right hand and forced Moetsch to sit on the floor behind a desk. The man ripped two telephones off the wall and used the torn wire from one of them to tie Moetsch's hands behind him.

The man in the yellow jersey jumped down on the inside of the counter, spun Dooner around and said, "Now, sit on the floor."

By this time the other robber had tied up the manager and was next to Dooner. He had the other telephone and its dangling wires in his hand. He said, "Put your hands behind your back."

She began talking rapidly. "I have a sore arm. I can't do that. I can't put my arm straight down. You don't want me to scream but if you put my arm behind me I'll have to scream. I'm not being smart. I'm not being fresh. Tie me in the front, tie me in the middle, tie me anywhere, but I can't put my hand behind my back because I will have to scream from the pain."

He shook his head. "All right, lady, all right."

He left her untied. She turned to watch the man in the yellow jersey. He had laid the pistol on the counter, pulled a brown paper bag from somewhere and was stuffing piles of currency into it. But the crisscross stacking made it difficult for him to hold the bag with one hand and grab crisscrossed stacks one-handed with the other. Stacks of hundred-dollar packs were spilling out of his grasp onto the floor, and he was scurrying, scooping up the scattered bundles of money. He saw her watching him.

"Lady, face that window!"

She looked away toward a back window facing the river.

A third, unnoticed phone began to ring. The blue-hatted man ripped it off the wall and wrapped the wires around Dooner's wrists, the phone dangling from her upper arm.

Someone banged on the front door that the two men had locked behind them. There was more than one person out in the corridor. Someone yelled to open up because he had only ten minutes to cash his check. Dooner looked around. The man in the yellow jersey said, "Lady, I said to face that wall!"

The banging on the door continued, with murmurings heard in the corridor.

Finally the two men had all the money. The bag was filled to the top. They tried to open the window overlooking the river.

The manager said, "You can't get out that way. The window's nailed shut."

The two men ran around the counter to the door where the banging continued. They whispered a moment to each other. The man in the yellow jersey, his gun now in his pocket, had the bagful of money tucked under his left arm.

Dooner was twisting her wrists through the loose telephone wires. Just as she got one hand free she heard the door slam shut. She shook the other hand free, ran to the door. A crowd of men waited to come in. She recognized Don Clemens, a press operator. She shouted, "Don, we just got held up! Yellow shirt, blue hat!"

Clemens ran down the corridor. Outside he saw a fellow worker in a car, Joe Pistelli. He jumped inside. "Joe, there is the fellas that are running, robbed the bank. Chase 'em."

The car took off after three men running toward the gate.

Dooner worked her way through the crowd in the corridor to the shipping office on the other side. She grabbed a phone and called the gate. "This is Rosemary from the credit union! We just got held up! Close the gates!"

The gateman shouted back, "They're just going through! They're just going through!"

Dooner went back to the credit union office and found the door had closed behind her and the spring latch locked her out. Her first thought was My God, my pocketbook is inside!

The car was right behind Lucky, Bruce and George. They had walked casually out of the credit union through the crowd waiting to get in but now they were running. Up ahead a guard was closing the gate and yelling to someone else.

Lucky looked behind as he ran. The car was pulling alongside.

Bruce said, "Keep going to the gate, man!"

Lucky yelled, "I'm going in the water!"

He put the bag of money on the ground and turned toward the river, ran across some railroad tracks and dove into the water.

George, the lookout, turned in the opposite direction and ran into a factory building, chased by twenty men.

Bruce looked around. The car was stopped and two men were getting out yelling. Ahead were a dozen men at the gate. He picked up the bagful of money. The men at the gate yelled, "Drop that bag! Drop that bag!"

The men at the gate were not armed. Bruce pulled out his knife and began running at the crowd at the gate, swinging his knife wildly in all directions, screaming obscenities. The swinging knife opened a path, he ran around the end of the striped gate and into the parking lot, where the driver had the motor running and the car in gear. In seconds they were lost in the narrow twisting streets. In the excitement at the gate George melted into a crowd of workers running into the street and walked off the premises.

Lucky swam through the dirty brown water just above a small dam. He pulled himself out on the other side among thick underbrush and ailanthus trees. He ran under transmission lines, across the Reading Railroad tracks, climbed up a steep hill toward the village. He was still in the foliage, his wet clothes clinging to him during the desperate uphill scramble. He looked up and down the street. Everything looked normal. Big yellow Philadelphia garbage trucks were rumbling toward the city incinerator. To the right was a long line of the yellow trucks parked by the Domino Diner. Lucky waited as casually as he could until he saw a black driver come out of the diner toward his truck.

Lucky asked if he could ride with the driver. He said he had been riding on his brother's bike when the bike fell over and he had gone into the water. The driver laughed and told him to jump in.

As the truck drove over a bridge toward the city zoo, Lucky looked out from the high cab. Police cars were speeding in the opposite direction, their red lights on, sirens screaming. He felt smug.

His partners—the getaway driver and Bruce—took their Oldsmobile to a block in North Philadelphia, picked up a friend's Chevrolet and drove to a nearby house. A short time later George, the lookout and owner of the getaway car, arrived.

Lucky by this time had reached his apartment. He changed clothes and tried to find his companions at the usual corner meeting places—

Diamond and Twenty-ninth, Ridge and Twenty-ninth. But he saw no one. The next day he had a friend drive him through the neighborhood until he saw one of the holdup party. He was taken to the house where the men had deposited the loot. They went into a bedroom and uncovered the paper bag with the money.

It was only half full. Lucky suddenly regretted leaving his pistol at home. "Where's the rest of the money?"

"What you talking about, man, 'rest of the money'?"

"The rest of the fuckin' money, that's what I'm talking about! That bag was full right to the top and now it's half gone!"

"Man, what you mean, 'half gone'? You dropped that bag and split and it was *all* gone. It was all over that fuckin' ground and I had to pick it up while I was running. I was fighting my way through fifty men while you was saving your skin splitting. You want the rest of that money you got to go back and tell the credit union. They picked up the money you dropped. So don't give me no shit. If it was up to you, we'd have nothing."

Lucky knew he had dropped the bag and hadn't looked back.

"Okay. Let's count."

They dumped the money onto the bed and stacked it in denominations: ones, fives, tens and twenties: $22,680.

They divided it four ways, each man carefully watching: $5670 each. A good score.

Within an hour they had all bought heroin and fixed. There was reason for euphoria. The day before Lucky had ridden to his task in a 1966 Oldsmobile, had collected $22,680 for twelve minutes' work, and then seemed to lose everything, riding back to town soaking wet in a Philadelphia garbage truck.

But it all ended well. He thought.

Lucky hid his money in wet clothes under a bathtub in the apartment of "Sarah," a woman he knew.

Lucky forgot about the Panther Party, about turning over all goods "captured in attacks upon the enemy," about eschewing narcotics, about living modestly. After the money was divided on Friday he took $1600 from his cache under the bathtub and bought heroin, lent some money to his brother and spent $1000 on sparkling new clothes, including two pairs of hand-made alligator shoes.

Unknown to him there were other events occurring. The night before, five hours after the robbery, police located the getaway car parked on North Douglas Street. Despite the crowd chasing the man with the bag of money who jumped into the getaway car, the car was reported on police bulletins as a 1968 steel gray Oldsmobile with Pennsylvania plates 694929. It was a 1966 brown and black Olds, license plate 6P4929. But once located, there seemed little doubt that it was relevant to the case. On the floor on the passenger side was a loose dollar bill, fourteen cents in change, and twenty five-dollar bills bound by a paper wrapper marked, "$100, 6-27-69, First Pennsylvania Co." It had been a remarkably sloppy crime.

The FBI took fingerprints and had the car towed away. They checked the ownership and the next day left word at the owner's home that they would like to see him. The owner went to the FBI office, accompanied by his lawyer, and asked for his car back, on which, he said, he still owed $2000 and was making payments of sixty dollars a month. The FBI interrogated him closely. He said he had heard gossip about the holdup but had taken no part in it. The FBI released him in the custody of his lawyer.

There was a police bulletin for the men who had been inside the credit union office:

> The Number One man, race, Negro; sex, male; age about 25; height, 5'7", weight about 140 pounds, slender, light complexion, thin mustache, normal Negro haircut, wearing yellow pullover V-neck sweater, dark trousers. Gun, small silver automatic.

Though he was twenty-two, not twenty-five, it was a better description of Lucky Johnson than the original description of the getaway car.

Plainclothesmen in unmarked cars, with indiscernible individuals huddled in the back seats, prowled the neighborhood Friday afternoon and Saturday with the indiscernible persons pointing out certain pedestrians and houses.

On Saturday Lucky was approached by two old acquaintances. One of them, a close friend, said he had heard about Lucky's big score and could Lucky lend him some desperately needed money. The man had lent Lucky money in the past. Lucky said he couldn't right at the moment because he didn't have any cash on him—he had, in fact, a hundred dollars—but as soon as he could get to Sarah's house he'd take some out of his cache. A few hours later police broke into Sarah's house and found $4000 under the bathtub. The old acquaintance with the borrowing friend had been a police informer.

On Sunday the owner of the car returned to the FBI office to say he knew some of the people involved in the holdup and had heard of the plans but insisted that he took no part in it.

On Monday morning Lucky, high on his plentiful supply of heroin, agreed to accompany his brother to the Veterans Administration office while his brother asked about a Marine check he had not received.

Probably because he was high on drugs, Lucky did not pay any attention to his surroundings. He did not notice the car parked behind them as he got into his brother's car, nor its careful trailing of them as they headed toward the VA building. Near Connie Mack Stadium they stopped for a traffic light. Lucky, gazing ahead in euphoria, noticed a darkening at his open window. He looked out. The barrel of a shotgun was two inches from his forehead. He looked toward his brother. Another man was holding a magnum pistol inches from his brother's temple. It was the FBI.

Lucky's brother was released by nightfall, having satisfied everyone that he had no involvement in the crime. Lucky pleaded not guilty and was held under $50,000 bail.

Bruce had left town at once on a bus to New York and lived high for a few weeks in Harlem. He bought a ring for $1500, had expensive women, bought expensive clothes, drank expensive drinks. When he returned to Philadelphia he stayed away from his old neighborhood and instead checked into downtown hotels as Mr. Love. By October he had run out of money, pawned his ring for fifty dollars, returned to his old neighborhood and was arrested. He, too, pleaded not guilty.

By December, Lucky learned something that confirmed what he had been told by the FBI but had not believed. Missing from the Concora Federal Credit Union was not $22,680 but $37,065.70. Someone had skimmed almost $15,000 before the loot was divided. He changed his plea to guilty and became a government witness. In addition to the other rules of the Panther Party he forgot the one about giving the police only your name and address.

In a January trial before jurors, Lucky was the crucial government witness, but he insisted on the stand that Leon, accused as the getaway driver, was not involved. Bruce's attorney argued to the jury that Lucky had lied about the matter, implying that if he was a liar about that he was a liar about Bruce. "He lied barefacedly and baldly to this Court."

The jury started deliberations at noon. At five o'clock they reported that Juror No. Six said he was not close to a verdict and the jury was discharged, the case a mistrial.

A year later the new trial was before Judge A. Leon Higginbotham, Jr., a prominent jurist who had been vice chairman of the National

Commission on Causes and Prevention of Violence.

In prison awaiting the second trial, Lucky learned that Bruce had changed his plea to guilty, was the government's star witness this time and, he was told, was putting all the blame on Lucky. Lucky assumed that he would testify that the accused getaway driver was involved while Lucky, under oath in the first trial, had testified that he was not.

On January 12, 1971, Judge Higginbotham signed the conventional warrant to get a witness out of prison for purposes of testifying, the warrant reading that the warden of Lewisburg Federal Penitentiary "produce the body of Allen Johnson on January 19, 1971." Officials regularly refused to believe that "Lucky" was a real name.

Lucky was not in the courtroom during the start of the trial but was detained in a holding cage in the courthouse. He was bitter and suspicious. His suspicions were intensified when he was forced to take part in a strange performance that the FBI and marshals would not explain. During the trial, while he waited in the holding cage, he would be taken out by a U.S. marshal, brought into the courtroom, and while the judge, jury, defendants, lawyers and spectators watched silently, he would be paraded by the marshal around the courtroom and then taken back to the cage. He was sure that he was about to be subjected to some additional penalty. He told the FBI agent and the prosecutor that he would not testify. They called him as a witness anyway.

Inside the courtroom he took the stand, accepted the oath to tell the truth, the whole truth and nothing but the truth, and turned to the judge. "I told the FBI agent I wouldn't give any testimony, not one. I don't even know why they are bringing me down here, Your Honor."

COURT: . . . If you testify, do you swear to tell the truth, the whole truth and nothing but the truth?

JOHNSON: If I say anything, it is going to be the truth. Your Honor, before the proceeding I would like to request counsel because I told him and him [pointing to the prosecutor and FBI agent] that I wasn't going to say anything up here because I think it is some type of harassment that is going on. They been bringing me down every day. My nerves are shot. I been going back and forth, back and forth. It is kind of depressing.

The judge told him that the only way he could legally refuse to testify was if he claimed that his truthful testimony would establish that he had committed perjury in the first trial.

Lucky said that was true. "I might perjure myself. See, the first time I was sort of on the nervous side and I may have said anything, you know . . ."

The judge asked if anything testified to under oath in the first trial might have been false. Lucky said it might have been.

Then there followed one of the charades common in criminal trials.

Prosecutors and accused citizens often make private deals, sometimes to speed up the process of justice and sometimes because the state has a weak case. The poor are particularly vulnerable in this plea bargaining because they are less likely to have bail to be free while awaiting trial and are kept in jails that are usually horrid. The longer the pretrial period, the more they endure the demoralizing atmosphere of the jail.

Once in court everyone is supposed to speak the spontaneous truth. If there has been a deal it is, in most places, an official secret, and the assumption of the court record has to be that no threats, no coercion and no promises were made by anyone to anyone. Certainly not by the government lawyers.

But Lucky broke the rules. He said in court, "The United States Attorney made a threat to me . . ."

COURT: Now just a minute!
JOHNSON: He said in relation to my parole—
COURT: Now just keep quiet! . . . You don't run this court!
JOHNSON: I am not trying to, Your Honor.

The Assistant United States Attorney prosecuting the case felt that the fragmented accusation by Johnson required an explanation. Victor L. Schwartz, the prosecutor, said that what Johnson claimed was totally false, that there were no threats, no promises, no coercion, that the prisoner's rights had been explained to him. The prosecutor said that he had told Johnson, "I would merely write a letter regarding a statement of fact to the Parole and Probation Board that he had an opportunity to assist the government and that he did indeed do so. I also told him—and I was not threatening him—I told him that, also as a part of the responsibility and duty of my position as an Assistant United States Attorney that if he refused to avail himself of this opportunity, it again was just a statement of fact—I would make this known to the Parole Board and the Probation Board."

Having made that perfectly clear, the prosecutor asked Johnson whether he participated in the robbery of the Concora Federal Credit Union on July 10, 1969.

"I refuse to say anything, you know, because it may incriminate me."

To the next sixteen questions Johnson replied, "I repeat myself."

Later, in a written order for the record, Judge Higginbotham wrote on the basis of more information:

> In the presence of the jury, Johnson was walked in by U.S. marshals and circled the trial area. Of course, the jury, both counsel and witnesses riveted their attention on him. No questions were asked of him, and the courtroom was quiet during Johnson's sojourn. Johnson made no comments during these "exhibitions" for purposes of identification. Understandably Johnson could have felt that he was like an object in the zoo being paraded for observation with no reason given for the parade. When he was finally called to testify, it was not surprising that in his own mind he might have felt that he had been subjected to harassment, for Johnson had testified in a prior trial where he had been subjected to dramatic, extensive and unsympathetic cross-examination. Moreover, he had already pleaded guilty to the crime and had been sentenced. When Johnson finally arrived at the witness stand in this case on January 26, 1971, it was at least the third time in three court days that Johnson had appeared in court.

To the prosecutor's threat of perjury charges against Johnson, the judge wrote:

> At this point, as a trial judge, I was faced with a difficult dilemma. Until this statement was made by Johnson, I had assumed that the witness was merely reluctant to testify because he thought he was being harassed. I did not think that he was basing his reluctance on any constitutional grounds. . . . I find that the admitted testimony of Johnson was but a "minor lapse" in a big and difficult trial.

The other people accused of conspiracy and the crime itself—originally eleven different charges against a total of six people, including the persons charged with hiding the men or their money—ended with dismissals except for the man accused of driving the getaway car, who was found not guilty of most counts and guilty, with a light sentence, of conspiracy.

Lucky Johnson's sentencing, despite his guilty plea and cooperation, took a tortuous if common course.

He had pleaded not guilty when arrested in July 1969, and he was interrogated over and over while he waited under $50,000 bail in Holmesburg prison.

In December he changed his plea to guilty. Judge Joseph F. Lord III, before whom he changed his plea, went through the conventional courtroom ritual:

COURT: Have there been any promises or threats or any inducements what-
soever to make this plea?

JOHNSON: No, there haven't, Your Honor.

It was a proper question by a judge and a conventional, insincere answer by the defendant.

A year later Bruce also changed his plea to guilty and he, too, went through the same ritual with the judge in his case. In the official court files there is a notation dated November 30, 1970, about the dropping of charges against a relative of Bruce's.

The Federal Bureau of Investigation has promised a crucial witness in exchange for his testimony, which is necessary to convict a major defendant in the bank robbery case, that the Federal authorities would not press charges against . . .

On April 20, 1970, after the first trial, Johnson was brought before the judge for sentencing. He was given twenty-five years under a code that sent him to a federal prison for a study and recommendation on, perhaps, a reduced sentence.

Judge Lord asked if Johnson wanted to say anything before sentence was imposed.

"Yes, I would. I would like to say if there is any way possible that I can possibly get some kind of a, you know, drug program for my drug addiction, if you do send me to—if you are planning sending me to the penitentiary, I would like to have some kind of drug reform act, if it is possible."

Johnson's lawyer, Hal F. Doig, pleaded that Johnson be sent to the public health hospital in Lexington, Kentucky, for addiction treatment, saying that Johnson had been addicted for at least four years. If that was not possible, the lawyer asked, could he be sentenced under the Youth Correction Act to someplace other than a penitentiary? "I feel that a flat term in the penitentiary would be ruinous to him."

The judge said he would write to the Federal Bureau of Prisons to ask them to focus on this in their recommendation.

He said he would send Johnson to Lewisburg Federal Penitentiary for a ninety-day study and recommendation to the court on final sentencing. His lawyer knew the prison better than his client. Doig protested to the court that when Lewisburg does the study required by law it routinely recommends half the maximum sentence.

Johnson went to Lewisburg. On September 9, 1970, he was brought back to court with the prison's evaluation and recommendation. Lewisburg said that Johnson was gregarious and cooperative, had an IQ of 114 and was interested in throwing off addiction. They recommended twelve years in the penitentiary, one half of the twenty-five-year maximum.

Attorney Doig protested the Lewisburg recommendation. He noted that despite the four months of evaluation the prison assessment was pretty much a mere copy of the information in the court's presentence investigation report. And he protested a sentence to Lewisburg:

> MR. DOIG: First of all, Lewisburg has a problem, as you may know. Parole is very difficult to achieve there. They have a problem of prisoners seeking transfers to Leavenworth and Atlanta, tougher institutions, but places where parole is achievable. I think it is not the place to sentence anybody to 12 years because it is so difficult to get parole.
>
> COURT: What I was going to do was sentence him to 10 years, to become eligible for parole after three years under Section 4208 (a) (1).
>
> MR. DOIG: Yes, but if he goes to Lewisburg under an (a) sentence or a (b) sentence, it doesn't matter. He is going to serve three-quarters of his time there just as sure—no matter how good he is, no matter what interest he expresses, he isn't going to get in anything less than three-quarters of his time. . . .
>
> COURT: I think you may be right, Mr. Doig.

Judge Lord sentenced Lucky Johnson to six years in the custody of the Attorney General of the United States under the Youth Correction Act "for treatment and supervision."

Bruce was sentenced to three and a half years. The man accused of driving the car was found not guilty.

On September 9, 1970, Lucky Johnson re-entered Lewisburg penitentiary on his final sentence, having already been behind bars awaiting sentence for one year and two months.

The judge had ordered "treatment and supervision" for drug addiction.

Lucky Johnson never received any treatment for drug addiction. There was no question that he had committed a crime, but so had ten other people involved in the same crime. One man was sentenced to one-third of Lucky's sentence and the others served no time at all.

Lucky Johnson had not been very lucky, nor had his regard for justice been heightened. Nor had it been strengthened by the treachery of the prison officials. That was why, perhaps, he wrote to me from segregation:

Sometimes I wonder if what I did was wrong. Even now I kind of believe I was right by my own standards. But that does not mean that I should continue to be as cruel and defective as this government.

16

PRISONER NO. 36035–133

He was sitting on his bunk listening to the familiar footsteps approach. It was Bixby on his way to the washroom. Eddie Mason knew it was Bixby, he knew Bixby was on his way to the washroom, he knew Bixby would have a brown leatherette shaving kit under his left arm, he knew what Bixby would say and he knew what he would say back.

Bixby looked into the dormitory cubicle. "Boy, you ain't never gonna make it looking like that."

Eddie said, "You don't look so fucking pretty yourself."

Bix said, "Hey, Charlie, look at Eddie. Looks like he been hit in the face with shit. Look at the fucking mug on him."

Eddie Mason said to himself, Same old shit, day after day, day after day.

Charlie came over. Eddie knew what he was going to say, too. "Hey, Motor Mouth, you got any sugar?"

"Yeah, I got some sugar. It's where it always is when fucking bums want it, and my name ain't Motor Mouth."

"Okay, dude, okay. Don't panic. I'll come back when I want it."

"You always do," Mason answered and said to himself, Same old shit.

He took off the long underwear he slept in, put on khaki trousers and shower shoes, picked up his shaving kit and headed for the dormitory washroom. He took an empty place next to Bixby. They saw each other in the long, dim mirror.

Bixby said, "Nigger, you ain't handsome."

"So what? I may grow up to be beautiful."

"How old are you?"

"Going on thirty."

268

Bixby peered in the mirror at Mason and shook his head. "You're a lying bastard."

Mason was youthful. His round face and mild looks gave a deceptive impression of pleasant adolescence. Mason said, "Shit, Bixby, you're old enough to be my grandfather."

"Fuck around, punk, and you won't never see thirty-one. Now take me, I'm thirty-two but I don't look a fucking day over twenty-one."

"Yeah?" Mason spoke through the lather on his face, "I can see you now, Bixby: 'Mirror, mirror on the wall, who's the handsomest of all?'

"And the mirror says, 'Snow White, nigger, and don't you forget it.' "

Bixby laughed and then looked serious. "I'd look a lot fucking prettier if those motherfuckers on the parole board hadn't fucked me out of two years I did on the street before they revoked. I do all right on parole for two motherfucking years before they violate me but I get no credit for it and I'm back in Lewisburg, gonna do twelve motherfucking years on a ten-year sentence."

It was a litany, a saying of beads, a ritual, an exhibition of wounds.

Eddie Mason pointed his razor at Bixby's image in the mirror. "Dig this shit. I go to the board in January '71. I make out my parole plan and I tell them I got a twelve-year detainer waiting for me in Jersey. Twelve years, and consecutive to this one. So they know that the fucking prison system somewhere—here, in Jersey—got practically my whole life, but it didn't make no difference to them. The suckers didn't even give me the consideration of an answer. All I get is a copy of their answer to the joint, 'Continue to expiration.' Nixon and Mitchell tell the fucking board they'll get higher salaries if they stop handing out paroles, so they take the bribe and stretch out our sentences. Now ain't that a bitch? They take money to fuck us."

It was true that the Attorney General's office had made clear to the United States Board of Parole that President Nixon would support a raise in salaries for board members if they would reduce the number of paroles.

Bixby shook his head. "Fucking cocksuckers. 'Continue to expiration, continue to expiration.' "

"Bix, I been in and out of these joints since I was a kid. I'm no angel but I'll be fucked if I let these suckers fuck with my future with this harassment bullshit."

"I dig it, Eddie."

"I got to quit. Every time I talk about these fucking joints I get sick to my stomach."

He went back to his cubicle. Charlie was sitting on the next bunk, sipping coffee. The public address made a hissing noise and Eddie Mason knew what it was going to say: "All industry shops to work. . . . Attention all quarters, shops out to work."

He was right.

Eddie called over to the next bunk, "Hey, Charlie, move it, punk. Ain't no hanging out, god damn it. The white man wants his day's work out of you."

"Fuck off, motherfucker. I heard how you work your ass down there in the press department. I hear you're the H.N.I.C."

Head Nigger In Charge was a stale joke.

"Yeah," Mason said, "I'm the fucking H.N.I.C. You heard The Man say it was time to go, motherfucker. Get your ass out there and hump."

"I'll hump your ass if you keep fucking with me."

"Why, ol' nigger Charlie can't take it."

"I can take it, punk."

"Shit, Charlie, you walk around the shop with your face all stuck out like you're gonna kill The Man himself, talking all that tough-guy shit. But, man, you ain't gonna bust a grape."

"I'll bust yo' ass, nigger."

"Listen to him. I ought to try your fucking skull with one of them pipes in the shop."

"Go ahead, punk. You won't have to worry none about no more motherfucking parole."

Eddie Mason buttoned his khaki shirt. It was the coated bitterness, the social grease, the joking clichés uttered to sustain amiable relations. But knowing what every response would be, knowing he would repeat his old lines, was depressing.

"Same old shit. Every day, the same old shit."

It was another episode in the bitter inevitability of his life scenario almost from the beginning.

Long Branch, New Jersey, has been a fashionable seaside summer home for Presidents, Ulysses Grant and Woodrow Wilson, for example. James A. Garfield, twentieth President of the United States, wounded mortally by an assassin in Washington, went to his house on the out-skirts of Long Branch to die. Edward Mason was born in Long Branch on February 15, 1942, but left there at the age of six months for the slower death of a black ghetto in Jersey City.

Death and violence were permanent members of the family. The Masons lived in the worst ghetto of New Jersey, between a city dump and a coalyard. The theme of ever-impending death and deliverance was strengthened by his mother's devotions at the Mount Olive Pentecostal Church, where sermons stressed sin and salvation, and where young Eddie learned to enter politely with his mother through the front door, pretend urgency for the bathroom, and sneak out the back door.

But death staked out all the doors in the Masons' lives. Of Mrs. Mason's twelve children, five died in infancy. When Eddie was six his father died of tuberculosis. In 1950, when Eddie was eight, a fifteen-year-old brother died of tuberculosis. When Eddie was nine his mother remarried, took a job as a cleaning woman in a funeral home and took Eddie with her where he watched his mother clean the embalming room with white corpses laid out on slabs.

When he was sixteen a probation officer's report said Eddie came from an "unkempt, disorganized, crowded" home in "one of the worst parts of the city," that he had no real memory of his father, that his stepfather was neglectful of his stepchildren, and his mother was "mostly interested in seeing how much welfare she can get." When Eddie was nineteen his mother, diabetic and paralyzed on the left side, stopped getting welfare. She died. When Eddie was twenty-three his stepfather died of pneumonia.

When Eddie Mason was five years old his mother, eager for him to get schooling, dragged him, frightened and crying, to first grade, where on the sidewalk entrance to the school he vomited from terror.

"You're going to get an education," she said and dragged him inside.

His teachers kept telling him that when he worked he did well, and his third-grade teacher said he could do eighth-grade spelling, superior reading but was slow on math.

But he learned mathematics in another school. His probation officer, in reports filled with contempt, said, "His only skills are cards, gambling, poker and dice."

All of these require, in addition to other less intellectual skills, complex and rapid mathematical calculations of odds, probabilities and sequential patterns.

He also learned the basics of physical life readily. At age five he had his first sex with a girl, a cousin, behind a garage near the railroad trestle. It was less than total intercourse, with pretentious simulations on his part, more going through the motions he had seen older children perform. His cousin talked about it and his mother whipped him.

Like most ghetto children he had to prove himself in a more public way than sex behind garages and a less passive way than in a classroom. He had to prove that he could fight and protect himself in gang fights, gang escapades and crimes. Can openers and sharpened screwdrivers were the initial weapons for self-defense.

By the age of seven he was going with an older brother and other older neighborhood kids on the Hudson Tubes to Thirty-third Street in Manhattan in order to steal from Macy's and Gimbels. Two of the kids would start a mock fight to distract attention from the others, who were slipping movie film, jewelry and cameras into slits in the linings of their coats.

By the time he was nine he was carrying a sharpened screwdriver as a weapon.

When he was ten he spent his first days in jail.

He and older kids in the neighborhood were in front of Macy's. They arrogantly walked to a sidewalk ice cream vendor, opened the door of his cart and took out packages of ice cream sandwiches. The vendor yelled and began chasing them The boys scattered. Eddie threw his ice cream away and ran. He stopped running in a strange neighborhood, totally lost. He walked around for hours looking for a familiar landmark to the Hudson Tubes or sight of his gang. He got more lost. As night began to fall he finally asked a policeman how to get to Thirty-third Street. The policeman asked what part of Thirty-third Street. Eddie was vague about his destination and about his own home address, so the policeman called a van to take the boy to the police station.

The police notified his home and sent him to the Manhattan detention center as a lost child to await his mother or stepfather. Nobody came that night or the next day or the next day. Inside the detention center he met older tough adolescents who challenged him to fights, one of them a vicious one over an extra piece of bread. For the first time he was alone against a hostile group and he learned deterrence to attack by instant defiance.

A week later his stepfather came to get him. Eddie was bitter at his abandonment. His stepfather said it should teach him a lesson.

The defense mechanism of aggression he had learned in the detention center was effective back home. He would pick fights, especially with older and bigger boys, though not with his own neighborhood gang, whom he came to value more than ever. He was still attending school, though spasmodically, and when he would see a fight at the other end of the schoolyard he would start one at his end without thinking why.

Sometimes he would spit on the nearest boy or push an older student to the ground, or simply tap the nearest shoulder and when the boy turned hit him on the jaw. He had always been taunted for being skinny and small and now when he started fights and defeated bigger boys he was praised by his gang and treated with deference. In later life he said it was not conscious but happened by reflex.

By now his neighborhood gang had a name, El Quintos, and had established liaison with a "brother club" in Brooklyn, the Chaplains. Gossip and occasional accounts in the newspapers brought the two gangs together. The Chaplains would come to El Quintos' parties in Jersey City and El Quintos would go to the Chaplains' parties in Brooklyn. Parties would be held in any hall available, or in someone's house while parents were away. Both gangs would discreetly hide their weapons someplace near the party, in the parked car of an older member, or under a tenement porch. Socializing with wine and marijuana created the atmosphere, but there was an underlying competition in cool toughness between each gang's president, war lord and war council. Fights inevitably broke out, first with fists, then, after a quick deployment near the hidden arsenals, with weapons. It was the most exciting event of the parties.

The highest values in the group, at least praised publicly, were chivalry in protecting a girl in one's own gang from others, gallantry in going to the assistance of a fellow gang member doing badly in a fight with a rival gang member, and valor in personal combat.

But chivalry, gallantry and valor did not extend to strangers, including handicapped old women. One day when he was eleven Eddie, walking on Van Horn Street in his neighborhood, saw ahead of him a heavyset woman with a bandage on her leg. Dangling loosely from her arm was a pocketbook. A perfect target. He ran by her and snatched the pocketbook off her arm and continued his dash up the street. The woman yelled and to his surprise chased him with remarkable speed. For reasons mysterious and astonishing to him the lumbering old lady was catching up with him and he had to wait until a passing car was almost next to him to run quickly in front of it, at risk of being run over but cutting off the pursuing old lady. He turned a corner, went through the pocketbook and found only seventy-five cents. He ran to his house. His mother, stepfather and sister were sitting on the porch.

"What are you running for?"

"Nothing."

He went upstairs to their flat. Moments later he heard someone say, "Did a little boy run by here?"

Then he heard his mother say in a cold, loud voice, "Edward!"

His mother came upstairs followed by the old woman. He had seventy-five cents in his pocket and admitted he had stolen it. Someone called the police. They took him to the Bayonne Parental Home, where he had to increase his power in resisting the advances of older boys even tougher than the ones he knew in his neighborhood. At the end of thirty days he was called before a juvenile judge, who said he was releasing him but warned him not to repeat his criminal ways.

By now he was more tough and embittered and began fighting with members of his own gang who were relatively young and vulnerable compared with the older boys he had contended with in Bayonne. He began to hang around with much older boys.

Between the ages of eleven and thirteen he did perpetual burglaries from stores and gas stations in Jersey City. He and older boys would jimmy open windows, or during the day fix a door so that the latch did not lock at night, or have one gang member ask the proprietor to show something in the back of the store while another emptied the cash register in the front.

As they became more cool and arrogant they developed another technique. A group of five or six older boys from the neighborhood would go to a white working-class neighborhood that was not so rich that they had air-conditioning or homes behind hedges and fences but rich enough to have houses with front porches and valuable portables inside. These were "hot day" exercises. They would wait until the height of summer heat in midafternoon when people were sitting on their front porches trying to catch some movement of air. Most of the boys would go down the sidewalk past the filled front porches, acting the white stereotype of blacks—jiving, zany and loud—so that the entire block stared hawklike at every boy in the crazy band trespassing in their neighborhood. While they watched, someone, usually Eddie, who was small and quiet, walked through the back yards, went into the back doors, looked quickly for pocketbooks, portable radios, wallets, toasters and other portable valuables. While the residents were keeping the sidewalk blacks under unremitting surveillance, Eddie would be quietly sneaking out their back doors.

Eddie remembers going into one home during a hot afternoon. He listened at the screen door for a moment and heard no one inside. He stepped inside and scanned quickly the kitchen, dining room and living room. The family members were sitting on the porch, hazily visible through the living-room curtains, his friends audible in their finger-snapping and high-pitched antics on the sidewalk. Nothing worth stealing downstairs. He walked quietly up the carpeted stairs. Sometimes wallets and pocketbooks were on bedroom dressers. He opened a door. It was the bathroom. A young woman about eighteen was sitting on the commode, her panties at her knees. She stared at him, paralyzed. She had brown hair, brown eyes and fair skin. He stared back. Neither could speak. He said softly, "Sorry," quietly closed the bathroom door, tiptoed down the stairs, out the back door and rejoined his gang three blocks away. Nothing came of that incident except a persistent memory of a strange encounter.

Other incidents did not go undetected. During that time he was arrested six times for breaking and entering and larceny, never for large amounts, but enough to bring police action. When he was thirteen he was sentenced as an incorrigible to the New Jersey State Home for Boys at Jamesburg. He escaped seven times. Once while he was a fugitive he heard that his mother was sick and he went home. An older brother took him back to Jamesburg. Another time after escaping he stole a car and went to Camden to achieve a certain notoriety among juveniles.

Eddie had escaped from Jamesburg with an older boy who had been in armed robberies and assaults and was considered dangerous. They abandoned their car in Camden and were walking on the street when a squad car pulled up and two policemen grabbed Eddie's companion, whom they identified at once. After his companion was taken away one of the policemen approached Eddie. Eddie gasped. It was Jersey Joe Walcott, also known as Arnold Raymond Cream, the oldest man ever to win the heavyweight championship of the world when, at age thirty-seven, he knocked out Ezzard Charles. Now, age forty-one and still a hero in boxing, especially among blacks, he was impressive-looking as a law officer in New Jersey.

Eddie was still staring at him when he heard the idol say, "What's your name?"

Eddie, still staring, said automatically, "Johnnie Smith."

That is the occasion on which Edward Mason, age thirteen, was defeated in one stroke by the former heavyweight champion of the world. Jersey Joe gave Eddie a sharp slap in the face that sent him spinning against a wall. "What's your name?"

"Eddie Mason."

They took him back to Jamesburg.

After he served his term, Eddie came out and at age fourteen was sentenced to the New Jersey reformatory at Bordentown for fighting. He served thirty days.

By age sixteen he knew many women and sex was a common occurrence. One girl in the neighborhood was highly developed, though very young, and among the gang was rumored to be sleeping with a boy in the flat upstairs while secretly having relations with her mother's boy friend. Eddie visited her and in the dark hallway made advances. When the advances got serious she objected. Eddie accused her of being a baby unable to do grownup things, and pressed harder. The girl continued to resist and began to cry. Eddie left but the mother's boy friend chased and caught him. He was sent to the New Jersey reformatory at Annandale for attempted rape.

When he was seventeen he became popular at parties, singing with two friends he had met at Bordentown. They did rhythm-and-blues and rock. On the way to a house party they saw a man and a woman fighting on the sidewalk. The man was demanding his car keys but the woman refused, keeping them in her bra. A crowd was watching the scene. The man lunged toward her. She threw her purse at him and hit him on the head. The purse fell on the ground, spilling its contents on the sidewalk, most noticeably a roll of bills and a government check envelope. Eddie snatched the roll of bills. He took a train to New York, where he bought marijuana, spent time with a prostitute and two days later, on a Monday, returned home in time to report to his job loading aluminum siding at a warehouse. That night two policemen knocked on his door and took him to a stationhouse. They kicked and beat him for a short time and then had him turned over to the court. He was sentenced for grand larceny to Bordentown reformatory on a sentence of five years–to–indefinite confinement.

Mason was paroled after two years and two months. Three weeks later his gang was fighting in Lincoln Park, the police arrived and Mason was arrested for assault and battery on a police officer, and he received another indeterminate sentence to Bordentown. He was paroled in December 1964.

There followed two years of gambling, hustling and alternating short-term low-paying jobs and living by no visible means of support.

In June of 1967 Mason was living in a Jersey City apartment with a woman, and on the morning of June 22 someone knocked on the door. Mason called, "Who's there?"

A voice said, "Are you Ed Mason?"

It was a familiar and predictable vignette. Any stranger, anyone asking your name, anything representing the outer world, any departure from familiar voices and familiar faces is a sign of danger. In this case it was the almost inevitable overtaking of Edward Mason in his contest with the law. As he put it in an affidavit to the court in 1967:

> I reside at 12 Fairview Avenue, Apartment 11, Jersey City, New Jersey. The apartment consists of four rooms: two bedrooms, a kitchen, a living room, and a bath. At about 9:30 A.M. on June 22, 1967, there was a knock on the door of the apartment and I called out, "Who is there?" and a voice answered, "Are you Ed Mason?" I opened the door slightly, and then the door was kicked in and four or five men came into the room with revolvers drawn.
>
> I asked who they were and what they wanted, and one of the men told me that they were agents of the Federal Bureau of Investigation. Before pushing their way into the apartment, they had not identified themselves as F.B.I. agents. One of the agents threw me up against the wall and put handcuffs on me. Another agent spoke out saying to the other agents, "Search the place and see what you can find."
>
> Thereafter the agents proceeded to go through every room in the apartment, opening all drawers of all chests and dressers and dumping the contents on the floor. They turned over the beds and pulled up the rugs. I inquired if they had a Search Warrant, and one of the agents replied that a Search Warrant was not necessary and that I was under arrest, but I was not shown any kind of Warrant whatsoever.
>
> The search of the apartment took about an hour, and when leaving, the agents took with them the following items which they had found in the drawers of chests and dressers in the apartment:
>
> 1. A .25 calibre automatic revolver.
> 2. A bankbook.
> 3. Birth certificate and other papers.
> 4. A book containing entries of paid bills.
> 5. A Bill of Sale for an automobile.
> 6. $52.00 in cash.

Edward Mason and his brother, Samuel Rochelle Mason, were indicted by a federal grand jury in Newark on three counts alleging that they had stolen $11,104.06 from the Bethune Branch of the Arrow Savings and Loan Association in Newark, a second count of doing it by personally intimidating three employees of the bank, and a third count of putting the employees in jeopardy of their lives by using a dangerous weapon.

A warrant was issued for their arrest on May 24 of that year. Sam went to Los Angeles, where he was arrested on June 22, a few hours after Edward, back in Jersey City, was seized by the FBI agents the same day.

The brothers claimed to be paupers, had court-appointed attorneys and fought all the way. Sam and Edward claimed to be in Jersey City at the time of the robbery in Newark. They questioned the accuracy of eyewitness accounts, the admissibility of evidence seized without a warrant and made several other defenses. The court permitted a private detective agency to be paid $265.46 for interviewing witnesses from the defense point of view. (The detective agency was J.F.K. Associates, Inc., a still prestigious set of initials in 1967. Its president was John F. Kelly.)

Six months later the brothers, after a relative had put up her home as collateral, were released on bail. One month later they were rearrested, Samuel charged with a spectacular robbery that allegedly took $122,830 from a bank in Paterson.

Edward Mason and a friend were indicted:

> . . . knowing that Samuel Rochelle Mason had committed a bank robbery . . . did knowingly and wilfully relieve, receive, comfort and assist the said Samuel Rochelle Mason in order to hinder and prevent his apprehension; that is the said . . . Edward Mason did convey the said Samuel Rochelle Mason by automobile from Jersey City, New Jersey, to Philadelphia, Pennsylvania.

Edward and his friend were also indicted on a second count alleging that they

> wilfully and unlawfully did possess the sum of $9,855 which had been taken and carried away, with intent to steal and purloin from the First National Bank of Passaic County, Riverside office, Paterson, New Jersey, a bank within the meaning of Section 2113 (f) of Title 18 U.S.C., and . . . Edward Mason then knew said money to have been so taken.

Edward insisted that Samuel came to his apartment one day with serious gunshot wounds and some money to be delivered to an uncle. By his account he took his brother to a doctor and the doctor told them that unless they got Sam into a hospital he would die from his wounds. They put him in Edward's car and drove him to Philadelphia. He knew that hospitals had to report gunshot wounds to the police, which is why Edward preferred Philadelphia to Jersey City for hospitalization. The Philadelphia hospital duly reported the wounds and the brothers were arrested in February 1968.

On this count Edward Mason again had a court-appointed lawyer. The lawyer was not paid by the word, as were the ancient English lawyers who placed into English and American laws almost synonymous words like "steal and purloin" to increase their income. Edward Mason's lawyer was paid by his time on the case, sixteen and a half hours, or $198.20.

A complicated set of maneuvers led to the dropping of the indictments for the Bethune Branch robbery, and Edward pleaded guilty to the second set of indictments.

At Edward's sentencing on May 9, 1969, his lawyer told the court, "I don't know whether I can say too much for Mr. Mason. I believe he was foolhardy in getting involved in this because he became involved due to the fact that his brother had, I believe, committed a crime. I think he pleaded guilty to it already, and Edward had been called by him or for him in order to help him out in a certain situation that he had become involved in. I think if it hadn't been for that, Edward would not have been in this matter at all."

The lawyer told Judge Lawrence A. Whipple, "He has been in prison now since February 12, 1968, awaiting detention, awaiting trial and sentence, and all I can say in regard to mitigation apart from what I have said so far is that I believe that he probably has seen the error of his ways, that he has spent enough time up to the present time, considering what has happened, and that he will avoid anything like that in the future. I think Mr. Mason himself may want to address the court."

Judge Whipple said, "Edward Mason, it is now my duty to call upon you and ask whether you wish to address this court before I pronounce sentence."

Edward Mason was as stoic as his lawyer. "Your Honor, I don't think that there could be anything that I could say that could justify my reason for being here. I do hope and pray that the court will take consideration for me, and grant me leniency."

Judge Whipple uttered the words "The sentence of this court is as follows: It is adjudged that you be committed to the custody of the Attorney General of the United States, and by him or his accredited representative to be placed in an appropriate institution for a period of seven years. At the same time, this court invokes Section 4208 (a) (2) of Title 18 of the United States Code. Counsel, explain that to him. Next case."

The U.S. Attorney prosecuting the case dropped the earlier bank charge and the later count that he did "knowingly and wilfully relieve, receive, comfort and assist the said Samuel Rochelle Mason," saying, "It is not in the best interest of the government to pursue this older charge, and the Justice Department has authorized the dismissal of this older indictment."

The earlier robbery was pursued by the State of New Jersey, where Edward Mason was found guilty and sentenced to twelve years, to follow the completion of his seven years in federal prison.

Edward Mason, in the life scenario that ordained almost every step of his childhood and adult life, was delivered to Lewisburg Federal Penitentiary on June 21, 1969. He had been arrested on the charge on February 15, 1968, his twenty-sixth birthday, a coincidence in the date though not in his career. On February 15, 1972, his thirtieth birthday, he had taken leadership in a prison strike, again a coincidence of birthdates but one of the few profound departures from the predictability of his life up to that moment.

17

PRISONER NO. 33074–136

"Zoia's" pregnancy could no longer be concealed and she was only sixteen. Her father, Sasha, a handsome man with an impressive history of philandering, was, of course, outraged. At first he said he would kill himself in shame. Then he said he would kill her. His wife sent the girl away for her own safety. Zoia, forever a romantic, named the baby after her favorite movie actors, Ronald Colman and Spencer Tracy, and her family's Russian name.

Her stepsister, Hulda, was twenty-one, married four years without children, so when Zoia gave up her rights to the infant, Hulda took possession of four diapers, enough baby food for two meals, and Ronald Tracy Filipchek, age ten weeks.

Thirty-six years later, when her "son" was in a federal penitentiary, my wife and I sat in the neat flowered living room of Hulda's cottage in Los Angeles while Hulda remembered those distant days. She was still youthful, though she had suffered much. She felt that she had been unwittingly trapped in a tragedy that started long before the first time she saw the baby in a Salvation Army foundling home.

Her first view of the infant shocked her: he was dark-skinned, black-haired and brown-eyed.

"I have always thought of babies as little blond babies."

Hulda has blond hair, fair skin and blue eyes.

"I don't particularly care for real dark people."

But she liked the idea of having a child. Her favorite expression to him for years was "How is my little adopted boy?"

She said, "He used to think that 'adopted' meant 'good.' "

He says he used to think "adopted" meant "dark-skinned."

She enjoyed his intelligence. He said "Mama" at four months,

"Dada" at five months, "eat" at nine. She thought physique was important and he was a big baby. Neighbors with children the same age would think theirs were sick, because Hulda's child, now called Duke, was so much bigger.

But she soon became sure that he was criminally inclined. Her overwhelming memory of him as a child was that he squirmed too much, that he was heavy to carry, that he was mischievous, always wanted attention, and from the age of three was, in her words, "maladjusted." She believed this "maladjustment" was genetic, from the "bad" or "dark" side of the family, and from the unknown father.

"I was worried from the time he was three. I was afraid he might be a criminal, so I was harsh on him. The fear that he might be a criminal was always on my mind."

She worried, too, because he insisted on playing with Mexican-American children who lived in another part of the neighborhood. She had moved only after making sure she was not in a Mexican neighborhood, buying a house on the white side of Third Street in East Los Angeles.

But the Chicano kids were nearby and she kept telling Duke that they were bad, that they were criminals who would end up in prison and that he would go to prison, too, if he played with them. She later said she should have known that his association with the Chicano children was inevitable. He had dark skin and so did they.

Hulda's husband, Bob Valentine, worked as a janitor at night and she spent as much time as possible with him during the day. The baby would compete for attention and she considered this another sign of his maladjustment.

Bob Valentine became hospitalized during the Depression and Hulda had to find a job. The baby was two years old when she went to work in a Hollywood laundry, thirteen hours a day for six days at sixteen dollars a week. She left the house before daylight and returned after six at night. Suddenly the child was alone, left with whichever neighbor would look out for him. Sometimes Hulda would come home to find that Duke had been out in the rain all day. He began to wet his bed for the first time since he had been toilet trained. Hulda considered it the first clear manifestation of his "maladjustment."

By the time he was six Hulda was telling him more often than before that he was not her child. "Zoia made you."

His first memory of Zoia was of a pretty woman, reddish hair, athletic figure and lively face. She laughed and hugged him. He said, "Race you around the block."

Zoia stood back in mock surprise. "All right. Ready? Go!"

They raced. He beat her but she was never far behind, laughing all the way.

But then Zoia would go away again, back to the Oakland side of San Francisco Bay, where she lived with her husband, trying to put her life together.

Hulda's husband was finally diagnosed as tubercular. His leaving for a sanitarium was hard for Duke, who regarded him as his real father, partly because Valentine, unlike most of the relatives he knew, was dark-skinned. The two had a warm relationship.

Duke used the last name Valentine until he was thirty.

When Duke was nine Hulda divorced the hospitalized Valentine. On his last visit to the sanitarium to see the man he considered his father, Valentine told him, "Duke, you're the man in the family now." Duke took the assignment seriously.

When Duke was eleven, already six feet tall, Hulda remarried. The honeymoon was to Yellowstone National Park. There was no alternative but to take Duke. The boy protested. At Yellowstone Park he continued to complain about the new man next to Hulda.

"He kept acting up. He was absolutely obnoxious. He kept acting up so bad that my new husband beat him. I guess Dukie never forgave him for that but my husband was so right to do it. The boy just aggravated us to the nth degree."

Might the boy have been jealous of the new man after being told he was the man of the house?

"I don't think so."

Hulda didn't like her stepfather, Sasha. He was a playboy, even at age sixty, a dominating man and, worst of all, "the dark one" in the family. But Duke had nothing but affection for the old man. The old man was always elegant, had a charm that captivated women and those men who did not happen to be suspicious husbands.

If Hulda visited her mother in the Russian flats, Sasha would announce, "Dookie and me are going to the beach." The two would get into the front seat of his 1941 Ford coupe, "the machine," and they would head for Pacific Ocean Park. Sasha would open all the windows, tune the Philco car radio to a classical station, turn up the volume full blast, especially if it happened to be Tchaikovsky, and head for the Pacific Ocean like a manic lemming. He knew only one speed on the machine—full. He careered down Santa Monica Boulevard, periodically going down the wrong side of the thoroughfare to bypass timid drivers observing the speed limit, interrupting his singing with the radio long enough to hurl Russian maledictions at the idiots who stood between him and the Pacific Ocean.

Duke was conscious of being "different" because he was adopted and because he was Russian. He was aware of "American" neighborhoods, which meant middle-class and not obviously "foreign" or Chicano or black. He flirted with "American" girls with success. He could pass because he was tall, his name was Valentine and the dark complexion was natural in Southern California beachboys.

He started first grade at Humphreys Avenue Grammar School, lying about his age because of his height. He became the star in baseball and soccer and protector of smaller classmates. He was praised by teachers for "leadership qualities." He liked school. His classmates and teachers liked him. So it came as a shock when his sixth-grade teacher told him that he would not remain with his class through the rest of his school career, that because he was so tall and doing well he was going to be skipped a grade. That meant going to a different school in a different neighborhood.

Kern Avenue Junior High School was a large school in a strange neighborhood. His status changed from an admired leader with many friends to a new and friendless kid to be challenged. His grades dropped. He joined the school toughs who achieved status with violence. Suddenly at eleven years of age he was drinking cheap wine, smoking pot and skipping school. It happened to be the same year Hulda remarried and brought a new man into their lives. The new "father" was an asthmatic Texan. From the start he and Duke were antagonists. After the honeymoon beating in Yellowstone National Park their relationship was physical and the tall eleven-year-old and his "father" often slugged it out in bitter fistfights, cursing each other. Duke spent less and less time at home.

When Duke was twelve one of his friends from Kern Avenue Junior High stole a new Ford and took Duke for a ride. Later the friend was arrested by police. For the first time police came to Hulda's door asking for Ronald Valentine. At police headquarters they insisted he had taken part in the theft. He insisted he hadn't. One of the policemen rolled a *Life* magazine tightly and smacked him on the head. "That's for getting smart." They booked him for "joyriding" and locked him up in Los Angeles County Juvenile Hall, where he had his first experience behind bars.

This was new for Duke but it was not new for his friends. Police arrests, lockups, jails and prisons were normal items for the local culture, no more remarkable than having a tetanus shot and requiring the same unflinching public poise, the lower-class bar mitzvah. This had not been true of Duke but he had been subjected, nonetheless, to a common ceremony. On the way to the beach, when he was four years old, they would pass a reform school in Whittier and someone would always perform the ritual of pointing to the institution and informing the youngest child present, "This is where you'll go if you aren't good."

When he was six they took Sunday drives and on the way they stopped on a hill to look at San Quentin prison. The usual adult admonition was delivered. But to the child San Quentin was a romantic fortress like the ones he saw in the movies where Jon Hall scaled the wall to save Yvonne De Carlo.

When an adolescent returned from reform school it was always a festive occasion, much like a hero's return from battle, with congratulations and much telling of tales from inside the wall, some of them true.

Duke's early incarceration and abandonment to await a hearing was not a disgrace in the eyes of his friends, but it changed his vision of himself.

In 1950 he spent thirty days in juvenile hall awaiting trial. It was not in the accepted surface culture of his friends to flinch before court decisions. But after being in jail four weeks, the night before his court appearance he lay in his bunk and prayed the prayer that has been uttered in a million children's heads: "Please God, give me one more chance and I'll never do it again."

The judge gave him two years' probation.

At age twelve Ronald Valentine had changed citizenship. He had been in a society where people are presumed ultimately law-abiding, where entanglement with criminal justice is a rare catastrophe and where the rewards for proper behavior are guaranteed. He passed into a different society where people are presumed to be lawbreakers, where arrests and jailings are common and where the rewards for proper behavior are so unreliable that attempts to achieve them are considered stupid. In his society he had proven he was no longer a child.

Within an hour Duke was smoking Fatimas, being slapped on the back by his friends, swapping tales of courts, reform schools and prisons, and erasing any memory of the earnest deal made with the deity the night before.

Back in Kern Avenue Junior High, the newly matured Valentine was a solid citizen in the society of toughness. Being ordered to the principal's office was a merit badge. He went there for fighting, smoking, truancy and cutting classes. A conference was called with the school principal, Duke's probation officer, Hulda and her husband. The probation officer said Duke was headed back to juvenile hall for violation of his terms of probation unless Hulda and her husband did something drastic. They promised to put him in that other institution of parental patchwork, the military school that is supposed to teach discipline, respect and lawfulness. There, in the eleventh month of his twelve-month enrollment an officer discovered him not only using obscene words but teaching them systematically to an eager class of his fellow cadets. He was expelled.

The authorities let him return to Kern Avenue Junior High. Six months later he was transferred to Andrew Jackson High School, one of Los Angeles County's "bad-boy schools." Ninety-five per cent of the students were blacks and Chicanos. One room was set aside exclusively for interviews with the Los Angeles Police and the Sheriff's Department.

Gang warfare and individual feuds were intense. Carelessness could result in being maimed or killed. Duke learned to carry a straight razor.

That year bore a special date. On August 20, 1952, he had his first fix of heroin. Self-contempt, despair and pain disappeared when the magic chemical entered his blood vessels. His friends gave him his first "junk," diacetylmorphine hydrochloride, the crystals distilled from opium, the juice of the lovely poppy, mixed with cheap powders, dissolved in water, sniffed or injected by hypodermic, with instantaneous impact on the central nervous system, a way, he would write later, "to die and yet to live."

When the chemical hit his blood stream he felt a sudden "rush" as though an elevator smoothly rose a thousand feet. The brain and sinuses pulsed. His eyes closed, his tongue searched for pleasant sensations. The rush lasted for several seconds, a phenomenon of novices that tempts them to deeper use and to fatal doses. After the rush a profound euphoria permeated Duke's being, a sense of serenity, a desire to lie down, a pleasant mild itching, now on one part of him and now on another. His eyes wanted to close, his head nodded. Cigarettes gave intense pleasure, fantasy shapes forming in the exhaled smoke. If it was good heroin the euphoria could last twelve hours. He learned that if he took small doses it produced spectacular satisfaction from sexual intercourse, but after a time he wanted only big doses. In the midst of the euphoria he might sleep.

Then he would awake. At first a general malaise, no more than an uneasiness. Then a feeling of illness that quickly intensified to pain, vomiting and terror at the unstoppable depth of the excruciating hurt. Unstoppable unless he quickly found another fix of heroin.

As his fourteenth year drew to a close Duke used heroin more often. He skipped school, then stopped altogether. His probation officer, Mr. Aaron, was a kind and patient man who knew something was very wrong. He told Duke and Hulda that unless something drastic happened Duke would go to juvenile prison. A month later Duke was in Zoia's home.

It was the first prolonged contact between Duke and his mother. She tried to please him. She told him she had tried unsuccessfully to regain custody of him. She hugged him often and cried as often. Her husband, an industrial foreman, tried to give Duke fatherly advice and be as relaxed as possible. They had a son, Duke's half-brother, Barry, who looked at his tall older brother with hero worship.

Zoia lived in a small but pleasant house in a graceful middle-class neighborhood. They had a barbecue, a patio and a red cocker spaniel. The neighborhood, in the California style, was graced by a variety of trees. The children of the neighborhood were proper, well-behaved, and wouldn't have recognized a straight razor if they saw one. It was the epitome of the American working-class dream. After one week he ran away.

Hitchhiking back to East Los Angeles was not hard. For two months he slept in hallways of buildings, untended garages and all-night pool halls. He spent the night of his fifteenth birthday sleeping in a parked car. He begged, played cards and performed minor thievery for food and heroin. Sheriffs looking for someone else came across him in the flophouse, and his heroin works—the eyedropper, burnt spoon and cotton. He was sent to Contra Costa County Jail near Richmond, since that was his last official address.

His mother visited him regularly. They became closer. When he was taken before a judge, Zoia pleaded for another chance. The judge did not agree and sentenced him to Preston until his twenty-first birthday, to be treated for narcotics addiction.

No one is certain what causes drug addiction. It has been epidemic in impoverished ghettos where there is despair and squalor. But it has also grown among the affluent where there is money and comfort. The best guesses are that addiction is more prevalent where drugs are easily available, where organized suppliers who start it can depend on growing sales through addicts who must spread the habit to make sales whose commissions will buy their own supply. The drug fixes itself most deeply in those who in their daily life do not experience trust or love or accomplishment or self-esteem. Whatever its causes, it is not suppressed by crude discipline—it is more prevalent in military forces than in civilian life. It is not cured by condemnation or degradation—that intensifies the desire to escape by drugs.

Preston School of Industry, a juvenile prison, is where the State of California, on orders from a judge, began what the court had called "treatment for drug addiction" for Ronald Valentine.

On his arrival Duke's handcuffs were removed and he was given two sets of blue khakis, underwear, boots, and a "whitewall" haircut, clipped close along the sides with a short stubble on top. He was led to "Diagnostic Clinic No. 1." Inmates were called "cadets." Every day in temperatures often above a hundred degrees they did close-order marching on a blacktop drill area. Boys unable to keep in step or respond quickly to drill commands were given a swift kick in the pants or slapped on the head. Silence was the rule during marching and while in the clinic dayroom and in the dormitory. One evening during the complete silence in the dormitory, Duke fell into a fit of uncontrollable laughter. The counselor called another staff member, who held Duke's arms behind him while the counselor slapped Duke's face for a few minutes until he agreed that what was happening at that moment was not funny enough to laugh about.

Duke was asked what vocation he wanted to train for. Hulda had paid a blind woman to give Duke piano lessons, and Duke had come to like music, especially jazz. He said he would like to be a jazz trombonist.

"Well, forget about playing jazz. It would take you into nightclubs and associations with people who take drugs."

A few days later he was told that he was too young for Preston and would be transferred to the Paso Robles School for Boys 200 miles away.

Paso Robles was a former prisoner-of-war camp from World War II, halfway between San Francisco and Los Angeles. While asleep each boy had to keep his head turned toward the counselor's desk. Anyone turning his head the other way would be knocked on the head. Anyone caught masturbating was publicly denounced and forced to stand at the head of his bunk while his sin was commented on. Duke was caught masturbating twice and decided the humiliation was not worth the joy (besides which, a priest had told him it would cause pimples, insanity, and deny him entry into heaven).

He met the classification committee, who asked him again what he wanted to train for. He said music. They assigned him to the vegetable garden.

One afternoon Zoia visited. She spent three hours, talking, joking and hugging Duke. She said she wanted him to come back to live with her and had visited the parole board to urge it.

In June of 1954 he was paroled to his mother's home. There the old uneasiness set in. He spent the hours listening to jazz on the radio and records, imagining himself playing trombone with Stan Kenton or Woody Herman. Except for the music he was bored.

When the parole officer visited, Duke asked to be transferred to Los Angeles, and his mother agreed because, she told the parole officer, Duke wasn't happy in her home. In mid-July he was back with Hulda and her husband.

One night he ran into "Brenda," whom he had known since they were eleven. They had spent years disliking each other. This time they liked each other and began dating. Her parents had moved from the old neighborhood near Duke's to Hollywood, and, becoming affluent, they gave Brenda almost everything she wanted. She could drive to East Los Angeles in the family car to pick up Duke. He liked her tomboyish good looks, her sense of humor, her irreverence. She had hazel eyes and long silky auburn hair. She liked what she called his "unusual maturity and knowledge," his dark good looks and his rebelliousness. His adventures in reform school fascinated her. They discussed psychology, which he had picked up from reform school "orientation" and books.

By this time he was back on heroin, though trying to use it sparingly. Brenda smoked pot and took Benzedrine pills but she said she drew the line at heroin. Duke shrugged it off, saying he could take it or leave it.

In September Hulda and her husband went on a week's vacation and Duke, Brenda and another couple had a party in Hulda's house. They played records, danced, smoked pot and popped pills until far into the morning. They were in poor condition to drive, so they stayed for the night. The other couple took Duke's bedroom. Duke and Brenda took Hulda's room.

The thought of being in bed with Brenda was exciting. They had petted but she had always resisted going to bed. They poured themselves another drink and sat on the bed talking. They petted. Duke pressed further. She resisted and pushed him away. He was frustrated, took a cold shower, lay down next to Brenda and went to sleep.

When he woke up he saw two sheriff's deputies standing over him. One of the deputies asked Brenda, "How old are you?"

"Sixteen."

Duke was booked for statutory rape and contributing to the delinquency of a minor. He went to the county jail. After he had been in jail a week, Brenda visited him. They had examined her and determined that there had been no sexual intercourse. But Duke was being held for violation of parole. At the parole office Zoia was present. The parole officer said he was determined to end the parole, but Zoia pleaded to let Duke stay free in her custody.

"Are you willing to live with your mother and stay out of trouble?" Duke nodded.

One week after he moved in with Zoia, Duke packed his bag and hitchhiked back to Los Angeles. He got a heroin fix from a friend. Minutes later he was strolling down a sidewalk when a sheriff's deputy called him over to his car. Duke ran. The deputy caught him and a month later he was back in Preston.

Brenda wrote regularly. He wrote back. He controlled his rebellious spirit in his desire to get out and see her. During this period he received the only letter sent to him by his grandfather:

Dear Dookie, You are my kin and it troubles me that you are in a concentration camp. You are my only kin to get in trouble with the police. You must learn to be a honest man. When they let you out you must work hard and obey the law. You must stop fooling with Mexican people. They only get you in trouble. . . . We send you $10. Sincerely, Sasha. P.S. Don't smoke cigarettes.

To his surprise, in April he was granted parole. He and Brenda became inseparable.

One night she confessed that while he had been in Preston she had started to use heroin. He was not shocked. There had been a sudden rise of addiction in his neighborhood, much of it among old friends who had started while in Japan with the Army. He and Brenda fixed together.

It was during this period that he heard again from Bob Valentine, Hulda's first husband. He had recovered from tuberculosis, had remarried and lived in Phoenix. They had dinner together and decided that Duke and Brenda would get married in Arizona. Hulda declined to come to Duke's wedding to a "Jewess."

After the honeymoon and a short experiment in Arizona living the couple moved back to Los Angeles. Duke got a job making cabinets for portable sewing machines and Brenda had a part-time job as a secretary. They bought an old Ford. It was decrepit enough so that one Sunday the rear license plate fell off. Duke was stopped by a sheriff who searched the car and then, in a new routine for all youths since the development of drug addiction, asked to see Duke's arms. He saw the needle tracks. He was booked for violation of the California Health and Safety Code, "marks of drug use."

Brenda was moving back with her parents. A week later she told him she was one month pregnant. The week after that, in October of 1955, at age seventeen, Duke was transported to Tracy, California, to the Deuel Vocational Institution, described in one brochure at the time as "California's newest and most modern plant for young adult offenders, located in picturesque San Joaquin Valley just an hour's drive from the Metropolitan Bay Area, specializing in up-to-date vocational training designed to return misguided youth, 18-to-26, to productive lives in the community at large." A less euphoric observer described it as a double fenced, gun-towered, multi-tiered, riot-gated, paranoia-drenched penitentiary with twenty prisoners assigned to aircraft mechanics school and 1500 to the mattress factory, mess hall and prison maintenance. Duke was assigned to the prison maintenance crew, painting.

Brenda wrote every day. Her obstetrician made her eat liver, which she hated. The baby was expected in June and Duke was determined to get out before the birth, and to impress the parole board when he had a scheduled hearing in February of 1956. So he worked hard and avoided the more troublesome inmates who had been his friends at Preston.

Once more, on April 6, 1956, when he was eighteen, there was release from an institution for "Ronald Phillip Valentine," his official name, "Phillip" from the transliteration of "Filipchek," which his family had started to use. After the required registration for the draft and a drink of vodka, he met Brenda and went to her parents' house, where they would live until he found a place. The first night her parents went to a movie and the couple had a candlelight dinner, danced to Errol Garner records and fell in love all over again. The next day Duke began eating liver to keep company with Brenda's agony. He hated liver, too.

Duke went to an employment office, where Columbia Studios called for extras to work two days for twenty dollars.

Ronald Tracy Valentine Phillips entered moviedom the next day. He played in the movie *Jeanne Eagels.* The more noticeable actors were

Kim Novak, Jeff Chandler and Agnes Moorehead. If one looked very closely, one might catch a tall, dark-skinned fellow in a crowd, one time wearing a straw hat in a summer scene, another time wearing a homburg in a winter scene.

His next role was as a car washer at a Bel Air establishment run by a cousin of Brenda's mother, where he starred in cleansing the Rolls-Royces, Alfa Romeos, and Duesenbergs of the rich. The pay was $1.25 an hour. He spent his day off, Monday, looking for another job. Arden Farms was willing to pay $2.50 an hour, with time and a half for overtime, to work nights at their Beverly Hills plant. He paid fifty dollars for membership in the International Brotherhood of Teamsters. Brenda and he saved money and in late May moved to a small apartment overlooking Sunset Boulevard. With some money her parents had set aside for Brenda they bought a seven-year-old Chevrolet.

In early June the baby was born, a healthy girl. The proud father bought himself a thirty-five-cent Garcia y Vega Banquet cigar and puffed it in slow self-congratulatory luxury, grateful for the survival of his wife, the birth of his healthy daughter and the end of his diet of liver.

The baby had colic. By the time Duke got home in the early morning, Brenda would be tired from walking the baby all night and he would take over. The woman in the apartment above was angry and foul-mouthed. When the baby would cry she would bang on the floor.

An "old feeling" began creeping into Duke's consciousness. It was vague but profound, a feeling of incompleteness, of something missing, of malaise. He solved it as he had before. He began using heroin again. Brenda also became bored and unhappy. Motherhood palled. The baby's constant crying unnerved her. They weren't having fun together. They began using heroin together. He knew he was headed for disaster but could not stop. He started to be late for work. He was fired. They both looked for work. She became a night carhop in Glendale. He would look for a job during the day, sneaking into East Los Angeles for a fix now and then, and take care of the baby at night while Brenda carhopped.

One night Brenda returned from Glendale to find Duke deep in a heroin dream state. She exploded in rage. They began shouting at each other. Long before, he had warned her never to call him a "bastard." This night she called him a bastard. He slapped her. She hit him with an iron ashtray. He walked out.

An old friend from Preston said he would buy him a fix from a woman he knew "who sells good junk." It was, Duke felt, a real favor.

Regular drug dealers don't sell to unaccompanied strangers. They went to see "Marian." The two men fixed together and the friend left. Duke felt happy and expansive. He looked at Marian. She was not unattractive, stocky, with black curly hair. And cold eyes.

She looked at Duke analytically. "Listen. You've got nowhere to stay, right? Well, I need someone around to keep things in line. A couple of guys tried to strongarm me for my junk last week and it was a bad scene. The Jaguar in that driveway I got from my last old man in a divorce settlement. It just sits there collecting dust because I don't know how to drive. If you're willing to keep order around here, and do some chauffeuring, you get all the junk you need, a private bedroom and no romantic involvement. What do you say?"

"You've got yourself a deal."

Marian was thirty-three, had been married four times, had worked as a prostitute in Palm Springs and was now a lesbian. She and Duke had a strictly business relationship. Each day he would drive her to the San Fernando Valley, where she picked up bags of heroin. Other than that Duke merely hung around to make sure the clients were not tempted to commit larceny. And giving Marian her fixes. In addition to not driving, she did not know how to inject herself. Duke learned to take long walks when Marian wanted privacy for sex, usually with a good-looking woman client. He liked neither Marian nor himself, but he liked the heroin that erased both dislikes.

Duke visited Brenda and the baby from time to time. He returned each time with profound self-contempt.

One night in May two men came to the door to buy heroin. Marian knew only one of them and asked him how come he brought a stranger. He assured her that the stranger was all right. After they left, Duke said, "Something tells me you made a mistake, sweetheart."

"Oh, for Christ sake, you're getting paranoid."

The next morning Duke was awakened in his room by the sounds of an argument in the kitchen. Duke went out and saw Brenda about to attack Marian. Duke stepped between them. He and Brenda went outside to a park.

"I don't want you living with that goddamn bitch," Brenda told him. "I want you to come back with me and the baby."

Duke said it was no use. He had a bad, bad habit and no way to support it.

"Well, I've got some money saved up. We can go to Phoenix. You've always liked Arizona. I can get a job as a carhop while you kick the habit. I can swipe my father's sleeping pills to help you over the hump and we can take the bus tonight."

Duke thought about it and agreed. He said, "I'll take some of Marian's dope, give it to you and you can taper me off with it. I'll pack my clothes and wait for you to call tomorrow."

Brenda said she couldn't call until late because she had to wait for her father to fall asleep. The money she had "saved" was in his wallet.

The next morning he drove Marian to the Valley again. He told her he was leaving.

That evening he packed, put on a pleated yellow shirt and his favorite brown silk tie, looked in the mirror and said to himself that everything was going to be okay.

He went to the kitchen and gave Marian her fix, but a very large dose. She mumbled, "Jesus Christ, I gotta cut that stuff. It's too good." She drifted into a dreamy sleep.

Duke went into her bedroom and took her packaged heroin, kept, as usual, in a condom. He came out and checked the clock. It was only seven o'clock. Brenda wouldn't be calling for a while. He went into the bathroom and injected himself, wrapped the works and the stolen heroin in his suitcase in the bedroom. He was about to close the suitcase when the doorbell rang. A bad time for a customer. Marian was rising slowly from the sofa.

"Let me handle this, Marian. You sit down and relax."

He asked through the closed door, "Who is it?"

"It's Ray. I want to score."

Duke didn't know any Ray. He was alarmed. He said, "Marian, do you know any Ray?"

She rose rubbing her cheeks with her palms. "No, baby."

The voice from the other side of the door said, "Hey, man. I was here last night with Sonny. I want to score a gram."

It was the man that gave Duke the bad vibrations. He turned to Marian with a warning look. "Tell him to come back tomorrow!"

Duke went toward the kitchen when he heard Marian unlocking the front door. She kept the chain on. Duke yelled at her, "Marian! Close that door! Tell him to come back tomorrow!"

Marian began talking to the man through the partially opened door when Duke heard a loud voice say, "Los Angeles Police Department! Open the door!"

Marian threw herself at the door, trying to close it. She yelled, "Duke, get rid of it!"

Before she said it, he had already begun to run toward the bedroom. As he ran through the kitchen, the side door of the house was smashed. Two detectives with drawn guns pushed through the broken wood toward Duke. One of them shouted at him, "Stop right there, you motherfucker, or I'll blow your head off!"

Duke pushed the man backward into his partner, slammed his bedroom door, grabbed the dope from the open suitcase. They were coming through the bedroom door when he ran to the bathroom, threw the heroin into the toilet, hit the handle and threw his chest over the mouth of the toilet bowl. A gun butt hit him on the back of the head.

When he became conscious he was sitting on the bathroom floor with one of the detectives holding his arms. Another detective was fishing in the toilet bowl.

"Got it, Ray?"

"Yeah, enough of it."

Duke's heart sank. One of the detectives looked down at him. "Don't you know any better than to run when a police officer tells you to halt?"

Duke dropped his eyes. He knew what was coming.

The detective said, "Well, I'm going to have to teach you a lesson, you stupid cocksucker!"

Duke lost count of how many times he was punched in the face. They dragged him into the kitchen, one detective pulling Duke by his brown silk tie. When they got to the center of the kitchen, one of the detectives punched Duke in the stomach.

"Remember this lesson, punk, the next time you think about pushing a policeman!"

They put one handcuff on his wrist and the other around the drainpipe of the kitchen sink, forcing Duke to sit on the floor. He looked at his shirt. Two buttons were torn off and the front was spattered with blood.

Marian was sitting at the table, her right eye swollen and dried blood along a cut on her forehead. They were asking about her connection. Duke's head ached. Then he remembered Brenda's phone call. The telephone rang. A detective answered, "Hello. . . . This is him. . . . What? . . . LAPD Vice Squad. . . . Hello? Huh, that sure scared the hell out of her."

Duke felt like crying. His eyes were swelling shut.

At the stationhouse they handcuffed Duke to a corridor bench. After a time a detective came to him and spoke gently. "Duke, it's Marian we want, not you. We know you're only a boot and shoe."

"Boot and shoe" is an impoverished off-and-on-again non-selling addict.

"We've got her for sale and possession. We've got you for possession. If you'll sign a statement saying it was her junk, we'll book you for marks and you'll be out in ninety days. What do you say?"

"Go to hell!"

"Okay, stupid." He turned as he got to the squad room door. "Bet you a buck she tries to lay the whole thing in your lap before it's over."

Ronald Phillip Valentine, age nineteen, was booked for possession of narcotics. He was taken to a dispensary to have the back of his scalp sewn. He was asked if he wanted to make a phone call. He declined. They locked him up.

What followed came through a haze of his beating and withdrawal symptoms. He found himself in the Hall of Justice waiting to be interviewed by an assistant district attorney.

Duke lay down on the bench. He felt pains and nausea and knew that he would soon be sick. He had a deeper "jones" habit than ever before and now he would have more excruciating jones "bones," withdrawal symptoms, than ever before.

He wondered briefly what Brenda was doing. Then he felt nausea again and dreaded the approach of symptoms.

"Valentine!"

He was handcuffed and taken to the district attorney's office.

Marian was there. "Jesus, Duke, you look a mess."

The district attorney asked questions to which Duke mostly grunted. He was aware that Marian was being too talkative. He felt the nausea getting worse. Outside after the questioning he sat on the floor with his head on his propped-up knees. He began getting hot and cold flashes. He was aware of being chained to a dozen other prisoners and taken into a courtroom to the jury box. A man who said he was the public defender said he was representing them at an arraignment and bail-setting. Duke's bond was $5000, Marian's $10,000.

On the tenth floor they were packed into a room to await booking. There were no benches and Duke sat on the filthy floor. Four hours later his name was called for fingerprinting. As the man was taking his thumb print Duke vomited on the desk.

The fingerprinter screamed, "Goddamn fucking hype!"

He was ordered to clean up his mess. He did.

The prisoners were put on an elevator to the eleventh floor for showers and body search. As they left the shower each man was sprayed with DDT. The smell made Duke vomit again. He cleaned it up again.

They were taken to the fourteenth-floor infirmary. A bored medical technician wearing a sheriff's badge ordered the prisoners to line up against the wall, drop their pants and hold their penises out for venereal disease inspection.

"Milk 'em for me, boys." Then: "Anyone with diabetes or epilepsy come over and sign here."

The prisoner assigned to take blood looked at Duke's arms. "Man, are your arms fucked up!"

"Yeah," Duke answered. "And I got a mean jones, too. Can I get something for jones bones?"

The jailer said, "Yeah. Run your head into the wall."

They were each issued a smelly mattress and a filthy cup and spoon. The jailer said, "If any of you sweet things are homosexuals, step forward."

One prisoner moved up and was taken to the Queen Tank.

Then they were taken to a detention room, where they slept on the bare floor.

Lights went on. Each prisoner was handed a dipper of warm mush, two pieces of bread and a cup of sweetened coffee. Duke gave his mush and bread to a shaking wino next to him. Rick, a friend from Tracy, was in the group and let Duke use his bunk. At lunch they were given soup and a piece of bread. Duke gave his to the wino. At four o'clock they got beans, tapioca pudding, bread and tea. This time the wino was already beside him to receive his gift.

The days remained hazy. He remembered trying to sleep, killing cockroaches but giving up and letting them crawl over food, face and hands, the Salvation Army singing hymns on Sunday morning when all had to remain silent. And each time he was tempted to eat he would vomit. Then diarrhea. His bones ached. His nose ran. By the eleventh day he was getting small periods of fitful sleep, a sign of the end of withdrawal symptoms. On the thirteenth day he kept down a full meal. He wrote a letter to Brenda.

On the fourteenth day he went to court. Marian was at the defense table with her private attorney. Duke laid his head on the defense table. Marian's bail was reduced to $1000.

A few days later he was told he had a visitor. It was Brenda. She was plainly under the influence of heroin. Duke pretended not to notice.

"What do you think they'll give you?"

"Oh, I don't know. Maybe a year at the honor rancho, maybe back to Tracy. Who knows?"

The twenty minutes' visiting time was soon over and she left. He sat on the floor. It's all over, he thought. Poor Brenda. Poor baby. What a pair she drew to.

A few days later he was called to the attorney's room. A balding man announced himself as Duke's public defender.

The public defender argued for a guilty plea because the case was hopeless. Duke's parole officer urged a guilty plea as a possible way of staying with the Youth Authority instead of going to an adult prison.

In court Duke pleaded not guilty and was assigned for trial August 13, three months after his arrest.

A week later he was visited by an elderly man who said he would deposit $10,000 in a bank under Duke's name and deliver the bankbook if he would plead guilty to the entire charge, exonerating Marian. He would also guarantee his child support while Duke served the prison sentence, and "business associates" would write letters to the parole board for an early release.

Duke said coldly, "Are you aware that sale of narcotics carries a term of five years to life?"

"Yes."

"The answer is no deal."

"Will you allow me to put some money in your jail account?"

"No thanks. I'm a good card player."

Duke settled down to watching traffic on the Hollywood Freeway, killing cockroaches, reading Frank Yerby novels, playing cards and wondering about Brenda and the baby.

An old friend from Tracy who lived on the East Side was booked into his cage. He brought news. Brenda was hooked on heroin and living with a man who gave her money for her habit. The baby was with Brenda's mother.

The public defender visited again. Marian had informed on her San Fernando connection, who had been arrested in a trap she helped set up. She was desperate to avoid the five-to-life conviction. The public defender recommended that Duke get out of the case as quickly as possible. Plead guilty. It's a first adult arrest, first felony at any time, only nineteen years old. Maybe no prison at all.

Duke thought a long time. "Okay, I'll change my plea."

"Good. Now you're getting smart. I'll contact the D.A. and have you in court by next week—and don't worry. It'll go easy on you."

Judge Clement D. Nye set sentencing for July 17. On that day the public defender informed Duke that Marian had been given five to life, suspended, and five years' probation. She would have to serve only ninety days in the county jail.

"That's unheard of for a sale and possession," Duke said.

"So maybe things will go our way," the public defender said.

In court the judge asked if Duke's change of his plea was the result of coaching from the public defender.

"No, Your Honor."

He was sentenced to ten years at Chino.

The public defender didn't meet his eyes. He said as they parted, "You won't have to serve it all, Ron. You'll be out in eighteen months."

It was August and the sheriff's bus was on the San Bernardino Freeway to the California Institution for Men at Chino. The air coming through the window felt good after three months of the stifling atmosphere of Los Angeles County Jail. When Duke saw the sign "Ontario-Chino Exit, ⅓ mile" his stomach tightened. He knew that the outside world was about to disappear. His eyes took in everything greedily—telephone poles, irrigation ditches, trees, cattle, clouds, railroad crossings, a gas station, corner grocery store, a pickup truck making a trail of dust, two dogs fighting in a ditch, a real estate sign—all the most ordinary things suddenly extraordinary and precious.

"State of California—Department of Corrections—California Institution for Men—Reception-Guidance Center. It Is a Felony to Bring Firearms, Narcotics, Alcoholic Beverages . . ."

Duke lit a cigarette and passed the pack around to the chained prisoners.

"All Vehicles Stop!"

A prison guard stepped aboard. He counted prisoners against a sheet in his hand. He lifted the sentry gate and the bus passed through a high chain-link fence with rolled barbed wire at the top. A guard in a gun tower moved a switch and an electrical gate opened. The bus moved into the dock of the yellow concrete prison.

"One chain at a time!"

The first six prisoners chained together moved off the bus. A guard counted them as they stepped onto the concrete floor. The sheriff removed the handcuffs, collected his chain and left.

"Okay men, remove all your clothes and put them with your personal property in the sacks provided. When your name is called bring your sack to the officer at the door, who will mark it with your name, and step into the next room for a skin search. If you wish to send your clothes and property home you may do so at your own expense. Otherwise it will be donated to the institution for use by inmates going to court or on parole."

When his name was called Duke stepped forward. A guard holding a flashlight said, "Bend your head down and rub your hands through your hair."

Duke complied, but with the traditional slave strategy, moving slowly as though confused about the order. After the skin search he moved to the next step.

He sat on the bench, still naked.

"Valentine!"

He walked to the sergeant's desk.

"Valentine?"

"Yeah."

"Yes, what?"

"Yes, I'm Valentine."

"Yes, *sir!* You will address all correctional officers as Mister, followed by their last name, or *sir!* while in this institution. Do you understand?"

"Yes . . . *sir.*"

"What do you want to do with your clothes?"

"You can have them."

"Your number is A-42815. Memorize it! Without it you're no one around here. Report to the clerk at the next desk."

Still naked, he went to the next desk, where a prisoner-clerk motioned him to sit down. The seat was still moist from the previous naked prisoner. The clerk put a form in the typewriter. Name, age, dependents . . .

"Religion?"

"No religion."

"You got to have some religion."

"Put down atheist."

"I can't. You got to be either Catholic or Protestant or—uh—Jewish."

"I don't believe in any God."

The clerk typed, "Protestant."

Still naked, he was fingerprinted.

He took a shower and went to the clothing counter.

He put on jeans and blue denim shirt. They stamped A-42815 on each shoe.

In the tradition of progressive penology the blocks of cages were called "halls" and had special names: Cypress, Palm, Sycamore and Madrone halls. Duke was assigned to Sycamore Hall. He was on the first tier. The door was opened electrically by a guard. Guards in

California are called "bulls" by inmates instead of the usual "hack" or "screw." The steel-barred door slid open. Duke, or Ron as he would be called hereafter, stepped inside. The door closed behind him. He took inventory:

A bunk bolted to the wall, a porcelain washbasin, a porcelain toilet with the last occupant's deposits, half a roll of toilet paper and a used paper cup.

He took off his shoes and lay down on his bunk. He thought of Brenda. And the baby. And ten years in this cage. He felt frightened and alone. He reminded himself of the public defender's words: he would be out in eighteen months. In time for his twenty-first birthday. He felt better.

At evening meal he met many old friends from reform school. It was the usual reunion. They provided him with *Life* magazines, cigarettes and advice. The master control locked down at five-thirty P.M.

Thus ended the first day of his rehabilitation.

He was in "reception" for six weeks, for physical exams, dental examination, IQ test, Stanford Achievement Test, Minnesota Multi-Phasic Personality Inventory and an interview with the staff psychologist. While still in reception his face swelled. The dentist said that a sloppy extraction in the county jail had ruined two more teeth, which he pulled. It left Ron with a large gap.

In mid-September a notice was posted showing prison assignments. He was going to Chino, across the street, the best assignment possible. It was an experiment in "prison without walls," with a cannery, furniture factory, school, library, hospital and a swimming pool constructed by prisoners. The prison farm extended as far as the eye could see. The grounds were more like a college campus than a prison. There were lawns, shade trees, a football field and six tennis courts.

They were handed a form letter signed by the warden: "Congratulations are extended to you on your arrival at C.I.M. That you were selected for C.I.M. indicates that you are a mature and responsible individual."

He was shown to his two-man cage. His cagemate was working in the fields, so Ron stretched out, looking at the fields through the windows. It would be easy to escape. He put the thought out of his mind. At four o'clock his cagemate, Benny, a Chicano, arrived. They shook hands.

They were having coffee when the evening guard appeared at the cage door. "Valentine?"

"Yes. Sir."

"Are you Mexican?"

"No."

"Well, the day officer must have figured you were and he's assigned you wrong. You belong with whites. I didn't think Valentine was a Mexican name."

"If my partner doesn't mind, I'll stay here."

"Okay. If you don't mind, I don't. It'll save me paperwork."

Benny didn't say anything. Ron said in Spanish, "That idiot must have just come from the mountains."

Benny grinned and said in Spanish, "He's a dog."

The next days were spent picking tomatoes. His hands turned green. A prisoner told him to wash them with a ripe tomato. It worked. They chased rabbits and snakes, waved at cars on the highway and got sunburned. On the weekend they lived in the swimming pool.

He was reassigned to the kitchen and vegetable-cleaning crew, where another prisoner, after a few days, asked Ron if he liked good books. He showed him a shelf in his cell: Ibsen, Dostoevsky, Kafka, Auden, Joyce, Proust, de Maupassant. He started to read. He met the prison librarian. It was the start of a long adventure into literature.

He had other good occasions. In January of 1958 he received a partial plate to plug the gap in his teeth. And shortly afterward Brenda visited with the baby. She had been to the public health service hospital in Kentucky to be detoxified. She looked wonderful. The baby was eighteen months old and walking. He and the baby were friends by the end of visiting time. Brenda said she would visit again in two weeks. They embraced and the baby gave Ron a chocolaty kiss.

Brenda came back in two weeks. She asked how long he thought he would be in. He said he went before the parole board in three months but he thought he wouldn't be released right away. She said she would return in two weeks. She did not. She didn't write.

A month later he developed a high fever and was hospitalized. While there, he got into the habit of reading the Los Angeles *Times* from front to back. On release he was given light duties and with much time on his hands he checked out a trombone and practiced under an oak tree, hoping that he sounded like Bill Harris. And he read voraciously. The new world of books absorbed him as much as music. He kept a Webster's collegiate dictionary for unfamiliar words. He would write the definitions in a notebook, memorize them and try using them in conversations.

One day he was reading the Los Angeles *Times*. In fine print under "Interlocutory Decrees" he saw "Valentine, Brenda vs. Ronald."

He was being divorced. That was the only notification he would receive until, months later, he was called to the prison office to sign divorce papers.

He turned his thoughts to other things. In May he went before the parole board. He was asked why he had used narcotics. He recited the usual speech—escaping reality—something he had read in a popular magazine. The chairman told him the real cause was his lack of church attendance. He was denied parole for at least one year.

Because of the aftermath of his illness he was still on light work when the August harvest began. All prisoners on light work assignments knew that with harvest there came the "shanghai," the recruitment of every available hand.

One afternoon Ron was called to the assignment lieutenant's desk. He was told that the doctor had approved his joining the field crews. Ron, a good poker player, decided to bluff. He refused to go.

A month later he was transferred to San Quentin prison.

As the prison bus rolled north through the Salinas Valley, Ron experienced motion sickness. The 350-mile trip between Chino and San Quentin required a stopover at Soledad prison. Cuffs and leg irons were removed and the men marched past local prisoners on the way to their overnight cells. Ron recognized familiar faces. A reform school friend shouted, "Hey, Valentine, you staying here?"

Ron waved back, still fighting back his nausea. "I'm going to the joint!"

The local prisoners looked back with the respect due someone who had made the bigtime, who was assigned to the toughest, most feared prison in the country. Young toughs boasted of their assignment to Soledad, but their distinction paled before San Quentin. That night Ron finally threw up in his cell toilet and discovered to his dismay that the partial denture that filled in his three front teeth had been flushed away.

The next day as they descended the Richmond–San Raphael Bridge, he began to recognize the landmarks of the auto trips of his childhood. They stopped at the sign: "California State Prison—San Quentin."

The massive fortress squatted on a rise that sloped down to the waters of San Francisco Bay. The inner gate opened and the bus ground slowly into the hundred-year-old fortress. A guard in a high tower leaned on a .50-caliber machine gun as he watched the bus go through.

After the preliminaries Ron was issued denim coveralls and boots with the upper fronts cut away. They stepped through a steel door with a bulletproof window. They were in the courtyard. To the left stood the Spanish Block, a nineteenth-century mass with three tiers of cages without plumbing that held long-term disciplinary cases. The doors were solid iron. Each cage had two metal buckets, one filled with fresh water for the punished prisoner, and one for his urine and feces. If he was uncomplaining and respectful he was permitted to refill and dump his buckets once a day. If not, one bucket slowly emptied and the other filled, until he met the behavior requirements.

More privileged disciplinary cases, sentenced to the hole for twenty-nine days or less, lived on the top floor of the "Shelf," next to death row, where they slept on concrete blocks, remained strictly silent at all times, and had only a Bible in the cell.

Ron was issued a sack containing a rule book, one earphone without headpiece, a paper cup, a metal teaspoon, a toothbrush and a razor. Issued once each month, with no exceptions made, were eight books of matches and one roll of toilet paper. When the roll of toilet paper ran out before the end of the month, which it always did, thirty-day-old *Christian Science Monitor*s were available.

On the way to the mess hall, the new men, easily identified by the preliminary issue of coveralls, walked by Four Post, the office used for shakedowns, interrogations and beatings. And then through the famous "big yard," an asphalt surface in a concrete canyon surrounded by high stone blockhouses. Half the yard was covered by a vast tin roof supported by rusty steel beams, and guarded by a network of catwalks patrolled by guards with rifles. Part of the uncovered yard was filled with constantly occupied domino tables.

As the new men walked across the yard a crowd of resident prisoners came forward for a closer look at the new fish. It was a familiar ritual. The new men were searched for a familiar face, a friend, an enemy, a known informer, or a young prisoner whose eyes betrayed timidity or fear and who therefore was a target for enforced homosexuality as a queen. Or some looked for a face that could still smile, eyes that were still not hard, hinting at a mind and heart not yet frozen by years of enforced stagnation, humiliation, violence and madness. Ron marched, watching the prisoners watch him.

"Ronnie Valentine, you motherfucker!"

A good friend from Paso Robles!

"Lenny, you son of a bitch! What's happening?"

Lenny walked fast to catch up enough to say, "I'll talk to you tomorrow when you get your clothes. Where's your house? I'll send you some cigarettes and coffee."

Then Lenny dropped back. Running, boisterous behavior or fighting could bring gunfire from a guard on the catwalk.

As they ate in the dining hall they were watched by an impassive guard above them on a catwalk, a rifle in the crook of his arm. As Ron put beans slowly in his mouth he was aware that the rifle was resting with its muzzle in his direction.

He and his assigned cage partner climbed the second tier of the massive south block, home for 2000 of the prisoners. His partner got to the cage first. "Dirty motherfuckers! They expect two men to live in that?"

The cage was four feet by nine, with a double bunk on the long side and two planks for shelves across the back. The cage was so narrow that it was necessary to brush against the opposite wall to walk. Ron lit a cigarette and looked around.

A toilet with a handle sticking out from a rough hole in the rear wall. A washbasin with a cold-water tap. A switchbox to plug in an earphone. Two nails in the wall. A sixty-watt bulb with a dirty pullstring.

He threw his cigarette butt into the toilet and pushed the flushing handle. Nothing happened. He pushed harder, with pressure in different directions. He finally got a trickle.

"Jesus Christ," he told his partner. "It's sea water."

Ron turned to the front of the cage—thirteen bars so close that only a hand and a wrist could pass between them. On the wall seen through the bars someone had thrown a bottle of black ink, making a large Rorschach on the concrete. He went back to his bunk and lay down. It sagged a foot under him. His spirits sank with it. It was the end of the world.

Blowing hand whistles woke him from his doze. Through the bars he saw prisoners in the yard lining up, carefully putting their feet between parallel dotted lines painted on the asphalt. Guards walked between the rows of prisoners to make sure no shoes protruded over the lines. Another whistle let one line at a time march to their cages. As the prisoners entered south block a wave of chattering noise ricocheted to fill the place, a sound that would continue until sleep. He noticed that prisoners would go to the single hot-water tap at the end of the tier carrying old vegetable cans with wire or string attached.

It was time for four o'clock count. Each prisoner had to stand behind his door for the count. If he did not stand he would be sent to the hole.

After count, the 5600 prisoners were released for supper. On his way back from supper Ron retrieved an old can from a trash barrel.

By five-thirty the prison was secured for the sixteen hours a day spent in the four-by-nine cages. Except for two added hours on Saturdays and Sundays.

An hour after lock-in a tier tender appeared at the cage. "Hot water?"

Ron put his washed-out tin can on the floor just inside the bars. The tier tender put the spout of his bucket through the bars and filled the can. "You Valentine?"

"Yeah."

He reached inside his shirt and pulled out some cigarettes and small packs of coffee. "From Lenny."

Ron took them and said, "Thanks. Something is wrong with our toilet. No water. Can we get it fixed?"

"Nothing's wrong with your toilet. Tide's out."

Instant coffee packs are standard social exchange in prisons, sold at commissaries and providing an occasional break of a cupful of warmth. Ron and his cagemate were drinking their warm instant coffee when a gurgling roar came from the toilet. Ron walked back and looked: muddy water, sand and a tiny minnow. The tide was in, the diurnal pulse conditioning the bowels of 5600 men to ebb and flow with the rhythm of the moon.

At eight-thirty the tier tender came by with the second and last portion of hot water.

"When do we shower?"

"Showers and underwear every Wednesday night."

It was Thursday.

Ron drank his coffee and read a month-old *Monitor* he had picked up at the head of the stairs. Then he took off his coveralls, pulled the light string and went to sleep. He awoke in the night being bitten. He pulled on the light and lifted the coarse tan sheet. Bedbugs. He put out the light and gingerly put his feet back under the sheet. He survived the first night.

After he emerged from "distribution" with his regular denim prison clothes, Lenny and a small group of old neighborhood friends went with him to the big yard for coffee and talk.

As they leaned against the north block wall, a loud voice called, "Dead man!"

Prisoners scattered in all directions, clearing a wide path. A guard walked through the parted humanity. Six feet behind was an over-weight, pasty-faced prisoner wearing brown leather slippers. Six feet behind him was another guard. The comfortable distance between the two guards and the pasty-faced prisoner was explained by the rifleman on the catwalk overhead who followed the prisoner through the sights of his rifle.

The prisoner in the brown leather slippers stared at the ground but looked up as he came by Ron. For some reason he nodded. He looked vaguely familiar. Ron nodded back.

"That's Caryl Chessman," Lenny whispered. "He's going to see his lawyers."

It was forbidden for any prisoner to touch or talk to a man on death row, who was, therefore, preceded with the loud warning "Dead man!" or "Condemned man!"

After the passage, prisoners regrouped and talked about Chessman. Someone said he had guts.

"You wouldn't be for him if he'd raped a woman in your family!"

"They ain't proved he done nothing, fuckhead. The cops in L.A. needed a quick scapegoat and they grabbed Chessman because he was an ex-con. The papers played up the 'Red Light Bandit' so much the squares had to have somebody to dildo themselves with. The fuckin' guy was framed."

"Bullshit! The guy's a fucking rapo!"

"Whatever the fuck he is, you got to give him credit for the fight he's making. He's taking on the whole fucking state machinery and cheatin' Sergeant Mesner out of his fifty bucks."

Sergeant Mesner, a guard at the prison, was the official state executioner.

"You wouldn't say that if he'd raped your sister, you phony mother-fucker!"

Ron didn't volunteer an opinion. But he decided he was on Chessman's side. The man had nodded at him.

At ten-fifteen the yard bulls blew their whistles for lunch. Everyone walked over to place feet between the white dotted lines. Waiting between the dotted lines would become hated during the cold, damp and windy winter months. Waiting for the whistle for their line to march to the mess hall, Lenny listed for Ron which of their former acquaintances had become "rats," informers, those who were suspected or known to have "turned out," become by choice or coercion passive homosexual partners.

After eating, they went to the ball-field bleachers in the lower yard. Lenny continued his briefing on how to get around rules and restrictions and where the danger points were. As they talked, a group of prisoners came in formation around the track. Ron was familiar with some of them.

"You remember any of those guys?" Lenny asked.

"Yeah," Ron said. He didn't want to talk about them. He thought they had been through enough. They had been preyed upon in reform school, used as messenger boys, been constant objects of ridicule, beaten frequently, and some of them raped by black gangs in Preston. They were now fanatical weight lifters; they tattooed themselves heavily and stuck together in a tight clique. They swaggered as they walked. They preached white supremacy and formed the nucleus of the prison "Nazi Gang."

Lenny showed Ron how to sneak into the three o'clock "construction work" crew for an illegal shower.

The yard bulls blew their whistles for four o'clock count. As he stood in line a fistfight broke out. Ron stood watching it, not noticing that other prisoners had scattered. He heard rifle fire and looked up to see the gunman on the catwalk holding his smoking rifle. Ron ran for cover. Guards rushed in and separated the fighting men. One prisoner kept trying to get at his adversary. The guards wrestled him to the ground and wrapped a leather belt around his neck until the prisoner began to go limp. The other prisoners began booing and cursing the guards. Five riflemen on the gunwalk fired warning shots in the air. The prisoners fell silent.

After supper Ron picked up another copy of the *Monitor,* a rag and a can of lighter fluid. Inside their cage he and his partner rolled up their bedding, put it on the toilet, squirted lighter fluid on the bedsprings, touched a match to it and stepped back during the burst of flames. They shook out their bedding to dislodge escaping bedbugs, made their bunks, scrubbed the cage with lye soap and settled back to their evening coffee.

Ron read the *Monitor:*

"Batista Troops Unable to Dislodge Castro Rebels."

His cage partner went to sleep early, so Ron pulled the lightstring and laid his ear and earphone on the pillow to listen to Friday night jazz with Gil Evans, Duke Ellington, Charlie Parker, Miles Davis, Count Basie, Art Tatum, Bud Powell, and Thelonius Monk, music that touched him, letting him listen in the dark, to help erase the sights and sounds of the daytime. He had survived his second day.

At eleven the next day he and Lenny went for Saturday movies in the north-block mess hall. Near them a "jocker," the aggressive partner in a homosexual partnership, escorted his "old lady," a subservient "female" partner who had plucked eyebrows, was perfumed, wore tight trousers and was referred to by the jocker as Lilly.

Prisoners pressed tightly against each other on planks, leaning on long tables. The lights went out and a Tom and Jerry cartoon appeared to applause and whistles. Partway through the cartoon there was a scuffle and a loud cry. Two prisoners, half bent over, ran to separate parts of the mess-hall crowd. The lights came on. Bulls ran to the assault area. Men stood on the benches to see better. A guard ran to a telephone and a few minutes later a stretcher was rolled in and a prisoner was carried out, blood gushing from his neck and chest. Everyone sat down, the lights went out and the cartoon resumed in time for the sight of Jerry rolling a lighted stick of dynamite under Tom, leaving Tom a charred mess, and bringing cheers from the audience. As each prisoner left the mess hall he was inspected by bulls for blood spatters.

During the movie Ron had missed another fight, in the yard, between two domino players. One prisoner had beaten another to the ground with a pipe for failure to pay five packs of cigarettes lost in their game.

Ron read another month-old *Monitor* that night in his cage. He had survived his third day.

Sunday was the same as Saturday except for half an hour listening to the Salvation Army band in the yard.

On Monday an eight-by-ten photograph of the prisoner killed during the mess-hall movies was posted on the yard bulletin board, cotton swabs protruding from his wounds. The prison authorities believed that photographs of dead prisoners killed in fights or in guards' gunfire discouraged violence among prisoners. Glossy photographs of mutilated dead prisoners appeared regularly.

Tuesday was the same as Monday, and Wednesday like Tuesday except that a hundred men were given fifteen minutes under eight shower nozzles. Thursday was like Wednesday without a shower. He had survived his first week.

Three weeks later he walked into the office of the classification committee. On one side was a civilian caseworker and a psychologist. On the other two guards. In the center a lieutenant. The lieutenant spoke. "Valentine, you have a big mouth. You're not in Chino or Tracy now. You're in San Quentin. And if you mouth off to my guards they'll knock your teeth down your throat. Do you understand?"

Ron smiled, exposing his missing front teeth. The psychologist chuckled.

The lieutenant wanted to leave him unassigned. The psychologist insisted Ron be given some job. There was shouting and arguing. A red-faced lieutenant said, "Valentine, I've got thousands of men in this prison who come to me on bended knee asking for jobs I can't supply. So you should be thankful that I'm offering you a job. Not only am I offering you a job, but I'm offering you a choice of two good jobs. You can work in either the laundry or the cotton textile mill. Which one?"

Lenny had warned him about the textile mill.

"I'll take the laundry."

Ron had survived his first month.

The days passed with punctuations in the sameness. He inserted numberless sheets into the hot mangle. He learned to steer clear of psychotic prisoners and psychotic guards. He developed an immunity to the dreary yard gossip, aggressions, insults and homosexual banter. He navigated the yard to evade the marksmanship of overfed seagulls.

He was partly protected from harassment from other prisoners by his distinction as one of the 500 most dangerous criminals in the California penal system, the "Penal 500" being those sent to San Quentin and once there being among the 500 classified for close custody.

His cage partner was a highly skilled robber—though not so highly skilled that he was at liberty—and entertained Ron with stories of his adventures and triumphs. He also criticized Ron for committing petty crimes. He pointed out that he had stolen $20,000 in one supermarket robbery, received an indeterminate sentence of five years to life and, with parole, would probably do no more prison time than Ron.

Ron provided himself with prison luxuries—bought tobacco, instant coffee, toothpaste and store soap—with proceeds of the traditional prison laundry racket. Instead of wrinkled clothes, he produced "bono-roos," starched and pressed blue jeans, for those who paid with tobacco, coffee, toothpaste and soap. He added to his income by winning at dominoes.

In early 1960 he was hospitalized for an operation to strip the saphenous vein of his leg. The hospitalization cost him his laundry job, and after his discharge he waited on the captain's porch for his new cage and job assignment. In the yard his eye was drawn to a figure pouring something from a can over his body. The figure sat down, and burst into flame, rose, and ran through the courtyard like a flaming cross. Ron had an impulse to run down and stop him but checked himself. The unwritten law of prison is never interfere with a prisoner who decides to commit suicide and "give their time back to them." A guard rushed toward the flaming man but he was driven away by the sweep of the flaming arms. Another guard moved behind and struck the burning figure on the head. The figure collapsed and the guards smothered the fire. A stretcher carried the charred form away. The next morning the San Francisco paper said it was a young man serving ten years for possession of three marijuana cigarettes, recently returned to San Quentin from psychiatric care at Napa State Hospital. He had ignited himself in protest against denial of parole for the fifth consecutive year. He survived with burns over most of his body and loss of his eyesight.

Ron remained unassigned. In April he got another partial denture. In May he appeared before the parole board for the second time. His parole judge was the former chief of the Los Angeles Police Department vice squad, who decided that a milk pasteurizer's license would help him earn an honest living and he should ask the prison classification committee to transfer him to the prison ranch. He said it would also be a good idea to attend church and group counseling. The parole decision was "Denied One Calendar Year."

That night Ron told his cagemate that the parole judge's advice would be perfect. "I could go to church and talk to God and they'd say I was praying. The next day I'd go to group counseling and say God talked to me and they'd say I was schizophrenic."

He was deeply bitter at the denial of parole.

At the prison classification board Ron repeated the recommendation of the parole board that he work in the dairy and added that he would like to do it. The board chairman said angrily, "Custody operates this prison, not the parole board." It was noted that Ron had no disciplinary reports, so his custody was reduced to Medium-A; he was out of the top 500.

His new cage in medium security in east block was luxurious. The shelves were metal instead of wood, the lamp fluorescent. Best of all was the view from the large barred windows of the east-block wall: the Berkeley hills and San Francisco Bay Bridge. At night the lights of the city and of the jeweled bridge reminded him that there was a life outside.

The new cage partner was a pleasant gentile whose job was clerk for the Jewish chaplain.

"Hey, Val, what religion are you?"

Ron looked up, irritated. He had his ear on the single earphone imbedded on his pillow, listening to a close Giant–Dodger game.

"What?"

"What religion are you?"

"None, man. Why you asking?"

"I thought maybe you'd like me to put you down as Jewish. That is, if you don't have no real religion."

Ron put his ear to the pillow for a moment, and asked, "Why would I want to do that?"

"Well, Jewish prisoners have two banquets a year, one coming up in September, and you can also get a few bucks from the Jewish Relief Agency if you don't have any loose money on the books."

"Hell, that's okay, but I don't know anything about Judaism. What if I get pinned down? And I don't want to go to services."

"You won't have to go to services."

"Okay, okay, put me down." And Ron turned back to the earphone. Willie Mays hit a three-run homer. Cheers and whistles came from Giants fans in the cellblock and Ron put away the earphone in disgust and went to sleep, for the first time as a Jew.

The days, the weeks, the months, the years went by in depressing vagueness. They blended into each other because the regimen remained unchanged, the concrete and steel and asphalt a seamless web, each contact a maddening repetition of a thousand others.

The violence continued with dreaded normality. A crowded yard, a scuffle, silence, turned heads, searching eyes, the scream of whistles, gunfire from the catwalks, a mass scramble for safety, a dying figure in denim dripping blood and spittle on the pavement, the stretcher, the thought "It wasn't me," a return to the interrupted conversation.

He saw an inmate try to commit suicide by jumping off a fifth-floor tier, hit the balustrade below and land on the concrete floor with blood flowing from his ears.

There was hardly a time when a gunman's rifle was not in view, even as Ron lay in his berth inside his cell.

Prisoners in the yard bet cartons of cigarettes on anything: a ballgame, dominoes, chess, handball, an election, who could throw a breakfast orange farthest, which of two seagulls on the ground would take off first, would a prisoner scheduled for execution get a last-minute reprieve.

Friday was the usual day for executions. Caryl Chessman had been confined to death row for twelve years. He had written books, won eight stays of execution and become a celebrity. But he was also an embarrassment to the criminal justice system. He was scheduled once more for execution, not on a Friday but on the first Monday in May.

The smart money in the yard said Chessman had run out of time and money and would be executed. At ten A.M. the death-watch sergeant took his position in front of the locked doors of the north block. As execution hour approached, the chatter in the yard subsided. At ten-thirty the sergeant opened the doors for resumption of normal business. The word was passed through the yards. Cigarettes changed hands. Chessman was dead.

Fellow prisoners got on Ron's nerves with their racism, their violence, their obscenities and their endlessly repeated tales.

The worst prison pressure weighed on him—the necessity to act and talk insincerely to conform with required behavior.

He plunged deeper into the world of books. San Quentin, surprisingly, had a good library. He read all of Hemingway, all of Dos Passos, all of Maugham. It opened new ideas and roles in life for the first time, but prison frustrated his desire to apply new insights to the real world.

He began looking for philosophies of inner survival. He listened regularly to a San Francisco disc jockey whose motto was "Out of the mud grows the lotus." Ron wrote it on a piece of paper and taped it to his cell wall.

Thoughts of his child came often. He had no word from her. Had no way of writing to her. He felt irresponsible and so depressed that he worked to suppress thoughts of her.

On impulse, Ron wrote to his mother. The next week she visited. The next month she brought her husband and son with her. They all came once a month thereafter. It was a new sensation. It broke the monotony and introduced a believable ingredient of a different world, a world without numbing sameness, without brutality, a world with affection.

In May Ron received a letter from Brenda. He sat on his bunk staring at the envelope. Why was she writing after so long a silence? He pulled the staple that reclosed the letter after the censor had read it.

> Hi . . . how are you . . . I'm doing okay . . . working as a secretary . . . saw Barbara and Doug last week . . . they send their best . . . well, considering your circumstances. I hope it's not going too badly for you . . . hope you'll answer . . . Love, Brenda.

No mention of her sudden and complete disappearance in 1958. No mention of the baby. Why did she write? What did she want? Why didn't she mention the baby?

He tore the letter into tiny pieces and flushed it down the toilet.

The next week he made his annual visit to the parole board. His judge this time was a former chief of police. "Young man, do you have difficulty understanding? The last time you were here the parole judge told you in no uncertain terms to get a pasteurizer's license, didn't he? Why haven't you made any progress in that area?"

Ron told him he had asked for it but the prison classification committee had refused.

"Do you want to stay here until 1967?"

"No, sir."

"Then you had better get yourself a job!" He flipped through the pages of Ron's file. "Another thing. I want to see some group counseling in this file. Do you understand that?"

The next day he received a notice: "Denied One Calendar Year."

The chief of classification called him in. "Valentine, we've an opening in the clothing factory."

"The clothing factory? I've heard that's a good place to work. Yes, I think I'd like that," he said insincerely.

"Good. And what about your group therapy?"

"I've been giving a lot of thought to my narcotic problem lately and I'm sure that group therapy will help me come to grips with my problem."

He hated himself.

"Well, your attitude has certainly changed for the better. Another year without disciplinary reports. That's good. I think you're ready for custody reduction. Continue going in the direction you're headed—it's the way to the front gate and a successful readjustment to society."

His new position at the clothing factory put him in command of a senile Singer sewing machine that regularly broke thread, jammed bobbins, slipped its belt, went out of timing—eight hours a day for three cents an hour minus 10 per cent toward the forty dollars he would get on parole day.

When the machine was being repaired he would go to sleep in the bottom of an empty clothing hamper. His boss asked him not to sleep at the machine because "it looked bad to visitors."

He received another letter from Brenda. Again he tore it up and flushed it down the toilet.

Two weeks later he received a memorandum from the warden:

> This afternoon I received a long-distance telephone call from your wife. Her letters to you are going unanswered and she is worried that you may

have fallen ill. I assured her that you were in excellent health. I'd suggest that you answer her letters.

Ron flushed the memorandum down the toilet.

Once a week he dragged himself to "group therapy." He would take a chair in the symbolic circle connoting intimacy and friendship. Most of the men regarded it as a humiliation endured in order to get parole. Ron gazed out the windows, yawned, smoked and wished the afternoon away. Prisoners learned phrases from Norman Vincent Peale, Dale Carnegie and Joyce Brothers, and used them to declare new insights into their own personalities, greatly pleasing the psychologist or staff member conducting the group. When the therapist probed deeper into what these meant in terms of the man's life, he was met with vagueness. Not even those playing the game wanted to risk saying something about their real life that might be used to extend their imprisonment or become a part of their personal record forever.

One day in August he was called for a visit. It was Brenda. He didn't want to see her. She didn't have the baby with her, which made him more angry. When he found the visit intolerable he said he was coming down with the flu and had to leave.

After less than six months the clothing factory cut back on production and he lost his job. He had more time for chess and a course in remedial math.

At his May parole hearing one of the judges, the son-in-law of a high state official, asked Ron, "You aren't planning on returning to East Los Angeles? With that trash down there?"

"The people down there aren't trash. They're poor but they aren't trash."

The chairman took the initiative from the son-in-law. "I've been reading a letter from your mother, Ronald, and she writes that she and her husband would like you to stay in their home until you get back on your feet. What are your feelings?"

"I'm not against it."

The next morning a clerk handed Ron a folded paper. What if he didn't make parole again? What if he had been fooled by the congenial manner of the chairman? He pulled the staple loose. "Release upon approved parole plan."

He felt a wild urge to dance and sing and call out. Then he had a second thought: What will I do when I get out?

He needed a job to get out. Zoia called his parole officer, a former

San Quentin guard, who said he knew some employers. Zoia's husband had friends in the maritime union. Ron wrote to a number of Bay Area firms himself. And waited.

The returns started to come in. The parole officer said things were slow and jobs a little tight right now. The friends in the maritime union said with his offense the Coast Guard would never grant a clearance. None of the firms he wrote to answered.

In early August he was checked out on parole. The clothing-room guard looked at him and at the racks of civilian clothing. "You're a tall one. What size jacket?"

"Forty, extra long."

"We got a forty-four regular."

It was a brilliant raspberry in color and more than wide enough.

At the gate a genial guard stuck out his hand to each prisoner and said, "Good luck."

After four and a half years of a dead world, the outside gave him a sharp sensory awareness, as though he were suddenly in the middle of brilliant colors and incredible sounds and exhilarating air. He felt wonderfully alive.

"That'll be seventy-five cents each, boys."

It was the tiny old woman who drove the only available transportation from the prison to San Raphael. Ron flipped the quarter change into the air and caught it.

The woman seemed to be driving at breakneck speed. Ron thought of the irony of being killed by a little old lady after surviving San Quentin. He looked anxiously over her shoulder at the speedometer. They were going only forty-five miles an hour. He hadn't been moving beyond a walk for over four years.

The man seated next to him said, "Hey, you wanna get a drink when we get into town? Maybe we could pick up a couple chicks in the bar?"

"No, no thanks. Why don't you ask one of the other guys?"

Then it dawned on him. He was now twenty-three years old, for the first time in his life old enough to buy a legal drink at a bar. He quickly forgot about it.

Entering the town, he took in everything that was new: stores, streetlights, parking meters, cars. At the Greyhound bus station he bought a package of chewing gum, something he had longed for. In prison chewing gum is forbidden. It can be pushed into locks.

Waiting for the bus to San Francisco, he pulled the parole agreement out of the pocket of his raspberry coat. He discovered that he had agreed not to enter into any contracts, including marriage, without his parole agent's permission in writing. Nor leave the country or state, or drive a motor vehicle.

He also discovered that he couldn't chew gum with his partial denture. He went to the men's room to free his teeth. When he saw himself in the mirror he gasped. The red tie and raspberry jacket were incandescent. He took off the red tie and carefully tied it in a four-in-hand knot around the Boraxo dispenser.

From the Greyhound bus to San Francisco he looked across the water at the disappearing pinkish brown cluster where four years of his life remained. Already it seemed unreal. He turned away. A pretty young woman sitting across the aisle smiled at him. He smiled back and she looked away. Her delicate features held his eyes. For years he had not seen skin and face shaped like that. There was an urge to reach out and stroke her cheek. He remembered the delights of women. Desire stirred powerfully. He fantasized wild sex with the girl and then looked back out the window. What if the bus crashed and he died before he had another woman?

Inside the bus station he had coffee and danish pastry at the lunch counter. He looked blank when the waitress asked him if he wanted cream for his coffee. He had always thought his first outside food would be a fabulous seven-course meal and now the danish pastry was almost too much. At the cashier's booth he handled his money awkwardly, counting change like a foreigner. He left the raspberry jacket on a coatrack in the bus station.

He started to cross the street and pulled back in panic. Cars seemed to be speeding. He couldn't judge their speed or his. In the big yard he had learned never to run for fear of being shot and now he no longer knew how to dodge cars. He waited for a crowd to cross and inserted himself in their midst.

His mother was surprised and delighted to see him so soon. His half-brother was overjoyed and begged to be taken to see the Giants play in Candlestick Park. Zoia's husband was cordial though Ron had the old feeling of being an intruder. That night he lay in bed and wished he had visited a prostitute.

In the morning he borrowed a sports coat from his brother and a tie from Zoia's husband. He registered at the state employment office in Berkeley and re-established his membership in the teamsters' hall in Oakland. Then he went to San Francisco's red light district and contracted for the services of a prostitute without the written consent of his parole officer.

The next day he got a one-day job washing windows in the Tudor mansion of a sugar heiress at $1.25 an hour, enough to take his brother to the ballgame the next day.

The following week he got a job at a Berkeley creamery by concealing his status as an ex-convict on parole. A month later, after the parole officer told the creamery, Ron was fired. He found a new job at a smaller creamery. He was the sole employee on the graveyard shift, opened the plant at eleven P.M., filled the orders for the morning drivers, and then at seven-thirty A.M., a half hour before the morning shift arrived, locked up.

Brenda called in December to say that she'd remarried. After extending sincere congratulations, he asked about the possibility of a visitation schedule with the child. Brenda said that it was out of the question. Ron hung up.

Life settled into a predictable pattern of work, bills, Sunday dinner with the family, and his first love: jazz. Evenings were spent at the local jazz clubs absorbing the sounds and alcohol.

In December the parole officer asked if Ron had informed his new employer that he was a convict on parole. Ron said he had not, seeing what had happened the last time. The parole officer took the initiative to tell the company. Ron was fired again. Without his parole officer's permission he went back to Los Angeles.

In Los Angeles an old friend from juvenile prison gave him his first fix of heroin in almost five years. They discussed how Ron could earn some money. The friend was supplying dealers with heroin. One dealer had taken three ounces worth $600 and was evading payment. The friend suggested that they collect the debt and divide the $600 equally. That night he was carrying two lengths of lead pipe when a Los Angeles Police Department cruiser pulled up and a voice told them to freeze.

Ron pleaded not guilty to a charge of violating the dangerous weapons act. He was sentenced to 210 days in the county jail. More important, he was returned to prison for violating parole.

He was entitled to an appearance before the parole board within a month of his new imprisonment. The day afterward he received their notice: "Denied One Calendar Year." He was assigned to Soledad rather than San Quentin.

In Soledad his bitterness at return to prison deepened. A year later he made his annual visit to the parole board. The parole judge wanted details of the 1955 statutory rape charge. Ron asked why he was going back so far and then explained that the charge was found to be untrue. The judge said, "Where there's smoke, there's fire, Valentine." The next day he received the hearing results: "Denied One Calendar Year."

In December he fought with a sergeant and was sent to O wing, where George Jackson was to spend so much time. Phillips was given a judo chop and put in a strip cage. After twenty-nine days in the punishment cage he was sent back to San Quentin.

In July 1964 he made his appearance before the parole board and was told, again, to get a milk pasteurizer's license. The next day he was handed the decision: "Denied One Calendar Year."

In October he was sent to Chino. He received a letter from Brenda. She was divorcing her second husband and wanted to visit and bring the child. They both visited. Ron fell in love with his nine-year-old daughter. They visited regularly and the parents talked about reconciliation.

The days became more relaxed. He was assigned to the officers' dining room, where the fringe benefits included good meals, short hours and luxurious stealing of officers' meats—of filet mignon, porterhouse steaks, lamb chops and shrimp. No liver.

When the jazz disc jockey on the institution's closed circuit radio was paroled, Ron took over. Every Saturday and Sunday evening he played his own favorites for his fellow prisoners—the compositions of Gil Evans, Quincy Jones, Oliver Nelson, Miles Davis, John Lewis and Duke Ellington. The radio program always included his taste for Ellington, Buddy Rich, Count Basie, Woody Herman, Stan Kenton, John Coltrane, Gerry Mulligan, Bob Brookmeyer, Art Tatum, Oscar Peterson, George Shearing, Charlie Parker, Dizzy Gillespie, Fats Navarro, Django Reinhardt, Claude Thornhill, Anita O'Day, Jimmy Rushing and his all-time favorite vocalist, Billie Holiday. The population told him his commentary was a smash hit.

Ron decided to complete his high school diploma requirements and was amazed at how much he enjoyed the English and mathematics that he had dreaded in school. He started to take care of himself physically, wanting to put weight on his string-bean frame. He did weight-lifting and used his position in the officers' dining room to drink half a gallon of melted ice cream every day. He soon increased his weight from 170 to 200 pounds.

One weekend Brenda failed to appear for her usual visit with the child. He wrote to ask what had happened. He didn't hear from her. He would not hear from her again for two and a half years.

When he made his next appearance before the parole board he asked to be discharged completely. The next day his notice said, "Denied One Calendar Year."

In February he was caught stealing sandwiches from the officers' dining room for the second time. He was fired and reassigned to the fields, which meant he had to give up his schooling. He refused the assignment and was sent back to San Quentin.

Back in San Quentin the classification committee left him "unassigned." He took up a career of his own. He was collection agent for the prison bookie, a prisoner who also ran the internal narcotics traffic. His pay for this work was seven cartons of cigarettes a week plus a paper of heroin worth ten dollars each Sunday.

Sundays were a euphoric haze, a desperate escape from the barbarities he lived with. Life in a maximum-security penitentiary was a daily assault on the sensibilities, a corrosion of sanity. Every day he would see the effects of prison's twisting of the human personality. Homosexual lovers embraced on stairways, in corners, copulating in the gym, school, workshop and chapels. He saw prisoners covered with their own feces and calling themselves "human turds." One drank his own urine from a hot sauce bottle. Another sat on the asphalt yard running his fingers over the spittle and phlegm of a recent passerby.

Porno peddlers collected cigarettes for photographs stolen from the medical department journals, photographs of breast and vaginal cancers.

A prisoner with a skin cancer that had eaten away his nose refused to wear his face mask in the dining room.

Even in the relative privacy of his cage, Phillips could not escape the madness. In the early evening the homosexual tier tender who had the privilege of selling black-market goods to locked-up fellow prisoners would call out, "Candy, coffee, sandwiches, pussy." For a sum slightly higher than the price of candy, the tier tender would drop his pants and place his buttocks close to the bars for quick anal intercourse and for a higher price oral copulation between the bars.

In November Ron was arrested with a pocketful of betting slips. He was assigned to sort underwear in the old dungeon.

A few months later there was a race riot, one that conveniently caused cancellation of an economy move that would have reduced the budget of the California Department of Corrections. Shortly after Governor Reagan announced a 10 per cent cut in the prison budget, with large reductions in San Quentin, a black prisoner was arrested in the dining room for getting a cupful of milk when he did not have a "milk card" signed by the prison doctor. He was taken to the hole and black prisoners gathered in the yard to protest.

Ron asked another white prisoner leaning on the mess-hall wall what was happening.

"Every goddamn nigger is on the warpath. They locked up one of the niggers and the rest of them think they're gonna get him out by protesting."

Ron walked across the west side of the yard toward the gate to his work assignment. A lieutenant was talking to a group of "Nazi" prisoners.

"I never thought I'd see the day when the niggers would run San Quentin," the lieutenant said. "You ought to go over there and crack a few nigger heads and put them back in their place. My guards ain't color-blind and they'll know who to hit when things get hot."

The racist gang spread among other whites and the Chicanos saying, "The niggers are going to attack us . . . they're going to take over this joint . . . get yourself a weapon . . ."

Mops, broom handles, mop wringers and knives were handed down from the mess-hall windows.

The outnumbered blacks seeing this began breaking up wooden benches that lined the wall to make clubs.

Two guards on the north-block gunwalk were setting up a portable movie camera. As Ron went through the gate to work he saw riot guards racing along the catwalk carrying Thompson submachine guns.

The report to the state house said that a full-scale race riot had broken out and worse bloodshed was averted only by dedication of the staff. The report also said that more trouble would occur if the guard work force were reduced. The governor instantly restored the 10 per cent cut in the prison budget.

A number of prisoners had been wounded by gunfire and one died of a heart attack. All were white.

It would make Ron suspicious thereafter of the source of prison strikes and riots.

A month before the completion of his sentence the parole board called him to a hearing and asked what his plans were. He told them it was none of their business. The next day he received his final notice from the California Board of Parole: "Denied—No Further Parole Consideration."

On the morning of August 5, 1967, ten years and four months after the night in Marian the dope peddler's house, he accepted a State of California going-away gift of forty dollars and a letter from Warden Louis Nelson.

Dear Mr. Valentine:
  Congratulations on the completion of your term. . . .

The California Department of Corrections, myself and my staff, would like to take this opportunity to wish you a successful readjustment to society.

Good luck . . .

He threw the letter into a trash can and headed for the front gate.

Within two hours he was injecting heroin. A friend in San Quentin was a pimp on the outside and had arranged a coming-out party for Ron. A statuesque girl, six feet two, was eager to have sex with a man who had been deprived of women for five and a half years. She was wildly stimulating to Ron, especially with her miniskirt, an invention he had not seen before. He went upstairs with her. But something else was even more immediately attractive, and before turning his attention to her he fixed with heroin. Within minutes he was too sleepy to have sexual intercourse. The next day he turned his full attention to the tall woman.

He headed, as always, toward East Los Angeles. Hulda hadn't seen him in ten years. When he walked in she didn't know who he was. When her husband said, "Duke!" she stared in disbelief and then rushed to him with a hug and kiss. They asked him to stay with them until he got a job and a place of his own.

Two weeks later he had a job at Crown Zellerbach Corporation loading railway cars at $2.89 an hour. Hulda lent him $500 for a used car. Two months later he traded it in for an expensive Austin-Healey 3000 sports car. He wanted some style and dash after the years of burial in prison. The bank officer who approved the loan was curious how a twenty-nine-year-old man had gone so long without establishing credit.

"Do you belong to a religious sect?" he asked. "Amish?"

He felt like a member of a strange sect, as though every stranger could tell by looking at him that he was a prisoner. Or an ex-prisoner. One day he ran into the old friend of the lead-pipe incident. It felt good to find someone who knew about him and accepted him and with whom he could communicate openly and frankly. He got another fix of heroin. As the heroin fixes became more frequent his paycheck became too small and he began stealing things from Hulda's house. Finally he joined two friends in robbing pharmacies of money and drugs. He didn't tell them he had never committed a robbery before. But they became weekly rituals successful enough to let Ron support his habit, make the payments on his Austin-Healey, quit his job and move in with a cocktail waitress from Texas.

In February his two partners in pharmacy robberies were arrested while leaving a savings and loan company. He became a lone wolf.

He used guns regularly, though he had a curious attitude toward them. He adopted them coldly, recognizing that if he carried one in a holdup he might use it. At the same time they revolted him. Robbing did not bother him as much as using a weapon. He was not sure why. It was no introspection about his robbery victims. He never thought of them as terrified human beings facing imminent death from the muzzle of his pistols. His disgust was with himself. It was part of a familiar cycle of fear of withdrawal symptoms followed by the euphoria that obscured reality, followed by guilt at his weakness, followed by fear of withdrawal, each cycle deepening both the self-contempt and the hunger for escape through chemical in the blood. He never robbed or took up a gun until he was on the verge of sickness from withdrawal.

He began, as did Irwin, with a prejudice against robbing women. Perhaps it came from Bob Valentine telling him twenty-five years before never to hit a woman. He rationalized it at the time as an analysis of the difference between men and women under stress. Men, he said, were more likely to have learned to obey authority through their military experience, and nothing exceeds the authority of a pistol aimed at the heart. Women, he insisted, were less predictable, either freezing or resisting. In the end, like Irwin, it became a distinction too subtle to worry about, and he robbed women bank tellers as often as he did men.

The precise places and times that he was said to have robbed banks are uncertain. They are spotted all over Los Angeles—Glendale, Santa Monica, Monterey Park. I was in California at the time, long before I knew Phillips. He robbed my bank.

Typical was the Garfield Bank in Monterey Park. On a Friday a friend from San Quentin "lent" him two pistols. Presumably detectable crimes had been committed with them and the friend wanted to get rid of them. Ron was sick from withdrawal. He sold the .25-caliber pistol at once and bought heroin with the proceeds. This carried him through the weekend. On Monday he began to feel withdrawal again. He had eighteen cents in his pocket and a quarter of a tank of gasoline in his Austin-Healey. He delayed through two o'clock, when he knew he was getting sick. And he knew the banks would not stay open much longer. Instinct led him to Monterey Park, a lower-middle-class community of civil servants who kept neat little lawns in front of neat little cottages. He walked down the street to get up his nerve. He walked into a Bank of America, lost his nerve and walked out. He looked down the street.

There was a modernistic clock with triangles for hands and no numbers but the time on it was clearly two-forty. Beyond the clock he saw a sign, "Police Station," with an arrow pointing down a side street. He looked at the clock again and realized that it belonged to a large brown sign that read "Garfield Bank." He ran into a supermarket, Fazio's Shopping Bag, grabbed a folded brown bag from a checkout counter and ran out to his car. He drove the car past a gas station to the parking lot driveway for the bank customers, parked the car at the exit of the lot where no one could get in front of him. He left the keys in the ignition, so that there would be no fumbling on the getaway, took the .38 pistol from his coat pocket and put it under his belt, put the paper bag in his coat pocket and walked toward the back door of the bank.

He had never been in the bank before. He used his forearm to pull the bronze door handles open. No fingerprints. The glass door bore the standard decal: "FBI investigates any robbery, burglary or larceny committed in this institution." Inside he turned momentarily to the left, toward a notary's desk, then to the right toward a teller. The bank was crowded as closing time arrived. As he approached the counter an officer of the bank moved away the "Next Teller" plaque from an empty window and said to him, "Can I help you?"

"Yes."

"Check to cash?"

"Yes."

"Okay."

He pulled the gun out of his belt with one hand and put the paper bag on the counter with the other. "Give me all your money. Quick."

The man stood motionless.

"I'm not fooling. If you want to see your wife and children tonight, put all that money in the bag fast and don't say anything."

The man started scooping the money into the bag.

To his right Ron noticed a woman at a desk in a glass booth staring at him, unable to move. He turned away to look at the teller. "Put that pile of hundreds in, too."

He grabbed the bag, put the gun back in his belt and forced himself to walk calmly out the back door. He used his forearm to push the door open. He could see his car parked at the end of the driveway, next to the street. He kept repeating to himself, Don't run. Don't run, you son of a bitch. Walk. Don't run.

He ran the last twenty feet. He turned the key, jammed the shift into second, screeched out of the lot, turned right and came to a red traffic light within easy sight of the bank. He knew that a bank robber is as likely to get caught running a red light as holding up the bank. So he waited. But it was excruciating. The light turned green and he drove quickly to the San Bernardino Freeway. He was sure that helicopters and police cars were waiting for him. But soon he felt the anonymity of the freeway and the soothing wind flowing through his hair.

At his apartment he ignored the girl from Texas and went into the bedroom. She had learned not to ask questions. The haul was $6800. Plenty for heroin and lots left over. He bought his fix. He lent the girl the Austin-Healey and bought himself a new Chevrolet for $3000 cash.

He was more deeply addicted than ever before. In early June 1968 he found himself unable to buy enough heroin. His dosages were getting dangerous. He needed to lower his threshold, and he admitted himself to the Rosemead Lodge, where addicts often paid to have themselves detoxified as painlessly as possible, at fifty dollars a day. He did not know it but police already knew that they wanted him. Tellers had identified him from police photographs and bank camera shots. He had no way of knowing how they discovered him, but on Friday, June 7, six men in civilian clothes came to his bedside.

"Ronald Valentine?"

He nodded. He knew already.

"Los Angeles Police Department."

When Ron left her house, Hulda gave up. She was determined never to see him again. A year after he was convicted as a bank robber, she wrote a poem:

TO A SON

Who came back so desperately
    in need of help
I hated to hurt again as the
    many wounds were now scarred from the past.
Again I helped and with my hope
    he tried.
Again we both lost.

On June 26, 1968, in Los Angeles, Ronald Phillips, the name he would use from then on, was indicted for robbing a bank and robbing with use of a dangerous weapon. The indictment said he robbed six banks. He pleaded not guilty. Like William Ryan Irwin's indictment, a few months earlier, Phillips' indictment was signed by the U.S. Attorney, William Matthew Byrne, Jr. Like Irwin, Phillips was represented at his bail hearing by appointed counsel, Veneto S. Tassopulos. The bank-robbing paths of Phillips and Irwin had crossed. They had even looked into the same banks. They were in the Los Angeles County Jail at the same time. But they were not to know each other for a while yet.

One month later Phillips changed his plea to guilty.

A month after that, on August 27, 1968, he was brought into federal district court for sentencing before Judge Harry Pregerson.

Phillips' appointed lawyer, Robert P. Mandler, made the usual plea for leniency: "I note that this defendant is thirty years old and his career, as such, began at the tender age of approximately fourteen or fifteen, when he began to experiment with narcotics. . . . Outside of the instant series of offenses, where possibly the habit became too much, for these fifteen years he had managed to support this thirty-to-fifty-dollar-a-day habit without getting involved in violence. . . . The picture is . . . rather typical, of the broken home, born out of wedlock, a broken home where the stepmother admits that she had to work outside the home and the defendant was left to whoever—let's see—quoting the probation report, 'Left to the care of whoever was around . . . he fell into the hands, at the age of twelve or thirteen, of some other undesirable elements . . .' "

The prosecuting attorney, Howard B. Frank, in response said that society was faced with too many bank robberies. "As I understand it, over 375 such robberies were committed in Los Angeles alone last year—"

Judge Pregerson interrupted: "That has nothing to do with my sentencing this man."

Judge Pregerson asked Phillips if he wanted to say anything before sentencing. Phillips declined.

"There being no sufficient cause why judgment should not now be pronounced, it is adjudged that the defendant is guilty as charged in count two of the indictment and he stands convicted. It is adjudged that the defendant is hereby committed to the custody of the Attorney General of the United States or his authorized representative for imprisonment for a period of fifteen years. It is further adjudged that the defendant shall become eligible for parole under Title Eighteen, United States Code, Section 4208 (a) (2) at such time as the Board of Parole may determine.

"This means that after a period of about five years if the Board of Parole feels that the defendant is eligible, he can be paroled."

Mr. Mandler stood up. "Your Honor, I think it is possible for the court to include in its order that he be given treatment for narcotics addiction at whatever facility he ends up at."

"That will be included in the order," the judge said.

In his formal commitment, "United States of America vs. Ronald Tracy Phillips," the judge wrote:

> The COURT RECOMMENDS that the defendant be placed in an institution where he may receive treatment for his narcotic addiction. Counts 1, 3, 4, 5, and 6 dismissed and defendant exonerated.

The Garfield robbery was one of the dismissed cases. Phillips had waived a trial and pleaded guilty to one of the robberies that was done without a weapon.

Phillips didn't know it on that day in August 1968, but neither the (a) (2) provision nor the conventional parole after five years of his fifteen-year sentence would do him much good. The prison system would have other reasons, unconnected with the safety of society or the stability of Ronald Phillips, to keep him in its grasp.

18

PRISONER NO. 33582–118

If a clerk in the Pittsburgh Home Savings and Loan Association had not decided to use pink cards to record mortgages, Ronald Tucker might not be in Lewisburg Federal Penitentiary.

The morning of May 31, 1968, was an irritating one for William Ray Bonnett, Jr., assistant secretary of the loan association. He was a mild-looking man with a 1950s haircut and brown-rimmed eyeglasses with a chain tying the ends together. He had not slept well the night before. As the morning wore on he was interrupted by petty supply problems. Bonnett was looking forward to lunchtime escape from his tiny office on the second floor to improve his mood when the phone rang.

It was a clerk in the mortgage department. "Ray, where are the pink index cards?"

"Pink index cards? I don't know where the pink index cards are! What in God's name do you need pink index cards for?"

"I need them for my work."

"We've got index cards all over the place. Why don't you just look for them?"

"I can't find any pink ones."

"Why do they have to be pink?"

"I'm putting all our mortgages outside Allegheny County on pink cards so I can spot them better right away. Ray, don't get sore but I've looked everywhere and all we have are white cards."

"All right, all right. I'll get some at lunchtime." Bonnett cursed to himself, There goes half my lunchtime.

He cut short his lunch period to stop at an office supply store. When he stepped into the store he cursed again. Customers were crowded against the counter. He stood in line impatiently. He was late by the time he had the packet of pink cards and he tried to walk rapidly down Wood Street, but even that was aggravating. The sidewalks, always crowded at lunchtime, seemed more solidly packed than ever. The closer he got to the bank the more dense the crowd. When he stepped into the street to walk, even that was full of people. He looked down the street and saw fire engines a block from the bank. The crowd was watching the excitement of a false alarm.

By the time Bonnett finally pushed through the doors of the bank he was perspiring and bad-tempered. The tellers' counters were triangular, the point toward the front doors on Wood Street, and the instant he unlatched the gate inside of the triangle he knew the tellers were not acting normally. He said to himself, Christ, what now! Everything's gone wrong today.

He looked around. Two of the women tellers were stuffing money into a paper bag. The third woman, standing as though paralyzed, looked at him wordlessly, her eyes wide with terror. She moved her eyeballs toward a customer at the counter.

Bonnett followed the teller's eyes. A young black man, with bulging eyes, wearing a trench coat and a beige fisherman's brim hat, his right hand in his pocket, was standing at the window. It was a holdup.

There are very precise FBI directions for behavior during a holdup and Bonnett knew them well. Each teller's money drawer contained five "bait" bills, their serial numbers recorded in the office, held by a metal spring clip at the back of the drawer, those bills never to be used in normal transactions. Only during a holdup would the teller pull out the bait bills, along with others, placing money with known serial numbers in the robber's loot. The bait money pulled out of its clip actuates a silent police signal and starts cameras directed at the scene.

Bonnett pretended not to notice the holdup and busied himself with papers. The tellers seemed to be following the FBI directions. Do as you are told by the robber. Don't be a hero. Always assume there is a gun even if one isn't showing. Don't try to hold back money. Don't challenge the robber. Don't do anything to make him nervous. Observe him carefully but unobtrusively, noting face shape, body shape, height and weight, any distinctive features like special haircut or scars. When you hand over the money look for tattoos and rings on the fingers. As the robber leaves watch the six-foot marker on the door frame to judge his height. If you can see outside, watch which way he goes, whether he gets into a car, what kind of car it is, and, if possible without running out or attracting attention, try to record the license plate. Then, without exchanging impressions with anyone else in the bank, take out the robber-description form kept in the files and instantly put down your personal recollection of the description of the robber and what happened.

But do not chase the robber!

Bonnett watched the robber leave the bank. The assistant secretary still had the pink cards in his hands. He looked down at the cards. Suddenly he was filled with anger and disgust. He threw the pink cards on the counter and ran after the robber.

The robber had turned left on Wood Street and was thirty feet ahead of Bonnett. The street was still packed because of the fire engines down the block.

Bonnett yelled, "Stop him! Bank robber! Stop that man in the brown hat!"

A few people on the street reacted in time to grab at the robber's clothing, slowing him down. The robber turned left onto Forbes Street, uphill, people still grabbing at him. He dashed off the curb and headed for the opposite sidewalk.

By now Bonnett was two feet behind him. He made a flying tackle. The bag of money flew out of the robber's hands and scattered onto the street. The men wrestled on the pavement. The robber twisted, trying to shed his coat, which Bonnett had in his hands. Bonnett could feel a gun inside the coat pocket. The robber wiggled free of his coat and ran uphill to the next corner, Smithfield.

For some reason the robber hesitated on the corner despite people yelling and running after him. He turned left onto Smithfield, but his hesitation was long enough to let Bonnett and a young man jump on him. Bonnett put a hammerlock on the robber. He and the young man, the robber between them, marched down Forbes Street toward the bank.

For the first time Bonnett looked at the robber at close range. He was only an adolescent. There was no more fight in him; his nose was bloody from the wrestling on the street. As they walked Bonnett could see money scattered over the street, gutters and sidewalks. An old man in a ragged coat and a growth of beard, the robber's hat in his hand, was picking up money and putting it in the hat and going to pedestrians, who were also picking up tens and twenties, which they also put into the hat.

At the corner of Forbes and Wood a motorcycle policeman, first on the scene, took over the teen-age robber.

Bonnett and the bank vice president went to Forbes Street to see about the money. The ragged old man seemed to have it all in the hat. Bonnett thanked him and said he would take the money.

The old man looked up indignantly. "I'm not giving this to no one but an officer of the bank."

"I'm an officer of the bank."

"You don't look like one to me, young fellow."

Bonnett went to the vice president and urged him to approach the old man. The vice president presented his card, the old man studied it carefully, studied the vice president carefully, and handed over the hatful of money.

A policeman asked Bonnett to come to the police station. He and the robber were in the back of one squad car, the two women tellers in another. Inside the cruiser there was no conversation. The young man's nose had stopped bleeding. His hands were cuffed and he sat silently looking out the car window.

At the station, FBI agents were waiting for them. By three o'clock there was a lineup with several men on the stage. Bonnett and the two tellers separately picked the same man as the robber. The young man was charged and held.

When the assistant secretary returned to the bank the vice president told Bonnett that he was grateful but he thought Bonnett was a damn fool for disobeying instructions and running after the robber. And he should call his wife at once; she had heard the news on the radio. His wife was pregnant with their sixth child.

Bonnett asked what happened to the money. They had counted it out. The robber had taken $3249, mostly in tens and twenties. It had been scattered all over Forbes Street. Every dollar had been returned. Some people had come to the bank to tell them they had helped pick up the money, and they were thanked. The young man who helped Bonnett hold the robber asked to have his sports coat replaced because of a tear and spots of blood from the robber's nosebleed. But they never saw the old man again.

The holdup had aftereffects for people at the bank. The first teller approached by the robber had been so thoroughly drilled not to use her bait money in the clip at the back of her money drawer that she left it untouched during the holdup. Later she was reminded that hold-ups were the special exceptions. The other teller did remove the bait money. Both women did not sleep well for weeks, and a year later were still having occasional nightmares about men with guns. Five years later any loud noise made the tellers shake.

Five years later Bonnett's hair still gets prickly every time he enters the main banking room. The night of the holdup he was greeted at home with relief and warmth, then taken to the kitchen by his wife, who told him, "Do you realize that we have a family? That chasing robbers is not a part of your job?"

There were, of course, aftermaths for the robber, Ronald Tucker. After he was booked, fingerprinted, photographed and identified in the lineup, he was taken to Pittsburgh Magistrate Court and arraigned on a state charge of armed robbery and receiving stolen goods.

That afternoon when he was trying to escape from the bank he had turned a corner and run up Forbes Street. He had hesitated at the next corner. If he had kept going up Forbes Street, in two blocks he would have run into the Allegheny County Jail, a grim granite fortress built in 1884, with medieval arched gates and windows opaque with grime and heavy screens. By nightfall he was in there, three blocks from the scene of his aborted crime.

That night there began for Tucker, as it does for most citizens arrested for a crime, a process unrecognizable as the justice described in their schoolbooks.

Ronald Lee Tucker, young, troubled, from a large stable family, undoubtedly did not plan to maneuver between jurisdictions. Few burglars and robbers do, except in sophisticated mystery stories. He did not know that robbing a bank used to be a state crime. The Wall Street crash of 1929 and the Great Depression caused banks to go broke and exposed them to internal robbery by bank officials. The New Deal regenerated public confidence in banks by creating the Federal Deposit Insurance Corporation; and because federally insured money was involved, Congress, with J. Edgar Hoover's prodding, created a new federal crime, bank robbery. The next year Congress did the same for credit unions and savings banks with the Federal Savings and Loan Insurance Corporation, whose offices are in the Federal Home Loan Bank Building at 101 Indiana Avenue, N.W., in Washington, D.C., which by coincidence also houses the headquarters of the Federal Bureau of Prisons.

When Ronald Tucker was indicted by a federal grand jury in June of 1968 the charge read that he had taken "by force and violence and by intimidation" money from an institution "the deposits of which were insured by the Federal Savings and Loan Insurance Corporation."

The indictment also said he had violated federal law by using "a dangerous weapon, to wit, a starter's pistol," a separate violation. Robbing the bank under any conditions had a federal maximum penalty of twenty years. If a dangerous weapon is used as intimidation there is an additional maximum penalty of twenty-five years.

There followed a jousting unseen by the public and contrary to the theory of the Constitution.

In the minds of most people never involved in a criminal proceeding there is a clear and simple system of justice. A crime is committed. A suspect is accused. The prosecutor informs the citizen which law he is alleged to have broken. In an open court hearing the citizen declares before a judge whether he did it or claims that he did not. If he claims he is not guilty, the state has to prove quickly beyond a reasonable doubt that the citizen is guilty. The Sixth Amendment to the Constitution guarantees that "In all criminal prosecutions, the accused shall enjoy the right to a speedy and public trial, by an impartial jury . . ." Before the speedy trial, the suspect may be free if the judge decides there is little chance of his fleeing before trial. If there is some doubt, the judge will jail him unless he can put up a stated amount of money to be forfeited in case he fails to appear. If found guilty, the convict may be placed on probation, able to live in the community under rules of good behavior and required to report regularly to a probation officer, subject to immediate imprisonment if he fails. Or he may be imprisoned.

It is a nice theory and millions of schoolchildren learn it every year. That is not the way it happens in real life.

Most crimes are never reported or recorded, so most crimes go undetected and the criminals continue to be free among us. Eight years ago the President's Crime Commission reported a survey of 1700 persons representative of the American population. Nine out of ten admitted committing one or more serious crimes punishable by imprisonment. Respectable middle-class burghers, clergymen included, were among the uncaught felons.

Of 1000 crimes committed, only 91 are reported to the police. The theory is that now the 600,000 police of all types in the country have been mobilized, there is one for every 334 men, women and children, and presumably one for every ten crimes reported. Not all police employees work on crimes, though crime is the most urgent legal problem in the country and plays some role in the spending of $17 billion a year, $3000 per serious crime reported.

The police and others insist that lax laws and lax courts are the cause of crime. But the vast majority of crimes covered by law, usually very stiff law, never even reach the courts.

Most of the other 909 unreported crimes are white-collar crimes that the middle-class society takes care of itself or ignores. Or they are illegal acts committed in areas not watched carefully by police, or which neither victim nor lawbreaker choose to make public. Or else the police do not bother making a report or arrest. A doctor's son taking a neighbor's car without permission and hitting a tree is probably turned over to his parents, the neighbor urges the police not to bring a charge and the "crime" is never reported. If a ghetto adolescent does the same thing it is almost invariably reported and adjudicated.

If out of 1000 crimes committed only 91 are reported, the police cannot be blamed for all of the hidden 909.

But with the 91 reported to them, the police do not do well. Of those, only 18 result in arrests. If police fail to solve 80 per cent of reported crime, they cannot reasonably attribute crime to lax courts or a permissive society. They know about the crime, they have been given billions of dollars in crime-control equipment, personnel and assistance in the last decade, and they simply fail to find even a suspect in 80 per cent of the cases.

The theory progresses. Presumably the arrest is made with good cause and charges are brought only after collection of sound evidence. But of these eighteen arrests, only one has enough evidence to result in either a guilty plea or a finding of guilt after trial.

After a finding of guilt, the courts pass sentence. Here, too, there is a civilized theory that each guilty person is punished according to the crime and the need for safety in the community. Across the top of the temple of the Supreme Court of the United States the theory is chiseled: EQUAL JUSTICE UNDER LAW. This, too, is not true.

If every guilty citizen committed the same offense under the same conditions with the same background of legal behavior, then, under the Constitution and the law and a decent social process, every guilty party should get about the same punishment.

But there is no equality under the law. It all depends on where you are and who you are.

If your offense is possession of marijuana, the average sentence is six months in Georgia and seven years in the District of Columbia. If you are guilty of forgery in southern Mississippi the average sentence is six months, and in Louisiana nine years. For transporting a stolen vehicle you will get eight months in northern New York and two and a half years in southern New York. For robbery, five years in Wyoming and twenty-five years in southern West Virginia.

It also depends on which judge you get. In 1974 fifty judges in the second federal circuit—Connecticut, New York and Vermont—were given the usual presentence information on twenty real cases, so all had the same information. They were asked what sentences they would give. Their sentences for the same crime with exactly the same background record of the offender ranged from twenty years in prison and a $65,000 fine to three years and no fine. On another crime the judges' sentences ranged from seven and a half years in prison to no prison. On a bank embezzlement case one judge gave two years in prison, and on the same case thirty-eight judges gave no prison sentence. On the same bank robbery case all judges gave prison sentences, but eight judges gave fifteen years or more and seven judges gave five years.

And it depends on who you are. Middle-class people, especially rich ones, are not in districts closely observed by the police, so they are not detected in many of their crimes. They tend to commit white-collar crimes because white-collar activity constitutes most of their money-making life, and white-collar crime is tolerated as the gray area of doing business. They also commit other crimes. They get drunk, they have fights in cocktail lounges, they use drugs. Cocaine is an after-dinner stimulant among the rich, hard-drug addiction is a significant phenomenon among doctors, alcoholism among clergymen.

If the crimes of the affluent are detected, they often have ways of interceding to cut short the criminal justice system. Influential friends convince the police that there is no good served by prosecuting. If the criminal justice system does prosecute them, the white-collar suspects have private lawyers who are well trained and take time to prepare and fight the case. They have the assumption of civilized behavior in the eyes of prosecutors and judges because they dress, talk and act the same way as prosecutors and judges.

Though all studies show that affluent middle-class people commit crimes at significant levels, the jails and prisons, with few exceptions, are filled with the poor.

The average sentence is one year for every $10 million stolen in white-collar crime and one year for every $682 stolen in "blue-collar" crime.

Unequal justice does not stop there.

It also depends on what color you are. The average white person's sentence for federal crimes is thirty-five months, for blacks forty-five months. Black first offenders get sentences that average eighteen months longer than white first offenders.

For every 1000 children picked up by police, twice as many blacks as whites are sent to court for a crime. In Los Angeles the maximum prison sentences go to black burglars twice as often as to white burglars.

The death sentence has always been the ultimate expression of racial malice in the American criminal justice system. In Florida in the last generation, for example, of 133 white men found guilty of rape, 5 per cent received the death sentence. Of the 152 black men found guilty of rape, 35 per cent received the death sentence.

Many prisoners claim they were "framed," that they were prosecuted with false evidence. Sometimes this is true, but most men in prison committed the crimes they were sentenced for. But almost every prisoner knows that he is being punished in ways that other kinds of people are not, that the criminal justice system is full of cynicism, of corruption unpunished, of unconcern with crimes committed by people with high status. Unequal justice and prejudiced punishment produce the massive disrespect for law that comfortable people—the beneficiaries of unequal justice—like to ascribe to "permissiveness" or "laxity."

Ronald Tucker was as clearly guilty of trying to rob a bank as anyone can imagine. A clumsy robbery ended when the robber, never lost sight of, was caught running away from the premises with the money in his hands, in sight of dozens of eyewitnesses. But he was then caught like a shuttlecock in legal maneuvers that have little to do with crime and punishment but with bureaucratic tournaments, employment levels in the court, and political power.

The night of his crime he was arraigned in a court belonging to the Commonwealth of Pennsylvania, which has its own laws covering everything it considers a crime, maintains its own police, its own jails, its own prosecutors, its own courts and its own prisons. It was to these that Tucker was delivered, with a state public defender, Richard Joseph, to act as his lawyer.

Twelve days later Pennsylvania authorities had a session in the Allegheny County Jail at which Tucker pleaded not guilty to two state charges of committing "armed robbery" and "receiving stolen goods," on or about May 31. The operative language of Section 3701 of the state law read "threatening another with or intentionally put[ting] him in fear of serious bodily injury" and taking away money belonging to another.

Two weeks later a federal grand jury indicted Tucker for the same crime under the Federal Criminal Code 2113, Section (a): "On or about the 31st of May 1968 . . . Ronald Tucker . . . by force and violence did take from the person . . ." plus the additional crime of using a dangerous weapon while doing it.

The next day the federal court issued a warrant for the arrest of Tucker, who was already under arrest for the same crime and was behind bars in the Allegheny County Jail.

He was charged by both the state and the federal government for the same crime.

The Fifth Amendment of the United States Constitution states, "No person . . . shall be subject for the same offense to be twice put in jeopardy . . ."

In addition to the wheels of justice being geared according to social class, affluence and race, they are also driven by the bureaucratic ambitions of legal systems to claim the bodies and political fruits of suspects in crime.

The federal police machinery has become a force in every community. The number of crimes that Congress has made federal has tripled since the turn of the century. It is a matter of geographical chance which courts will claim the criminal and what kind of sentence, imprisonment and treatment he or she will receive for the same crime. On the surface local detectives and federal agents cooperate, and in actuality they often do. But beneath the surface there is an endemic competition for claiming crimes and what goes with them—criminal justice budgets and jobs. The race for money and jobs includes local police, state police, county police, FBI, Treasury agents, postal inspectors, the Secret Service and a growing number of federal offices with police and punishment powers. And the organized employees of local, state and federal prisons.

They and lawbreakers are caught in a geographical game of chance.

If an armed robber holds up a supermarket in New Florence, Pennsylvania, he violates a state law with a maximum penalty of twenty-five years. If he holds up a bank across the street he violates a federal law with a maximum penalty of forty-five years, because money in banks is insured by a federal agency and money in a supermarket is not.

If a person in Philadelphia knowingly cashes a false check on a bank 300 miles away in Pittsburgh, he has violated a state law with a maximum penalty of two years and a $5000 fine. If he cashes the same kind of check that happens to be on a bank five miles away in Camden, he has violated a federal law with a maximum penalty of ten years and a fine of $10,000, because Camden is across the state line.

Ronald Tucker was charged with a federal crime and a state crime arising from the same incident.

While he waited inside Allegheny County Jail, the ceremonial papers moved in and out of offices, following systems designed to keep things orderly and to perpetuate the ancient procedures of the English Crown to restrain secret handling of imprisoned citizens, but conducted in a culture of Latin, Anglo-Saxon and esoteric forms and language that are beyond the average citizen.

The United States Attorney wanted Tucker moved six blocks from the jail on Ross Street to the federal courthouse. He filed the proper message with the judge.

> WHEREFORE, your petitioner prays Your Honorable Court for a Writ of Habeas Corpus Ad Prosequendum in this behalf, direct to the Warden of Allegheny County Jail, Pittsburgh, Pennsylvania, and to the United States Marshal for the Western District of Pennsylvania, commanding them to have the body of Ronald L. Tucker before this Honorable Court . . . on August 13, 1968 . . .

Judge Wallace A. Gourley wrote underneath, "Granted."

More paperwork flowed from the judge's chamber and the clerk's office to the warden of the jail, since each time a prisoner moves and changes hands he is signed for as carefully as though he were a shipment of gold, with never a moment when he is not under the custody of a known person whose official duty is not to lose him.

On August 13 Tucker was delivered to the federal court. That court assigned a different lawyer, John Gedid, a Pittsburgh attorney, to defend Tucker. Gedid asked for a session to reduce the $5000 bail and possibly release Tucker. He told the court that Tucker was only eighteen at the time of the offense, was nineteen now, had never been charged with an offense before, had six brothers and sisters who had not been in trouble, and lived with his parents, who agreed to take custody and responsibility for their son's showing up in court. The judge said he would hear arguments of the matter two weeks later, during which time Tucker remained in jail.

In the meantime, more paper moved:

"United States of America vs. Ronald L. Tucker, Criminal No. 68–158, Writ of Habeas Corpus Ad Prosequendum" was not personal. It only meant that it was the 158th federal criminal case processed in the Western District of Pennsylvania in the year 1968.

"Habeas Corpus," Latin for "You have the body," ordered an individual out of jail to be presented to the court, in this case for a stage of prosecution.

The writ went on in even grander style as a note to the warden up the street.

United States of America
Western District of Pennsylvania

THE PRESIDENT OF THE UNITED STATES

To: Warden, Allegheny County Jail, Pittsburgh, Pa., United States Marshal, Western District of Pennsylvania

Greetings:

WE COMMAND YOU to have the body of Ronald L. Tucker . . . before the court.

The special form was given to Anthony J. Furka, the chief United States marshal for the district, who gave it to a deputy, Raymond E. Echement, who took it six blocks up the street and gave it to Robert Ritzel, supervising clerk of the jail, who accepted it on August 26 at eleven A.M. in the name of his warden. The deputy marshal recorded a three-dollar fee, which meant that three dollars was transferred from one set of books within the United States Department of Justice to another.

The date was postponed a day, which meant another order from THE PRESIDENT OF THE UNITED STATES, another trip up the street, and another theoretical three dollars.

In a twenty-minute session the federal court told Tucker he was charged with bank robbery, heard his plea of not guilty, reduced the bail to $3000, of which the required 10 per cent was paid on the spot to the clerk. Tucker's father and brother signed the judge's conditions of bail in addition to the promise of $3000 for forfeiture and the $300 down payment if they did not produce their son Ronald at the appointed time.

The conditions of the defendant's release to be further premised on the oral comment made in court at the time of the hearing as to the limitation on the activities of the accused, his manner and way of life, and his use of alcoholic beverages. He is to be at home at 11:00 P.M. each night and is to attend church each week. [Signed, Chief Judge Wallace A. Gourley.]

But as soon as this order was issued Tucker was back in jail as a state prisoner.

Tucker had been accused by the Commonwealth of Pennsylvania of another violation of law four months before the bank robbery. On February 6, 1968, someone had entered a business office and taken a wallet containing two dollars from a pocketbook. On March 26 Tucker was arraigned on charges of larceny and receiving stolen goods, the two dollars. At a preliminary hearing on April 11 Tucker pleaded not guilty, was remanded to the grand jury, which would decide whether the evidence against him was strong enough for a trial, and was released on $500 bond. It was while out on this bond that he held up the Pittsburgh Home Savings and Loan Association seven weeks later.

On September 13 the state grand jury dismissed the pocketbook theft charges against Tucker, the equivalent of finding him innocent, without sufficient state evidence to have him stand trial. Despite this, he remained a state prisoner accused of bank robbery.

Three days later there was another federal petition and order from the court, on mimeographed paper, from "THE PRESIDENT OF THE UNITED STATES" demanding delivery of the body of Ronald L. Tucker from the county jail to the federal courthouse for trial on September 19 for robbing the savings and loan association. A deputy United States marshal, John M. Milanovich, walked six blocks to the county jail, delivered the writ to Warden William B. Robinson "personally" and once more noted a three-dollar fee to be transferred from the courts to the marshal's funds.

"PRESIDENT OF THE UNITED STATES" notwithstanding, Warden Robinson had a problem. The Commonwealth of Pennsylvania considered Tucker their prisoner for robbing the savings and loan association. James Dunne, first assistant district attorney for the state, told Tucker's federal attorney, John Gedid, that the state refused to relinquish custody of Tucker until he was tried or would plead guilty to the state charge and that there could be no federal trial until the state had completed its business with the defendant for the same crime.

So Tucker, while in Allegheny County Jail, in possession of a release under bail from a federal court, was simultaneously the prisoner of the Commonwealth of Pennsylvania and the prisoner of the United States Government.

On October 22, 1968, Ronald Tucker was called before Judge Loren Lewis of the Pennsylvania courts. With Attorney Joseph as his counsel, Tucker withdrew his previous not guilty plea and pleaded guilty to robbery and receiving stolen goods at the Pittsburgh Home Savings and Loan Association. Maximum sentence could be twenty years for the sentencing. Tucker went back to Allegheny County Jail.

One month later another deputy United States marshal, John Lellech, made the six-block trip again from the federal courthouse to the jail and left a writ from THE PRESIDENT OF THE UNITED STATES with "Warden William Robinson personally" to deliver the body of Ronald Tucker to federal court the next day at ten A.M. Marshal Lellech noted a three-dollar fee.

On November 27, 1968, Ronald Tucker was delivered to the federal court before Judge Louis Rosenberg. With Attorney Gedid as his counsel, he withdrew his previous not guilty plea and pleaded guilty to violating U.S. Code 2113 (a), robbery of a bank.

He had used a gun to rob the bank. The federal law makes it a separate offense even if the gun is fake and even if it isn't brandished by the robber. In his sentencing, the judge would mention a gun. But in the private bargaining before the trial, to persuade the suspect to plead guilty, the gun part of the crime was conveniently dropped.

Tucker and the judge went through the familiar ritual. The federal prosecutor asked Tucker, "Has anyone, whether in or out of law enforcement, your attorney or any other person, made any threats or promises to you in order that you plead guilty in open court now?"
"No."

JUDGE: Did anyone promise you anything?
TUCKER: No.
JUDGE: Is anyone forcing you to say what you are saying now, that you are guilty?
TUCKER: No, sir.
JUDGE: And you are doing it because you want to do it?
TUCKER: Yes.

As of that moment, Ronald Tucker was guilty in the state court of robbing the Pittsburgh Home Savings and Loan Association on May 31, with a maximum possible sentence of thirty years, and he was at the same time guilty in the federal court of the same crime, with a maximum possible sentence of twenty years.

Pennsylvania, having put Tucker through its system first, deferred sentencing and conceded the prisoner to the federal government. It did not have to do so under any law or procedure at the time.

The state judge said he would let the state sentence run concurrent with any federal sentence, double jeopardy forbidden by the Fifth Amendment.

In federal court Judge Rosenberg asked Tucker if he had anything to say.

Tucker was brief. "Well, it was a big mistake I made and I deeply regret what happened. That is all."

The judge was not impressed. "Why didn't you regret it before and not do it? You did some planning on it. Well, you went out there and had the gun for several days and then you decided, according to the report—according to the version that you gave to the probation officer, you obtained a starter pistol from a friend—that is different from a toy pistol—for a few dollars, kept the starter pistol at home concealed under a mattress about three or four days before the event."

The judge looked at the presentence investigation report that every federal judge gets from the probation officer before passing sentence. In most courts it has a strong influence on the judge. It is supposed to be a careful and factual life background and evaluation of the prisoner, but in most cases busy probation officers rush through a few interviews and repeat the school and criminal record. They are notorious for errors of fact.

The judge finished reading the report and looked at Tucker. "He was thinking about the possibility of robbing a bank but is not certain as to why he wanted to do it. He said he was confused on the day he committed the offense. He walked from the Hill District to downtown Pittsburgh. En route he picked up a paper bag and wrote the note— so you did do a little planning on it, didn't you?"

"Yes, I guess you could say so."

"Well . . . there was a reason why you wanted to do it. You don't know why?"

"No."

"You haven't been very good at employment, have you? Your employment record is very bad. Since 1962 entering Aaron Hill Junior High School, transferring to Fifth Avenue, March 30, 1966, you must have had at least a dozen jobs, didn't you? Small jobs. Went back again to a certain prior job and the work was either not done satisfactorily or you didn't attend very well, didn't do good work. Oh, you can do good work when you did appear. Excessive absenteeism seems to be the big reason. But in one place at the Carnegie-Mellon University your work was unsatisfactory. You were dismissed there.

"All right, it seems to me that your mother thought you needed psychiatric examination. She told you to go to the Western Psychiatric Institute, didn't she? You went there and on two occasions you saw two different doctors?"

"Yes."

"And all you wanted was a letter to take back to your mother that you had been there. . . . Do you think you need psychiatric examination?"

"I wouldn't know."

"You don't know that? Well, we will find out. I will agree with you, Mr. Gedid, that he does need a study here. The report itself seemed to indicate it but I wanted to verify it with this young man and hear what he has to say."

The judge ordered Tucker sent to Lewisburg Federal Penitentiary for a three-month study and recommendation. On May 12 he was back in federal court in Pittsburgh for sentencing. In a last-ditch plea for leniency, his attorney had two men testify to Tucker's background.

Edward C. Dean, a recreation leader in the Pittsburgh black district, said, "Well, I have been knowing the gentleman for fifteen years. He is an outstanding athlete and a real good leader of boys. . . . He has a very good chance of being an outstanding basketball player. He is a born leader with the boys."

G. Harold Griffin, associate director of the community center in Tucker's neighborhood, said he had worked with Tucker daily. "I always considered him an outstanding person. He never gave me any difficulties whatever . . . he has a lot of leadership personality and I would say he is an outstanding person. I think he has an awful lot of leadership ability."

Judge Rosenberg was sarcastic. "Will you call bank robbery leadership?"

"No, Your Honor."

"So much of what you have already said doesn't count except the fact that he was one of those children who might have come along in the right way except that he became a bank robber."

Tucker was asked what he had to say.

"I believe that I made a big mistake at the time. I feel different than I did at the time the crime was committed. I understand more things than I understood at the time."

The judge said, "Go on."

"I believe that I can be rehabilitated and do something worthwhile in life if given a chance."

Judge Rosenberg noted that Tucker came from a good family and apparently was the only member who had ever been in trouble with the law. Was that true?

"Yes."

"You were the one who got into fights?"

"Not too often."

The judge nodded. "Ronald, I don't believe that you are ready for society yet. I think you need some more growing up. I think that you are in a position where you can really and, according to this report, really benefit from real direction and proper guidance, proper training, or that you can be what your parents intended, that you should be a good citizen living in a normal community. You had twelve employment positions in the last two years. Some of them were stable and some paid pretty well but you had no interest in them. You indicated to the officers that where you studied that you have some resentment toward authority. What is that resentment?"

"I don't recall."

"You have high intelligence. . . . The Youth Correction Act . . . means that now that you are going to be in the right hands, get the right control and the right direction and the right teachings. . . . Very lenient, instead of sending you to prison for fifteen or twenty years, we will let the authorities deal with you in the proper fashion because you are a young man yet."

On May 12, 1969, almost a year after his crime, Ronald Tucker was sentenced: four to six years, to be released when the authorities believed him ready.

The theory of the Youth Correction Act is that sentences are not fixed but permit the parole board to release the young offender when he is "ready," before he is immersed in the life of adult criminals in prison, making certain that youths caught in federal crimes, especially first federal offenders like Tucker, would serve shorter sentences than adults.

But, of course, it doesn't work. The year Tucker was due for release, young people paroled under the "lenient" Youth Correction Act served 10 per cent longer sentences than prisoners serving old-fashioned adult sentences.

Tucker ended up in an adult penitentiary—Lewisburg.

19

PRISONER NO. 37102–133

Horatio Alger, Jr., author of the New Testament in the American Dream, imbedded the gospel of financial success in the national soul through books called *Luck and Pluck, Slow and Sure, Strive and Succeed.* His work so profoundly instilled in millions of American youth the doctrine of shrewd service to the rich that his name became confused with the heroes of his novels, and today a socially approved rise from rags to riches is said to be "like Horatio Alger." This prophet of law, order, hard work and conforming success was himself a personal wreck. He was born on Friday the 13th, left Harvard Divinity School because of a homosexual episode, patrolled Broadway in wig and silken cape, lived in Manhattan with a series of young boys, and died broke in 1899 after his discharge from a mental hospital.

One of his biographers, John Tebbel, wrote:

> A psychoanalyst searching for clues to what was eventually the total disorganization of Horatio Alger's personality would have to look no further than to the classic psychologic mainspring of human mental ills, the man's father and mother. In Alger's case, these two represented between them nearly all the ingredients necessary to guarantee their son a maladjusted life.

For those who see biological inheritance as condemning individuals to recycled fates of their ancestors, the case of John Thomas Alger, car thief, burglar, robber, bad-check artist and perpetual jailbird, might seem to confirm predestination by genes. He is a member of the family descended from Horatio Alger, Jr. His troubles may have been compounded by the high expectations for all sons created by Horatio's fiction. But they were not created by Horatio's genes. It is not clear whose genes he carried. It was by pure chance that he entered the tribe of Horatio Alger, a random entry produced by the need of an unknown teen-age girl to escape gossip, his birthday fixed by the girl's insistence on attending graduation exercises of her high school class.

The girl had arrived pregnant in a Boston hospital from a northern Vermont town. The father, unknown, was presumed to be a visiting sailor, now disappeared in the last years of World War II. Her Boston doctor was approached by another doctor who told him that the child, when born, would be taken by a couple who lived in Brockton, Massachusetts, a city of shoe factories between Boston and Cape Cod.

The couple, approaching middle age, were childless and didn't want to wait years for usual adoption procedures.

The adoptive father, Thomas Alger, was one of three brothers who inherited the Alger Paper Box Company in Brockton. One brother, Joseph, was in New York City, a painter and writer, author of a popular book, *Get in There and Paint*. Another was Thomas, a heavy-set Yankee with sensitive, troubled eyes, who preferred music, reading, studying nature and restoring pianos, who agreed to remain at the factory during the labor shortage of the war. His wife, a former vaudeville singer from England, was forty-two, five years older than Thomas, eager to bring up a proper child.

Mr. and Mrs. Alger had a farm in Epsom, New Hampshire, so after the doctor told them the baby would be born in June, Mrs. Alger waited in New Hampshire while her husband worked in Brockton.

Unknown to them, the pregnant girl insisted that she attend her graduation exercises in early June. The doctor induced labor at eight months, producing a four-pound, one-ounce boy around midnight of May 19, 1945.

The next morning Mrs. Alger, bicycling to a telephone in the general store, skidded to the ground and broke her finger. Mr. Alger, calling from Brockton, said, "The baby is born. It's a boy."

She got first word of her child while in pain from her broken finger.

They named the child Jonathan, meaning "Gift of the Lord." They made plans for him to be a perfect son. When the baby reached five pounds they took him to Epsom, where the local paper ran a social item:

> Mrs. Alger and her adopted son, 4-month-old Jonathan Alger, were given a surprise party and baby shower by a dozen neighbors at their home in Epsom Center. . . .

The faded clipping was shown to me by Mrs. Alger as we sat in the living room of their cottage on a quiet side street in Brockton. She brought out an elaborate bound baby book, the gift of a friend of Al Jolson from her vaudeville days. The entries showed the baby's first word ("hello") at four months, his first walk at twelve months, the events through infancy recorded on rose-decorated pages full of the pride and wonder of new parents.

But pride and wonder ended with the last pages of infancy. The story of their son's life thereafter flowed in a bitter conversational stream throughout that dark Massachusetts day, from early afternoon, through tea in the kitchen, until we sat, the three of us, around the kitchen table with the dark falling outside, the room, the memories, the three of us overflowing with pain, bitterness and bewilderment.

They were so sure they had done all the right things. But a moment later they would be tortured, especially Thomas Alger. Perhaps they hadn't. No, they had done everything they could. They had planned great accomplishments for their new child. They believed discipline was the key to character; they obeyed the injunction "Spare the rod and spoil the child."

Mrs. Alger was still indignant at more liberal theories. "Those were the days of Dr. Spock and his permissiveness. But I can tell you, we weren't permissive."

Like millions of other parents, they would let the infant scream for hours but not touch him until the proper time in his schedule.

The Epsom farm had 120 acres surrounded by open fields, and when he was two Jonathan began exploring. If he left the yard Mrs. Alger would cut small branches to switch the child on the legs. The boy would shout back with angry tears. One day she saw his red cap moving up a hill a mile away. She retrieved him, switched him, and that night Mr. Alger built a chicken-wire pen twenty feet by ten, and four feet high. The child, two and a half, pushed against the wire, crying and screaming, but they would not let him out. He spent two days crying in the small prison before they abandoned the project.

He developed a lifelong wanderlust which they saw as one of many pathologies.

The Algers believe that 90 per cent of an adult's character is the result of genetic inheritance, and they clearly believe that their son's natural parents were deficient.

They feel that his natural mother's willingness to give him up meant that she rejected him in his prenatal state, transmitting this feeling to the unborn child.

Mr. Alger said, "It was a forced birth a month early. That's how it all started."

From that time on, they feel, a series of events confirmed the genetic predestination.

Back in Brockton they took him shopping. He liked to run in and out of the racks, so they put a bell around his neck to reveal his location and discourage his playing in the store.

"We would see kids who were bratty, running around and knocking things over and their mothers would just ignore them. We never did."

Thomas Alger said that proudly. And then his square face clouded. He leaned against the refrigerator and rubbed his hand under his chin to the back of his neck and shook his head slowly. "But, hell, maybe that was wrong. Maybe we should have let him run free, like the other kids."

Mrs. Alger sat erect in her chair at the kitchen table, shaking her head in absolute rejection.

They kept track of a series of events in childhood, each of which convinced them and their relatives that the child was already condemned by bad genes.

When he was five years old the family had a party attended by a sixteen-year-old daughter of a relative. The girl had noticeable breasts and Jon was observed to be looking at the girl quite often. A relative took Mrs. Alger aside and said there was no doubt that the boy had a psychotic obsession with sex and should be seen at once by a psychologist. Mrs. Alger took him to a psychologist who declared that they had a perfectly normal child. They concluded that the psychologist was incompetent.

In retrospect, the Algers see the beginning of school as confirmation of the child's future fate.

"On his first day of school," Mrs. Alger said, "the teacher had forty-two children. Jon came home and said he had made three friends. All three were adopted. Every one of them. They were drawn to each other."

On that first day Mrs. Alger went to school and showed the boy the way home.

"But after school he didn't show up and didn't show up. Tom had to go looking for him. You know where he found him? He found him in a colored person's house, the lowest trash possible, over the railroad tracks, eating supper.

"The second day of school a man drives up to the house and lets Jon out of his car. Jon had gone home with a boy with a deaf mute father."

They saw grave significance in these visits to people they regarded as inferior.

"He has felt insecure from before the time he was born," Mrs. Alger said. "I believe prenatal influence builds up."

"The mother's mind can affect the unborn child," Mr. Alger said. Mrs. Alger nodded in agreement and added more events:

"When he was seven he was at a boy's house where the other boy was having a bath. Both boys took their clothes off and got into the bathtub together. I had to go right over to the other boy's mother and speak to her about letting such a thing happen."

When the farm failed, Mr. Alger went back to work in the family box factory. In school Jon became the classroom clown, ignoring studies, creating scenes.

When he was seven he threw a rock through a church window. His father installed the new glass personally. John Alger remembers his mother saying about the incident, "Your real father must have been a no-good s-o-b."

When he was eight he needed dental work and he remembers his mother saying, "Your mother must never have taken care of her teeth."

Mrs. Alger said, "By the time he was eight years old, I could see that he was not developing into an acceptable human being. The school psychologist interviewed Jon for forty-five minutes and then told me, 'Don't expect too much of Jonathan.' "

Mrs. Alger replied immediately, "He doesn't steal."

She says the psychologist answered, "He will."

When she tells this story, Mr. Alger adds, "Now *that* psychologist was a real pro."

Those who see crime arising from permissiveness, lack of church, and relaxed parental discipline would have no criticism of the Algers. They never spared the rod. The boy was constantly reprimanded for departing from strict behavior. They held him to inflexible standards of propriety. He and his family were regular members of the Episcopal Church. If relatives or teachers found the boy at fault, the parents were quick to punish.

His first genuine police record was the result of the family insisting on official punishment. When an abandoned house in the woods caught on fire, apparently as the result of play by Jon and some of his friends, his father drove him to the police station and said, "My son lit that fire."

His first police record, made when he was eleven, reads, "Malicious destruction of property."

He was placed on probation.

It was during this period that he became aware that his parents were living separately. He was sent to Camp Yomechas (YOung MEn's CHristian ASSociation). He ran away so often that the camp would not take him back. The parents came back together. The boy evaded his household chores. When school started he didn't do his homework. Acrimony between son and parents increased.

The family moved and he changed schools, but each time he was an irritant in school. The parents decided on a cure. Some parents choose military school to "teach discipline" to children. The Algers, with an upper-class background, chose a religious private school, Episcopal, of course.

St. Andrew's School, in Barrington, Rhode Island, a fashionable suburb of Providence, was considered a privileged assignment for a young man. But the rebellious child was more impressed by the fact that he was not sent seventeen miles farther to the south, to the tip of Newport, Rhode Island, location of the gothic spires of St. George's School, one of the academies for America's aristocracy, particularly its Episcopal aristocracy, to which Jonathan's father and uncles had gone. (His father's celebrated ancestor had not gone to St. George's; Horatio was a Unitarian.) Instead of being impressed with the social superiority of his academy compared to Brockton High School, Jon was impressed with its social inferiority compared to St. George's. He resented most of all being sent away.

He was in St. Andrew's two years, during which time he ran away three times. About his St. Andrew's experience he wrote bitterly to his mother, "I was just a toy for you until I grew up and your baby toy wore out. You pushed me out of the house."

His mother said, "I did it out of love."

He was expelled from St. Andrew's. He went back to public school. He was suspended for hitting a teacher. Jon claimed the teacher hit him first.

While he was still suspended from school, Jonathan Alger spent his first night in a jail. He and two other boys were on the way to the weekly record hop in St. Paul's Episcopal Church when police arrested them for stealing money in an empty house along the way. They were locked in the stationhouse overnight and arraigned in Plymouth County Court the next morning. Jon was ordered to stay in jail over the weekend. Mrs.

Alger demanded the house keys from him. On Monday he was sentenced to his first penal institution, the Lyman School for Boys, a hundred-year-old juvenile prison in Westboro, Massachusetts, twenty-five miles west of Boston.

Alger's most vivid memory of Westboro is the aftermath of his helping two boys escape. He was reassigned to Cottage 9, the discipline center. Juvenile prisons tend to call their buildings "cottages," their jailers "house fathers" or "house mothers."

As he walked into Cottage 9 his house father asked, "What's your name?"

"Alger."

Alger remembers a blow to the side of the head and waking up moments later on the floor, his head aching and his pants wet.

His house father was standing over him. "That's just so you won't think of doing anything like you did in Cottage Three. And address me as 'sir.' Sit in that chair."

He sat in a wooden library chair facing the wall.

His punishment was shoveling coal in the boiler room from eight in the morning until four in the afternoon. At four he would shower and eat.

At dinner the boys stood until the house mother sat. They said grace, were forbidden to talk during the meal unless they raised their hand, and everything on the plate had to be eaten or the house mother or house father handed out punishment. Alger remembers that his punishment for not eating one meal completely was to kneel on the cottage floor with a broomstick underneath his shins.

He was in Lyman School nine months. When the parole board was about to consider his release, his parents arranged for him to be admitted to a special "bad boys school," St. Francis' Episcopal Home in Bavaria, Kansas. They picked him up at Lyman School and took him directly to Logan International Airport in Boston. The boy, now sixteen, changed planes at O'Hare Airport in Chicago by himself and flew to Kansas City. From Kansas City he took a bus to Salina, 180 miles away, in the center of the state. In Salina the school picked him up and took him to Bavaria, a tiny town ten miles farther.

St. Francis' Home was different from Lyman, disciplined but not brutal. Boys received demerits for insolence, profanity and making their beds sloppily. They were required to work off their demerits by marching, shoveling manure on the farm, or washing dishes—chores called, in the medieval manner of a religious establishment, "scribe duty."

There began letter-writing between parents and Jon, or "Jake" as he preferred. He had come to hate the name Jonathan. The letters followed a cycle that remained through adulthood. He would write with warmth. He would give his parents advice—on house repair or car selection or the stock market—based on the latest thing he had heard or read. Introduced, at first in passing, would be a request for something—money, clothes, a guitar. When the desired object was not delivered, a relentless campaign would continue day after day in letters, coupled with the start of recriminations against his parents, ranging from mere rebukes for denying him what he wanted at the moment to shrewd thrusts at their weaknesses and troubles. Then the desired gift would arrive and his letters would be ecstatic, expressing gratitude not just for the gift but for the luck he had in such loving parents. He would often promise them huge rewards for their thoughtfulness, suggesting that he had made connections or was at the start of a career that would provide his parents with great riches.

As his possible release from an institution approached, he would ask for them to tell the authorities that he would return home with a guaranteed job. His parents were increasingly reserved about his return. There would begin another cycle of profound denunciation, accusing them of abandonment and of being the cause of his forthcoming death by suicide or homicide within the institution. He would periodically announce that the letter they were now reading was the last they would ever get from him.

Then the parents would relent and say he could come home to Brockton. There would be a resumption of Jake's letters of joy and loving gratitude, with predictions of a brilliant career for himself after he returned home and plans for lavish retirement in which he would support them.

Then another cycle would begin.

The weeks before his birthday, May 19, were always the start of a campaign. He wrote from St. Francis' Home on April 7, 1962:

> Dear Mom & Dad . . . I would like a portable typewriter or a used television for my birthday. . . . Father John said I could have you send me a carton of Lucky when ever you want. I'm 16 and almost 17. . . . It will be awful if I don't get home for summer vacation, because Kansas is so bare of trees, lakes, grass and everything.

While he was in Kansas he acquired his first tattoo, reflecting his religious training and his rejection of the name his parents gave him.

On his left arm is a cross with "John"—not "Jon"—in green.

The boys were bused to the Salina High School every day. He got average grades and played baritone trumpet in the school band. Shortly after his birthday he and another boy walked into town after school, found a new car with the keys in it and drove around the surrounding countryside until they needed gas. They broke the rear window of a closed gas station, took thirty dollars from a cash register and headed east with John driving. A state police car chased them at high speed, John wrecked the car and both boys were arrested.

In Salina jail police discovered John was on parole from Massachusetts. He was put on an airplane for Boston and once more he changed planes unaccompanied at Chicago. He thought of what he would say to his parents when they met him at the Boston airport. He was looking for them as he walked down the ramp of the plane when he heard someone say, "Jonathan Alger?"

Two men who said they were from the state police put handcuffs on him and drove directly to Lyman School. Two weeks later he was "promoted" to Shirley Industrial School for Boys. Lyman was for boys twelve to fifteen. Shirley was for boys fifteen to eighteen. John was sixteen. He spent the summer pulling weeds on the institution's lawns and was paroled home after six months.

His father drove the family Pontiac to Shirley to pick him up. Father and son shook hands. His father said, "Well, let's try it again."

As they drove, they made small talk and then turned to what lay in store for John. His father said it was important that there be a job, and if he liked the idea, John could help repair player pianos and reed organs. By this time they had reached Concord, historic landmark of the American Revolution, but known to generations of Massachusetts youth for Concord Reformatory, a great red-brick pile surrounded by iron, and now an adult institution called Massachusetts Correctional Institution. As they drove the rotary by the prison, the father said something to the son. The father remembers it as "When you get in there, bub, we won't visit." The son remembers it as "Here's your next stop. And you can bet your ass if you come here I'm not going to visit you."

Mr. and Mrs. Alger were renting an apartment on Main Street, Brockton. When they got home his mother hugged and kissed him. "Glad you're back. We've got roast beef tonight."

They had bought a daybed and made up the living room as his bedroom. He worked in a shoe factory for three months with take-home pay of seventy-five dollars a week. One evening a friend John had met in the Shirley Industrial School dropped by and asked him if he wanted to ride. At three o'clock in the morning the police were at the door asking to see John. They had picked up John's friend sleeping in a stolen car and the friend said John had been with him.

Mrs. Alger burst into tears, ran into her bedroom and slammed the door. Mr. Alger, John remembers, shouted, "I'm getting sick of this shit! Here we go again!"

The next day John appeared in Plymouth County Court on his first adult charge, using a car without authority of the owner. He was sentenced to ninety days in the Plymouth County Jail, an institution on Obery Heights, overlooking the bay where Pilgrims were said to have set foot on Plymouth Rock. His father made his own pilgrimage to Obery Heights to visit the son and bring him cardboard on which to practice a new skill. An old wino serving a recurring sentence in the county jail had taught John how to do commercial lettering.

From the county jail, in May, John, age seventeen, wrote to his father:

> . . . your the only person that can understand me. Don't tell mom that I'm writting [Alger had a lifelong habit of spelling "writing" with two t's] you because she will just get upset at you and start complaining about me.
> [He advised his father to buy Xerox stock, predicting a mushroom rise.]
> I guess you are done with me just like Mom is, I called you last Sat but you weren't home and so I had to talk to mom and it wasn't very pleasant at all. I can talk to you more easy than mom and you are more understanding than she will ever be. . . . Do you and mom argue when I'm not home, if so maybe it isn't me that made you and mom fight. At least I always thought it was my fault. . . . I don't think a boy can be on his own until he is 21 years old . . . nobody wants me. . . . I don't know what to do. . . . Love Jake. PS. Write, Write, Write.

John served his time and was released. The policeman who had arrested him was a free-lance sign painter and got John a job in a supermarket at seventy-five cents a sign. A cousin got him a job at D. D. North, a commercial sign-painting company, where John learned how to put up neon signs, weld steel braces and use heavy tools.

He began to date a girl who lived with her mother, and soon John decided he needed an apartment of his own. He discovered that living alone entailed unforeseen expenses for rent, food and furniture. A friend he had met in Shirley became his roommate and they undertook a new set of enterprises—burglaries, robberies and car thefts.

The burglaries were in homes, doctors' offices, garages, veterans' clubs and gas stations. The car thefts from the street were always cars with keys left in the ignition. The locations were in towns of southeastern Massachusetts, along the approach to Cape Cod. He tells of one period when he made what he called mafia connections and put car theft on a more scientific basis.

In the morning a man whom he knew only by a first name would telephone, "John, I want a '63 Mercury convertible." Alger would go to the General Electric plant in Lynn, on the north shore of Boston, and comb the assembled hundred of parked cars until he found the desired car, or one like it. At first he either found cars with keys in them or used a coat hanger to open the locked door and cross the ignition wires. Later he was given ten rings with fifteen keys each to open and start any American-made car. He recounts driving the stolen cars to Pawtucket, Rhode Island.

If the car met the desired specifications, they would duplicate the keys, and the man would attach his prearranged new license tags and rivet a new serial number strip to the doorjamb. He would pay John $300.

From time to time John and his friend stole cars for convenience rather than profit. In the spring of 1964 he and his partner decided to take their girls to California. They stole a Chevrolet in Brockton, picked up the two girls and headed west on the Boston–Worcester road. Refinement in planning was not typical of either partner. They ran out of gas about four A.M., sputtered into a roadside rest area and waited. After a long wait a Chrysler New Yorker slowly drove into the rest area. An elderly couple were alone in the car. The old man walked beside a bush to relieve himself. John put a knife against his neck and took away the man's car keys and about $125. The two men and their girls drove off in the Chrysler. For some reason the Chrysler, though fairly new, stalled. While they had the hood up, a state police cruiser went by at high speed, slammed on its brakes and started backing rapidly. The four ran into the woods and scattered. The sky showed signs of dawn when John heard dogs barking—bloodhounds. He hid underneath a heavy low bush. In minutes a lathering, trembling bloodhound, straining at his leash, found him.

The policeman holding the leash had his gun out. "Come out with your hands up and when you get out, stand up and don't move."

He was taken to the old jail on Summer Street in Worcester, charged with armed robbery and car theft.

The Algers dreaded looking into their local paper, the Brockton *Enterprise*. Both sides of the family are prominent in the city. Periodically a story about John's crimes humiliated them.

Mrs. Alger said, "When we read in the paper that he had held up an old couple and took their car . . ." She shook her head.

Her husband said he had talked to John in jail by phone. "I said to him, 'If anybody my age stopped to take a leak, if it had been me, I could drop dead from a heart attack just from the fright of it.' You know what he said? 'Oh, I didn't do it, Pa.' That made me sick to my stomach. That was it for me. I have turned into an intolerant, cranky old man."

John spent twenty-six days in the Summer Street jail, and though Worcester is only fifty-two miles from Brockton the Algers did not visit.

On May 12 John wrote from Summer Street jail:

> Dear Mom & Dad, there must be something wrong above my shoulders, and this time I'm getting more and more dangerous. . . . I've heard that you both don't want anything to do with me anymore. So let's draw everything to a close. . . . I can't blame you for giving up on me, cause I've been nothing but trouble since I was 10. . . . I must be off my rocker for pulling an armed robbery on a man 66 years old. . . . Your troublesome Son, Love Forever, Jake.

Six days after his son's nineteenth birthday Thomas Alger received a letter from the superintendent of the Massachusetts Correctional Institution at Concord:

> Dear Sir: Please be advised that your son, John Thomas Alger, was received here on May 22, 1964 as C#39623. He was sentenced from the Worcester Superior Court to serve 5 years indefinite.

John's partner received five years also. John's girl friend, who was pregnant, received probation, as did her sister.

John believed that if his father had found him a job in Brockton before sentencing he would not have gone to prison. He wrote the first of many letters from "Box 00," the not-so-anonymous address for Concord prison. His letters were a combination of conciliation and hidden rebuke. He began with his lifetime greeting:

> Dear Mom & Dad, I hope this letter finds you both in the best of health, as for me I'm fine. . . . I'm not mad at Dad for not getting me that job so I could have got off probation. . . . I have to have a job and a place to stay

before November, 1964 . . . When you address my letters, the Box number is 00 not 39623, that is my con number. . . . Mail me my baseball glove. . . .

In Concord he made concrete culverts for the Massachusetts Highway Department at seven and a half cents a day. He practiced boxing in the prison gym and wrote that when he got out he would enter the Golden Gloves tournament. By July he was bitter at his parents' spasmodic letter-writing. He knew how to play on their guilt. "This will be my last letter unless I hear from you. . . . You are my parents and I thought you cared." Ten days later they visited him.

Relations improved with his parents. They arranged for a job offer from D. D. North to help him make parole. He was now working in the prison paint shop making traffic signs for the state.

His mother had brought him a manual guitar and he had obtained a small book of chords. He began a letter campaign for an electric guitar. "Just lend me the money for the guitar, and I'll repay you. . . . I swear to God Almighty that I'll repay you as soon as I'm released."

If months went by without a visit he would write:

I'll just spend Sunday walking around in circles talking to myself. . . . It seems that you have forgotten that this is your son and that you and I belong until death. . . . If you don't have someone pulling for you on the street, you come out hard as stones, with hate in your mind for the people that could have helped you, and sat back and laughed!

Within a week he was writing a pleasant letter announcing that when he got out he wanted to go into missionary work. "I've always wanted to be a priest of the Episcopal Church but I really never had the nerve to tell anyone. . . . If this don't work out on the missionary work, I'd still like to have a guitar."

A month later he repeated that he wanted a Vega guitar, in time for the prison Christmas show. A month after that he had his guitar.

But his parents said they didn't want him to come to their home when he got out. He began another letter campaign. "I haven't been home for Christmas in the last 4 years. . . . I HATE IT!!!" A little later: "Would like to live at home and *not* go drinking, nightclubbing and racing. If you give me this one more chance . . ." In January he wrote, "In May '64 you said I was always welcome home, 9 months later, 62 days before I see the board you say I'm not welcome home." He announced, "I'm looking out for Jonathan Thomas Alger and I'm changing my name, too. . . . I'm going to forget everyone I ever knew. . . . Everyone go to hell, I don't need you anymore. . . . Love, Jake."

As his parole hearing approached he intensified his letters, sometimes appealing, sometimes threatening. He wrote to "Dear Mom & Dad" saying he had saved all their letters, including their statements about his coming home. "On 10–17–64, mom, you said, 'It won't be long, do your best, we're doing ours.' On 11–28–64, Dad, you said, 'Of course your welcome, you're always welcome home.' Mom, 12–22–64, you told me, I can't come home. Dad, on 1–25–65, you said, 'Forgive me but I haven't the will or intestinal fortitude to be pushed around anymore. I'm just too old and tired.' " John told his parents that if they did not let him come home he would show all their letters to the parole board members.

A week after that letter his parents visited and the three of them talked about buying a new house. A few days later he found they had told the parole officer that they did not wish him to live at home and he wrote a letter saying he didn't need them anyway, a friend had found him a job as a sign painter at the Boston dogtrack, signed, "your son (adopted)." Shortly before his board appearance he escalated the pressure. He shrewdly demanded a copy of his birth certificate.

> There's no Jonathan Thomas Alger on the records for May 19, 1945, or around that date in Boston City Hall. Something's fishy. I wasn't adopted through an adoption agency in the Boston area. So let's bring it out of the dark. I've known this for about a year now, but I was waiting for the right time to question you about it. . . . Who are my parents? You know. I want to know! . . . This may be my last letter.

The Board of Parole postponed consideration of parole for another year. In the same letter that he told his parents of this he asked for a Fender electric guitar. In another letter he said the Fender Stratocaster guitar "would make a wonderful 20th birthday present. . . . I've calmed down, and have adjusted. . . . I don't hold any remorse against anyone. . . . Your new son, Love Jake, P. S. May 19–birthday!"

He wrote that he knew 400 chords. "I got my guitar book, 2400 chords, Duane Eddy, Bodidly and Chuck Berry." On May 19 he thanked them for the new guitar. It was not a Fender and he wrote admiringly of it, but "I've named it the Mystery Master because it hasn't a name or anything."

But in June he wrote bitterly:

> Your letters are full of troubles, and getting troubled letters in prison make a man go crazy. I've got troubles, bills, and I don't complain, it's life.

I realize your just putting it off about my coming home. . . . Your trying to keep me here . . . because of the past. . . . My question shouldn't take any thought, its either yes or no . . . if no, let's say goodbye. I'm *just* your son, Love Jake. [Three days later] I can't accept the fact of your disowning me. . . . Sorry for that last letter.

He wrote to his father, who was alone in Maine, "I seem to get along great with you when Mom isn't around, probably because your a guy, not a broad."

To his mother he wrote, "I received your letter yesterday and was very upset over it. Because they take photostatic copys of those kind of letters and the parole board reads them. . . . So please don't write rotten letters like that cause it will get me another setback. . . . Write soon, Love Jake."

A week later, telling them that his parole was set back again, he good-naturedly asked for an amplifier with reverberation, because "I intend on making this my life, with music."

In July he urged them to get someone in Brockton to commit themselves to giving him a job so that it would impress the parole board at his next hearing. He also said they would have to let him live at home, otherwise the board would not consider his case.

By now his parents were bitter almost beyond recall. They were untouched by his promises and disgusted with his friends. His father told me, "The boy has a built-in insecurity. He feels he has to prove himself. He had the ability to pick hoodlums for friends. Maybe I'm a snob but his friends were always from the bottom of the barrel."

His mother agreed. "They were dirty, unintelligent, the lowest kind of people. He always wanted to buy his way. He didn't attract real friends, always the scum."

John continued to press them to relent. "I've seen enough to make any man go straight. . . . I won't have time to find friends with the plans I've got. Like woodworking and taking guitar lessons. I'd like to start a little guitar repair shop." His parents relented again. He wrote them, "I'm about the happiest person in this place because you said in your letter that you think I'm really trying to go straight and live a better life. . . . I just want to come home where I belong and do the things a young man should do." A month later the joy was still in the letters. "In due time I'll be an average human being, and not an animal." He asked a week later, "When you said you thought I'd learned my lesson, does this mean you are willing to get me out by Christmas? . . . We'll live as a happy family once again. . . . I'm staying home most nights and watch TV, or work another job at night."

In October of 1965 he was paroled to the Plymouth jail for eventual discharge. In early November his father picked him up at the county jail and drove down the hill, through the historic town of Plymouth and home to the new house in Brockton. For November and December things went fairly well, with jobs here and there. In January John began stealing cars, burglarizing gas stations and veterans' clubs. He and a partner were burglarizing a gas station in Norwell, ten miles from Brockton, when a police car drove into the station and they were both captured. John was arraigned for two burglaries, one larceny and a stolen car. He was back in Plymouth County Jail.

He wrote a letter:

> Dear Mom & Dad, Well, I guess this letter will just make things worst. But what can I say that you haven't heard before.

Then he criticized his parents for doubting his love for a girl he had dated during his few months at home, and "trying to ruin our marriage to be." He was sharpest with his mother:

> I never brought a girl home before because you'd . . . call her a tramp and say she must be pregnant. . . . I love her and if I can just keep her until I get out I know we'll make it. Yes, she might be pregnant but I don't care. . . . If you haven't the nerve to admit you are wrong, just please leave us alone. It might be too late. If so, THANKS PARENTS. . . . If I lose [her] I intend to pull a horror show and break a few heads. [He repeated words he said he remembered them saying.] Remember, "I'll pack your bags," "I'll call the parole officer," "Lazy no-good excon." Wonderful words to hear. Thats why I'll never come home. So it isn't all my fault! . . . Maybe [we] can show you a granddaughter by next spring.

Three weeks later relations were better and John was contrite. He said some important friends of his were arranging bail and a job to persuade the parole board. Then he mentioned the girl he had said was pregnant, whom he would marry and with whom he would present his parents with a grandchild. "As for her, well, like with every beginning there is an end."

On March 7, 1966, John wrote a letter to his father full of advice. He told him that he should promote his piano repair business by putting a player piano on the street playing automatically as an advertisement. He told his father, "Don't give up," telling the older man that his son had faced problems and conquered them and so could the father. It sounded like a father writing to his son in jail.

It was strange for another reason. A few hours later Jonathan Thomas Alger escaped from Plymouth County Jail.

On a Monday night police visited the Alger home to say that their son was an escapee. The next afternoon the Brockton *Enterprise* carried a page-one story:

> A Brockton youth, Jonathan T. Alger, 20, formerly of 1627 Main St., is still the object of an area search by state and local police today following his escape from the Plymouth County Jail about 6 P.M. Monday.

The next morning the mailman delivered the letter written just hours before the escape expressing confidence that his father could conquer his problems even as the son had.

The explanation of how Alger conquered Plymouth County Jail varies. Alger has one memory, jail records another. Alger has a lively imagination, fed by years of absorbing jailhouse legends, the boasts of inmates about their exploits—of insults to police, defiant speeches to judges, often exaggerated or fictional, feeding both the ego and the need for survival in prison by projecting an image of indomitable toughness and incomparable cunning. And his profound need for acceptance.

Alger's memory is that the Monday night of his escape he was swinging barbells made of tin cans filled with concrete when one of the cans hit the jail wall, cracking open a hole in the cinder-block interior. Looking inside, he saw two wires, one red and one black, which ran toward an electric door leading to the outside. He heated a butter knife over book matches until it was hot enough to burn the insulation around the wires. He held the metal knife across the bare spots, shorting the wires, and the electric door clicked open and he walked out.

Jail records and the memory of a jailer differ. "We were building the new addition and we kept telling the construction crew, 'For chrissake, will you pick up your tools at night when you're through?' But, no, four o'clock would come and they'd drop everything, hammers, jimmy bars, hacksaws, everything. And the worst thing was they had to break a big hole in the outside wall. We'd ask them to seal it up careful every night. But, no, they'd just put up a sheet of plywood with a two-by-four to brace it in position on the other side.

"So what does Alger do? He finds a hacksaw blade and saws enough of the bars inside to weaken them and push them wide with his hands. When he gets to the wall, he just pushes that stupid piece of plywood and walks out. The prisoners were escaping in droves all the time they were building the addition."

The jail had no electric door until the year after Alger escaped.

A close friend from Concord lived with his girl in Brockton. Alger moved in with them, emerging only at night. Four days after his escape, he, his friend and two other young men stole a car with keys in it. They had an idea for a large burglary: the safe at D. D. North, where Alger once worked. With an acetylene torch they cut an eighteen-inch square in the outside steel jacket of the safe. Inside was a thick layer of concrete. They worked on the concrete with hammer and chisel until they reached an inner jacket of steel. This was penetrated by the acetylene torch, but the flames set fire to papers inside the safe. A fire extinguisher grabbed off a wall ended that threat. They withdrew a steel cash box, pried open the locked lid with a screwdriver and counted the proceeds: $12.90.

Twenty minutes after the break, inside a nearby apartment, Alger and his three friends were drinking and arguing so loudly that it attracted the police. They were charged with breaking and entering in the nighttime, larceny, and stealing an automobile. On May 17, two days before his twenty-first birthday, Alger was sentenced to four to eight years in the maximum-security adult prison at Walpole, on the outskirts of Boston.

He wrote to his parents:

> I guess you're both through with me. . . . I can't blame it on anyone but myself and I'm not blaming either of you. You both gave me everything I could need to go straight.
>
> [He said the last girl he had been in love with had written to give him hell.] She's really too good for a guy like me, but I can't settle for less than the best. Sure I live like a bum, act the part also. But, when it comes to clothes and a woman, I got to get the top shelf.

Three days after his sentencing he wrote from Walpole to rebuke them for not visiting him:

> I myself, if my son fouled up and got life, I'd fight and visit him every week, until either he got out or past away. But I guess we're not alike in many ways.

His father wrote a distressed letter. The son replied:

> Dear Dad, I received your very upsetting letter a few days ago . . . more worries make the time go much harder. Please when and if you write don't talk about death unless one of you is very ill.

In June he was transferred to Concord. In July his parents visited him and brought him his guitar. In July he heard that his latest girl was pregnant. "If I had known . . . I would have married her." He said if he had married her and the baby was a girl he would name her Tracy Lee or Caprice, if a boy, Thomas, after his father.

He began a new letter campaign for a $220 Fender guitar and amplifier. He also asked for fifteen dollars to repair an expensive watch he owned. "I just won't wear a cheap Timex." He got the guitar for Christmas. He explained his need for money:

> I've little things that are a must with me, like new clothes and a new car, nice girls and stuff like that. . . . [He told them that if he was paroled they need not worry, he didn't want to live in Brockton anyway.]
>
> I can't see myself going out there and . . . living in a 1-room furnished dump, putting in a 40-hour week in some sweat shop, coming back to my little pad and eat a can of Campbell Beans and then go to bed at 6:30 cause there's nothing to do. This isn't for me. [He demanded that they commit themselves to fight for his release and support him or reject him flatly.] If you brought me into the world, you'd act different.

In May 1968 he received his high school equivalency diploma. "Don't be surprised if I hold a degree by 1972. I'll be 27 and mature enough to really make something of myself." He invited his parents to the high school diploma graduation exercises at Walpole in June.

The diploma ceremony was clearly an occasion of enormous pride for Alger. He sent the diploma home and wrote, "Did you put it on the television or something or over a door where guests will bang their heads on it!"

Later when he asked his mother why she didn't write about joyful memories, she wrote back:

> There is very little in this "memory file" that brings me joy. . . . I cry for your wasted years, I cry because when other mothers speak with pride of their accomplishments, I sicken with fear and apprehension for you and your future. Perhaps you *have* grown up and matured. I believe you are trying now; I believe that *you* believe you'll never foul up again and your father said before he left yesterday, "I think he might be all right now." That's a big statement coming from your father. Don't let him down, again, his heart couldn't stand it. As for me? I'm your mother—I will always love you. Don't let yourself down, son. You've got to make it. Mother.

This stimulated more plans in him and he wrote in his euphoric style of what was in store for him if he finally got to a halfway house in Boston:

> I'll be going to classes during the day for 5 hours, and nights from 6 P.M. till 9 P.M. go home and study, sleep, work, eat, etc. for two years, then I'll be in a position to be accepted by people.

On August 7, 1968, he wrote to say he had been granted parole to a halfway house.

His father drove him to the halfway house in Boston, a place where he could live and be supervised, as though in prison, but be free during the day for study or work. He was enrolled in Franklin Institute but his major effort was playing bass guitar in a rock band in downtown Boston clubs. He started using drugs, heroin a few times, was frightened by it and shifted to cocaine. The parole board disliked where he was working and said he would have to find a place that served no alcohol and was not frequented by people with criminal associations. He shifted to a Beacon Street discotheque.

Three Boston snowstorms in the winter of 1968–1969 blew away his resolve for spartan living, all-day classes and all-night studying. He had met a girl, "Marlene." He was driving a new GTO stolen in Rhode Island and equipped with fake papers. Making a screeching exit from a restaurant parking lot, he was stopped by a police cruiser and charged with driving without a license and being a parole violator. He made bail, was set down for hearing the next morning. That night he was on the way to Florida in the GTO with Marlene beside him.

On March 5, 1969, he wrote his mother and father from Fort Lauderdale:

> Dear Mom & Dad, this letter is going to make you wonder, but its the truth so forget any predrawn conclusions.
> [He said his parole was about to be revoked, Marlene was all he cared for and so now he and Marlene were living in Fort Lauderdale.]
> If Parole asks, you don't know where I am. . . . I'm old enough to live a private life. . . . Parole isn't anything but trouble. . . . I hated the thought of going back to prison for something foolish. So unless I come back to Mass. they can't touch me. . . . I hope you'll understand without too much of an argument. . . . Love as Always, Jake.

Marlene wrote a P.S. "Come on down!"

His account of the Fort Lauderdale period describes living in a beach

hotel, earning $400 a week playing from eight-thirty P.M. to three A.M.
in an exclusive club, of separating from Marlene when she became
jealous of other women surrounding him, of a rich older woman who
fell in love with him, who owned "an air-conditioned vinyl-top Chrysler
LeBaron Imperial with white leather upholstery."

And suave rackets with a new partner, "Howie."

Howie was from western Pennsylvania and could do everything from
con rich women to pick locks in stores, by the Fort Lauderdale account.
This included using a van with "Al's Pool Service" painted on the side
by Alger, of driving by security guards at exclusive protected neighborhoods, ringing the doorbells and asking if they wished pool service. If
the answer was yes, they would make a date and never show up. If there
was no answer they would take the address and name and call from a
public phone; and if there was still no answer, they would back the
"Al's Pool Service" van into the back yard near the pool, up to the
sliding glass doors, and empty the house of everything valuable that
would fit into the truck. Jewels were fenced and national credit cards
sold to a syndicate for $100 each. The cards were then flown the same
day to the West Coast for use before the credit company computers
could cancel the numbers.

Despite the glamorous accounts of high-level hedonism, summer
found Alger and Howie in Beaver, Pennsylvania, not one of the nation's
pleasure domes. It is midway between Pittsburgh and Youngstown,
Ohio, a smudge on the carbonized corridor of compacted industry
along the banks of the Ohio River.

Here, too, the account glows with big hauls and important criminal
connections, of rented trucks to steal whole schoolrooms full of electric
typewriters, of feeding the black market in stolen Xerox machines, of
fencing a stolen microfilming device worth $5000 to a modern-minded
bookie who computerized his records, of acting as guerrilla fighters
between two gangs warring for control of Beaver County industrial-mill
betting tickets, of robbing one lottery operator of $44,000 at the invita-
tion of the rival gang, who provided Alger and Howie with inside
information and official police protection, with a net to them of $10,000
each. But when the FBI arrested Alger it was for cashing a false check
in the amount of $216.34 at the Economy Supermarket in Beaver Falls,
Pennsylvania.

In September 1969 the Algers in Brockton received a telegram from
their long-silent son saying he needed $200 at once for a car payment
during a Labor Day weekend when a big paycheck for him was not

available. In fact, he needed it to try to make bail. He was in jail, in trouble with both the federal and Pennsylvania state governments.

Pennsylvania had arrested Alger for burglaries in Beaver County, and while being held for these he escaped the easygoing Beaver County Jail twice. Once, as a trusty with easy access to the outside grounds, he had merely walked off the premises and kept going until he got a ride to Ohio, where he was arrested by the FBI. Returned to Beaver County Jail, he escaped a second time with two accomplices by beating up a guard, after which he was captured.

Someone had burglarized a Beaver painting company and stolen their check-writing machine and a book of their checks. Whoever did it used the check-writing machine to stamp out payroll-like checks taken from the stolen book of company checks. John Alger cashed one of those checks in a supermarket that, unfortunately for him, used an automatic photographing machine for every customer who cashed a check in the store.

It was also Alger's misfortune to have used a check from a bank that the painting company had ceased using six months earlier. It was further complicated by the fact that the now defunct bank account was not with a local bank but one located in Wilmington, Delaware.

The result was that the check bounced, having been drawn on a closed account. It went back to the supermarket, which had a photograph of Alger signing the check, and because the check had crossed a state line to Delaware before being returned uncashed, it was a federal offense.

A federal court issued a warrant for the arrest of John Thomas Alger, also known as Paul Vander Warren, a false name he had adopted. He was arrested, extradited to Pennsylvania and charged with transporting forged securities in interstate commerce.

After complicated appeals and delays, he was sentenced to five years at Lewisburg. He was delivered to Lewisburg to start his sentence in February of 1971, to suffer the harsh penalties meted out to low-level check cashers.

In August 1971 Alger received a reply from the U.S. Board of Parole denying his application and putting off for another year consideration of his early release. He wrote in black marking pencil across the form, "Fuck it," and then wrote the judge who sentenced him, John Miller, asking for release on the basisof an inaccurate presentence report, saying he had "a girl whom you've just received a letter from. . . . I've a woman who is very much in love with me, and I the same."

Marlene, abandoned in Fort Lauderdale, had, nevertheless, written to Judge Miller.

> Now, John has had two long years to think about all of this, and I firmly believe he has come to realize he will never have me and his illegal wrongdoings at the same time. It's one or the other.
> [She was sure he had learned his lesson and would make a wonderful husband and father.]
> I'm willing to take full responsibility for his actions and if he by any small chance should "slip up" again I wish you would have me locked up also. . . . When all of this is finally over, and John is released, would you give me the honor of having you perform the ceremony. I'm really serious.

The judge did not reduce the sentence and Marlene married someone else. John Thomas Alger began his incarceration a year before his election to the first committee ever to represent striking prisoners at Lewisburg penitentiary.

PART FOUR

Prisons are an environment created totally by the state. If in this institution uncivilized things are done, it is not because prisons have failed but because society is becoming uncivilized.

If prison cruelties are excused in the belief that they match the crime of the prisoner, the state is telling the prisoner that cruelty is legitimate. If the state commits cruelties but pretends to the public that it does not, the state is instructing the criminal that cruelties by stealth are acceptable cruelties. If an individual damages another and in retaliation the state demonstrates new forms of damage to its prisoners, the state has added to society's repertory of human destruction.

20

"ADJUSTMENT"

One at a time, each committee member was called out of his segregation cage, escorted down two flights of stairs to the basement and told to wait outside the concrete chamber.

Inside, a gothic scene awaited the prisoner. A long bare table occupied the center, one chair at its head at the far end, one at the near end, one on the left side and two on the right side. In the far corner sat a functionary with the apparent role of secretary, though he did not always take notes. In the near corner an officer stood guard. The seat on the right side of the table was occupied by Captain Dodd. In the two chairs opposite him were a doctor representing the medical department and a caseworker representing the classification and parole department.

At the head of the table sat the chairman, Associate Warden Cansler, dressed in black—black suit, black shirt, black socks and black shoes. The only relief from blackness was diagonal silver stripes on his black tie.

A fluorescent lamp gave everyone a deathly pallor.

This was the adjustment committee.

"Adjustment committee" is one of many inspired names created by the Federal Bureau of Prisons. Just as prisons are "correctional institutions" and guards "correctional officers," the punishment board for prisoners who break rules is the "adjustment committee."

Its decisions can have grave consequences, more than most courts on the outside. By a finding of guilty it can add years of imprisonment and make parole impossible. If it condemns a prisoner to "indefinite segregation" it can drive some men mad, giving the committee members power of sanity and insanity and in some cases life and death. A significant number of prisoners condemned to indefinite segregation

371

become permanently psychotic—Charles Manson before he formed his "family," for example—and a significant number commit suicide.

Punishment boards of some kind are inevitable. Rules will be broken and intolerable acts short of crimes will be committed. Prison boards might be considered teaching models of the sanctity of law, order and concern for justice: the accused would know the rules he is expected to obey, be informed ahead of time of accusations against him, have an opportunity to defend himself by calling witnesses, not have his accuser be his judge, and if found guilty be punished in ways that are consistent with making him respect law and will not violate the Eighth Amendment of the United States Constitution forbidding cruel and unusual punishment.

None of the committee prisoners awaiting their turn in the concrete room had ever seen printed rules for Lewisburg penitentiary or been told them orally. Later when a judge asked a prisoner how a new man learned the rules the man answered, You do something, the guard arrests you, you are taken before the adjustment committee, you are punished, and then you know that particular rule. Associate Warden Cansler told the same judge that even he had never seen a copy of the institution rules.

None of the committee prisoners had been told what rule they were accused of breaking. Each would hear it for the first time when he entered the chamber and was asked his claim of innocence or guilt. He had no right to call witnesses or bring in other evidence that might support a claim of innocence. In most cases the officer charging him with the infraction sat on the board deciding whether the charge was justified. If the prisoner was found guilty he was sent to a board that could lengthen his time in prison and threaten his sanity.

The prisoner had no rights. As Mr. Cansler told one Lewisburg prisoner, "When the judge raps that gavel down on you, boy, you lose all your rights. Anything you get after that is a gift."

Later a judge was to ask Cansler what would happen if an inmate denied the charge against him. The associate warden's reply was a clear and honest statement of the working of justice within the prison system: The word of the staff is always taken; if by some chance the prisoner was innocent he would still be punished.

"Here you would be in the position of having an officer that . . . either seen this incident take place or . . . heard this incident take place. In other words, he has a personal knowledge of it. The lieutenant has investigated it and certainly he has substantiated what the officer has charged the man with . . . so that there is no doubt left in it."

The judge was puzzled. But what if the lieutenant who makes the independent investigation found that the original accusation was wrong?

Cansler: "I think he [the accused prisoner] would be guilty but we try to make every effort to give him leniency as far as the penalty is concerned."

There was the case of John Moore, a thirty-seven-year-old Philadelphian serving ten years for possession and sale of marijuana. He was unrelated to the Richard Moore of the prisoners' committee and there was no problem of mistaken identity. Richard Moore was punished under his prison identity, No. 70209–158. John Moore was processed elaborately in and out of the prison under his prison identity, No. 37483–133. That was also the number under which charges were brought on the official Federal Bureau of Prisons form for "Misconduct Report."

A few days after committee members were charged with "inciting," noncommittee members who had attracted attention for some reason were brought into the concrete chamber. For the first time John Moore heard the chairman read the accusation.

Date of Offense, February 15. Place of Incident, warehouse platform. Charge: Attempting to incite a work stoppage. A senior officer specialist who observed the offense wrote the charge as read to Moore:

> This date, at approximately 12:20 P.M., the above captioned inmate delivered a very radical speech from the warehouse platform. There were approximately 150–200 inmates gathered in the open area between the Industry building and warehouse platform. It is my personal opinion this inmates speech had a direct effect in causing the large number of inmates to refuse to report to their assigned details.

Underneath was "INVESTIGATOR'S REPORT: Facts are as stated above. The radical speech delivered by this inmate did indeed have a direct effect on those inmates who had gathered in the Slot." It was signed, "G. C. Baker, Lieutenant."

At twelve-twenty P.M., when speeches were being made on the kitchen platform, John Moore was handcuffed in an automobile of a U.S. marshal somewhere between Philadelphia and Lewisburg. Since February 8 he had been in Montgomery County Jail, twenty miles outside Philadelphia, the nearest facility where he could be kept while awaiting a court hearing on an appeal of his sentence. On the 15th he was being returned to Lewisburg. He arrived sometime in midafternoon and, in the regular procedure, was immediately placed in temporary segregation, as are all incoming prisoners while they are processed for return to the main population. However, his processing was delayed because, some officers told him, "an incident" was in progress. It was not until four P.M. that he was released from a segregation cage to go to the evening meal. At the evening meal it was clear that something unusual was happening and he kept trying to find out what, getting confusing answers.

Moore's job was in the library, taking care of prisoners' correspondence courses. He handed out the mailed assignments, graded papers and kept records, usually in the evenings. But at the mess hall an officer told him to return to his quarters and he did. In the evening he heard the public address system telling prisoners to go to the auditorium to elect a committee. He hesitated to go. Some men in his quarters said it might be a trap. When officers urged the prisoners to go he did, but only in the last minutes, and he left early.

On the 26th he and all the other prisoners were still locked in their cages when they were told that the prisoner committee had been disbanded. He was asked to sign a statement on his willingness to go back to work. He told the interviewing caseworker that the announcement had said there could be "serious consequences," including loss of good time and punitive transfers, and he'd like to talk to his lawyer first, especially since he had an appeal pending. The caseworker said, "That's a no answer," made a notation and left. The next day Moore was taken to S-1 segregation. For a week there were four men in his cell. The first night there was no mattress for him and he slept leaning against the concrete wall. He had no pants, just shorts, T-shirt and a blanket. Among the men was Singleterry, the man without clothes. One main meal was two kernels of corn, three peas, a slice of bread and butter. Contrary to law, he was denied legal materials for his appeal. He asked the segregation officer and the caseworkers and nothing happened. He wrote to the associate warden and nothing happened. He wrote to the warden and nothing happened. He wrote to the judge in Philadelphia and the day the judge wrote back to him Moore was released from segregation.

On March 3, Moore was called to the adjustment committee. Chairman Cansler read a charge accusing him of making a speech on the platform.

He said to Chairman Cansler, "Do you realize that I wasn't even in the institution when all that was taking place?"

Cansler made no response. Moore was also charged with refusing to work. He was found guilty of both charges.

The next day, by now released from segregation because of the judge's letter, Moore asked to see the warden. The warden, Captain Dodd and two other officers were interviewing men still holding out against going to work. But the warden agreed to see Moore. Moore explained to the warden that he wasn't inside the prison at the time he was accused of making a speech inciting the work stoppage. The warden looked to Captain Dodd. Dodd nodded that Moore was right. The warden said he would wipe out the charge and guilty finding and expunge Moore's record. It was a great relief to Moore. He was not punished further, though his record remained unchanged.

Or take the case of John Alger, who, when Captain Dodd asked Phillips to start taking down grievances on the platform, handed Phillips a ballpoint pen.

The reporting guard who viewed the scene wrote the charge read to Alger when he was called into the concrete chamber:

> This inmate climbed upon the warehouse platform and delivered a "no work" speech to approximately 150–200 inmates who had gathered in the open area between Industry and the warehouse platform. His speech had the desired effect on those who listened as they refused to report to their assigned details.

It was properly signed by the guard who observed it.

It was also verified by Lieutenant G. C. Baker, who investigated the report:

> Facts are as stated above. Alger had a strong influence on other inmates as they appeared to follow his leadership. Placed in Administrative Segregation pending appearance before The Adjustment Committee.

Alger, of course, had not spoken a word from the platform.

He was found guilty, continued in segregation and referred to the Good Time Forfeiture Board.

The adjustment committee continued to grind out its justice.

After the prison returned to work, a second charge was brought against committee members: "Conduct prejudicial to the Good Order, Security and Safety of the Community and the Security of the Inmate Population."

> A member of the so-called first committee, subject deliberately refused on more than one occasion to present grievances to the administration although having previously expressed to the administration that the sole

purpose for which the committee was formed was to present the grievances of the inmate population for my [warden's] and others consideration. The action in concert with other members of the committee prolonged an emergency at the U.S. Penitentiary, Lewisburg, Pennsylvania, threatening the security of the institution and the safety of the staff, the inmate population and the community.

When the charge was read to them by Chairman Cansler it was, like all charges, new to them as of the moment they were asked to reply to it. Most answered more or less as Irwin did. He told the adjustment committee that the grievances were about ready on Friday, but the administration, which had promised round-the-clock sessions for the committee, refused to honor the promise and so shared in the failure to get completed grievances. In addition, the election to the committee was on orders of the administration, which used the public address system and personal persuasion to get prisoners to the auditorium and ordered them to elect the committee. The committee had permission to collect grievances representing the complaints of the 1491 prisoners, and had been promised no reprisals. Irwin told the adjustment committee, "As far as I could see, I was following the orders of the administration and was following their instructions to represent the men. It was the warden who ordered us to do that. And it was the warden and Captain Dodd who promised us there would be no reprisals if there was no violence."

Alger told the adjustment committee he was critical of his committee. He said that only five members of the committee were sincere and the rest were just griping, and he said that it was his opinion as a member of the committee that the population should continue to work while the committee negotiated. This did not spare him.

All committee members in segregation were found guilty and sent to the Good Time Forfeiture Board.

The Good Time Forfeiture Board hears appeals from the adjustment committee, and if it upholds the guilty decision of the "lower court" it fixes punishment. Its chairman is the same chairman as the adjustment committee's, Associate Warden Cansler. Associate Warden Cansler as chairman of the Good Time Forfeiture Board seldom decides that Associate Warden Cansler as chairman of the adjustment committee was wrong.

The Good Time Forfeiture Board makes a delicate improvement over the justice process of the adjustment committee. It informs the prisoner that it is a meeting of the board, that it is empowered to hear charges and evidence against him, will listen to his defense if he has any, that he may have a full-time member of the prison staff defend him, and the board will make recommendations to the warden for forfeiture of all or part of his accumulated good time.

Though the chairman did not say so, more was at stake than just loss of "good time," substantial as that might be. If even one day of good time should be withdrawn, the United States Board of Parole will not accept an application for parole. Parole on some sentences is possible after a few months, in all cases after a third of the sentence. Irwin, for example, had 588 days of good time at stake, or more than a year and a half off his twelve-year sentence. He had begun his federal imprisonment in early 1968. He had a perfect record as a prisoner, without misconduct reports, with excellent work records and full-hearted involvement in all self-improvement programs. He should have been eligible for early parole because he had an (a) (2) sentence, and certainly by 1972, when he would have served the usual one-third of his sentence, when all prisoners are theoretically eligible. But if the board took away any good time he would never be eligible for parole as long as even one good-time day remained withheld. He would get out not in 1972, or with ordinary good time in 1975, but in 1980.

So when William Irwin appeared on March 9 before Associate Warden Cansler's Good Time Forfeiture Board, what was at stake was his prime of life, whether he would be released from prison that year or eight years later. No law enforcement officer, no prosecutor and no judge has such arbitrary powers for guaranteeing imprisonment as Associate Warden Cansler and his superior, Warden Alldredge, held over their prisoners.

It is significant that the adjustment committee hearings had found most prisoner committee members guilty on February 22. Two days later, when they were called out of segregation to resume their meetings, with the hope that the strike would end, these members had over their heads guilty findings by the adjustment committee and were yet to meet the Good Time Forfeiture Board, which would hand out punishment. As a committee of negotiators with the prison officials they were now in the position of being condemned to prolonged imprisonment if they did not "negotiate" to the satisfaction of the warden and his deputies.

On March 9 Irwin pleaded not guilty to both charges—inciting a work stoppage and threatening the safety of the prison by failing to present grievances. No one had ever heard of a rule about failure to present grievances as a cause for punishment. Neither was there a rule at that time making work compulsory.

Irwin asked to be represented by his friend the chief of classification and parole, Olymp Dainoff.

After Irwin and Dainoff spoke, Dainoff told the board that he would not say anything about the guilt or innocence of Irwin but simply speak to Irwin's character as he had known him. He did say that he felt that Irwin admitted his desire for the strike to occur but felt the second charge was unfair. Dainoff told the board that Irwin was ready for release from prison, was almost destroyed by the continued lengthy postponements of parole by the parole board, and that Dainoff suspected that this was what lay behind Irwin's involvement in the strike.

Irwin then took over his own defense, according to the official record, talking to the only man who made any difference on the board, Chairman Cansler.

> IRWIN: One other thing. I'd like to mention that I have been doing time for the past 25 years and this is the first time I have been before a disciplinary board for any reason. I have always managed to control myself very well and if you check my record you will see that it is an exemplary record and that I consider this thing that I did the other day an emotional thing. If I had been using my head I would not have been up there, but I was upset, I was angry, and I said things that I knew were going to cause me a lot of trouble and will cause me a lot of trouble.
>
> CANSLER: In regard to the two charges against you, you were a member of the first committee. Is that correct?
>
> IRWIN: Yes.
>
> CANSLER: As a member of that committee, did you individually or collectively with the committee ever present grievances to the Warden or his committee?
>
> IRWIN: That depends. One of my major grievances was that we weren't considered a legal body. We were just there together and had no rights. To me that is a very strong grievance. . . . If you don't already know, I was strictly against bargaining until this was straightened out . . . I still feel this way. If that is wrong, then it's wrong, that's all.

Other members of the board wanted to know how it was he got elected to the committee. Irwin reminded them that Mr. Cansler had ordered prisoners to the auditorium for the purpose. A member of the board, Dr. Louis J. Oropallo, chief medical officer of the prison, kept pressing the point: "Was there any leadership in all this?"

> IRWIN: I feel if we're gonna talk about who was responsible for this committee I feel that Mr. Cansler is just as responsible as anyone else. . . .

I feel that Mr. Cansler is responsible at least as much as I am for what happened. . . .

CANSLER: This Board will make a recommendation to the Warden regarding forfeiture of any, all, or none of your good time.

The board voted unanimously to take away 482 days of Irwin's good time.

The board was particularly interested in Irwin, as chairman. But they were also interested in Phillips, who in addition to being sophisticated was, judging by his behavior and the secret letters of informers on the committee, part of the hard core holding out for negotiations. They also knew that he had accumulated 416 days of statutory good time.

On March 8 he was called to a special office where Chairman Cansler, Associate Warden C. A. Cramer, and B. J. Clendenning, superintendent of industries, sat as the board.

Cansler handed him the written charge, told him the function of the board and that they would decide how much good time to take away and what other punishment he would get. Did he have anything to say?

Phillips said he declined to take part in the proceedings, that he considered them a charade. "I intend to go to court over your taking away good time that I have already earned and doing it for following your own instructions about representing the prisoners."

Cansler smiled. "You can take it to court twelve times if you want and you're going to lose every time."

"Then I'll take it a thirteenth time."

Cansler stopped smiling. "Phillips, are you mentally competent?"

Phillips had long ago learned not to answer questions too quickly, to search mentally for ulterior meanings. He speculated that this was a veiled threat, that if the board decided he was not mentally competent they could keep him in the worst hole, the bare tiled solitary cage where they held violently disturbed prisoners. Or they might send him to the psychiatric prison at Springfield, Missouri, where he might be subjected to mental and psychological experiments. He followed his instinct for direct answers.

"Whether I'm mentally competent is of no concern to this committee. One way or another it would make no difference to you. You are not a legal body and I am not a psychologist or psychiatrist."

Cansler turned to Clendenning and asked if in Clendenning's opinion this prisoner was mentally competent. Clendenning said he did not feel competent to judge. Cansler pressed him, saying he had to express an opinion because it would decide whether Phillips was sane enough to face these charges. Clendenning was uncomfortable and under the stare of the associate warden said that, well, he didn't think Phillips was acting normally, the way he was answering the questions.

Cansler turned to Cramer. Cramer quickly said he thought Phillips was normal. Cansler shrugged and said, Okay, we decided you're competent to face these charges. The board took away his 416 days of good time.

The prize the associate warden awaited was Joel Meyers. They knew he was a communist, that he was one of the most articulate and tough members of the committee, that he was a draft evader, and that he held them in contempt. He had been on the platform, therefore "inciting." He had been a member of the committee and therefore had not turned over grievances, thus "prejudicial to . . . good order." He had done table-hopping the night of the 25th against the orders of an officer.

On March 8 Meyers had 213 days of accumulated good time that they could take away from him, a sixth of his whole sentence.

Cansler made his opening speech, including the right to have a staff member represent him, and asked for Meyers' response. Meyers said he was not guilty of the charges. He declined the use of a staff member for defense because a staff member worked for the members of the board and would only do what they needed to preserve their jobs, which was to be a part of the railroading process.

Cansler made a remark about Meyers' radical politics.

The official record says only, "During the hearing, Meyers verbalized profusely regarding irrelevant information, tending toward revolutionary type statements of a nonspecific nature."

It was remembered by others, including Meyers, with more detail.

Cansler said they would decide how much good time to take away and added sarcastically, "You want to quote from one of your books now?"

"Well, I'll quote your book about my book."

"What do you mean, my book?"

"Well, the Bible. That's your book, isn't it?"

"That's right . . . New Testament!"

"Well, in the New Testament it says that Jesus said, 'Cast not pearls before swine.' "

The members of the board looked at each other, startled. Cansler said slowly, "Are you saying that we're swine?"

"You said that."

They took away the 213 days and recommended continued segregation.

They were almost as interested in Clarence Jones. He was imposing, had strong political and black nationalist opinions and was a potential leader. He, too, by informers' letters, was a strong member of the prisoner committee.

When he was shown the charges by the board he said they were false and trumped-up, and that he needed legal representation. Cansler informed him that he didn't need a lawyer. Jones said he would like to see the policy statement governing operation of the Good Time Forfeiture Board, since he had never been before one in his life and wanted to know the rules. Cansler read a few statements from a document. If that was the policy statement, Jones said, could he read it for himself so that he would know what the policy permitted an accused prisoner to do.

Cansler said Jones had no need to read the policy himself. "You have the right to be represented by a full-time staff member. Do you want to avail yourself of that right?"

Jones said that would be futile. "I can't get justice from a full-time employee of the prison. Can I have a prisoner represent me?"

"That won't be necessary," Cansler said.

"Well, then will you let me read the policy statements about this board, so I can study them? And will you let me take time to read the charges? This is the first time I've had an opportunity to see them in writing, and if you're forcing me to represent myself, could I at least study the charges?"

"Will you be ready to represent yourself tomorrow?"

"I'm forced to. I'm not ready because I don't know what these proceedings are all about."

The next day he was called back and asked if he was prepared. Jones said he was not.

They took away 200 days of accumulated good time.

All the board punishments went to the warden, and the warden, with all of them, softened the blow with a device that kept a hold on the men but had the appearance of justice tempered by mercy.

The warden's ratification of his board's punishment of Jones, as it was with the others, read:

> Subject is to forfeit 30 days S.G.T. for the following major misconduct report of attempting to incite a work stoppage. The forfeiture of the remaining 170 days S.G.T. is suspended for a period of six (6) months from the date of the original report by the Warden on the specific condition that no further major misconduct report is incurred by Jones. If a major misconduct

report is incurred within the stipulated six (6) months, the remaining 170 days S.G.T. are forfeited. [Signed] Noah Alldredge.

The 30 days withheld unconditionally still kept the committee members from eligibility for parole. Unless the prison system sometime, someplace restored those thirty days, there could be no parole, which usually represents more time in prison than accumulated good time.

On the other hand, if any staff members reported a major misconduct, whether or not it was subsequently found to be true, the additional 170 days of good time would be lost as well.

This completed the lesson of the Federal Bureau of Prisons in respect for law.

After the hearings a friendly guard passed the word to them in their segregation cages. Cansler had told another officer, "There are five of those radicals who are never going to leave segregation."

In some of the federal prisons men had been in solitary confinement for five years. Most committee members had seen prisoners demented by endless segregation, wrecks in catatonic paralysis, or screaming animals, laughed at by guards, prodded, beaten, splashed with water. One was in Lewisburg.

They had to do something.

21

HUNGER AND THE FBI

Weeks passed in the segregation cages and committee members began to feel the hopelessness of abandonment. The rumor had grown that eight of them, not five, would never leave segregation. Some of them —Irwin, Jones, Phillips—had more than ten years to go and they were haunted by remembered sounds of demented prisoners unhinged in segregation.

They gradually obtained their personal effects, Irwin his AA books and his Bible, Phillips his philosophy books, Alger his law books, Jones and Johnson their black nationalism literature, Meyers his regular edition of *Workers World.* Eventually they were given fifty minutes a week of exercise outside their cages and ten minutes a week for a shower.

They "fished," used scrounged pieces of string to drop bits of food or literature to hospitalized prisoners on the floor below them, or receive the same from the S-2, S-3 and S-4 prisoners in the cages above them. Written messages were exchanged among themselves inside pages of books and magazines carried by orderlies. In emergencies they could make string out of mattress material, tie soap to the end for weight, wrap a message around the soap and, swinging the string like a pendulum, wait until it glided past the small opening of a nearby cell where the recipient could catch the soap.

They talked to each other, though with difficulty, shouting through the narrow opening in the cage door to unseen companions across the corridor. Some adjacent cages had outside windows close enough for conversation.

They had small ceremonies. On February 27 Phillips in his cell heard Lucky Johnson call out to Lumumba Jones. "Hey, Lumumba!"

"Yeah, Lucky."

"Guess what? Today's my birthday!"

"Well, I wish you a happy birthday, brother!"

Lucky was twenty-five.

Phillips was about to call his congratulations through the hole in his door when suddenly he stopped. February 27 was his birthday, too. "Hey, Lucky!"

There was no answer. Phillips never could shout loud, and talking through the small hole across the corridor in the echoing concrete cageblock was a strain. He tried to make his voice more distinct.

"Hey, Lucky!"

"Yeah, Ron."

"Guess what? Today's my birthday, too!"

"Hey, man, that's cool. Happy birthday!"

Phillips was thirty-four.

The block soon rang with "Happy Birthday," like a matrons' afternoon at Schrafft's. Except for an occasional "Well, happy fucking birthday, man!"

The strike, they remembered, had started on Eddie Mason's birthday. It was a question how many birthdays would pass in segregation.

There was a literal breakthrough when Irwin and Phillips, now warm friends in adjoining cages, found a crack in the plaster and concrete. By diligent digging they enlarged the crack to make a hole half an inch wide.

Phillips was ecstatic. "I could actually see Billy's eye and he could see mine. When we talked we could watch each other through the hole. It was wonderful. We'd cover the hole when we were through, but now when we talked to each other we'd uncover it and actually see the other human being we were talking to."

But the dreary days went on and the prison administration remained unbending. Lucky Johnson, bitter and emotional, attracted the attention of all the S-5s, including one prisoner unconnected with the strike. He proposed a hunger strike. The strike would force the prison to act. It might attract attention on the outside and get help for their case. Some of the prisoners were close to fasting anyway, including Lucky. Fasting had a special fascination for prisoners who looked for any area of life where they could exert personal control. Refusal of food was one of them.

Tucker was for it. So were Jones and Mason. Alger said he would go along and Meyers was willing to try it. Irwin was against it. He had seen prisoners in other places on hunger strikes and he said they didn't gain control, they lost it. They got irritable and weak and began quarreling with each other. Phillips was against it. He argued, as usual, with clever and erudite reasoning, that a hunger strike would be counterproductive, but the simple truth was that he was dismayed at the idea of not eating.

The majority voted to do it, and on the same day they began refusing the trays shoved through the feeding slots of their cages. Except for Irwin, who took his trays and threw the contents to the birds. By now it was spring and he was watching a nest of sparrows.

Unfortunately, the terms of the hunger strike had not been determined ahead of time. Fasting meant different things to different people. For some it meant drinking only nonnutrient liquids. For some it meant only coffee and fruit juices. For others it meant taking no official food but using food ordered from the commissary. And Irwin was right, there were arguments. Irwin dreamed, to his surprise, of cole slaw, Phillips of everything except liver and tapioca.

The effects of fasting developed quickly. At first there were hunger pangs, dizziness and fatigue. But about the third day the sensation of hunger ended and a new exhilaration was felt. Discovery that the body if supplied with fluids can survive and the spirit can be sustained had a stimulating effect on group morale.

Alger wrote to his parents:

> I'm over withdrawal symptoms and cruising along fine. . . . You get an acid taste in your mouth, which I have, when burning up fat. . . . I topped out at 137 when I came into segregation 83 days ago . . . I weigh about 120 or 118 now. I'm very pale and look like hell, but feel pretty good.

The prison took notice. After seventy-two hours without food intake, fasting prisoners, according to regulations, must be placed in the hospital.

Alger wrote his parents:

> . . . yesterday they hospitalized all of us according to law. We are given urine tests every morning, temperature and pulse regular, and weighed every day. I weigh 117 pounds . . . the slimmest I've ever been, but I feel good, drinking a lot of water and liquid.

A few days later he wrote to Brockton, "Dear Mom and Dad, greetings from your 115 pound son," and a week after that:

> Two weeks today with no solid food, just liquids. . . . Tomorrow is my birthday, or whatever! It means less and less each year. It doesn't mean

anything to anyone. . . . I haven't written lately because I've noticed that
when you fast, your mind wanders.

Assignment to the hospital meant that for the first time in months
the men could be together, in sight of a complete human being, able to
talk conversationally and in private. They were in a locked and guarded
ward but inside was open, with rows of beds. For some reason, guards
put Alger and Tucker in separate locked rooms but after the first day
the other committee members protested and the Alger and Tucker
doors were left unlocked. The men had access to the hospital supply
of chess sets, Monopoly and Scrabble. Meyers and Jones were hard to
beat in chess, though Irwin was challenging. Phillips had an unbroken
record of winning at Scrabble. But mostly the men talked, feeling a new
excitement after weeks of hearing only disembodied voices echoing
through concrete corridors.

Their weight continued to drop. Loose pants became a badge of
honor. They discussed body chemistry and a strategy of maintaining
themselves above the threshhold of medical urine and blood readings
that would permit the prison to force-feed them intravenously. A package arrived mysteriously from the kitchen—seven pounds of wheat
germ and a gallon of honey. Books delivered from the magazine cart
that went by daily often contained encouraging notes from the population.

Camaraderie deepened. The eight members selected for special punishment happened, presumably by chance, to be four blacks—Johnson,
Jones, Mason and Tucker—and four whites—Alger, Irwin, Meyers and
Phillips. Though, with the Bureau of Prisons' sensitivity to public
relations, it was speculated that it had become an equal opportunity
punisher. Among almost all the committee consciousness of color disappeared.

Hunger and weakness took their toll and caused occasional outbursts
predicted by Irwin. The arguments were usually about rules of the fast.
Some men most eager to start the fast were discovered eating candy bars
from the commissary. And there was one quick racial incident.

Tucker remained an enigma. He had adopted the Muslim name
Yousuf, and he was vocal against bourgeois society, repeating Marxist
clichés so often that even Meyers thought it amusing. But Tucker was
also vocal from time to time on his hatred of white society.

Tucker had grown up in the Hill District of Pittsburgh, the black
ghetto, in a family with middle-class strivings. The Hill District is

surrounded by evidence of the futility of normal ambition.

In prison he had become increasingly anti-white, perhaps because his first venture into serious crime had had such a bizarre ending, his careening through the criminal justice system so enraging, his imprisonment so unexpected and the impact of his act on the white victims so unknown to him, that the law and its system remained a malign white mystery.

Tucker was irritable from hunger, too. He was serious about the fast. He was the youngest of the eight, twenty-three years old, facing an indeterminate sentence under the Youth Correction Act, which meant that while he was limited in the total number of years he would serve, he never knew when within those years his release would come. It was hard for him to believe he was in prison anyway. He did not have the long recorded career of trouble with the law that most of the others had. Even his arrest for the sentence he was serving at Lewisburg was somehow unreal.

One day Tucker called Mason, Johnson and Jones into his room to discuss strategy for the fast. There was an argument. Hearing it, Irwin wandered in and started to speak. Tucker interrupted him, saying coldly, "This is no concern of yours. This is just between us."

Everyone else in the room was shocked. "Between us" clearly meant "between us blacks."

Irwin said, "What do you mean 'just between us'? Since when have we stopped acting together? We've stood together in this thing from the start and why the hell are you trying to divide us now?"

The other three men agreed. They insisted that Irwin and any of the others should be a party to anything said. But Irwin was hurt and, as was his habit when angry or hurt, he walked away. Jones followed him and said it was just hunger nerves.

On the other hand, Lucky Johnson was the hero of all for organizing the hunger strike. He had brought them together, physically and emotionally.

It was a high point of his rebellion against white society, against the system that had put him in prison. The treatment of the committee, the reprisals after the early promises, had convinced him that the law meant nothing, that whoever had force made up his own standards. The government, he believed, had behaved worse than he had.

"These people are really too much," he wrote to me from segregation. "I have no intention of violating their laws any longer. But I will survive! Sometimes I wonder if what I did was wrong. Even now I kind of believe I was right by my own standards. But that does not mean I should continue to be as cruel and defective as this government."

But Lucky's antagonism toward white criminal justice had no effect on his loyalty to the rest of the committee, including Meyers.

Meyers, small, white, draft evader and communist, was liked by most prisoners but hated by others. A hulking black orderly in the hospital had taken a strong dislike to him and one day began goading Meyers to fight. The words "commie Jew" floated over a nearby chess game. Lucky Johnson stood up, disturbing the board, and walked toward the two men. As he walked he flipped a dental cap off a front tooth. A gang fight early in his career had broken the tooth now protected with the precious cap that covered it. When Lucky Johnson flipped off his tooth cap it meant he was ready to fight. The orderly left and never harassed Meyers again.

After Meyers had been in segregation a month, before the hunger strike, he was permitted to see his wife in the visiting room. The same day another prisoner, a white orderly in S-5, also had a visit. They were being escorted together back to S-5 when one of the guards told Meyers, "Don't trip on the stairs." Meyers looked quickly for a blow from the guards or a shove onto the floor. The guards didn't move and in a second Meyers understood why. He felt a hard punch in the head from behind. It was the orderly. The prisoner hit him again. Meyers stood still, knowing what would happen if he hit back. The guards watched without moving until the other prisoner took a third punch at Meyers. Then they stepped between the two men impassively and continued up the stairs. Nothing happened to the other prisoner. He kept his job as orderly on the S-5 floor.

The official "Segregation Report" for that period recommended that Meyers be transferred to another institution. "This recommendation," the segregation officers wrote the warden, "is based on the fact he was recently assaulted by another inmate, which reflects his inability to get along with his peers."

The hunger strike eventually ended, a few men at a time, the impact of the fast diminishing and with it the strain of living on fluids and wheat germ. They were returned to S-5 cages on the second floor and began once again communicating by disembodied shouts out the small holes of their doors, by notes passed in magazines, by messages swung on string.

But shortly after the hunger strike there was a message unlike any that had passed before.

It was about ten o'clock in the morning. Segregation orderlies—

prisoners selected to work for the guards—roll food carts, clean up, hand out clothing to incoming prisoners. They tend to feel superior, to side with the officers and to look down on segregated prisoners, particularly the ones up in S-5 who were "radicals." Committee members expected little from orderlies.

But shortly after nine o'clock one morning an orderly slipped a note under Irwin's door: "Alger's downstairs talking to the FBI."

It was not unusual for the men to be called out of segregation from time to time. By now they could have visitors in the visiting room. Some could go to sick call. Or an attorney might visit.

But this was something special.

Irwin thought about it. Alger was someone who could be warm and friendly. He responded to whatever was around him. He had become radical in his talk since his segregation. But if a guard engaged him in conversation through the opening in his door Alger would reverse his opinions. He wanted to please everyone.

The note could be true.

Irwin had a matchcover in his cell. He printed in big letters on the back of the matchcover:

                              F B I

He went to the opening in his cell door. Members of the committee had been shuffled in their cell assignments and now Lumumba Jones lived directly across from Irwin. Irwin and Jones, totally different personalities, had developed respect for each other.

Irwin called out, "Lumumba!"

Jones came to his cell window. "Yeah, Billy."

Irwin held up the matchbook cover. The corridor between rows of cells was about five feet wide, the light pale. Jones squinted through his granny glasses. Irwin held the matchcover as steadily as he could as Jones's eyes focused on the small message. Irwin saw Jones's lips slowly spell out the letters silently: F-B-I.

Immediately Irwin took down the matchbook cover and held his forefinger to his lips for Jones not to say anything out loud.

Jones formed a word with his lips: "Who?"

Irwin listened to make sure no one was walking in the corridor and whispered across the five feet, "Alger."

Jones's eyes opened wide and the two men stared at each other silently across the gloomy emptiness.

Irwin put his finger to his lips again and Jones nodded and disappeared from his cage door.

Irwin sat on his bunk. He noticed the loose plaster on the wall. He took down the cover of the "telephone" that connected him with Phillips' cage. He called in a whisper, "Ron!"

Phillips' eye appeared at the hole.

"Can you hear me?"

"Yeah, Billy. What's up?"

"I just got a note. Alger's down talking to the FBI."

"How do you know?"

"An orderly just slipped me a note."

"How the hell does he know?"

"It was down in the basement."

Phillips was skeptical. "FBI doesn't talk to guys down there. You know that, Billy."

"Yeah, but what if he is?"

"Be careful, Billy. Have you told anyone else?"

"Just Lumumba."

"Okay. Don't tell anyone else until we know for sure. It could be wrong."

Irwin put the piece of plaster back in the hole.

Ten minutes later there were footsteps in the corridor. Sounds echoing in the corridors were continual and most prisoners remained where they were, in their bunks or sitting in their chairs or looking out the window. But this time three faces appeared in the door openings: Irwin, Jones and Phillips.

It was not Alger but a prisoner-orderly from the hospital on the floor below. During the hunger strike they had become friends. Irwin called him over. "Can you go to the basement?"

"If I have to. What's the score, Bill?"

"The FBI's supposed to be down there talking to people. Find out who they're talking to."

The prisoner walked away. The three faces disappeared from their doors.

Several minutes later the prisoner returned to Irwin's cage. He whispered through the door opening, "You're right. The agents are in one of the basement rooms and guys are sitting on the bench outside waiting to go in."

"Who?"

"Well . . ." The orderly looked around carefully and spoke even more softly. "Alger and Wolcott are sitting on the bench waiting to go inside." The hospital orderly disappeared.

Immediately Jones appeared at his wicket. Irwin nodded solemnly to him. Jones's face looked grim and disappeared.

Irwin opened the hole in the wall. Phillips was already there, waiting. Irwin whispered, "It's true. Him and Wolcott."

Wolcott had been released from segregation almost at once. There were few doubts about his role, either among the committee or the population.

One day Phillips had been standing at his cage window watching a prisoner play on the miniature golf course below. It was forbidden for either man to attempt speaking to the other. The golfer seemed to have trouble at his game directly under Phillips' window, cursing loudly, exhorting the ball to behave.

"Motherfucking pill, get into the fucking barrel. Can you hear me, motherfucking ball?"

Phillips coughed loudly, indicating he could hear.

"All right, now, all right! Line it up, motherfucker, into the hole this time! Guys in the shops beat up Wolcott. Get in there, now, fucking bastard!"

Phillips leaned out farther and hunched his shoulders in a gesture of "What happened?"

The golfer took a swing that sent the ball only a few feet and cursed again.

"Son of a bitch bastard ball! Threw a fucking blanket over him and kicked the shit out of him. Now get into the fucking hole, you little motherfucker!"

Phillips coughed loudly again. The golfer stood with his head cocked, eying the ball, but his vision included Phillips at his window. Phillips was shaking his head firmly and waving his palms in crisscross fashion, forming the word "no" with his lips.

Within hours the committee had sent a message to friends in the population to leave Wolcott alone, that hurting him would only hurt members of the committee and their cause.

But Alger. He was one of them, loyal to them, part of their planning and complaints and frustrations. He had been vociferous in his solidarity with the committee.

Irwin looked at Phillips through the hole. "Now what?"

"Wait until he comes back, Billy. The FBI could be talking to him about something else. Why not wait until he gets back and see what he says?"

"Well, if he's snitching what the hell do you expect him to say? 'I'm snitching'?"

"No, but if he volunteers that he was called down to see them, then it might be on the up and up. He'll be honest with us."

Irwin was silent for a moment. "And if he doesn't volunteer it?"

No answer came from the other side. Irwin put the piece of plaster over the opening.

Phillips and Alger had adjoining cages, their outside windows close together. They could talk confidentially to each other and often did.

At ten-thirty the three faces watched Alger being escorted back to his cage. He went between Irwin's and Jones's cages, past Phillips' and into his own. The corridor echoed with the guard's keys jangling, the opening of Alger's cage door, its slamming shut, the turn of the key again and the receding footsteps of the guard.

Irwin waited. From time to time he went to his door. He saw Jones waiting. After a while Irwin took the loose plaster from the hole in the wall.

"Ron!"

Phillips' eye, untypically dull, appeared at the hole.

"What did he say, Ron?"

"He didn't say anything."

The two men pulled back until they could look into each other's eyes. Prison informers are frequently killed.

Irwin sat in his cage silent and troubled. The usual place for FBI agents from Lewisburg to talk to prisoners was in the warden's office. Few prisoners walk the corridors of the administrative complex, and there are many reasons why a prisoner might enter the section leading to the executive offices. The FBI has good reason for making certain that their informants are not observed.

So why, Irwin asked himself, would they let men sit on a bench in plain sight of other prisoners who know that the agents are using the room inside for questioning?

On the other hand, why didn't Alger tell them when he got back? If the agents called him down and asked him questions about the committee members and he didn't tell them anything, why wouldn't he tell the men as soon as he got back?

He remembered that on the first day Alger had somehow just appeared in the auditorium and been elected. He had been in self-appointed control of the microphone that first afternoon with Wagner and Wolcott. Wolcott! He was with the FBI at the same time!

They knew about Wolcott for certain. And now Alger?

Slowly the thought crystallized. They had both informed, they were no longer useful and now the FBI deliberately had them sit outside the agents' room to be seen by the population. Irwin thought to himself, They're setting them up to be killed. They can't use them anymore. So they get them killed or beaten up and they have another reason to keep us locked up in segregation forever.

The more he thought about it the more sense it made to him.

An undefined anger grew in him and, by habit, he consciously controlled it. If there was hate involved, he immediately told himself, he must love the person he hated. God works in mysterious ways.

Maybe Alger was just busy and waiting for a chance to talk about it. Maybe his speculation was all meaningless because he was assuming that Alger wasn't being open about it.

He went to his wicket and called into the corridor, "Hey, Alger!"

He could see the faint shadow of listening shapes behind Jones's wicket and he thought he heard an unusual number of other men moving toward their wickets. He called again, "Hey, Alger. It's Bill."

"Yeah, Bill."

"What's going on in the outside world? Where'd you go this morning?"

"Oh, I got a visit from the Christian Science reader. I'm kind of into that now."

"Shit, John, all that time?"

"Yeah, Bill. We rapped a lot. It's better than sitting up here rotting."

Irwin grunted and went back to his window. This was serious. He was still standing at his window when he heard Phillips poking at the plaster in the hole. Slowly Irwin went to his bunk and removed the plaster.

"Billy, take it easy. We've got to know a lot more about this before anyone does anything foolish. He may be frightened. Do you think he's going to yell into that corridor for everyone to hear that he's been down seeing the FBI?"

"But, Ron, Ron, you and him talk all the time. He didn't have to be yelling it down no corridor to come to your window and tell you, did he? No. He didn't tell you a damn thing."

"Look, Billy. This is your exercise day and they've been letting you out with Joel. Tell him about it and talk it over."

Irwin listened carefully. He had come to be surprised at the accuracy of Meyers' predictions of official behavior and by his reasoning power.

"Okay. But I'm telling you, Ron, we got a shitload of trouble."

"Talk it over with Joel if you see him."

Irwin put the plaster back. Meyers was on the opposite side of the corridor, always at the end of the line of segregation cages to give him minimum contact with the rest of the committee. It was a joke among the committee members that the cage assignments showed what theory the administration had about the committee. At the moment they had Meyers between Dr. Z and Scully. Dr. Z they considered crazy and Scully totally unpolitical. They let Meyers and Irwin exercise together because they thought Irwin disliked Meyers.

That afternoon Meyers and Irwin were let out together for their one-hour-a-week exercise and shower. As they started their brisk walk around the gym Irwin started to tell him about Alger.

Meyers said, "Yeah, I heard already."

"How the hell did you hear?"

"All the guys know. Like the whole population must have seen them sitting down in the basement. It's the same as Grand Central Station."

"You know he lied about it," Irwin said.

"Yeah, I heard him."

"So what do we do with a snitch? He's right here with all of us. When we send messages to each other he's in on it. We all had good time withheld, we got all that other good time hanging over our heads if we get busted for any infraction. They want any excuse they can get to keep us locked up forever. And we got this guy who's been in the middle with us talking to the FBI and lying about it."

Meyers was quiet as they walked briskly in the small recreation area for segregation. Meyers walked with a slight waddle. Now he listened to Irwin carefully and was silent for a while, his short legs moving more rapidly than Irwin's long ones.

"Maybe he's scared."

"He had a chance to tell me. I asked him."

"But maybe he needs someone to help him get over it. I'll say, 'I heard you saw the FBI. What's going on?' "

Irwin was angry. "I'm surprised, Joel. We got someone right in our midst and you're not upset at all. You're making him out to be an okay guy."

"Bill, we should direct our anger at the torturer, not the tortured. Alger's being victimized just the way we are. They know they can put pressure on him and that hurts him more than it does most people. Whatever goes on, they're the ones who are doing the manipulating. Do you think they had them sitting out in front where everyone could see them by accident? They're anxious to see Wolcott and Alger get killed.

If that happens, then we'll look like animals and the administration will look good."

They walked in silence for a time. Irwin asked how the other men felt.

"Lucky and Yousuf are pretty sore. We got to talk to them, Bill. You talk to them, I'll talk to them, Ron has got to talk to them and I think Lumumba will talk to them."

"Joel, I've been in joints a lot longer than you have and I can tell you it ain't easy to reason with people about something like this. Everyone feels threatened and if they divide us this way a lot of guys will want to take direct action."

Meyers shook his head. "Listen. What do we gain by hurting this kid? He's being exploited by them. They're the ones who we ought to be angry at, not Alger."

They showered quickly. Their hour was over.

As pairs of men were released for their weekly fifty minutes of exercise and ten minutes of showering the debates went on.

Before the week was over Alger was called out of his cell again. Nobody had said anything directly to him, but tension in the S-5 wing was palpable. When Alger came back Lucky Johnson yelled out, "Hey, Alger, where you been?"

"Had to see my lawyer. I'm fighting a Penn state detainer and I think I got them over a barrel."

Two days later Alger was called out again.

When he got back, Tucker asked him where he had been. He said he saw his lawyer again, that his detainer fight was getting hot.

When a friendly orderly came by, Tucker asked him to find out what lawyers had visited the prison that day and if the FBI was still holding sessions in the basement. The orderly came back later and said he couldn't tell about lawyers but the FBI was still down there.

The next day Phillips was in his cell reading Carl Jung's *Memories, Dreams, Reflections* when he heard someone calling softly at his outer window. "Ron."

Phillips went to his window. It was Alger. If both men reached out of their windows they could touch, and Alger silently handed Phillips a note and withdrew to his cage.

Phillips took the note to his chair. It was on lined notepaper folded tightly in quarters. It said he trusted Phillips and wanted him to know what had been going on. He had been called down to see the FBI who were investigating suspicions that Alger and another prisoner had forged the prison librarian's name on book orders. The note said that he didn't want to talk much about it because he didn't know if it would hurt the other man. But he wanted Ron to know that he wasn't telling the FBI anything about anyone on the committee.

Phillips reread the note two or three times. He felt it was probably true. Alger was easily pressured and they had probably used him. But he was also easily frightened and knew how most prisoners would react to it. It could be that he was lying, he could be "dropping a dime" to the FBI. He doubted it, but either way, why not take it at face value in the absence of anything else? He didn't have to write that note if he didn't want to.

Eventually, Phillips went to the bunk and poked at the hole in the plaster. Irwin opened the hole and looked through. Phillips read him the note. Irwin asked if he believed it.

"I think it may be true. Billy, he may just have played himself out. He might have been scared and lied about it the first day, got stuck with the lie the other days and then had it work on his mind all this time and now comes clean on his own. And even if that isn't the case, what difference does it make?"

"I suppose not a hell of a lot. We got nothing to hide. But a snitch could take perfectly innocent things and make it look bad if they was really pushing him."

They whispered back and forth for a time and came to a decision between the two of them. Do nothing to hurt Alger. Don't fight or argue with him. Be careful what you say in front of him. But let everyone know that they are hurting the cause if they hurt him. They used a phrase of Meyers': "Sympathize with the tortured, not the torturers."

As the exercise days went through their weekly schedules, private communications spread the argument. The Meyers-Irwin-Phillips consensus became the group consensus. And except for a momentary later verbal exchange between Tucker, Johnson and Alger, the problem of the FBI was put behind them. The committee remained supportive of Alger and he of them.

It was easier to do this, perhaps, because there finally came an idea for delivering them from their segregation and a way to strike back at the Federal Bureau of Prisons.

22

THE DREAM

All prisoners have a dream: They have been unjustly punished and a courageous judge sets them free.

Committee members in their Lewisburg segregation cages began to dream. They had no illusions. They knew that prisoners send floods of paper ranging from pitiful notes to proper legal writs to hundreds of judges and receive back a simple "Denied." They knew that in cities and towns near big prisons the local courts are like an extension of the prison administration. Federal judges' chambers are usually in the local post office–and–courthouse, on the same floor as the FBI and the U.S. Attorney; they walk in and out of each other's offices, go to lunch together and chat about legal people and cases. A judge can enter his courtroom with a mind set, consciously or unconsciously, by the gossip with his friends in the courthouse building. His office neighbors never include prisoners and their lawyers.

Besides, the traditional attitude of courts to complaints about prisons has been what legal literature calls "the hands-off doctrine": Whatever prisoners might claim about illegal acts by prison authorities, it is not up to us—judges of a court—to tell prison keepers how to run their institutions.

Committee members knew, too, that if by some miracle a local federal court accepted a prisoner's case, it was a habit of the Bureau of Prisons to transfer the prisoner to another jurisdiction, disrupting his case. Or to punish him more severely. Or to promise him a reward if he dropped his suit.

The Bureau of Prisons did that with Arthur Burghardt Banks and made a mistake, a mistake that produced one of those spectacular episodes that keep dreams alive. The Department of Justice, the FBI

397

and the Bureau of Prisons had not taken into account a Minneapolis federal judge named Miles W. Lord.

While prisoners in Lewisburg were striking, Danbury's were doing the same. One of Danbury's leaders was Banks, a black Broadway actor sentenced for draft resistance and outspoken—in a deep and commanding voice. As a result of the Danbury strike, Banks was transferred to Terre Haute, notorious for racist guards, where he was beaten and Maced. When he tried to defend himself he was charged with assault upon a federal officer. When he began to collect sworn statements on official lying, the Department of Justice, the FBI and the Bureau of Prisons tried to prevent his completing the damaging depositions. The Bureau of Prisons in its attempt to obstruct the process transferred Banks to another of its prisons in Sandstone, Minnesota, which is how, two years later, on September 19, 1974, a U.S. Attorney from Washington, the defense attorney, Morton Stavis of Newark, and Banks himself found themselves before Judge Lord in Courtroom 1 of the United States Courthouse in Minneapolis.

Confronted with an actual court hearing on the embarrassing facts, the Department of Justice made a deal. If Banks would plead nolo contendere, no contest, to the assault charge, they would parole him. But if he didn't they would send him back to Terre Haute and all that that meant in the basement of the penitentiary. The nolo plea required an explanation by the defendant.

Banks stood before Judge Lord.

BANKS: I have been in a federal penitentiary, Judge Lord, for 27 months. At Danbury . . . I was in their solitary confinement unit for four months. At Terre Haute maximum security penitentiary at Terre Haute, Indiana, I was in their solitary confinement unit for almost 17 months . . .

Judge Lord, the whole thing about slavery is that slavery makes thoughtless human beings . . . and when I went to prison I resolved then and there that I would keep my First Amendment rights and any other rights that I possessed as a human being.

When I went to jail I found that not only theoretically but practically speaking I was not a citizen or a human being. I was beaten on August the 22nd, 1972. Have you ever been maced, Judge Lord? . . . I was maced, twice, three times, four times, by federal prison guards. I was maced again when they had the handcuffs on me and then beaten again, beaten again, and then I retaliated—I certainly did—but very limitedly because I couldn't see, I couldn't hear. They sprayed mace into the orifices of my eyes, my ears, into my mouth, all over my chest, and they finally got me down on the floor of G block, solitary punitive confinement in that penitentiary, they beat me again and threw me stark naked into a cell.

I had no medical treatment for 48 hours, I had no clothes, I had nothing to swab my body with—nothing.

You ask why I plead nolo contendere? There is a taint and a dirty, filthy smell about the plea of nolo contendere, especially after the problems with the former Vice President of the United States, Spiro T. Agnew, isn't there? . . .

You asked, Judge, why I wanted to plead nolo contendere. Because Judge Noland out in Indiana has denied me a hearing on my depositions, because Judge Noland out in Indiana and a few other members of the United States Department of Justice have denied my taking depositions in a civil matter. . . . The prison runs the town—the prison runs the town.

JUDGE LORD: That is what it does in Stillwater, but I didn't know it did in Terre Haute.

BANKS: In small towns, Judge Lord, the prison has incredible economic sway and political influence . . .

They have dispersed my witnesses to the far corners of the United States. . . . Witness Jamie Jenkins was approached by an officer named Ray Stevens and told in 1973 that "If you go up there for Banks, nigger, I will declare that you're perjuring yourself."

Witness William Clayton . . . was approached by two agents of the Federal Bureau of Investigation, one agent by the name of Rosenbaum, and he was told that they were members of the Defense Committee to Free Arthur Burghardt Banks. When the ruse failed, Mr. Clayton said, "You're not really from anything to free Banks. Who are you?"

"We are with the FBI. But we want to know what your feelings are about the Banks case. You are about ready to be paroled. You don't want to say anything like that, do you? You don't want to have anything to do with this case, do you?"

When we were taking depositions on August 28th, 1974, in the habeas corpus matter . . . an agent of the Federal Bureau of Investigation by the name of Smiley told a guard, an officer named Turpen, that he had better not know anything with regard to the Banks case, said in the outer offices of the law firm in which we were taking depositions. . . .

I saw men beaten in solitary confinement Block L, Judge Lord, and complained about it. I went to the Associate Warden about it. I did my Christian and my legal duty and I said, "That man was beaten by prison guards." I didn't say that I was beaten by prison guards. I said that Paul Cook was beaten by prison guards, and they refused to hear me. . . .

. . . you see, Judge Lord, my case is not simply a matter of . . . assault. . . . My case is the issue of the penitentiaries and the entire slavocracy of the Federal Bureau of Prisons. . . .

You see, the Federal Bureau of Prisons in fiscal year 73–74 made seventy-two million dollars on convict slave labor. Why am I in trouble with the Federal Bureau of Prisons? Precisely because—and I admit it now—I was a leader among 12 other men of a strike at Danbury . . . where we opposed not only prison conditions but slave labor wages, no inmate representation and no educational facilities that were any good to us. . . . Since then, I saw my whole life turn upside down. . . . They want me in solitary confinement, they didn't want me to have the attorney of my choice, they wanted to return me to my adversary, to transfer me, to keep me from my witnesses, to harass and abuse my witnesses . . . because I am articulate, because I am strong and because, Judge Lord, I am black, and proud of it—proud of it.

The U.S. Attorney said, sarcastically, that he could not match the dramatics of Banks, but he denied that he had agreed in the judge's chambers to get a parole for Banks if Banks pleaded nolo, because "the Parole Board is an independent body."

The judge said, "Mr. Nixon didn't conceive it to be an independent body when he announced that from now on all paroles would be harder to get . . . the Department of Justice . . . acts both as the keeper of the key that holds the man in prison, and has within its confines the Board of Parole as a part of the Department of Justice; so they are the 'keeper-inner' and the 'letter-outer.' And then their attorneys call the shots before every court in the country. And they just have not been fair to this man. . . . It's the John Mitchell syndrome . . . which is to put everybody in jail except the speaker."

The judge spoke to the defendant: "Arthur Burghardt Banks . . . The Court accepts that plea, and as punishment for the offense the Court finds that you have suffered enough and that your sentence has already expired . . . while you were in solitary you were serving the sentence . . . which means that you are not sentenced at all, you have no punishment."

And Arthur Burghardt Banks, brought to court in chains, walked out of court and out of the Bureau of Prisons a free man.

That is the rare case that keeps alive the dream. But there are thousands of anonymous cases that are killers of the dream.

In 1972 there was another kind of communication with federal judges, this one from the Trailblazer Jaycees Legislative Reform Committee at Leavenworth Federal Penitentiary, which used the legal form a "Petition for Equitable Relief" to urge passage of a congressional prison reform bill as relief from

The humiliation of our souls and degradation of our physical beings which we suffer from constant and prolonged confinement, with little or no hope of again being recognized in that capacity which our Constitution guarantees us cannot be revoked.

Among those who received this petition was the Honorable William Harold Cox, Senior Judge of the United States District Court in Jackson, Mississippi. On August 10, 1972, Judge Cox wrote a letter on his official judicial letterhead to the warden of Leavenworth, whose prisoners had sent the petition.

Dear Sir:

I am today in receipt of the enclosed piece of trash sent me as Chief Judge of this Court which I am handing you for your proper action in the future. It is nothing short of shameful, if not disgraceful, that criminals in a penitentiary can be allowed such leisure as to draft such worthless material designed and intended solely for propaganda purposes. It is my firm conviction that those criminals should be put to work and worked and not allowed to roam at large through a law library and annoy and harass some Federal judge.

Obviously no rehabilitation has been accomplished on these criminals who do not even realize that they are in the penitentiary for the commission of a crime against society. Certainly they should not be accorded the privilege of wasting paper and using the mails without charge for the purpose of disseminating such propaganda. It certainly falls on deaf ears in my case because I firmly believe that every criminal up there is there because he richly deserves it. It is surprising to me that even the criminal mind should be so stupid as to think that his incarceration is in violation of any part of our Constitution. These criminals and such concepts of justice make it perfectly apparent that the Supreme Court grievously erred in negating capital punishment.

Yours very truly,
HAROLD COX

Between Judge Lord and Judge Cox there are many shades of judges, and the committee members in segregation at Lewisburg had no illusions that a miracle was at hand. But dreams are sometimes the alternative to psychotic despair. So the committee members dreamed.

When Meyers' wife, Pamela, visited, she asked when the men would get out of segregation. He didn't think they ever would unless something unusual happened. The press had been denied access to the men. The strike was over. The rumors were bad. They would probably be transferred to the most unpleasant places around the country. Why didn't she ask Leonard Kolleeny, a New York City lawyer who had represented radicals, if he could bring a lawsuit? Kolleeny said he would bring an action on behalf of the Prisoners Solidarity Committee, Joel and Pamela's political group, but he needed help.

Lewisburg prisoners had already written to Professor Herman Schwartz at the University of Buffalo Law School, head of the ACLU Prisoners Rights Projects, and known to prisoners everywhere as one of the outside people called for by prisoners in Attica. Schwartz agreed that the case seemed worth pursuing. A young ACLU lawyer, Michele Hermann, twenty-eight, a recent graduate from Yale Law School, worked on the case full time. Before joining the ACLU legal staff, she had done legal aid for prisoners but she had never tried a case or cross-examined witnesses. Kolleeny did not charge for his services, nor did the ACLU or Schwartz.

The first problem was basic. They wanted to bring a class action on behalf of all Lewisburg prisoners improperly punished, but it was hard to get proper names and identities. Culled mostly from Pamela Meyers' memory, the first petition to the Middle District of Pennsylvania listed as plaintiffs a group of men with nicknames, and wrong names: "Fred Tucker," "Bill Irwin," "Clarence Jones Lumamba," "Yousef Lucky Johnson," "John Mason," "Frenchie Buyse" and "John Moore."

The defendants were Noah Alldredge, warden; Norman Carlson, Director of the Federal Bureau of Prisons; and Richard G. Kleindienst, Acting Attorney General of the United States.

Eventually the plaintiffs were properly named: Joel Meyers, Ronald Phillips, Ronald Tucker, William Irwin, Clarence Jones, Lucky Johnson, Richard Moore, Edward Mason, Michel Buyse, John Alger, Walter Scully, William Genco and James Hilty.

To the prison's surprise, the petition was accepted for formal hearing instead of getting the usual summary dismissal by the Lewisburg court. The case went to a judge from Scranton, William J. Nealon, forty-eight, a liberal Catholic appointed by President Kennedy. Judge Nealon had heard criminal cases against Lewisburg prisoners. In one a potential witness had been murdered; the judge had ordered announcements over the penitentiary's public address system for eyewitnesses in the case and promised protection. Prison officials hoped this would give Judge Nealon a proper view of prisoner treachery.

In due time Noah Alldredge received a legal communication that began remarkably like the one that started inmate Joel Meyers to prison. It began

GREETINGS:
You are commanded to . . .

The order demanded the production of the prisoner-plaintiffs in District Court at the post office building in Lewisburg at ten A.M. on March 29, 1972: "HEREIN FAIL NOT, AND DO RETURN MAKE HEREOF."

A few days before the March 29 hearing, three of the most militant committee members dropped out of the suit—Scully and his two friends, Genco and Hilty. It was not an accident. Scully's later sworn testimony described the events.

A week before the hearing Scully was called out of his segregation cage and into a room where he found Hilty alone. They talked for two hours. Scully was told that Hilty and Genco had dropped out of the suit, and Hilty said Scully should, too. The reason: the trial was a communist plot and before it was over the government was going to show in court that it was a communist conspiracy.

Scully asked if Hilty had proof of this. Hilty told him to speak to Captain Dodd, who could show him something interesting.

The next day Scully was called out of segregation again. This time Captain Dodd was in the conference room. Dodd said that Scully might change his mind about staying with the lawsuit if he saw some special documents.

"Okay, where are they?"

"Lieutenant Baker has them and tomorrow morning he can show them to you."

The next morning he was called again from segregation. Lieutenant Baker had copies of *Workers World,* Meyers' political paper. He showed Scully a letter Meyers had written to the paper with the signature "Comrade Joel." He showed him another letter from Lumumba Jones to the paper that started "Revolutionary Greetings."

Scully interpreted it from the witness stand: "Now to me, 'Comrade Joel' and 'Revolutionary Greetings'—that always brings to mind 'Communists.' Now, I've got nothing against the Communists. . . . That's their beliefs, and I don't want to go down to court under any banner, because even when I was on the street I wasn't Republican or Democratic. I didn't vote, you know, because I didn't get a chance because of my prior record . . . and I didn't want to get involved in anything so I came up and told the committee members. I said, 'This is the way it is. I will not go down to court under those conditions if it's going to be made into a big communist conspired thing.' "

Scully told the prison staff he would withdraw from the lawsuit. The next day he was released from segregation. Hilty and Genco had already been released from segregation. Every prisoner remaining in the lawsuit remained in segregation.

The suit challenged the constitutionality of conditions and procedures in the penitentiary, saying that the charges against the committee were untrue and unfair, that punishment procedures violated rules of fair process, and the punishment of indefinite segregation was cruel and unusual and therefore unconstitutional.

The day of the first hearing was gray and cold. The sight at the start brought grim stares from the stolid burghers around the Lewisburg post office and courthouse. Dozens of young people, members of the Prisoners Solidarity Committee, from New York City, marched around the courthouse before the trial started. They wore Army jackets and dungarees, Mao caps, the young men with long hair, headbands and beards, the young women in Army jackets and dungarees, most carrying bedrolls or old canvas knapsacks. They held high a banner—"Tear Down the Walls"—and chanted, "Prisons are the concentration camps of the poor."

They marched in a town that voted for Barry Goldwater for President in 1964 and three to one for Richard Nixon in 1968 and would again in 1972. As they went around the courthouse they passed through a municipal parking lot past a symbol of Union County solemnity, an Amish black wagon parked carefully within the diagonal lines of a parking space, its horse tied to the parking meter and the parking meter properly filled with enough coins for ninety minutes.

On the second floor the young people crowded into the government-green plaster of the outside corridor and then into the dignified contrast of the courtroom of dark paneling and checkered marble floor.

Before long the spectator seats were full. On one side were the hairy young people from New York, green parkas and bedrolls underneath their benches. On the opposite side of the spectator section sat off-duty prison guards and their wives, dressed as though for church, the men in shiny suits, the women with stiff hairdos. The two groups of spectators looked like separate guests of bride and groom in a hateful wedding.

As each prisoner began his testimony, off-duty prison officers whispered to their wives.

On one side was the government counsel, Clair Cripe, now general counsel of the Federal Bureau of Prisons, a round-faced man with a

Lincolnian beard, and Julius Altman, Assistant U.S. Attorney from Scranton, a jovial bureaucrat in glasses who did most of the questioning.

On the plaintiffs' side on the first day was Herman Schwartz, professorial, in contrast to Kolleeny, who looked deceptively like a tired man who had seen too many trials. And Michele Hermann, earnest and nervous.

But the people bringing the lawsuit were not in the courtroom. They were manacled together in a back room, too dangerous, the marshals said, to be loose. Judge Nealon ordered them unshackled and brought in.

Entry of the prisoners brought something like a whispered cheer from the right side of the spectators' section and glares from the left. Jones, tall and dignified, Meyers with a demonic grin, Phillips smiling and philosophical, Irwin formal and serious. They were ushered into the jury box, to the red-leather seats. Several of the men quietly ran their hands over the leather. It was the first time in years most of them had sat in an upholstered chair.

The prisoners looked in open wonder at the paneled walls, the soft indirect lighting in the ceiling, the polished brown and tan checkerboard design on the courtroom floor. With the exception of six hours, they had spent the last 960 hours locked alone in their barren six-by-fourteen cages. Now they were in an elegant palace of justice. They had all seen courtrooms before, but usually in a rush and never as prisoners bringing their keepers to testify under oath, never before as an escape from hopeless isolation.

The first witness was Phillips, whose testimony gave the basic story from the prisoners' point of view. He quoted Captain Dodd at the kitchen dock on February 15 promising no reprisals: "There will be no reprisals because of this incident. . . . Please keep it nonviolent. We're opening up the recreation and auditorium. If you want, you can all go up there and have a general meeting amongst yourselves."

He described the official announcements on the prison public address system instructing the population to elect a committee to represent them.

The next witness was not a prisoner. Kernahan Buck was a young Kennedyesque aide to Congressman William Anderson of Tennessee. Anderson had taken a personal interest in the prisoners, one of the unorthodox acts—like criticizing J. Edgar Hoover—that would cost him the next election.

Buck described two contrasting experiences. The prison had insisted that men in segregation were well treated, with good sanitation and care. Buck had notified the Bureau of Prisons at ten A.M. on March 9 that he would like to interview a few of the segregated committee members. He gave Warden Alldredge their names ahead of time. He was granted that "courtesy" given members of Congress and their aides. He arrived at the prison at three-thirty P.M. and met the committee members whose names he had given the warden five and a half hours earlier. Those prisoners were clean-shaven, wore neat clothing and had obviously bathed. Buck left the prison.

The next day, unexpectedly, he returned with no advance notice and asked to see the rest of the committee members from segregation. These men, he testified, "were unshaven, filthy and looked like they had been wearing their clothes for a week or more."

The prison staff had consistently said the committee had failed to compile grievances in a form that could be given to the warden. Buck said that the warden had told him that when he finally disbanded the committee on February 25 "there was no list of grievances being prepared, but he said he couldn't prove it."

Buck produced the list of typed grievances on the stand.

Buck's documents originated with stencils given him by Meyers during Buck's visit to segregation. The grievances Buck had in his hand were neatly typed and lacked only the signatures of the committee members. Later the government questioned the authenticity of the stencils on grounds that neither in Room 14 nor in segregation did the committee have access to a mimeograph machine, and these grievances in the courtroom were mimeographed.

Cansler testified, "They could have went out of segregation in longhand for all I know." John Wagner had typed the stencils in his cage through the night hours of February 24 and 25, describing it in the April-May 1972 issue of *Penal Digest International.* But before the trial ended, Wagner was transferred to a federal prison far from the jurisdiction of Lewisburg.

Buck had brought me the stencils shortly after March 10, after he returned from his visit to Lewisburg. The stencils were clean, completely typed, and not yet inked or mimeographed.

To everyone's surprise the hearing was not completed on March 29, and the judge scheduled a second session the next day.

Committee members testified to their feeling of entrapment, a feeling deepened by something they learned for the first time from the testimony of Captain Dodd.

At the initial gathering of industry workers at the kitchen dock on February 15 no one had made a move to take leadership. A black prisoner finally stood up and called for grievances, urging the men to express themselves and to stand up for what they believed was right. Most of the committee members assumed that he was one of the original ringleaders, so they responded. In court they discovered that he was not a "ringleader," as Phillips and Irwin had supposed, but a prisoner following instructions of Captain Dodd.

Dodd testified, "I ran across an inmate . . . a black inmate, and I asked him what was going on, and he said he didn't know. I said, 'Well, get up there and ask them what are they doing out here; what are they standing around about.' I thought maybe this might bring the leaders out, whoever was organizing this, which it did."

It was a bitter discovery. It deepened their sense of treachery by the administration. Urged by a man under instructions of an officer to come forward and speak their minds frankly, they had come forward and spoken their minds frankly. These were the speeches that formed the first half of the charges for which they were serving indefinite segregation—inciting a work stoppage by making speeches from the kitchen dock.

At first, the Bureau of Prisons denied that there had been any promises of no reprisals. Cripe, the Bureau of Prisons attorney, announced in court, "We challenge the fact that there was any guarantee by the administration or any indication of no reprisals." He said flatly, "There was no guarantee of no reprisals."

Captain Dodd, on the stand, contradicted his lawyer. He said there was a promise but it was conditioned on a committee turning over grievances. This was crucial. Eight of the committee members remained in isolation on the charge of failure to turn over grievances.

The captain testified, "I told them as long as they maintained themselves in a nonviolent manner and give me their grievances, I would pass them on to my superior, and I certainly wasn't going to take any sort of reprisals against them."

Warden Alldredge, under oath, also contradicted Cripe. Alldredge agreed there had been a promise but said it had been on condition of peacefulness by the prisoners, which he conceded had been the case, but also on turning over grievances, which had not happened.

Wasn't it strange, the officers were asked in cross-examination, that at the kitchen dock at one P.M., on February 15, before there was any thought of a committee, before there had been any request for an election, before the formal listing of grievances had even been considered by the original strikers or the officers, that a no-reprisal pledge had been made with a condition of a committee turning over grievances? And that no prisoners, sympathetic or not to the strike, could be produced who heard that condition to the pledge?

It was strange. It was also unfortunate that the court did not have in its possession, because it did not know of its existence and the government did not volunteer it, the confidential "incident report" Warden Alldredge made to Director Carlson in Washington the day after the scene at the dock. He wrote, "Captain Dodd agreed to this request on their word that they would remain nonviolent."

There was no mention in the detailed official report of any other condition to the promise of no reprisals. That report, written in the early afternoon of the 16th, came after the final election of the committee.

The sense of entrapment deepened as the account by the officers confirmed that they had ordered prisoners to the auditorium in the evening and told them to elect a committee, that the committee had been given no prior deadline but had been disbanded and punished the first day, that on their recall a week later they were told they could meet round the clock and a few hours later were thrown into segregation because they were still meeting.

At the time, the undisputed militant leader of the committee was Scully, with his friends Hilty and Genco.

As Officer Young had written in his memorandum to the warden after observing committee meetings:

> Scully then took the floor and it became apparent rather quickly that he was the actual leader of not only the group but the population as well.

And now Scully, Hilty and Genco, as a reward for dropping out of the lawsuit, had been released from segregation.

Shortly after the trial started, Hermann learned that letters between lawyers and prisoners in the lawsuit were being seen first by the prison staff. She asked in the judge's chamber for assurances that the traditional confidentiality between lawyers and clients would be respected in their mail. Cripe refused.

Hermann was astonished: "You mean they cannot write to me as their attorney?"

Cripe replied, "Of course not. That's not permitted by Bureau of Prisons policy."

Hermann successfully pleaded with the judge that it was unethical and unfair that the people being sued would be able to read letters about the case from the people suing them. Judge Nealon ordered the prison to deliver legal letters in the case without interception by the penitentiary.

The reaction in the prison was reflected in a curious Lewisburg official memorandum. On April 21 Associate Warden Cansler issued his memo to "All Concerned":

> We are in receipt of a Court Order from U.S. District Judge Nealon to the effect that the below listed ten (10) inmates will be permitted correspondence with the below listed five (5) attorneys, uncensored and unopened.

This might ordinarily be considered sufficient orders in a militarylike institution. But experience with differences between official Bureau policy and actual practice behind the walls explained the last paragraph of Cansler's memo that seemed to say, "We really mean this." It said:

> All personnel are cautioned that this mail is to be unopened and we are under a Court Order to insure this. Any opening of this mail would of course place the institution in contempt of court.

The prisoners' lawyers feared another Bureau practice. The case could embarrass the penitentiary. A common reaction of the Bureau of Prisons to prisoners bringing embarrassing lawsuits is transfer of the prisoner to a distant prison, out of the jurisdiction of the court about to hear damaging testimony. Judge Nealon granted a petition forbidding transfer of the ten prisoners until he issued his decision in the case.

Testimony from the highest officers of the prison continued to have an unreal quality, as though the official transcript for Civil Suit 72–132 had been drawn from Alice in Wonderland.

First, Associate Warden Cansler testified under questioning from the judge that if an accused prisoner before the adjustment committee turned out to be innocent "we would try to make every effort to give him leniency as far as the penalty is concerned."

The judge pursued the matter. If an officer reports something that later seems to be wrong and in conflict with the prisoner's testimony, why doesn't the board have the accusing officer appear?

Mr. Cansler said it was not worth the trouble. "Our officers work around the clock seven days a week. The man he reported for an infraction, say in the evening, when he comes before the adjustment committee, this would be in the morning. This officer is at that time off duty, so that this would involve overtime . . . to get the officer back in before the committee."

At one point Cansler was asked if a particular man had been punished. He said, "He spent a time in the segregation unit—if you call that punishment."

Cansler said that when prisoners came before the Good Time Forfeiture Board they could have any full-time employee of the prison act in their defense. The prisoners' lawyers insisted that a full-time employee was not likely to anger his fellow officers by asserting that they were wrong or lying, that under the best of circumstances defense of a prisoner by a member of the prison staff would be ineffectual.

To prove their point, the prisoners used the example of the most sympathetic high employee they knew, Olymp Dainoff, chief of classification and parole, who had agreed to "defend" Irwin. Irwin insisted he had done nothing wrong and was being charged for following official orders. But Dainoff had told him not to dispute the accusation and merely let Dainoff testify that Irwin was generally of good character.

Irwin took the stand to describe the failure of his best friend on the staff to make a vigorous defense on the facts. As he started to speak he looked distressed. It was much like his reaction when he faced the warden in Room 14. He started: "Mr. Dainoff . . ." He stopped, said softly, "This man has been good to me," and choked emotionally. The judge called a recess. A few minutes later Irwin gave a straightforward and unemotional account of his limited defense by Dainoff. It was a small, touching episode. The prison would use it for retaliation afterward.

Then there was the matter of records kept at the penitentiary.

The prison was proud of its records. It had a meticulous ledger showing every time a segregation prisoner showered, shaved, exercised, whether he did it voluntarily or not. Lieutenant Baker, adjusting his glasses, confidently read from the stand examples of the records:

> Alger . . . a shower on 2/21, a shower on 2/24, a shave on 2/9, shave on 2/22, cleaned his cell, 2/20, shower on 3/3, shave again on 2/26 and on 2/29, and a cell clean on 2/26. . . . Phillips showered 2/24, offered a shave and refused on 2/19, shaved voluntarily on 2/22, cleaned his cell on 2/20, on 3/3 he showered, 2/26 he shaved, 2/29 shaved, 2/26 cleaned cell.

But when the judge asked Chairman Cansler how often the adjustment committee finds a prisoner innocent of a charge, the associate warden said he couldn't tell.

JUDGE NEALON: Don't you keep any kind of record in your office as to the functioning of your committee . . . ?

CANSLER: No sir, I do not.

JUDGE NEALON: . . . two or three years from now . . . there's no way you could determine what action was taken by the Adjustment Committee?

CANSLER: That's correct.

The findings of the adjustment committee, sent to the Good Time Forfeiture Board, had added years of imprisonment to men's lives, without a meaningful record. The prison kept records of the length of prisoners' beards, but not of their condemnation to isolation.

At the end of the first day, the prisoners were jubilant. It seemed to them that the original bland denial of everything by the prison system had fallen apart.

Toward the end of the second day, a disturbing new factor emerged. McAllister, the honor-dorm orderly who had remained mute when asked if he would sign the back-to-work agreement, told of conditions of the hole, of crowding, naked men, starvation diet, Macing.

The judge let testimony go beyond five P.M. After a brief recess for supper, he let it go on into the night—he was worried about perjury. One side of this case was lying under oath.

The session lasted to an extraordinary forty-five minutes after midnight. Almost everyone was exhausted. Emily Cadden, the stenographer, had been taking notes since nine-thirty that morning. Julius Altman, the U.S. Attorney, was bitter because the night session had made him miss the first Passover ceremony in his new house in Scranton. The judge's clerk, driving Mrs. Cadden home to Scranton, struck a deer, making a total wreck of his car. It was not a night for final clarity.

The prisoners were exhilarated. The word of their keepers, for the first time in their experience, had been put under oath and, it seemed to them, found false.

It was May 12 before the case reconvened for its third day. Judge Nealon called scheduled witnesses before him. He was solemn. "I am concerned about the direct conflict in testimony and . . . I may consider directing the Grand Jury or a grand jury . . . to investigate the possibility of perjury, obstruction of justice, or any other related crimes that may be committed in the courtroom."

The prisoners in the red chairs smiled with excitement.

Fourteen prisoners who had been in S-1 segregation testified to nakedness, filth, painful heat or cold, starvation quantities of food, beatings, Macings and denial of emergency medical treatment.

Prisoner Thomas J. Bullock testified that some time late Saturday or early Sunday he was called from his quarters in F block at the west end of the prison, had his clothes stripped and was marched naked the length of the prison corridor to the segregation basement.

"They twisted my arm behind my back and marched me across the Red Top and down to segregation. . . . They were punching me in the head, calling me 'nigger,' 'instigator.' . . . Officer Walburn . . . would get me near the doorway and say, 'Watch out for the doorway,' and then he would run me into the doorway."

Bullock said he was put into his segregation cage naked and was given no clothes by officers for a day and a half.

Officer Walburn testified that it was not he who had taken Bullock to segregation. But the prison had no record of who did. It was impossible to determine the names of officers involved. The government did not produce any officer who had taken Bullock to segregation.

But they did produce Robert D. Warfield, senior officer specialist in charge of segregation, to deny everything.

Question: "There was no instance where a man came in and didn't get any shirt or pants?"

Answer: "No."

Question: "And there was no instance where a man came in naked?"

Answer: "No."

The judge, fearful of perjury, said witnesses could not hear each other's testimony, a move to prevent false supporting statements.

Officers had denied almost everything. They insisted that there was no nakedness and that temperatures in the S-1 cages were kept scientifically even.

Officer Warfield changed his testimony under cross-examination. On the last day of the trial he said most of the S-1 cages had four or five men in them and "most of these men were in the state of undress in these particular cells." He explained: "When you have four or five people in a cell like that, it's not uncommon for a man to take off his T-shirt if it's exceptionally warm and finds it uncomfortable."

Later in the day Frank Nickerson, chief of mechanical services at the penitentiary, said there could not be excessive heat or cold in the basement cages because "an air recovery unit . . . thermostatically controlled . . . changes air every twenty minutes" and that a thermostat set at sixty-eight degrees varies no more than "five degrees at the most."

It turned out that there were between forty and fifty sets of segregation clothing available but during the weekend in question 130 men were put in segregation.

Earlier in the trial, Cansler testified, "No man was put in segregation nude." And Lieutenant Baker, when asked, "Could there have been men put in there in . . . underwear?" answered, "That's not possible."

Later asked if "a man could have been naked from Saturday until prior to seven-thirty Monday morning?" Officer Warfield, in charge of segregation, replied, "I suppose it's possible."

The weekend the prison was forcing men to sign statements agreeing to work, fifty-six prisoners were put in the fourteen one-man cages, the others in E and F dormitories. The worst complaints of beating, Macing and starvation diets were in the S-1 cages.

Cansler was asked why some men were selected for S-1 and others put in the dormitories. He said the S-1 prisoners were the "hot ones." Asked to define "hot ones" he said, "You can take almost any employee out there and hand him a list and he can run down and tell you the troublemakers in that list."

Some of the "hot ones" in S-1 that weekend had unblemished disciplinary records.

The jamming of prisoners into the tiny basement cages raised the logistical problem of how they slept, walked or ate in a compartment bearing a slab bed, a toilet, sink and less remaining space than a conventional bathroom. Yet officers insisted that every prisoner in the S-1 cages had a mattress. A blackboard and chart paper brought into the courtroom to demonstrate how five six-foot mattresses could be put into a six-by-fourteen cage left some question. The judge made a date to visit one of the cages and have five mattresses put inside.

When the official party went to the hole at the penitentiary there was a familiar smell: fresh paint. The cages were spotless. They opened an empty cage. Five mattresses were put in. Five people got in, the judge, his clerk, a lawyer from each side and a lieutenant. One person in the party was sure the case was over. When the door was shut there was no room for the five people to move and it was hard for them to walk with mattresses crawling up the walls. Faces became red and a sense of desperate claustrophobia seemed to overcome all five.

It was in a crowded S-1 cage that prisoners claimed to have been sprayed with Mace.

I remembered asking Warden Alldredge three months earlier about this rumor.

He had replied indignantly, "Mace is not used in this institution!"

Now Officer Warfield was being asked under oath whether Mace had been used during the episode.

"I used what we refer to in the institution as 'Federal Streamer.' "

The warden had been technically correct. The irritant-paralytic Mace-like agent used by the Federal Bureau of Prisons happens to have the brand name "Federal Streamer."

The prisoners' claim that the S-1 cages were filthy was denied. On the second day of trial Lieutenant Baker had testified that each occupant "is furnished with necessary equipment—mop, bucket, dust pan, brush . . . in all stages."

A government affidavit from the orderly with that responsibility was shortly thereafter put in the record:

> It was my duty to be certain the inmates confined in Stage 1 section of segregation received the necessary sanitation materials, i.e., mop bucket, toilet bowl brush, mop, water, scouring powder, etc. for the purpose of individual cell cleanup. During the period of work stoppage this program was continued and each cell was cleaned.

The prisoner-orderly who swore to the affidavit had asked for a special early release date for college admission. It had been pending for some time. The day he signed the affidavit he received his special early release date.

After the judge announced that he feared perjury was being committed by someone, Officer Warfield was called back to the stand, was read the orderly's affidavit and was asked, "Is that an accurate description of that week in Stage 1?"

He said it was not.

The starvation diet for men in S-1 was a long controversy.

Lt. Baker swore, "I can testify that they received the normal ration of food . . . more than adequate rations." He said they were served on paper plates with wooden spoons shoved through a food slot in the lower portion of the cage door. The food came down in a hot food cart, was put on the paper plates by officers, and if a food cart ran out of hot food "absolutely there would be a second or third trip."

There were 130 men in segregation cages, all of them served by one hot food cart that held sixty-five servings. Lieutenant Warfield, who had not heard Lieutenant Baker testify, was asked how many food carts were brought to segregation during that period and his answer was "one hot food cart." There were no second or third trips to replenish food.

Most of the segregation food orderlies testified to the portions described by the prisoners in segregation—a biteful of meat, three or four peas, a square inch of cheese.

Orderly Colburn testified that an officer named Stahlnecker parceled out the food and put in the small portions, saying as he put in the tiny bits, "This is too much for him . . . he'll get fat."

The judge asked him if the officer had really said, "This is too much; we can't give them this because they will get fat"?

"That's right."

The government did not call Officer Stahlnecker to testify.

Most of the prison officers who testified smiled condescendingly each time attorney Hermann asked a question, amused by a young female attorney. This included an officer named Robert Diverf, a guard in segregation who put food on the paper plates. She carefully took him through the process of putting food on the plates for the S-1 prisoners. Mr. Diverf, smiling confidently, described heaping portions of everything. She asked about how high the plate would be heaped before being put through the food slot. He held his hands about ten inches apart. The prisoners laughed. The food slot is five inches high.

Testimony on medical care upheld the prisoners' claims. Dr. Budin, general medical officer of the penitentiary, agreed that Prisoner Spencer had a bad heart, and the diabetic Gunderson had insulin shock caused by reduced food. He testified that he had been informed of such problems but he did not examine the men. Some days after the complaint, the doctor ordered a reduced dosage of insulin for Gunderson to take into account the seriously reduced food intake that segregation officers swore did not exist.

In Judge Nealon's chambers Cripe told the judge that he would have produced witnesses to refute prisoner testimony but some of his potential witnesses had been threatened with death by the plaintiffs. Hermann said this could not be so because the plaintiffs had been locked in segregation continuously. Cripe noted, correctly, that it was easy for men in segregation to get word to the rest of the population. Hermann absented herself from the chambers and returned after several minutes. She said that every plaintiff had offered to take a lie detector test on whether they or anyone they knew had in any way threatened potential witnesses. Cripe said he would drop the subject.

Another subject came up in the judge's chambers: the real reason for the indefinite segregation of the eight prisoners from the committee. Cripe told the judge, "The warden has indicated to me . . . as far as he's concerned the eight who are still there still belong in segregation and should not be returned to the population at Lewisburg, and on information he has received, the type of social correspondence they are sending out indicates they are still dedicated to radical type union action."

The rumors had been true. The eight would never get out of isolation.

Denial of parole, withdrawal of good time and condemnation to indefinite segregation had not been imposed because they had taken a strong part in the strike negotiations. Scully, Genco and Hilty had done that, too.

Nor were they being kept in segregation for their committee activities. The other committee members had long ago been released.

Nor were they condemned because they had been violent or threatened violence. One man on the committee, voted down by everyone else, had proposed to seize Associate Warden Cansler as hostage and kill him. He was not among the men condemned to indefinite segregation.

Their special punishment had a special origin: the FBI and the Bureau of Prisons read their mail and disapproved of their political ideas.

The trial ended. The prisoners were returned to their cages, certain they had won. Under agreement with the court they could not be transferred until Judge Nealon handed down his decision. They waited. No decision came down. John Alger quietly withdrew from the suit.

On June 16 Judge Nealon handed down his decision. Perhaps by coincidence his decision was announced the same day as Judge Robert C. Zampano's on a related case in the Danbury strike. Both judges denied the prisoners' complaints.

Judge Nealon conceded that there were some troublesome points in Lewisburg's handling of punishment within the prison but they were excused because of emergency conditions.

He found prison officials' testimony credible and disbelieved the prisoners', which was, he said, "greatly exaggerated and inconsistent." He gave as an example testimony by prisoners that one man was part naked for two or three days while another prisoner in the same cage said it was for only a day and a half.

He said food was sparing but not so much as to be cruel and unusual under the Eighth Amendment. He was struck by lack of exercise given segregation prisoners, but "fortunately this policy has been changed somewhat drastically" by giving prisoners two hours of exercise a week instead of one.

Concentration of men in the hole "does cause me some concern . . . although I cannot conclude . . . that it rose to the level of cruel and unusual punishment."

Lack of a procedural safeguard in punishment by the adjustment committee and Good Time Forfeiture Board "causes me some concern although I do not believe it is constitutionally required."

It was a classic judicial decision in the doctrine of "hands off"—the people who run prisons are experts who operate under difficult conditions, so they must always be given the benefit of the doubt.

Judge Nealon's decision accused the committee of bad faith, citing Irwin as testifying that he had never seen the printed list of grievances. This misquoted Irwin, who said from the stand, "We were going to give them to him [the warden] that day. . . . I wasn't interested in the technicalities of typing. . . . Meyers had the stencils." The judge had no verbatim testimony when he wrote his opinion. The court stenographer suffered a heart attack and the transcript was delayed a year.

The Court of Appeals generally supported Judge Nealon, except that it said the procedures used by the adjustment committee and Good Time Forfeiture Board were unconstitutional. All punished committee members were entitled to new hearings. The Court of Appeals added that prisoners asking for new hearings took the risk of receiving harsher punishments in their second hearings. The prisoners understood the hint. None asked for new hearings. Besides, by that time the Bureau of Prisons, released by Judge Nealon's decision, had already taken its next step: the prisoners were in special caged buses, U.S. marshals' cars or otherwise in the process of being scattered to other prisons throughout the United States.

23

EXILE

Lewisburg penitentiary acted quickly, not like Governor Rockefeller in Attica with massive killing, but by the quiet killing of an opportunity to substitute reason for violence inside prison walls. The Lewisburg strike was the longest in federal history and completely nonviolent on the part of prisoners. It may be the last peaceful prolonged strike a penitentiary can expect. The message to prisoners from the Bureau and the courts was clear: Nonviolence does not pay.

Significantly, it is the same message society gave to the ghettos, slums and barrios in the 1960s: If you burn and smash we will pay attention to your grievances; if you remain peaceful we will reward you with neglect.

Most American prisoners, like most of "the dangerous eight," came from these ghettos. They survived there because they learned to be distrustful and violent. They were the products of abandoned households, oppressive schools, economic injustice. Acceptance of the Lewisburg grievances would not have changed that. It would have merely diminished the role of prisons as graduate schools of treachery and violence. The best prisons in the world will not change crime. As long as society sustains injustice, and promotes materialism and violence, there will never be enough prisons to contain the results.

There is no need for lawlessness to go unpunished in a humane system. Under the most just society some individuals will harm their neighbors. A small proportion will be physically dangerous and be imprisoned. The answer for the others is not long sentences in massive fortresses but social sanctions in the community with which they are supposed to learn to live in peace. In prison they learn only savagery so that the moment of peril to society is not when a lawbreaker emerges from his cage but the moment he is put in.

Most men, women and children now incarcerated should be in the community, but with supervision where it is needed to repair past failures in education and work. If they have damaged or robbed others, they should make reparations out of their own income, not only because it is a reasonable demand but because it establishes a more wholesome relationship between victim and victimizer and sensitizes offenders to what they have done to innocent victims. Reparations to victims, according to ability to pay—the rest paid by government—would also diminish the present outrageous difference in punishment for white-collar criminals, who generally are let go, and blue-collar criminals, who go to prison.

For offenders who are physically dangerous or repeat serious crimes after supervision in the community, there should be imprisonment. But it should be in small facilities near the offender's home city, near the specialized help needed in the institution, and with the prisoner in maximum responsibility for his own behavior. This would not require the bureaucratic empire that now operates the federal fortresses in the countryside. Instead, the Federal Bureau of Prisons should be an agency placing the small number of prisoners who need incarceration in small prisons operated by states and localities, paying the costs for each prisoner, provided the local facility was small enough—no more than forty or fifty inmates—and had a humane and useful environment. It would be a major stimulus for states and localities to make their own prisons rational and humane. Only where localities refused to meet these standards should the government build its own places. There are, already, too many competing systems of jails and prisons in the United States.

The Federal Bureau of Prisons did not suspend its revenge upon the prisoners who led the committee and brought the Bureau into court. The Bureau's retaliation had its aftereffects, some good, some bad, some amusing, some tragic. The eight are bitter about being caged in isolation, not for anything they did in the strike but because they used their constitutional right to sue the prison and because of their ideas, ideas that ran the gamut from Meyers' Marxism to Irwin's religious salvationism turned toward helping prisoners.

The eight remained certain that what they did was profoundly important to their lives, giving them self-control and selfless commitment that was new to most of them.

They were soon separated. Tucker completed his sentence in May, before Judge Nealon's decision. Two weeks after the decision, Mason was turned over to New Jersey authorities to serve a state sentence awaiting him there.

Meyers was scheduled to complete his maximum sentence on July 15, a Saturday. The officer in charge of receiving and discharge is ordinarily off on Saturday, so prisoners scheduled for Saturday release are usually let go on Fridays. Meyers was told he would leave on Friday. Shortly before that date his radical paper announced that Meyers would be released on July 14—Bastille Day, commemorating release of prisoners at the start of the French Revolution. Meyers was told that plans had changed, that the discharging officer had decided to work on Saturday. Only after a protest was the release rescheduled for Bastille Day. Meyers returned to New York and party work. His marriage ended soon afterward, a casualty, as marriage usually is, of prolonged imprisonment.

The other five, still in extended custody of the Bureau of Prisons, were transferred to penitentiaries all over the United States.

Phillips, first, like the other four, in a special prison bus, and then in marshals' cars, spending most nights in filthy county jails along the way, took two and a half months to reach the McNeil Island penitentiary near Tacoma, Washington. His official history thereafter was uneventful except for three things. He was punished twice more, once because he joined another prison strike out of principle, and once when he was standing at his place of work in the dental laboratory in Leavenworth penitentiary and refused an order to turn his back while guards dragged in a badly hurt prisoner the guards had beaten. The third event was an offer to reduce his sentence if he would submit to readdiction of drugs for the purpose of medical experimentation. He refused.

Jones was sent to Marion, the grimmest of federal penitentiaries, with the worst record of killings, insanity and suicides. I visited him there once. Moments after I left he was called to the associate warden's office and interrogated on our visit, which was proper and unexceptional, and threatened with punishment if he ever saw me or wrote to me again. Shortly afterward I was notified that I had been removed from his visiting list. When I inquired, the prison said it was because of my profession, presumably meaning a journalist working for a newspaper. I informed them that I was no longer a journalist working for a newspaper. The answer was another refusal to let me visit because I did not know the prisoner before his incarceration. Jones continued to write and he continued to be harassed, including being caged in Marion's notorious segregation unit.

Johnson was sent to the Terre Haute penitentiary, a place with a reputation for guards who hate blacks. His most notable experience, apart from the daily avoidance of racist guards, was his unexpected meeting with his old warden, Noah Alldredge, who had been transferred to Terre Haute from Lewisburg.

Alger and Irwin were sent to the federal psychiatric prison at Springfield, Missouri. The decision of committee members to forget Alger's suspected conversations with the FBI was justified. Whatever happened in those interviews, Alger did not satisfy the authorities. They did everything they could to prevent his parole. An official Parole Progress Report from Lewisburg, dated June 29, 1972, said, "The most noteworthy occurrence in Alger's case since he was last seen by the parole board is his continuing participation in an anti-administration inmate group . . . aimed at inciting a work stoppage."

Alger, of course, had been exonerated of the charge of inciting the work stoppage.

The parole report also said, "Records indicate . . . that he spends inordinate amount of time in legal pursuits. His visiting records also indicate a great amount of time with visiting lawyers."

The Lewisburg report to the parole board concluded, ". . . it is recommended that favorable parole consideration be deferred at this time."

The assignment to Springfield frightened both Alger and Irwin. It is a psychiatric prison, and at that time the Federal Bureau of Prisons bristled with experimental psychiatric procedures frankly verging on "brainwashing," complete with punishment cages, beatings, drugs and psychological torture to break down individual personalities. For Irwin, already the victim of prison electroshock, the prospect held special terrors.

The two men's fears were heightened when at every stop at a jail on the way to Missouri they were separated from other transported men and placed in psychiatric cages.

They would have felt even more fear if they had known the confidential notation in each of their jackets, forwarded to the prison in Springfield but kept secret from the prisoner:

ALGER, John T. 37102–133 and IRWIN, William R. 36234–133— Springfield . . . two members of the group involved in the work stoppage.

Although neither Alger nor Irwin can be considered psychotic or certifiable, we believe that the emotional problems which they displayed during these episodes and during the subsequent court appearances may receive some attention if they are at Springfield institution.

It is not clear what was meant about Alger's "emotional problems," unless it was an ultimate refusal to inform. But for Irwin it seemed certain to mean the occasion when he found it hard to confront Warden Alldredge in Room 14 and choked emotionally in testifying about Olymp Dainoff in the courtroom, both men he felt personally warm toward at the time, but both of whom were representatives of the prison system whose policies he had committed himself to change.

Both men were received at Springfield and assigned as psychiatric cases. Intervention of lawyers and friends may have been influential in preventing actual treatment of them as psychotics.

Different fates awaited prisoners not on the committee but involved in the strike.

Dr. Z ultimately was released and was found occupying a narrow office in a building squeezed between pornographic movie houses on Forty-second Street in New York City, quarters marked "Father Bernarr," and a placard announcing that volunteer donations for counseling were a mandatory $2.50, backed by a poster with a mosaic tablet engraved "Thou Shalt Not Exploit Thy Minister."

Anthony DiLorenzo, the prisoner selected by the warden to break up the strike, was immediately transferred to the honor camp at Allenwood, even though he was classified as "dangerous" by the FBI and had served only one year of a ten-year sentence. Four months later he was said to have a toothache, and although Lewisburg has an elaborate dental clinic and laboratory, DiLorenzo was permitted to see his private dentist. Perhaps by coincidence, the Department of Justice, at the end of a three-year investigation, issued an indictment of three men on union extortion and freight theft conspiracy. One of the men was Anthony DiLorenzo. The indictment was issued late in the morning of July 26, 1972. Early in the morning of July 26, 1972, Anthony DiLorenzo was permitted to leave the custody of the Federal Bureau of Prisons in order to visit his dentist on Long Island, unescorted, and he has not been seen since.

Robert Wolcott, who sent secret letters to the warden during committee meetings, was transferred to Danbury prison and was released on February 16, 1973, anniversary of the first meeting of the committee he had served as secretary. According to the official report of the Los Angeles medical examiner, seven months later, on August 15, 1973, Robert Wolcott, as tragic a victim of prison as anyone he had been forced to betray, placed a .38-caliber revolver to his right ear and killed himself.

AFTERWORD

On November 9, 1975, almost four years after the Lewisburg strike, the Central Susquehanna Chapter of the American Civil Liberties Union sent out the following appeal:

> Lewisburg Federal Penitentiary has 16 cells in the basement of disciplinary segregation. . . . The basement cells are extremely poorly ventilated. The windows are sealed, barred and painted over. . . . Four of the 16 basement cells . . . have toilets which can only be flushed from the outside by the guard if and when he has time and inclination. There is no wash basin but rather a hole in the wall with a small pipe, the flow of water again being controlled by the guard. A prisoner wanting a drink may have to wait for hours. Recently toilet paper has been given out in small amounts. A man with a sinus condition, lacking a handkerchief, needed all his paper to blow his nose. Not only did he have to live in close proximity to his own waste for hours at a time in an unventilated or poorly ventilated cell, but he was unable to use paper after defecating, or to wash his hands except during his semi-weekly shower. . . . In addition there have been complaints about short rations of food; lack of exercise; a cell being filthy . . . arbitrary closing of the small opening in the door which is the only connection with what little outside world beyond the cells is available, and which has profound psychological effect. . . . We have an ever increasing number of requests for help from prisoners. . . . We must win this suit. . . .